E–Logistics and E–Supply Chain Management:
Applications for Evolving Business

Deryn Graham
University of Greenwich, UK

Ioannis Manikas
University of Greenwich, UK

Dimitris Folinas
ATEI Thessaloniki, Greece

Managing Director:	Lindsay Johnston
Editorial Director:	Joel Gamon
Book Production Manager:	Jennifer Yoder
Publishing Systems Analyst:	Adrienne Freeland
Development Editor:	Austin DeMarco
Assistant Acquisitions Editor:	Kayla Wolfe
Typesetter:	Alyson Zerbe
Cover Design:	Jason Mull

Published in the United States of America by
      Business Science Reference (an imprint of IGI Global)
      701 E. Chocolate Avenue
      Hershey PA 17033
      Tel: 717-533-8845
      Fax: 717-533-8661
      E-mail: cust@igi-global.com
      Web site: http://www.igi-global.com

Library of Congress Cataloging-in-Publication Data

E-logistics and e-supply chain management : applications for evolving business / Deryn Graham, Ioannis Manikas and Dimitris Folinas, editors.
    pages cm
 Includes bibliographical references and index.
 Summary: "This book explores the creation of integrated supply chains, the developments of virtual business, and the processes of re-engineering for business development"--Provided by publisher.
 ISBN 978-1-4666-3914-0 (hardcover) -- ISBN 978-1-4666-3915-7 (ebook) -- ISBN 978-1-4666-3916-4 (print & perpetual access)
1. Business logistics. 2. Electronic commerce. I. Graham, Deryn, 1961-
 HD38.5.E4736 2013
 658.70285--dc23
                2012051621

British Cataloguing in Publication Data
A Cataloguing in Publication record for this book is available from the British Library.

In memory of Albert Graham
(1932 - 2012)

Table of Contents

Section 1
The Concepts of E-Logistics and E-Supply Chain Management

Section 2
E-Logistics and E-Supply Chain Management

Section 3
Evolving Business

Detailed Table of Contents

Section 1
The Concepts of E-Logistics and E-Supply Chain Management

Chapter 1

Deryn Graham, University of Greenwich, UK

Whilst the field of Logistics has existed for a considerable time, the concepts of E-Logistics and E-Supply Chain Management are relatively new. Supply Chain Management development can be traced back to the use of modern logistics (circa 1980s). In the early days, logistics was considered not to make much of a contribution to profitability and given little capital investment. Process and delivery cycle times were long and global competition virtually non-existent. Modern Supply Chain Management (SCM) is comprised of five stages: Management, Warehousing and Transportation, Total Cost Management (TCM), Integrated Logistics Management, SCM, and e-SCM (Ross, 2003). This chapter presents an overview of the concepts, contents, and the aims of this book.

Chapter 2

Sudhanshu Joshi, Doon University, India

The objective of the chapter is to formulate a supplier integration strategy with the aim to optimise the supply chain in Fast Moving Consumer Goods (FMCG) Sector using a literature-based approach. There is a scarcity of research inputs that study the impact of supplier integration on optimisation of the Value Chain. The chapter emphasizes the integration of supplier relationship practices and their impact on the optimisation of the Value Chain. FMCG industry based on the value chain is defined, and an e-collaborative framework is introduced. The framework is primarily based on factors comprising the supplier integration strategy, i.e. information sharing, e-business systems, and policy-based supplier selections that have a positive influence on the long-term lean manufacturing adoption in FMCG firms. Implementing supply strategy in practice requires the collaboration of manufacturers and suppliers using e-collaborations.

This chapter investigates the extent to which the Greek Third-Party Logistics (3PLs) companies use the internet in order to provide information and on-line services to their customers. It is based on the findings of a survey that examined the Web presence of 3PL companies in Greece. Thus, the websites of these companies were contacted and evaluated against a specific questionnaire that consists of two main categories of questions: the scope of logistics services which 3PLs provide, and the Internet practices and technologies that the examined companies use in order to support the identified logistics services. The findings of the survey reveal the effort that 3PL companies in Greece have applied in order to effectively and efficiently support their provided services via the Internet. Furthermore, they support the belief that adaptation and application of the Internet best practices and innovative technologies turns out to be beneficial for all the parties involved in the examined business sector.

Section 2
E-Logistics and E-Supply Chain Management

Chapter 4

The concept of lean thinking is—despite its prominence as waste reducer and value creator—still mainly applied to the manufacturing environment. Whilst investigations on applicability to the service industry are advancing fast, little has been distributed for the area of procurement. This development is opposed by trends of increasing degree of outsourcing and related high portions of procurement of up to 60% of a company's total value creation. The mismatch in terms of lack of strategic attention on lean procurement on the one hand and the responsibility of this function for the majority of a company's value creation on the other, combined with the simultaneous trend of establishing "miracle cures" in the form of e-procurement gave rise to the interest in determining the stake of buy-side systems in the leanness of procurement processes. For this purpose, a case study approach was adopted focusing on the central questions of what lean means for procurement, which measures could portray leanness in this instance, how the stake of buy-side systems can be reflected in the performance indicators with separate consideration of repetitive processes in operational and strategic purchasing, in order to finally attribute a clear enabler role to IT for achieving leanness in operational procurement. This finding has been reached by the means of an objective research approach, relying on quantitative methods such as KPI measurement for data collection and regression analysis for the interpretation of correlation between the variables. As such, this chapter has not only a high value for practitioners by providing a baseline for benchmarking lean performance of e-procurement, by supporting system investment decisions, or by simply facilitating decisions on adapting existing IT solutions. It also proves as enrichment to the existing theoretical body of knowledge filling into the aforesaid gaps of lean procurement and putting—at least for procurement processes—an end to the discussion as to whether ERP systems and lean thinking are reconcilable or not.

Chapter 5

The evolution of e-business has enabled the development of e-marketplaces facilitating the transactions among existing and potential supply chain members on an integrated platform. E-auctions are already considered a critical process for the selection of transport providers, but have not yet been systematically integrated in the 4PL concept. Specifically, a 4PL provider must add value to the e-auction process by assessing, in prior, the capabilities of potential transport providers through an e-negotiation process in order to justify its administrative role. The aim of this chapter is to present a hybrid e-auction-negotiation model, managed by a 4PL provider aiming to improve the transport provider selection process.

Chapter 6

The aim of this chapter is to showcase the potential of new, Cloud-based, Information and Communication Technology (ICT) platforms for transport logistics chain management. The related literature is analysed from five perspectives. First, by examining supply chain issues relating to integration of core processes across organizational boundaries, through improved communication, partnerships, and cooperation. Second, from a strategy and planning perspective, by examining supply chain management as an IT platform dependent business practice. Third, by considering implementation issues using agent, as well as Web service technologies. Fourth, by considering the impact of new trends in service computing built around technologies, such as Semantic Web services and Service Oriented Architecture (SOA), on transport logistics. Finally, the chapter proposes a Cloud-based SOA software platform as an enabler for lowering transaction costs and enhancing business opportunities through service virtualization in shipping transport logistics. The operational aspects of shipping transport logistics management are illustrated using a business case that shows the opportunities for increased collaboration through Cloud-based virtualized services.

Chapter 7

The successful control of the physical flow of the products along the supply chain and product safety assurance depends on the existence of an efficient traceability system. This system must be able to identify each and every single unit produced and distributed from farm to fork. In this chapter, the authors present a Web-based application that enables quality, origin, and processing-related data entry in real time. The application's theoretical background lies on the Traceability Data Pool (TDP) model described in the literature and aims to offer a practical solution for traceability support, especially for the stakeholder operating in the supply chain base, such as the farmers and agricultural cooperatives. This activity-oriented Web application connects field treatments with the rest of the supply chain without implementing additional physical labelling. This application aims at integrating the existing labelling systems implemented in different levels of the supply chain, under a common standard virtual crop codification following the produce along the supply chain, from farm to fork, thus achieving total traceability.

Chapter 8

This chapter provides a framework and discusses the integration of Customer Relationship Management (CRM) and Supplier Relationship Management (SRM) systems in e-ERP environments in supply chains. Currently, the economic environment enterprises are operating in is extremely competitive and influenced greatly by Information and Communication Technologies (ICT). ICT can be an enabler of business performance but also an obstacle if these technologies are not managed carefully. Enterprises are implementing integrated CRM and SRM software in order to remain competitive, but high rates of failure indicate that the implementation of these solutions is not straightforward. In this chapter, organizational issues concerning the integration of CRM, SRM, and ERP software in supply chains are discussed. This chapter aims at informing managers, scholars, students, and researchers of the issues involved, and identifying critical factors of success for enterprises adopting and implementing integrated CRM/SRM solutions.

As supply uncertainty increases in recent years, it is of great importance to manage multiple suppliers, monitor, and warn the supply process of problems to achieve supply coordination in the assembly system in case of supply risks. This chapter analyzes the uncertainty factors and emergence mechanism of supply uncertainty in the assembly system. To achieve supply coordination, the monitoring operation mode under uncertain delivery in the assembly system is constructed. Under this circumstance, suppliers can be classified into four categories, and monitoring tactics are provided for supply coordination. Additionally, case-based reasoning is presented to monitor and warn the supply process with detailed steps and methodology, which are conducive to finding similar cases to provide warning insights and suggestions.

The purpose of this chapter is the thorough observation of supply chains within the broader geographical area of Northern Greece in order to recognize whether organizations formulate and use KPIs in order to evaluate performance. The essence of developing useful KPIs with regard to supply chain performance is the identification of the gap between planning and executing while KPIs also give an indication about areas that are in need of corrective action. However, due to the fact that the Greek region has maintained narrow manufacturing activities as a result of its economic situation in the past five years, the research is focused on that part of the supply chain associated to logistics and customer service.

Section 3
Evolving Business

Chapter 11

Zenon Michaelides, University of Liverpool, UK
Richard Forster, University of Liverpool, UK

This chapter reviews the potential benefits and challenges of introducing Radio Frequency Identification (RFID) technologies as a means of e-enabling logistics supply and distribution systems. It introduces RFID and associated technologies as a catalyst for e-enabling optimised supply and distribution activities. In particular, the emerging role of RFID in integrating logistics supply chains is considered key to aligning tasks and achieving operational efficiencies. Other benefits include better visibility resulting from proactive task and process management, and improved risk assessment associated with better data accuracy/quality. In addition, the optimisation of planning and control functions is enhanced through the introduction of key RFID technologies and their integration into logistics systems and operations. Finally, the use of RFID technologies is reviewed in a variety of diverse sectors and areas, from assisting humanitarian efforts through solutions aimed at recovering from the effects of natural disasters to providing accurate and effective methods of recording race times for the Los Angeles marathon.

Chapter 12

Agorasti Toka, Aristotle University of Thessaloniki, Greece
Eirini Aivazidou, Aristotle University of Thessaloniki, Greece
Antonios Antoniou, Aristotle University of Thessaloniki, Greece
Konstantinos Arvanitopoulos-Darginis, Aristotle University of Thessaloniki, Greece

In the modern world, companies are investigating state-of-the-art practices to optimize both the cost and operational efficiency of their supply chain. Cloud computing emerges as a meaningful technology that could contribute to this optimization by providing infrastructure, platform, and software solutions for the whole supply chain network via Internet. The utilization of cloud-based services in supply chain management leads to financial and operational benefits, while at the same time potential risks and limitations should be taken into account by all supply chain stakeholders. In this chapter, an overview of cloud-based supply chain management is addressed. At first, a brief introduction to cloud technology is provided. Then, the application of cloud computing on supply chain activities is presented, while positive and negative aspects of adapting this technology in modern supply chains are discussed. The case for Third-Party Logistics (3PL) service providers is specially addressed. Finally, conclusions and future research steps are presented.

Chapter 13

Victor Chang, University of Greenwich, UK, University of Southampton, UK & School of Computing and Creative Technologies, UK
Gary Wills, University of Southampton, UK

This chapter proposes a new Supply Chain Business Model in the Education domain and demonstrates how Education as a Service (EaaS) can be delivered. The implementation at the University of Greenwich (UoG) is used as a case study. Cloud computing business models are classified into eight Business Models; this classification is essential to the development of EaaS. A pair of the Hexagon Models are used to review Cloud projects against success criteria; one Hexagon Model focuses on Business Model and the other on IT Services. The UoG case study demonstrates the added value offered by Supply Chain software deployed by private Cloud, where an Oracle suite and SAP supply chain can demonstrate supply chain distribution and is useful for teaching. The evaluation shows that students feel more motivated and can understand their coursework better.

   Dimitrios Terzidis, ELT Sales Consultant, Greece
   Fotios Misopoulos, University of Sheffield, Greece

This chapter's concern is the impact of new technologies in the supply chain of the English Language Teaching (ELT) book market. The chapter's research starts with a literature review that presents the modern technological solutions for an educational system that can alter the book market's supply chain. The electronic teaching and reading facilities can reduce costs of production and distribution, but they can also become an ecologically friendly solution to the environmental problems that the world faces today. The statistical analysis of questionnaires has resulted in the Greek ELT market not being willing to change the existing supply chain operations of the ELT sector. Even though the market does not believe that the use of new technologies can result in the replacement of printed books, there is a trend of using them because they provide marketing benefits to their users. This trend can become the reason of a new era within the ELT book market's supply chain operations.

   Yong Lin, University of Greenwich, UK
   Zhenkun Zhou, Huazhong University of Science and Technology, China
   Li Zhou, University of Greenwich, UK
   Shihua Ma, Huazhong University of Science and Technology, China

ERP system plays a critical role in gaining competitive advantages; however, the implementation of the ERP system is a critical success factor but a difficult process to both the software providers and the buyers of the ERP system. Designing and delivering the implementation services becomes a key challenge to the ERP suppliers. This chapter applies modular logic into service design in order to reduce complexity and increase the service variety and quality, and develop a conceptual structure of service supply chain for delivering ERP implementation services.

Foreword

by Zongwei Luo

Traditional Logistics and Supply Chain Management (LSCM) aims at movement of goods and services from one end of a chain to the other through different stages so as to improve the efficiency, productivity, and profitability of the entire process. Spanning across the economic function of the value chain of a product or service, LSCM has been instrumental in connecting and smoothing business activities, forming various kinds of business relationships among LSCM participants. Relationship management in LSCM increasingly becomes one of the core functions in today's marketplace for companies to strive for business competiveness to meet the dynamic economy calls for innovative logistics operations and supply chain management to address uncertainties and improve efficiencies for business agility. E-Logistics and E-Supply Chain Management (e-LSCM) provides technological solutions with electronic LSCM infrastructure and networks that can support interconnections among LSCM participants and enable them to collaborate in a much more efficient and effective manner with provisions of agile and responsive planning and business decisions capabilities.

Key technological and business enablers for e-LSCM includes Radio Frequency Identification (RFID) technology, Cloud computing and infrastructures, service innovation, and advanced business analytics. They are critical to develop infrastructural, application, and management technologies for e-LSCM related processes and services, leading to, for example, shorter lead times, reduced working capital needs, and closer customer relationships. E-LSCM will ideally enable informed decision-making and better market adaptation capabilities for companies to strive for business competeness and sustainability in the fast changing business environment.

This book titled *E-Logistics and E-Supply Chain Management: Applications for Evolving Business* has 15 well selected chapters to give students, researchers, and practitioners a critical understanding of current academic and pragmatic approaches to e-LSCM. Among those, 3 chapters are devoted to the introduction of the concepts of e-LSCM, 7 chapters are devoted to the examination of various elements of e-LSCM, and 5 chapters are devoted to solution enablers for evolving business. With good balanced materials, this book would serve well as an aid to readers who like to read introductory materials of e-LSCM and to those who like to gain deeper insights in specific focused areas of e-LSCM.

Overall, this book provides updated materials disclosing innovative findings for e-LSCM. As e-LSCM not only helps enterprises to improve their business processes today, but also enables them to adopt technological solutions in the future, it supports business evolutions, especially enabling innovative business models for creating value for customers. This book on e-LSCM would, of course, help readers to gain understanding and insights in this important yet fast developing field.

Zongwei Luo
University of Hong Kong, China

Zongwei Luo *is a Senior Researcher at the E-Business Technology Institute, The University of Hong Kong (China). Before that, he was working at the IBM TJ Watson Research Center in Yorktown Heights (NY, USA). He also served as the Affiliate Senior Consultant to ETI Consulting Limited. His research has been supported by various funding sources, and his research results have appeared in major international journals and leading conferences with 5 books and over 100 papers published, including an IEEE International Conference best paper award. He is the founding Editor-in-Chief of the International Journal of Applied Logistics and serves as an Associate Editor and Editorial Advisory Board member in many international journals. Dr. Luo's recent interests include Internet of things and Cloud computing, service science and computing, innovation management and sustainable development, technology adoption and risk management, and e-business model and practices, especially for advanced manufacturing, structural health management, and logistics and supply chain management.*

Foreword

by Michael Bourlakis

It is well documented that innovations in Information and Communications Technologies (ICT) have had a profound impact on firms. It has also been argued that information technology related business changes are greater than the changes caused by the industrial revolution. Unsurprisingly, in the past few years, we have witnessed the increasing role of ICT within logistics and supply chains, and many academics and professionals have noted that without the use of ICT, modern logistics and supply chain systems would not be able to operate successfully. More importantly, in many contexts, ICT and its applications offer a competitive advantage to companies, such as increased operational efficiency, improved responsiveness, as well as better integration, alignment, and collaboration with other supply chain companies.

This book is titled *E-Logistics and E-Supply Chain Management: Applications for Evolving Business*, and therefore, it aims to analyse many key innovation and changes emanating from the use of ICT within logistics and supply chains. The book contains three major sections ("The Concepts of E-Logistics and E-Supply Chain Management," "E-Logistics and E-Supply Chain Management," and "Evolving Business") and fifteen comprehensive chapters detailing a plethora of ICT features including Web applications, e-procurement, cloud computing, ERP systems, and RFID, to name a few. The authors have also carefully selected these book chapters, as they represent many different industries and sectors, such as logistics services, transportation, shipping, education, and e-learning. They have also examined the application of ICT in relation to many topical supply chain issues, such as collaboration and integration, outsourcing and 4PL, leanness, traceability, and CRM, and have provided many new, original, and interesting insights to the issues explored.

Based on the above, I believe that this book is a welcome addition to the current logistics and supply chain management literature. It will serve sufficiently the undergraduate and postgraduate student market, and many researchers and practitioners will find this book extremely beneficial. Most impressive is the breadth and depth of the ICT issues covered. These issues are not discussed on a "stand alone" basis, but are fully incorporated in a range of logistics and supply chain contexts and issues.

To conclude, I have no reservations to recommend this book to anybody interested in E-Logistics and E-Supply Chain Management.

Michael Bourlakis
Chair in Supply Chain Management
Brunel University, UK

Michael Bourlakis *graduated with a B.Sc. in Business Administration from Athens University of Economics and Business and completed MBA and PhD degrees at University of Edinburgh. Michael has produced more than 170 publications including journal papers, book chapters, and conference papers. His papers have appeared in leading supply chain management, marketing, and business journals, such as Supply Chain Management: An International Journal, International Journal of Logistics: Research & Applications, International Journal of Logistics Management, European Journal of Marketing, Journal of Marketing Management, Journal of Business & Industrial Marketing, Environment & Planning D, Technological Forecasting and Social Change. He has received funding from various bodies including the European Union, Food Standards Agency (UK), and Regional Development Agencies (UK). Michael is on the Editorial Board of six journals; he is a member of the European Technology Platform (Food for Life, European Union) and the Academic Committee of the Chartered Institute of Logistics & Transport (CILTUK). From January 2013 onwards, he will serve as a joint Editor-in-Chief for a leading logistics journal, International Journal of Logistics: Research & Applications.*

Preface

INTRODUCTION

Logistics and Supply Chain Management has been a vital part of every economy and every business entity. Supply Chain Management encompasses the management (including the planning, design, implementation, and control) of all of the logistics processes (including procurement, warehousing, inventory control, manufacturing, distribution, and sales order fulfillment functions) of a business. Both sciences have become prestigious research fields in the past few years. More than 75 journals include these terms in their titles (Folinas, 2012).

Whilst the field of Logistics has existed for a considerable time, defined as: "1. The science of the movement of supplying and maintenance of military forces in the field; 2. the management of materials flow through an organization, from raw materials flow through to finished goods; 3. the detailed planning and organization of any large complex operation" (Collins, 1990), the concepts of E-Logistics and E-Supply Chain Management are relatively new. Supply Chain Management development can be traced back to the use of modern logistics (circa 1980s). In the early days, logistics was not considered to make much of a contribution to profitability and given little capital investment. Process and delivery cycle times were long and global competition virtually non-existent. Modern Supply Chain Management (SCM) is comprised of five stages: Management, Warehousing and Transportation, Total Cost Management (TCM), Integrated Logistics Management, SCM, and e-SCM (Ross, 2003).

Evolutions in electronic business, especially business models relying on new developments in logistics and supply chain management, challenge traditional channels for creating value for customers. The adoption of electronic supply chain models not only helps enterprises to improve their business processes today, but also enables them to incorporate new technologies for e-commerce solutions in the future. This book examines how organisations are restructuring their supply chains in order to accommodate new technologies and new ways of doing business on the Internet. In particular, it explores the creation of integrated supply chains, the development of virtual business communities, and how business process re-engineering and business operations re-orienting enable dynamic responses to new customer demands.

The aim of this book is to give students, researchers, and practitioners a critical understanding of current academic and pragmatic approaches to E-Logistics and E-Supply Chain Management. With this book, readers should be able to:

- Assess the structure, nature, and management of e-logistics and the changing external environment in which businesses operate;
- Evaluate the tools and techniques logistics managers may use to measure cost and performance;

- Examine the role of logistics in ensuring customer satisfaction in different areas of business activity;
- Evaluate logistics trade-offs in relation to integrated strategy;
- Debate the impact of logistics decisions on the environment and global industries;
- Analyse the contribution of e-business logistics to competitive strategy, productivity, and value advantage;
- Judge critically concepts and methods applicable to the implementation of e-logistics;
- Identify how major functional areas within business influence e-logistics; and
- Engage in and reflect upon problem solving in e-logistics.

The book contains 15 excellent chapters (organised in 3 sections) that examine most of the key aspects of E-Logistics and E-Supply Chain Management. The first section examines the Concepts of E-Logistics and E-Supply Chain Management:

- Introduction to E-Logistics and the E-Supply Chain
- E-Supply Chain Collaboration and Integration
- Information Technology (IT), Electronic Commerce, and Supply Chain Management (SCM)

The second part of the book looks at the elements of E-Logistics and E-Supply Chain Management:

- Procurement
- Distribution and Transport
- Fulfilment
- Traceability
- Customer Relationship Management
- Supplier Relationship Management
- Enterprise Resource Planning

The final part of the book on Evolving Business discusses the future research directions for E-Logistics and E-Supply Chain Management.

- Radio Frequency Identification in the E-Logistics Interface
- Cloud Computing in Supply Chain Management
- Data Modelling and Information Logistics
- The Evolution and Impact of IT on Logistics and SCM: E-Production
- Future Considerations: Sustainability and Reverse Logistics

This book is considered to be of aid to the following prospective audiences:

- First of all, students (both at final year Undergraduate and Postgraduate level) who study Business, Computer Science and Information Systems, Logistics, and Supply Chain Management.
- Moreover, researchers in the above fields.
- Practitioners that either hold a position in the logistics system of companies/organisations or work in third-party logistics services providers.

The Editors' intention was to help the above groups by giving them an easy to read and understand book with the right depth and the right amount of topic coverage.

ORGANISATION OF THE BOOK

The book is organised in three sections. Each section refers to a specific area regarding E-Logistics and E-Supply Chain Management.

Section 1: The Concepts of E-Logistics and the E-Supply Chain Management

The first section serves as an introduction to E-Logistics and E-Supply Chain Management. Its three chapters synthesize the literature and provide definitions of E-Logistics and E-Supply Chain Management as well as analyse the main concepts and parameters.

Chapter 1: *Introduction to E-Logistics and E-Supply Chain Management.* This chapter provides an introduction to the E-Logistics and the E-Supply Chain Management paradigm. It presents definitions and an overview of Logistics and Supply Chain Management and the logistics processes of the supply chain, expanded upon in the subsequent chapters that provide empirical evidence through case studies, such as those from India, China, Europe, and the UK, which are presented and analysed.

Chapter 2: *E-Supply Chain Collaboration and Integration: Implementation Issues and Challenges.* The objective of the chapter is to formulate a supplier integration strategy with the aim to optimise the supply chain in Fast Moving Consumer Goods (FMCG) Sector using a literature-based approach. There is a scarcity of research inputs that study the impact of supplier integration on optimisation of the Value Chain. The chapter emphasizes the integration of supplier relationship practices and their impact on the optimisation of the Value Chain. FMCG industry based on the value chain is defined, and an e-collaborative framework is introduced. The framework is primarily based on factors comprising the supplier integration strategy, i.e. information sharing, e-business systems, and policy-based supplier selections that have a positive influence on the long-term lean manufacturing adoption in FMCG firms. Implementing supply strategy in practice requires the collaboration of manufacturers and suppliers using e-collaborations.

Chapter 3: *Web Applications for the Outsourcing of Logistics Services.* This chapter investigates the extent to which the Greek Third-Party Logistics (3PLs) companies use the internet in order to provide information and on-line services to their customers. It is based on the findings of a survey that examined the Web presence of 3PL companies in Greece. Thus, the websites of these companies were contacted and evaluated against a specific questionnaire that consists of two main categories of questions: the scope of logistics services which 3PLs provide, and the Internet practices and technologies that the examined companies use in order to support the identified logistics services. The findings of the survey reveal the effort that 3PL companies in Greece have applied in order to effectively and efficiently support their provided services via the Internet. Furthermore, they support the belief that adaptation and application of the Internet best practices and innovative technologies turns out to be beneficial for all the parties involved in the examined business sector.

Section 2: E-Logistics and E-Supply Chain Management

The logistics and management functions are the main topic of this section. Functions, such as procurement, distribution and transport, traceability, customer relationship management, supplier relationship management, and enterprise resource planning, are discussed in this section based on real life examples.

Chapter 4: *Measuring the Impact of Tools on the Leanness of E-Procurement Processes.* The concept of lean thinking is—despite its prominence as waste reducer and value creator—still mainly applied to the manufacturing environment. Whilst investigations on applicability to the service industry are advancing fast, little has been distributed for the area of procurement. This development is opposed by trends of increasing degree of outsourcing and related high portions of procurement of up to 60% of a company's total value creation. The mismatch in terms of lack of strategic attention on lean procurement on the one hand and the responsibility of this function for the majority of a company's value creation on the other, combined with the simultaneous trend of establishing "miracle cures" in the form of e-procurement gave rise to the interest in determining the stake of buy-side systems in the leanness of procurement processes. For this purpose, a case study approach was adopted focusing on the central questions of what lean means for procurement, which measures could portray leanness in this instance, how the stake of buy-side systems can be reflected in the performance indicators with separate consideration of repetitive processes in operational and strategic purchasing, in order to finally attribute a clear enabler role to IT for achieving leanness in operational procurement. This finding has been reached by the means of an objective research approach, relying on quantitative methods such as KPI measurement for data collection and regression analysis for the interpretation of correlation between the variables. As such, this chapter has not only a high value for practitioners by providing a baseline for benchmarking lean performance of e-procurement, by supporting system investment decisions, or by simply facilitating decisions on adapting existing IT solutions. It also proves as enrichment to the existing theoretical body of knowledge filling into the afore said gaps of lean procurement and putting—at least for procurement processes—an end to the discussion as to whether ERP systems and lean thinking are reconcilable or not.

Chapter 5: *A Hybrid E-Auction/Negotiation Model as a Tool for 4PL to Improve the Transport Provider Selection Process.* The evolution of e-business has enabled the development of e-marketplaces facilitating the transactions among existing and potential supply chain members on an integrated platform. E-auctions are already considered a critical process for the selection of transport providers, but have not yet been systematically integrated in the 4PL concept. Specifically, a 4PL provider must add value to the e-auction process by assessing, in prior, the capabilities of potential transport providers through an e-negotiation process in order to justify its administrative role. The aim of this chapter is to present a hybrid e-auction-negotiation model, managed by a 4PL provider aiming to improve the transport provider selection process.

Chapter 6: *The Use of Cloud Computing in Shipping Logistics.* The aim of this chapter is to showcase the potential of new, Cloud-based, Information and Communication Technology (ICT) platforms for transport logistics chain management. The related literature is analysed from five perspectives. First, by examining supply chain issues relating to integration of core processes across organizational boundaries, through improved communication, partnerships, and cooperation. Second, from a strategy and planning perspective, by examining supply chain management as an IT platform dependent business practice. Third, by considering implementation issues using agent, as well as Web service technologies.

Fourth, by considering the impact of new trends in service computing built around technologies, such as Semantic Web services and Service Oriented Architecture (SOA), on transport logistics. Finally, the chapter proposes a Cloud-based SOA software platform as an enabler for lowering transaction costs and enhancing business opportunities through service virtualization in shipping transport logistics. The operational aspects of shipping transport logistics management are illustrated using a business case that shows the opportunities for increased collaboration through Cloud-based virtualized services.

Chapter 7: *A Web Application for Supply Chain Traceability.* The successful control of the physical flow of the products along the supply chain and product safety assurance depends on the existence of an efficient traceability system. This system must be able to identify each and every single unit produced and distributed from farm to fork. In this chapter, the authors present a Web-based application that enables quality, origin, and processing-related data entry in real time. The application's theoretical background lies on the Traceability Data Pool (TDP) model described in the literature and aims to offer a practical solution for traceability support, especially for the stakeholder operating in the supply chain base, such as the farmers and agricultural cooperatives. This activity-oriented Web application connects field treatments with the rest of the supply chain without implementing additional physical labelling. This application aims at integrating the existing labelling systems implemented in different levels of the supply chain, under a common standard virtual crop codification following the produce along the supply chain, from farm to fork, thus achieving total traceability.

Chapter 8: *E-Enterprise: Organisational Issues of CRM, SRM, and ERP Systems Integration.* This chapter provides a framework and discusses the integration of Customer Relationship Management (CRM) and Supplier Relationship Management (SRM) systems in e-ERP environments in supply chains. Currently, the economic environment enterprises are operating in is extremely competitive and influenced greatly by Information and Communication Technologies (ICT). ICT can be an enabler of business performance but also an obstacle if these technologies are not managed carefully. Enterprises are implementing integrated CRM and SRM software in order to remain competitive, but high rates of failure indicate that the implementation of these solutions is not straightforward. In this chapter, organizational issues concerning the integration of CRM, SRM, and ERP software in supply chains are discussed. This chapter aims at informing managers, scholars, students, and researchers of the issues involved, and identifying critical factors of success for enterprises adopting and implementing integrated CRM/SRM solutions.

Chapter 9: *Monitoring and Warning Mechanisms of Supply Coordination in the Assembly System under Delivery Uncertainty.* The objective of this chapter is to explore the emergence mechanism of supply uncertainty in the assembly system, analyse the uncertainty factors and characteristics of the assembly system, which is different from the series system and the distribution system, and find the consequence of supply uncertainty in the assembly system. On that basis, to achieve supply coordination, the monitoring operation mode under uncertain delivery in the assembly system is constructed. The most important goals are to find the proper monitoring mechanism and warning model of supply coordination in the assembly system. This chapter contributes to the literature by analysing and finding the emergence mechanism of supply uncertainty in the assembly system, which is a bit different from the uncertainty in other supply chains. The investigation of many automobile companies supports this analysis. The proper monitoring mechanism of supply coordination is proposed and case-based reasoning is applied to monitor and warn the supply process in the assembly system under supply uncertainty. Based on a vast investigation of the automobile industry in China, such as the Jiangling Engine Company, Shen Long Automobile Company, General Motors' Corporation in China, Dongfeng Automobile Company, etc., the quantitative data among these companies was collected and compared. Qualitative analysis is then used to find the uncertainty of the assembly system. Based on logic reasoning, the mechanisms of the monitoring and warning model are proposed. Case-based reasoning is conducted to find the similar case to provide the warning insights and suggestions. Results show that supply uncertainty factors in the assembly system is a bit different from the series system and the distribution system. The manufacturer can classify the suppliers to cope with supply uncertainty while the different warning levels can be adopted accordingly. Case-based reasoning can be presented to monitor and warn coordination of supply process in the assembly system. As supply uncertainty increases in recent years, results and some mechanisms proposed from this chapter provide insight for the manufacturer for how to manage the multiple suppliers, monitor and warn the supply process to achieve supply coordination in case of supply uncertainty. Consequently, the manufacturer should know the emergence mechanism of supply uncertainty in its assembly system and take effective policies to prepare for the supply risks during the purchasing period.

Chapter 10: *The Strategic Contribution of ERP Systems to the Formulation of Non-Financial Key Performance Measures (KPIs) in Logistics Activities: An Exploratory Study in Northern Greece*. The purpose of this chapter is to make a thorough observation of supply chains within the broader geographical area of Northern Greece in order to recognise whether organisations formulate and use KPIs (Key Performance Indicators) in order to evaluate performance. The essence of developing useful KPIs with regard to supply chain performance is the identification of the gap between planning and executing, while KPIs also give an indication about areas that are in need of corrective action. However, due to the fact that the Greek region has maintained narrow manufacturing activities as a result of its economic situation in the past five years, the research is focused on—but not limited to—that part of the supply chain associated with logistics and customer service. With respect to the diversity of the sample researched, which is categorized into four groups—namely LSPs (Logistics Service Providers), wholesalers, retailers, and service companies—some trigger outcomes have been obtained regarding the manner through which those companies are manipulating their information flow—either through their ERP (Enterprise Resource Planning) or another IS (Information System). Within this context, it is also observed whether ERPs are utilized in order to assist and support the design and deployment of KPIs in the framework of performance evaluation with regards to key and support logistics activities.

Section 3: Evolving Business

For anyone who needs to understand the future challenges of logistics and supply chain management, the examination of case studies seems to be a very useful tool. These cases refer the future practices of logistics and supply chain management to various business sectors.

Chapter 11: *The Use of RFID Technologies for E-Enabling Logistics Supply Chains*. This chapter reviews the potential benefits and challenges of introducing Radio Frequency Identification (RFID) technologies as a means of e-enabling logistics supply and distribution systems. It introduces RFID and associated technologies as a catalyst for e-enabling optimised supply and distribution activities. In particular, the emerging role of RFID in integrating logistics supply chains is considered key to aligning tasks and achieving operational efficiencies. Other benefits include better visibility resulting from proactive task and process management, and improved risk assessment associated with better data accuracy/quality. In addition, the optimisation of planning and control functions is enhanced through the introduction of key RFID technologies and their integration into logistics operations. Finally, the use of RFID technologies in a variety of sectors and areas is reviewed, from monitoring the supply of perishable goods to the distribution of pharmaceutical products, to tracking livestock "from farm to fork."

Chapter 12: *Cloud Computing in Supply Chain Management: An Overview.* In this chapter, the use of cloud computing is presented in supply chain management and more specifically in the case of third party logistics service providers. At a first level, the chapter demonstrates what cloud technology is, how it can be used in supply chain management, as well as its benefits compared with other systems. Furthermore, the chapter outlines the implementation of cloud computing in the case of third-party logistics companies, especially from the perspectives of cost effectiveness and real-time visibility of shipment and inventory between companies and their customers.

Chapter 13: *A University of Greenwich Case Study of Cloud Computing: Education as a Service.* This chapter proposes a new Supply Chain Business Model in the Education domain and demonstrates how Education as a Service (EaaS) can be delivered. The implementation at the University in the UK is used as a case study. Cloud computing business models are classified into eight Business Models. This classification is essential to the development of EaaS. A pair of the Hexagon Models is used to review Cloud projects against success criteria; one Hexagon Model focuses on the Business Model and the other on IT Services. The case study is used to demonstrate the added value offered by Supply Chain software deployed by private cloud, where Oracle suite can demonstrate supply chain distribution, is useful for teaching. The evaluation shows that Students feel more motivated and can understand their coursework better supported by statistical analysis. A strategic plan of using enterprise SAP (Systems Applications Products) for supply chain in higher education is in place to improve teaching and learning where SAP is more suitable for delivery of teaching activities and content. It is believed that adopting an appropriate EaaS and the right technologies such as SAP will help this and other universities to improve learning efficiency and quality of teaching.

Chapter 14: *Investigating the Effect of E-Learning Technologies on Supply Chain Activities: The Evidence of ELT Book Market.* This chapter is concerned with the impact of new technologies in the supply chain of the English Language Teaching (ELT) book market. The chapter's research starts with a literature review that presents the modern technological solutions for an educational system that can alter the book market's supply chain. The electronic teaching and reading facilities can reduce costs of production and distribution, but they can also become an ecologically friendly solution to the environmental problems that the world faces today. The statistical analysis of questionnaires has resulted in the Greek ELT market being unwilling to change the existing supply chain operations of the ELT sector. Even though the market does not believe that the use of new technologies can result in the replacement of printed books. There is a trend of using them because they provide marketing benefits to their users. This trend can become the catalyst of a new era within the ELT book market's supply chain operations.

Chapter 15: *ERP Implementation Service Supply Chain: A Modular Perspective.* ERP system plays a critical role in gaining competitive advantages; however, the implementation of the ERP system is a critical success factor but a difficult process to both the software providers and the buyers of the ERP system. Designing and delivering the implementation services becomes a key challenge to the ERP suppliers. This chapter applies modular logic into service design in order to reduce complexity and increase the service variety and quality, and develop a conceptual structure of service supply chain for delivering ERP implementation services.

Deryn Graham
University of Greenwich, UK

Ioannis Manikas
University of Greenwich, UK

Dimitris Folinas
ATEI Thessaloniki, Greece

REFERENCES

Folinas, D. (2012). A framework for the management of logistics outsourcing life cycle . In *Outsourcing Management for Supply Chain Operations and Logistics Service* (pp. 24–38). Hershey, PA: IGI Global. doi:10.4018/978-1-4666-2008-7.ch002

Hanks, P. (Ed.). (1990). *Collins dictionary of the English language* (2nd ed.). London, UK: Collins.

Ross, D. F. (2003). *Introduction to e-supply chain management: Engaging technology to build market-winning business partnerships*. New York, NY: The St. Lucie Press.

Acknowledgment

The editors would like to express their gratitude to a number of people who have contributed to the completion of this book in various ways and to thank them all for their assistance and encouragement.

First, we wish to thank all of the authors for their excellent contributions to this book. All of you also served as reviewers for manuscripts written by other authors. Thank you all for your contributions and your constructive reviews.

Second, to our colleagues and Editorial Advisory Board (EAB) members: Dr. Hamid Allaoui and Dr. Gilles Goncalves, for their support during the reviewing process.

Finally, we would like to express our gratitude to Zongwei Luo and Michael Bourlakis for their prompt response and support.

Special thanks to the staff of IGI Global for their continuous coaching and guidance. Thank you Hannah and Austin!

You all helped to make this book a reality!

Deryn Graham
University of Greenwich, UK

Ioannis Manikas
University of Greenwich, UK

Dimitris Folinas
ATEI Thessaloniki, Greece

Section 1
The Concepts of E–Logistics and E–Supply Chain Management

Chapter 1
Introduction to E–Logistics and E–Supply Chain Management

Deryn Graham
University of Greenwich, UK

ABSTRACT

This chapter provides an introduction to the E-Logistics and the E-Supply Chain Management paradigm. It presents definitions and an overview of Logistics and Supply Chain Management, and the logistics processes of the Supply Chain.

INTRODUCTION

Logistics and Supply Chain Management has been a vital part of every economy and every business entity. Supply Chain Management (SCM) encompasses the management (including the planning, design, implementation and control) of all of the logistics processes (including procurement, warehousing, inventory control, manufacturing, distribution and sales order fulfillment functions) of a business. Both sciences have become prestigious research fields in the past few years. More than 75 journals include these terms in their titles (Folinas, 2012).

The objectives of this chapter are to define and provide an overview of concepts and terms, namely; Logistics, Supply Chain Management, E-Logistics and E-Supply Chain Management (E-SCM). The chapter describes the logistic processes of Supply Chain Management, the relationships between Information Technology (IT), and resulting trends such as greater Supply Chain Integration and Collaboration.

MAIN FOCUS OF THE CHAPTER

Issues, Controversies, Problems

The field of Logistics has existed for some considerable time, defined as: "1. The science of the movement of supplying and maintenance of military forces in the field; 2. the management of materials flow through an organization, from raw materials flow through to finished goods; 3. the detailed planning and organization of any large complex operation" (Collins, 1990, p. 903). This

DOI: 10.4018/978-1-4666-3914-0.ch001

definition is indicative of the age and military origins of the term, the latter two definitions are more appropriate to modern business. The second definition describes supply chain management, minus the important references to information and information flow.

Whilst the field of Logistics has been in existence for some considerable time, with strong military associations, the concepts of E-Logistics and E-Supply Chain Management are relatively new. In the early days, logistics was considered not to make much of a contribution to profitability and given little capital investment, process and delivery cycle times were long and global competition virtually none existent.

Beginning with the early days of production systems, the history of production systems has moved on from the limitations of production and supply famously coined by Henry Ford: "Any customer can have any car painted any colour that he wants, so long as it is black". Kiichiro Toyota, founder of Toyota, started with the production of 20,000 vehicles a year, a very far cry from the production figure at the Ford plants. Identifying that in order to best raise efficiency levels when starting out from limited production volumes, it would be necessary to eliminate stockpiling in the production process, and to achieve this it would be necessary to ensure the Just-In-Time (JIT) supply of parts to all segments of the manufacturing process. Thereby, reducing stockpiling and the need for warehousing of parts, driving out waste, etc. JIT was developed by the Japanese and first used for Toyota. With JIT, supplies and components are "pulled" though the system when and where needed.

Manufacturing processes can involve push or pull production systems. Push is based on sales forecasts which in turn push products into the warehouse, this is also known as "make to stock" and is based on an estimate of how many products might sell. Production of parts pushes the production of the end product. Conversely, Pull systems (the opposite of push), is when a product is made only when a customer order arrives. It is based on actual demand in the market, and is also known as "make to order". In this case, demand for parts pulls the manufacturing of parts for the end product.

The Push system is not used much as it requires companies to hold massive amounts of stock which will increase warehouse inventory costs. Holding stock will also cause other problems such as stock obtaining defects due to long periods of being on the shelf, this could lead to problems further in the supply chain as damaged stock could be used in production which will produce a bad quality product and the whole production process will have to stop until fixed.

Pull is the most used in mass production with reduced warehouse costs as well as less inventory being held (material is only needed when orders come in). An example is Dell computers, which makes computers to order (specification) when ordered. Pull systems produce products with a short lead time, the time between receiving and delivering the order.

The concept of Lean Management also originated at Toyota in Japan. Lean Management provides a competitive edge by eliminating waste, with the aim that every step adds value to the process.

A Supply Chain is the chain of activities from the raw materials to the customer, a classic supply chain description is: "Farm to Fork". A typical supply chain involves activities such as sourcing the raw materials, transporting the raw materials for processing, transporting the processed goods for warehousing, before transporting the goods again for packaging, packaging the goods, transporting the packaged goods to a central distributor, before finally transporting the finished goods to local retail outlets and ultimately customers.

A Supply Chain can be defined as the sequence of an organisation. The sequence refers to the facilities (warehouses, factories, processing centres, distribution centres, retail outlets and offices), and functions and activities (purchasing, forecasting, inventory management, information management, quality assurance, scheduling, production, distribution, delivery, transport, supplier management, and customer management).

Supply Chain Management development can be traced back to the use of modern logistics (circa 1980s). Supply Chain Management relates to an organisation's operations, involving the optimisation of material and information flows for that organisation. This management is achieved through the use of business applications software, such as Enterprise Resource Planning (ERP) systems for example.

The two kinds of movement in the supply chain are material and information flows. Material flow is the flow of materials from suppliers to customers, via manufacturers, assemblers and distributors. Information flow is bidirectional throughout the supply chain. The information flow is equally important to the material flow and is enhanced by the use of IT to gather customer demand information for instance to upstream supply chain functions and subsequently pull (demand-driven) supply chain operations.

Information Technology (IT) encompasses software (applications), hardware (including computers, scanners, etc.), firmware and middleware, as well as the network infrastructures (internet, intranet, etc.), platforms and operating systems, and the World Wide Web (WWW). The Internet refers to the physical network (infrastructure), connecting computers across the globe, using WAN (Wireless or Wide Area Networks). The Intranet is the internal network connecting computers within an organisation, using Local Area Networks, or LANs. There is also the Extranet which is a network that uses the Internet to link multiple Intranets. The World Wide Web (WWW) is essentially the main technique for publishing information on the Internet, displayed on web pages and accessed via (Web) browsers.

The objectives of supply chain management are to get the right products, in the right quantities, to the right place, and at the right time, at a minimal cost. The primary goal is to eradicate waste of all forms, where supply chain entities touch, such as logistics, inventory, procurement, customer management, product development and financial functions. A second goal is to abandon vertical integration (vertical integration is expanded upon later), divesting non profitable functions, and collaborating with supply chain partners. Thirdly, there is the explosion of global trade, internet technologies and international logistics. The internet has opened up markets to the smallest of companies, allowing them to have a web and therefore a market presence. Fourthly, today's market place requires companies to be agile and efficient with shorter times frames for services, product mixes and volume and variety changes, leading to the spawning of virtual organisations, for example Amazon. Finally, applying the technologies; tools centred on the Internet for competitive advantage, thus transforming all functions of SCM to the Web and in addition, the Cloud, thereby generating new sources of competitive advantage through cyber collaboration, enabling joint product innovation, on-line buying, markets, network planning, operations management, and customer fulfillment.

The elements of SCM are:

- Demand
- Production
- Procurement
- Distribution
- Fulfillment

Logistics is a primary activity in the Value Chain.

There are conflicting objectives between companies in the supply chain; rapid response to the market, minimum variance between products, minimum inventory, the aim for quality (Total Quality Management [TQM]), and product lifecycle support (reverse logistics – working backwards to improve logistic processes in the product lifecycle).

Within each company in the supply chain there are also conflicting objectives: Marketing objectives include the rapid introduction of new products, new products requiring short (but usually unknown product lifecycles), and the provision of a high variety of products. There can be problems with raw materials procurement, difficulties in forecasting quantities to be ordered and increasing transportation costs. There can also be production problems, with long production lead times and high production costs.

These conflicting objectives have led to a drive towards supply chain integration. There is a common belief that managing the entire supply chain as a single entity can significantly improve cost and service performance. Integration is the process by which parts of a whole become more connected so that they are in effect less "part" and more "whole," i.e., such that functions formerly carried out by one part are carried out by others, and usually vice-versa. Supply chain integration is the process of transformation or "rationalisation" of the supply chain by which functions are redefined and redistributed so that these are carried out faster, cheaper, better (more quality, i.e. meeting requirements of the "customer," who is the next "receiver" in the supply chain).

In order to achieve an integrated supply chain, a baseline of the current material flow within the supply chain needs to be established to enable functional integration. For example, a supply chain involving the functions of: Purchasing (of raw materials), Material Control, Production, Sales and Distribution (to customers: Customer Service), can be integrated into three main functions: Materials management, Manufacturing Management and Distribution. These three functions can be integrated internally or externally to the organisation.

Barriers to internal integration include the organisation's structure (e.g. department centric), the availability of comparable and valid measurement systems, inventory ownership, information technology—compatibility and use, and knowledge transfer capability—is such information flow possible? Integration can be backwards or forwards, and vertical: From or to the raw materials (suppliers) to or from the finished goods (customers), requiring the ability to produce goods previously purchased, raising the issue of make or buy ("Make-buy"). Successful supply chain management requires mutual agreement on goals, trust, and compatible organisational cultures.

Integrated supply chains offer opportunities:

- The generation of accurate pull data (demand).
- A reduction of lot size (production) and Vendor Managed Inventories (VMI).
- **Postponement:** Keeping the product generic as long as possible.
- **Channel assembly:** Sending individual components and modules rather than finished goods to the distributor.
- **A drop in shipping and special packaging costs:** The supplier will ship directly to the end consumer, rather than to the seller.
- **Standardisation:** Reducing the number of variations in materials and components.
- **Electronic ordering and funds transfer:** "Paperless" ordering and 100% material acceptance, payment by "wire."

Supply Chain Management began from the late 19th century to the early 1960s, with the decentralisation of logistics, to then focus upon Total Cost Management (TCM), before the consideration of Integrated Functions (during the 1980s). In the mid-1990s these concepts, such as integrated logistics were consolidated, leading to Supply Chain Management. Today, the internet has changed SCM radically to E-SCM with the evolution of E-Marketplaces and exchanges, collaborative planning and fulfillment management (Ross, 2003).

SOLUTIONS AND RECOMMENDATIONS

Modern Supply Chain Management has arisen in response to modern critical business requirements, the extension of available tools for modern enterprise management providing sources of cost reduction and process improvement. Available tools such as those for ERP (Enterprise Resource Planning), TQM (Total Quality Management) and BPR (Business Process Reengineering). SCM is comprised of five stages: Management; Warehousing and transportation; Total Cost Management (TCM); Integrated Logistics Management; SCM; and e-SCM (Ross, 2003).

E-Commerce or Electronic Commerce can be considered as "all electronically mediated transactions between any organization and any third party it deals with" (Chaffey, 2011, p. 10). A subset of E-Commerce is Social Commerce, where site owners incorporate reviews and ratings into a site. Linking social networking sites aids understanding of customer requirements with a view to converting this information into sales. E-Business (Electronic Business) is "the transformation of key business processes through the use of Internet technologies" (Chaffey, 2011, p. 12).

Laudon and Laudon (2011) describe E-Commerce; digital markets and digital goods, from the perspective of management information systems. They describe the impact of E-Commerce technologies on the world markets and collaborations for B2B (Business to Business) E-Commerce.

Logistic processes are now also prefixed be "E", for example E-Procurement. Electronic Procurement relates to "the electronic integration and management of all procurement activities including purchase request, authorization, ordering, delivery and payment between a purchaser and a supplier" (Chaffey, 2011, p. 355).

The common denominator for all E-Logistics processes namely the "E" is the exploitation of technology to give a competitive advantage and to add value. Improvements in the available technologies have led to vast increases in information and knowledge acquisition, and new concepts such as Big Data (massive repositories of data) and Cloud Computing. The Cloud Computing model, more commonly referred to simply as Cloud Computing or "The Cloud", provides access to "clouds" of shared computing resources such as storage and applications, over a network, usually the Internet. The future appears to see more delegation of technology provision and management through Cloud Computing, as well as greater marketing opportunities (E-Marketing) and e-tailing (on-line retailing) and m-commerce (mobile commerce), etc., with more internationalisation and globalisation.

Evolutions in electronic business especially business models relying on new developments in logistics and supply chain management challenge traditional channels for creating value for customers. The adoption of electronic supply chain models not only helps enterprises to improve their business processes today, but also enables them to incorporate new technologies for E-commerce solutions in the future.

Organisations are restructuring their supply chains; in order to accommodate new technologies and new ways of doing business on the internet. In particular, this has led to the creation and adoption of integrated supply chains, the development of virtual business communities, business process re-engineering and business operations re-orienting, enabling dynamic responses to new customer demands, and new customer or consumer behaviour, segmentation and values. In order to respond to new customer demands, new models such as Cloud Computing and new resources, such as Big Data, have been created.

An area this book does not discuss is the realm of Social or Ethical considerations. The Internet and WWW have had huge implications for society and its behaviour. Historically technological progress and innovation has always taken precedent over social and ethical concerns, but real issues do exist. Cloud Computing for instance, raises again worries about security and the right of access to certain data, and whether or not, some data and services should be cloud-based with commercial proprietors as the custodians of such information and resources.

The E-Logistics and the E-Supply Chain Management paradigm is expanded upon in the subsequent chapters that provide empirical evidence through case studies, such as those from India, China, Europe, and the UK.

FUTURE RESEARCH DIRECTIONS

E-Logistics or Electronic Logistics is part of an "E-genre," which includes E-Learning, E-Business, E-Commerce, etc. All of these terms essentially refer to the major and significant employment of IT for that domain. In the case of E-Logistics the use of IT has been manifold, from software applications; databases, data warehousing, knowledge bases, data mining, etc. to the use of Radio Frequency Identification (RFID), the Internet and the World Wide Web. However, the greatest impact of IT has been the change of the material flow in some cases, for example the production of music, newspapers and books, from a "material" (a physical product) to data (an "electronic" product). This means that E-Logistics has become Information-Logistics with E-Products, E-Production and E-SCM in the literal sense.

CONCLUSION

E-logistics and E-Supply Chain Management have affected the structure, nature and management of organisations, changing the external environment in which businesses operate. New tools and techniques have been needed for logistics managers to use to measure cost and performance, and in assessing the role of logistics in ensuring customer satisfaction in different areas of business activ-

ity, evaluating logistics trade-offs in relation to integrated strategy and enabling the debate on the impact of logistics decisions on the environment and global industries. This has facilitated the analysis of the contribution of E-business logistics to competitive strategy, productivity and value advantage and judgment of critically concepts and methods applicable to the implementation of E-logistics. It has also led to the identification of how major functional areas within business influence E-logistics, the engagement and reflection upon problem solving in E-logistics.

The book is comprised of chapters that subsequently examine most of the key aspects of E-Logistics and E-Supply Chain Management, organised in three sections. Each section refers to a specific area regarding E-Logistics and E-Supply Chain Management. This first section serves as an introduction to E-Logistics and E-Supply Chain Management. The three chapters synthesize the literature and provide definitions of E-Logistics and E-Supply Chain Management, as well as analysis of the main concepts and parameters.

The second part of the book looks at the logistics and management functions of E-Supply Chain Management: Procurement; Distribution and Transport; Fulfilment; Traceability; Customer Relationship Management; Supplier Relationship Management; Enterprise Resource Planning, with discussions in this section based on real life examples.

The final part of the book on Evolving Business discusses further the future research directions for E-Logistics and E-Supply Chain Management: Radio Frequency Identification in the E-Logistics interface; Cloud Computing in Supply Chain Management; Data Modelling and Information Logistics; The evolution and impact of IT on Logistics and SCM; E-Production; Future Considerations of Sustainability and Reverse Logistics. This section describes the future challenges of logistics and supply chain management, the examination of case studies providing a very useful tool in this endeavour. These cases refer the future practices of logistics and supply chain management to various business sectors.

REFERENCES

Chaffey, D. (2011). *E-business & e-commerce management: Strategy, implementation and practice* (5th ed.). Upper Saddle River, NJ: Prentice Hall.

Folinas, D. K. (2012). *Outsourcing management for supply chain operations and logistics service, handbook*. Hershey, PA: IGI Global. doi:10.4018/978-1-4666-2008-7

Hanks, P. (1990). *Collins dictionary of the English language* (2nd ed.). London, UK: Collins.

Laudon, K. C., & Laudon, J. P. (2011). *Managing information systems: Managing the digital firm* (12th ed.). Upper Saddle River, NJ: Pearson.

Ross, D. F. (2003). *Introduction to e-supply chain management: Engaging technology to build market –winning business partnerships*. New York, NY: The St. Lucie Press.

KEY TERMS AND DEFINITIONS

Big Data: Essentially massive repositories of data.

Cloud Computing: The Cloud Computing model, more commonly referred to simply as Cloud Computing or "The Cloud", provides access to "clouds" of shared computing resources such as storage and applications, over a network, usually the Internet.

E-Commerce: E-Commerce or Electronic Commerce can be considered as "all electronically mediated transactions between any organization and any third party it deals with" (Chaffey 2011, p. 10).

E-Logistics: E-Logistics or Electronic Logistics is part of an "E-genre", which includes E-Learning, E-Business, E-Commerce, etc. All of these terms essentially refer to the major and significant employment of IT for that domain. In the case of E-Logistics the use of IT has been manifold, from software applications; databases, data warehousing, knowledge bases, data mining, etc. to the use of Radio Frequency Identification (RFID), the Internet and the World Wide Web.

Electronic Procurement: E-Procurement relates to "the electronic integration and management of all procurement activities including purchase request, authorization, ordering, delivery, and payment between a purchases and a supplier" (Chaffey, 2011, p. 355).

E-Supply Chain Management: Applying the technologies; tools centred on the Internet for competitive advantage, thus transforming all functions of SCM to the Web and in addition, to the Cloud, thus generating new sources of competitive advantage through cyber collaboration, enabling joint product innovation, on-line buying, markets, network planning, operations management, and customer fulfillment.

E-Tailing: On-line retailing.

Extranet: A network that uses the Internet to link multiple Intranets.

Information Technology (IT): Information Technology (IT) encompasses software (applications), hardware (including computers, scanners, etc.) firmware and middleware, as well as the network infrastructures (internet, intranet, etc.), platforms and operating systems, and the World Wide Web (WWW).

Integration: The process by which parts of a whole become more connected so that they are in effect less "part" and more "whole", i.e., such that functions formerly carried out by one part are carried out by others, and usually vice-versa.

Internet: The Internet refers to the physical network (infrastructure), connecting computers across the globe, using WAN (Wireless or Wide Area Networks).

Intranet: The Intranet is the internal network connecting computers within an organisation, using Local Area Networks, or LANs.

Logistics: "1. The science of the movement of supplying and maintenance of military forces in the field; 2. the management of materials flow through an organization, from raw materials flow through to finished goods; 3. the detailed planning and organization of any large complex operation" (Collins, 1990, p. 903).

Social Commerce: Where site owners incorporate reviews and ratings into a site. Linking social networking sites aids understanding of customer requirements with a view to converting this information into sales.

Supply Chain: The sequence of an organisation. The sequence refers to the facilities (warehouses, factories, processing centres, distribution centres, retail outlets and offices), and functions and activities (purchasing, forecasting, inventory management, information management, quality assurance, scheduling, production, distribution, delivery, transport, supplier management, and customer management).

Supply Chain Integration: The process of transformation or "rationalisation" of the supply chain by which functions are redefined and redistributed so that these are carried out faster, cheaper, better (more quality, i.e. meeting requirements of the "Customer", who is the next "receiver" in the supply chain).

World Wide Web (WWW): Essentially the main technique for publishing information on the Internet, displayed on web pages and accessed via (Web) browsers.

Chapter 2
E-Supply Chain Collaboration and Integration:
Implementation Issues and Challenges

Sudhanshu Joshi
Doon University, India

ABSTRACT

Formulation of supplier integration strategy is essential to optimize the value chain. In the chapter, the authors review the literature on integration of supplier relationship practices and its impact on optimization of value chain. The review is based on e-collaborative framework for optimized value chain, which comprises the supplier integration strategy, i.e., information sharing, e-business systems, and policy-based supplier selection have positive influence on the long-term planning and supply chain practices. The chapter reviews 368 articles on empirical research in e-collaboration and supply chain management. It finds the majority of authors are using a combination of the entity of analysis, while still focusing on the firm level rather than the network level. In this, another encouraging fact is that most of the authors prefer to consider a combination of various elements of exchange in their analysis. The potential limitation of the study is that it does not attempt to trace out trends using regression techniques. The extension of this study could be statistically testing the figures observed in this chapter and setting a grounded theory approach for future research in e-collaboration and supply chain.

INTRODUCTION

Supply Chain Management (SCM) collaboration includes logistics, transportation, strategic alliances, industrial marketing, purchasing, economics and organizational behavior (Kern and Willcocks, 2002; Zheng et al., 2000), describes a wide variety of transactional to relational business relationships at firm level.

Co-operative supply chain relationships achieve benefits for the participants (Christopher, 2005; Stevens, 1989), however, it is also apparent that full SCM implementation is not being achieved (Kempainen and Vepsalainen, 2003). This is because partners are still taking a short-term view, often in the face of increasing market-place complexity and uncertainty and are limiting the extent to which they extend their collaborative

DOI: 10.4018/978-1-4666-3914-0.ch002

focus (Fawcett and Magnan, 2002). SCM can be seen as an integrative, proactive approach (Matthyssens and Van den Bulte, 1994) to manage the total flow of a distribution channel to the ultimate customer-like "a well-balanced and well-practiced relay team" (Cooper and Ellram, 1993).

The advent of e-business has created several challenges and opportunities in the supply-chain environment. The Internet has made it easier to share information among supply-chain partners and the current trend is to try to leverage the benefits obtained through information sharing (also called visibility) across the supply chain to improve operational performance, customer service, and solution development (Swaminathan and Tayur, 2003). A key feature of SCM is an early decision to reduce the number of suppliers in the chain (the elimination of multiple sourcing) (Ellram, 1991) because maintaining close, intense relationships can be very expensive in management effort (Cavinato, 1992; Langley and Holcomb, 1992). The intention is to have no more "partners" than necessary and to work more closely, effectively, and over the longer term (Peck and Juttner, 2000; Scott and Westbrook, 1991) with those who have the most critical impact on the overall operation (Cooper et al., 1997).

Giannakis and Croom (2004) propose an SCM paradigm conceptual framework, the "3S Model" containing the synthesis of business resources and networks, the synergy between network actors and, the synchronization of operational decisions. The International Marketing and Purchasing Group's dyadic interaction approach summarized by Kern and Willcocks (2002), supply chain integration reviewed by Fawcett and Magnan (2002) and, networks of relationships described by Harland et al. (2001) and Kempainen and Vepsalainen (2003) all suggest that exposing the relationship management aspects of supply chain relationships and their impact on performance (Giannakis and Croom, 2004) is highly problematic.

In Fast-Moving Consumer Goods (FMCG) sector, this collaboration aspect has been ex-

pressed through the Efficient Consumer Response (ECR) movement. ECR encompasses multiple technological and managerial innovations which aim to transform retailers, distributors, and manufacturers into more efficient inter-linked organizations placing special emphasis on collaboration (JIPOECR, 1995). One of the first forms of supply-chain collaboration has been the practice of Vendor-Managed Inventory (VMI) or Continuous Replenishment Program (CRP), as it is often called in the context of grocery retailing, where the buyer shares demand information with the supplier who, in turn, manages the buyer's inventory. The practice of Collaborative Planning Forecasting and Replenishment (CPFR) has extended this collaboration to include the exchange of forecasts based on widely shared information (usually Point-of-Sales [PoS] data and promotion plans), having a more strategic focus and placing more emphasis on the demand side. Primarily, For an effective Supply Chain in a FMCG Industry, the existing supplier relationship is combination of 3Cs—Cooperation, Coordination and Collaboration and Open Market Negotiations among suppliers (as mentioned in Figure 1), and there is wide range of attributes covered under it, including Price Based discussions, Adversarial relationships, Supplier selection and Contracts, Information Exchanges using WIP Links and EDI and Supply Chain Integration using Joint Planning and Technology Sharing.

More specifically, the Supplier relationship practices including VMI/CRP has been implemented at the level of the retailer's central warehouse, based on the daily sharing of the warehouse inventory report data and orders information. Most CPFR initiatives also focus on the central warehouse rather than on store replenishment, and deal mainly with mid-/long-term replenishment planning for promotion items and new product introductions. The VMI/CRP practice has been extensively studied by researchers but mainly from the perspective of evaluating the impact of information sharing on supply-chain performance rather

Figure 1. Supplier relationship based on cooperation, coordination, and collaboration (3C) (source: adapted from Spekman et al., 1998)

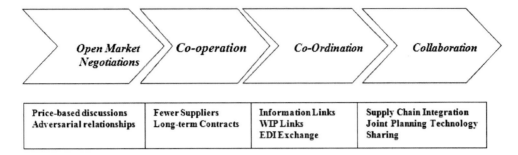

than from the Information Technology (IT) implementation perspective.

Furthermore, studies on CPFR mainly define it as a new practice and discuss its adoption or evaluate its business impact. Vendor-Managed Inventory (VMI) is gradually becoming an important element of supply chain management strategy of organizations.

REVIEW OF LITERATURE AND RESEARCH METHODOLOGY

A comprehensive and critical literature review of empirical research work in the areas of Supply chain management, e-Collaboration, Supply Chain Integration, Customer Relationship Program (CRP), Vendor-Managed Inventory (VMI), Continuous Replenishment Program (CRP), Collaborative Planning Forecasting and Replenishment (CPFR), and e-commerce, Point of Sale (PoS). A Step-by-Step approach was adopted for literature review (also illustrated in Figure 2):

Step 1: The assessment period of articles is between 1994 to 2006, a 12 year timeline was selected (based on availability of research work). The year 1994 was taken as the base year for data collection as the first research based on E-collaboration and Supply Chain practices was first appeared in 1994 (Dunn et al.1994). The year 2006 is chosen as the terminating point of data collection for providing a landmark to end data collection.

Step 2: The articles were collected from four major management science publishers viz. Ebscohost, Science Direct, Taylor & Francis, Emerald Insight.

Step 3: Filtration of the search string "e-collaboration and Supply chain" among selected management and technology databases. Burgess et al. (2006) and Soni et al. (2011) adopted similar approach for review based research.

Step 4: Flynn et al. (1990) explained that any empirical research article can have one or more of the following empirical research designs viz. single case study, multiple case study, panel study, focus group and survey. We selected empirical research articles from the selected population of journals on the similar lines.

Step 5: Classification of the articles is based on following parameters: Empirical research growth in SCM.
  ◦ Purpose of empirical research
  ◦ Citation index per sub topic searched (see Tables 1 and 2)

Figure 2. Literature review methodology (adopted from Soni and Kodali, 2011)

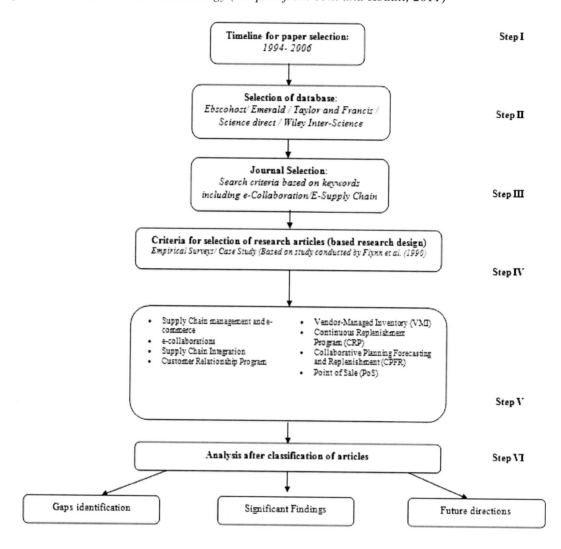

SUPPLY CHAIN MANAGEMENT RELATIONSHIP

Within the supply chain, the need for much closer, long-term relationships is increasing due to supplier rationalization (Refer. Figure 2 and Table 3) and globalization and more information about these interactions is required (Wilding & Humphries, 2006).

Studies including Wilding & Humphries, 2006 demonstrated that the existing theoretical model including Williamson's economic organizations failure framework could provide powerful insights

into the research subject and especially revealed the important part played by co-operation, co-ordination and collaboration (C3 behavior) in reducing the inherently negative effects of close proximity and limited choice relationships (see Figure 4).

The research specifically tested the well-accepted Williamson's economic organizations failure framework as a theoretical model through which long-term collaborative relationships can be viewed.

There is a strategic dimension into the network of organizations (Refer Figure 3) that are involved in the up-stream production and downstream distribution processes and activities focused on the satisfaction of customers and maximization of both current and long-term profitability (Christopher, 1992, 2005; Cox and Lamming, 1997; Harland, 1996a; Kempainen and Vepsalainen, 2003) preliminary meant for reduction in inventory, to increase customer service reliability and build a competitive advantage for the channel (Boddy et al., 2000; Cavinato, 1992; Fawcett and Magnan, 2002; Hines and Jones, 1996).

From the Supply Chain Restructuring perspective, vital feature for an effective Supply Chain is to reduce the number of suppliers in the chain (Ellram, 1991). The adverse relationship leads to extensive loss in management objectives (Cavinato, 1992; Langley and Holcomb, 1992). There was an immense need to be identified toward "lean partners" to work more closely, effectively and for longer duration and its impact on overall operation (Scott and Westbrook, 1991; Cooper et al., 1997; Peck and Ju ttner, 2000). Functional framework was analyzed by Harlan, 1996 and Hines and Jones, 1996 between Japanese Lean automotive Producers and their western counterparts. Inter-organizational Strategic alliances emerged as key tool of Confliction Resolution & Competitive Intelligences (Anscombe and Kearney, 1994). Further extension to this study was giving by Bechtel and Jayaram (1997) and Perks and Easton (2000) who suggest that SCM provides business environment in which firm closely co-operate rather than compete to achieve mutual goals and are incentivized to join in collaborative innovation (Harland, 1996a).

The concept of VMI as tool for strategic partners' role to share confidential demand information and to cater uncertainty by replenishing inventory orders (Cooper and Ellram, 1993; Lamming, 1993; Benchtel and Jayaram, 1997).

Researchers explained Supply Chain Integration as an overview towards the need for closer relationships, including supplier' trust, commitment, co-operation, co-ordination and collaboration between supply chain members to ensure the success as per objectives (Christopher, 2005; Hines and Jones, 1996; Spekman et al., 1998). Supply Chain Collaboration increases the scope of its operations and minimizes the confliction among the partners and act as tool to tackle operational problems (Sako et al., 1994). For better profitability & performance close long-term relationships between customers and suppliers is suggested (Giannakis and Croom, 2004).

Lamming et al. (2001) cited that by instrumentalising and developing the unique capabilities of partnership, it is possible to create a guard from system-level forces. Supplier relationship management is based on function of Partnership, whose success depends upon the duration to build trust (Sako et al., 1994). When mistrust is entrenched, a shift from adversarial to co-operative relationship styles is extremely difficult. Moreover, Macbeth and Ferguson (1994) and Kern and Willcocks (2002) propose that despite the availability of modern information systems, the practice of managing supply chain players is wasteful of resources and drags performance backwards rather than promoting continuous improvement. Furthermore, Cooper et al. (1997) believe that achieving true supply chain integration is "a lofty and difficult goal" and research indicates that companies continue to struggle to operationalise SCM principles such that they support dynamically changing business influences (Braithwaite, 1998). We conclude that since SCM appears to implicitly require a move towards a limitation of the number of market players involved – small numbers, effective supply chain relationship management presents a more complex set of challenges to achieve success.

COLLABORATION CHALLENGES

Academics have used a number of approaches within SCM research to capture perspectives containing the key facets of inter-organizational,

Table 1. Literature review and research contributions

Author (Year of Publication)	Period	Reviewed Journals	Sample Size	Area of Research
Dunn et al. (1994)	1986-1990	N/A	N/A	Types of research in SCM
Croom et al. (2000)	Not restricted	Not restricted	84	Suggests the way of reviewing literature critically
Ho et al. (2002)	N/A	N/A	N/A	State of empirical research in CPFR based SCM
Carter and Ellram (2003)	1965-1999	JSCM	774	Types of research, methodologies used and data analysis techniques in JSCM
Gammelgaard (2004)	1998-2003	IJPDLM, IJOPM, JBL, JOM and IJLM	N/A	Prevailing schools of thought
Frankel et al. (2005)	1999-2004	JBL	108	Types of research approaches including CPFR/VMI etc
Sachan and Datta (2005)	1999-2003	IJPDLM, JBL and SCMIJ	442	Analysis of references on the literatures on Supplier relationship using ecommerce
Kovacs and Spens(2005)	1998-2002	IJLM, IJPDLM and JBL	N/A	Analysis of methodologies applied in different subfields of SCM
Halldorson and Arlbjorn (2005)	1997-2004	IJLM, IJPDLM and JBL	71	Analysis of types of research
Reichhart and Holweg (2006)	2004	JOM, IJOPM, MS, IJPR, JBL and IJPDLM	89	Analysis of methodologies applied in different sub-filed of SCM
Spens and Kovacs (2006)	1998-2002	IJLM, IJPDLM and JBL	378	Analysis of types of research
Burgess et al. (2006)	No Restriction-July 2003	Not restricted	100	Analysis of object of study and methods applied.
van der Vaart and van Donk (2008)	Not restricted	IJOPM, IJPDLM, IJLM, IJPR, IJPE, Interfaces, JBL, JOM and MS	36	Survey research in Supply Chain Integration
Wolf (2008)	1990-1996	IJLM, IJPDLM, IJPE, IJPR, JBL, JOM, and PPC	282	Analysis of the nature of SCM research
Fabbe-Costes and Jahre (2008)	2000-2006	IJLM, IJLRA, IJOPM, IJPDLM, JBL, JOM, SCMIJ, Transportation Journal and Transportation Research- Part E	38	Studies the link between supply chain integration and performance
Giunipero et al. (2008)	1997-2006	IJOPM, IMM, Management Science and Decision Sciences	405	Carried out review of 405 articles focusing on categories covered within the SCM literature, various levels of the chains examined and sample populations and industries studied as well as research methods employed

BPMJ-Business Process Management Journal, CCE- Computers and Chemical Engineering, CIE- Computer and Industrial Engineering, EJOR- European Journal of Operational Research, EJPSM- European Journal of Purchasing and Supply Management, IJLM-The International Journal of Logistics Management, IJLRA- International Journal of Logistics Research and Applications, IJOPM- International Journal of Operations and Production Management, IJPDLM- International Journal of Physical Distribution & Logistics Management, IJPE- International Journal of Production Economics, IJPR- International Journal of Production Research, IMDS- Industrial Management and Data Systems, IMM- Industrial Marketing Management, JMTM- Journal of Manufacturing Technology Management, JOM- Journal of Operation Management, JSCM- The Journal of Supply Chain Management, LIM- Logistics Information Management, PPC- Production Planning and Control, SCMIJ- Supply Chain Management International Journal

Table 2. Literature review and research contributions

Journal Name	1994	1995	1996	1997	1998	1999	2000	2001	2002	2003	2004	2005	2006	Empirical Research Articles
BPMJ	0	0	0	0	0	0	1	1	0	1	2	2	0	7
TR	0	0	0	0	0	1	0	0	2	3	0	0	0	6
CCE	0	0	0	0	0	0	0	0	0	0	0	0	0	0
SCMIJ	0	0	6	2	7	4	4	3	3	6	10	9	16	70
PPC	0	0	0	0	0	0	1	1	1	0	6	1	2	12
EJOR	0	0	0	0	0	0	0	0	0	0	5	1	4	10
EJPSM	1	3	1	0	4	3	8	6	2	1	0	0	0	29
IJLM	0	1	2	3	1	1	0	4	2	1	5	5	4	29
IJLRA	0	0	0	0	0	3	2	1	3	4	5	5	4	27
IJOPM	0	0	0	1	0	2	1	6	4	3	4	5	6	32
IJPE	0	0	0	0	0	1	1	0	5	4	11	7	7	36
IJPR	0	0	0	1	0	0	1	0	4	1	2	7	1	17
IMDS	0	0	1	0	0	0	0	0	0	1	2	1	3	8
IMM	0	0	0	1	0	0	2	1	1	4	3	3	2	17
JMTM	0	0	0	0	0	0	0	0	0	1	2	2	3	8
JOM	0	0	1	0	0	0	1	2	5	2	2	9	5	27
JSCM	0	0	0	0	0	3	2	1	3	1	1	4	1	16
LIM	0	2	2	0	1	0	1	0	2	0	0	0	2	10
OMEGA	0	0	0	0	0	1	0	0	0	2	0	1	3	7
Total	1	6	13	8	13	19	25	26	37	35	60	62	63	368

operational, and inter-personal dynamics. Giannakis and Croom (2004) propose an SCM paradigm conceptual framework, the "3S Model" containing the synthesis of business resources and networks, the synergy between network actors and, the synchronization of operational decisions. The International Marketing and Purchasing Group's dyadic interaction approach summarised by Kern and Willcocks (2002), supply chain integration reviewed by Fawcett and Magnan (2002) and, networks of relationships described by Harland et al. (2001) and Kempainen and Vepsalainen (2003) all suggest that exposing the relationship management aspects of supply chain relationships and their impact on performance (Giannakis and Croom, 2004) is highly problematical. The literature also contains examples of research describing relationship behaviors between one/many buyers, one/many sellers and dominant market "players" in both public and private sector situations. Within the marketing literature Porter's (1980) five forces model of competitive advantage considers short-term, arms-length competition and the exercise of market power by limiting competition through the creation of barriers to entry (Rugman and D'Cruz, 2000). Cox et al., (2000) alternatively see the combination of resource utility and scarcity creating a power regime in which the involved parties will employ adversarial/non-adversarial and arms-length/col-

Table 3. Transaction alternative between businesses, consumers and governmental organizations (source: Chaffey, 2012)

Consumer or Citizen	Business (Organization)	Government
Consumer-to-Consumer (C2C)	**Business-to-Consumer (B2C)**	**Government to Consumer (G2C)**
eBay	Transactional: Amazon	National Government Transactional: Tax-Inland Revenue
Peer-to-Peer(Skype)	Relationship Building: BP	National Government Information
Blogs and communities	Brand Building: Unilever	Local Government Services
Products Recommendations	Media Owner: News corp.	
Social Networks: MySpace, Bebo	Comparison Intermediatry: Kelkoo, Pricerunner	
Consumer-to-Business (C2B)	**Business-to-Business (B2B)**	**Government to Business (G2B)**
Priceline	Transactional: Euroffice	Government Services and Transactions: Tax
Consumer- Feedback, Community and Compaigns	Relationship Building: BP	Legal Regulations
	Media Owned: eMap Business Publications	
	B2B Marketplaces: EC21	
Consumer to Government (C2G)	**Business to Government (B2G)**	**Government to Government (G2G)**
Feedback to Government through pressure group or individual sites	Feedback to Government Business and Non Governmental Organization	Inter-government Services
		Exchange of Information

Figure 3. Supplier-relationship optimization model

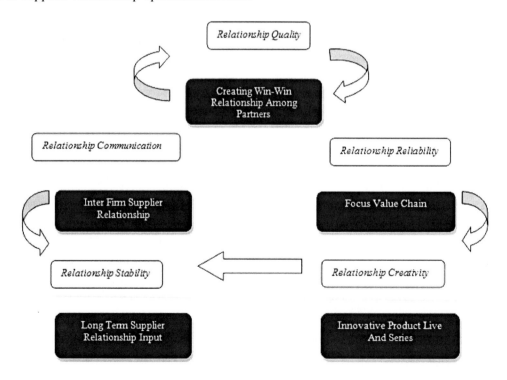

Figure 4. Alternative strategies for modification of the e-business supply chain (source: Chaffey, 2012)

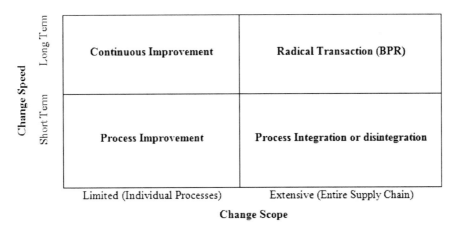

laborative arrangements depending on their relative power positions (Refer Table 4). In the 1990s, UK motor industry supply chains, employing economic power was a driving objective to achieve the "vantage point" (Lamming, 1993). Examples of small numbers or monopoly (Fishwick, 1993), and strong market power relationships between dominant firms are also found within the retail sector where major supermarkets such as Walmart with their own brands, fought "price wars" with global companies such as Coca Cola and Pepsi. Eventually, the balance of power was restored to prevent intense, adversarial influence from destroying long-term relationships (Christopher, 2005). In the public sector, Harland et al., (2000) revealed that UK health authority procurement

Table 4. Strategic options for e-partnerships

Sno.	Partnering Arrangement	Technical Infrastructure Integration	Examples
1	Total Ownership (More than 51% Equity in Company)	Technical Issues in Merging Company Systems	Purchase of Booker(Distribution Company Iceland (Retailer), Since 1996 CISCO has made over 30 Acquisition (not all SCM- Related)
2	Investment Stack (Less than 49% Equity)	Technical Issues in Merging Company Systems	Cisco has also made over 40 investment in hardware and software suppliers.
3	Strategic alliance	Collaboration tools and Groupware for new product development	Cable and Wireless, Campaq and Microsoft new e-Business solution a-services.
4	Profit Sharing Partnership	As above	Arrangement sometimes used for IS outsourcing
5	Long Term contract	See Above. Tools for managing Service level Agreements (SLAs) Important	ISPs have performance on SLAs with penalty Clauses.
6	Preferred Suppliers	Permanent EDI or Internet EDI Links setup with Preferred partners	Tesco Information Exchange.
7	Competitive Tendering	Tender issued intermediary or buyers' website	Buyer arranged auctions
8	Short-term contract	As above	As above
9	Sport Markets and Auctions	Auctions at Intermediaries or buyers website	Business to Business Marketplaces, Example www.freemarkets.com

relationships contained distinctive features such as dedicated suppliers with reduced availability of alternatives and, where the government made the rules and could sanction anti-competitiveness. Parker and Hartley's (1997) recommended that the UK Ministry of Defense (MoD) should accept that its major procurements operated under monopoly or near-monopoly conditions rather than attempting to maintain a competitive semblance. They concluded that adversarial competition should be abandoned and collaboration based on long-term, trusting relationships should be established.

These examples suggest, regardless of power or sector consideration, collaboration is preferable to adversarial competition, however, managing close proximity as illustrated in Figure 5.

McDonald et al. (1997) and Moorman et al. (1992) view C3 behavior as similar or complementary, co-ordinate actions needed to achieve mutual outcomes with reciprocation over time and rather than pure exchange, are used to create real value as an organizational competence know as "collaborative advantage". Morgan and Hunt (1994) and Oliver (1990) describe the importance of pursuing mutually beneficial interests but additionally emphasize the fundamentally co-operative nature of business life characterized by balance and harmony. Moreover, this powerful combination of behavioral variables can often lead to the discovery of even more successful ways to co-operate and new objects of co-operation (Doz and Baburoglu, 2000). C3 behavior is,

therefore, essential to maintaining a successful business partnership (Metcalf et al., 1992; Rugman and D'Cruz, 2000), especially when linked with commitment to the achievement of shared, realistic goals (Lewin and Johnston, 1997; Sheth and Sharma, 1997). As already mentioned, in the quantitative data analysis C3 behavior appeared to make a strong contribution to relationship success. However; effectiveness could be reduced when the sincerity of the other party's intentions was doubted. The overwhelming majority of respondents placed strong emphasis on personal relationships ("hitting it off") (Gulati, 1995; Kempainen and Vepsalainen, 2003) and culture-matching (relating to the way the other side do things) (Moss Kanter, 1994). This counters the enlightened, self-interest approach (Faulkner, 2000) and underlines the central importance of commitment and trust to relationship stability and productiveness (Morgan and Hunt, 1994). Excellent, long-term commercial arrangements, frequent, interactive, open communications, and constructive conflict that supported repeated cycles of exchange, risk-taking and successful fulfillment of expectations were also described as important contributors (Doney and Cannon, 1997). These appeared to strengthen the willingness of parties to rely upon each other and to develop adaption and interdependence (Eisenhardt et al., 1997; Madhok, 2000). However, opportunistic behavior such as adversarial bidding, inflexible and unduly bureaucratic commercial prac-

Figure 5. Integrated e-procurement mechanism between buyers-supplier

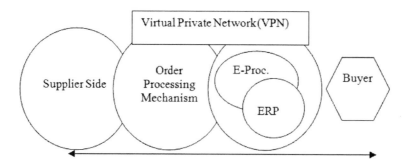

tices, unwillingness to share proprietary data and uncaring use of power were clearly evident and potentially capable of undermining relationship-building (Humphries and Wilding, 2003; Faulkner and de Rond, 2000; Palmer, 2001).

The literature says comparatively based on empirical research about the relationship dynamics within long-term, closely collaborative, dyadic relationships. We hypothesized that this proximity could generate both positive and negative feedback behaviors. Our research detected a spectrum of these phenomena and the managers in many cases clearly understood the limitations on their freedom and were employing C3 behaviors to improve the performance of their partnerships. The literature is generally aware of these dynamics but our contribution to theory is a research methodology that allows them to be exposed in an integrated manner and comes close to provide a balance of results using Giannakis and Croom's (2004) "3S" SCM paradigm conceptual framework.

PRACTICAL IMPLICATION OF E-COLLABORATIONS

Humphries and Wilding (2004a) and Spekman et al. (1998) suggest that co-operative, co-co-ordinating and collaborative behaviors involve working together/jointly to bring resources into a required relationship to achieve effective operations in harmony with the strategies/objectives of the parties involved, thus resulting in mutual benefit. McDonald et al. (1997) and Moorman et al. (1992) view C3 behaviour as similar or complementary, co-ordinate actions needed to achieve mutual outcomes with reciprocation over time and rather than pure exchange, are used to create real value as an organisational competence know as "collaborative advantage". Morgan and Hunt (1994) and Oliver (1990) describe the importance of pursuing mutually beneficial interests but additionally emphasize the fundamentally co-operative nature of business life characterized

by balance and harmony. Moreover, this powerful combination of behavioral variables can often lead to the discovery of even more successful ways to co-operate and new objects of co-operation (Doz and Baburoglu, 2000). C3 behaviour is, therefore, essential to maintaining a successful business partnership (Metcalf et al., 1992; Rugman and D'Cruz, 2000), especially when linked with commitment to the achievement of shared, realistic goals (Lewin and Johnston, 1997; Sheth and Sharma, 1997).

DISCUSSION

This chapter, through a systematic and critical review of e-collaborations and supply chain research literature based on few parameter including Supply Chain Integration, Customer Relationship Program (CRP), Vendor-Managed Inventory (VMI), Continuous Replenishment Program (CRP), Collaborative Planning Forecasting and Replenishment (CPFR), Point of Sale (PoS) provides insights into the growth of empirical research

The review enables to brief present status of e-SCM practices in the current set of existing literature. The gaps that were identified and the significant findings of the review will be discussed in the subsequent part of this section.

Findings

1. Empirical research in Supply Chain based e-collaborations is growing and shows highest growth during period of 2000-2004. Theory building is most popular among SCM researchers while theory verification is also on the rise but percentage wise the rise is very slow and gradual. Wallenbergburg and Weber (2005) pointed out that despite debate in the field of logistics and SCM, research on methodology and theory development still lacks the focus. They also advocated that theory development (or theory build-

ing) will advance, as shown in the field of marketing research, through a rigorous empirical research approach.

2. In the review, 115 issues were identified out of which performance measurement, supply chain integration, status of SCM in a field or industry or nation, relationship management, information sharing and commitment, collaboration, strategy formulation, IT, green supply, quality, supply chain practices, incentives, identification of barriers for SCM, critical success factors, design of supply chain and selection of type of supply chain were most visited issues by researchers. Many researchers have even tried to analyze these often visited issues by researchers. Many researchers have even tried to analyze these often visited focal issues in their literature reviews, van der Vaart and van Donk (2008) performed a review on survey-based methodologies on supply chain integration, similarly Fabbe-Costes and Jahre (2008) analyzed the relationship between performance of supply chain and supply chain integration Issues like "status of SCM in a field, industry or nation" also gained appreciable attention in article by Arlbjorn et al. (2008) (status of Nordic research in logistics and SCM), Bales et al. (2008) (development of supply chain in aerospace sector). Brun et al. (2008) (logistics and SCM in luxury fashion retail). Mangan and Christopher (2005) (Supply chain Management of future), McMullan (1996) (SCM practice in Asia-Pacific) and last but not least Sahay et al. (2003) (architerture of Indian supply chains). Also, relationship management was widely researched in SCM by various authors like Benton and Maloni (2005) (power-driven buyer-seller relationship), Boger et al. (2001) (supply chain relationships in Polish pork sector), Kwon and Suh (2004) (factors affecting trust and commitment in supply chain relationships),

Parry et al. (2006) (to core competence posted by developing closer supply chain relationships), etc.

3. Harland (1996) distinguishes four main uses of the term "e-Collaboration in Supply Chain":

a. Internal supply that integrates business functions involved in the flow of materials and information from the inbound to the outbound end of the business;

b. E-Collaboration using web technology as the management of supply relationships;

c. E-commerce as the management of inter-business chains, and

d. E-Commerce and Supplier/Vendor Relationship as strategic management of inter-business networks.

Among these four uses strategic management as a major function SCM is apparent. Macbeth and Ferguson (1991), Cavinato (1999) and Bechtel and Jayaram(1997) had devoted their study explaining strategic nature of SCM and concluded that majority of functions in SCM are performed at strategic level. On the other hand, the under-explored area of organizational behavior can also bring stronger theories in SCM as emphasized by the works of various authors such as Ellram (1991) (industrial organization),Co and Barro (2009) (stakeholders theory),Knoppen and Christiaanse (2007) (supply chain partnering) and Wilding Willamson organizational failure framework). According to Ketchen and Giunipero (2004), the idea of a supply chain organization has been presented but this has yet to be systematically investigated (Giunipero et al., 2008).

4. Regarding level of analysis at network level, out of 80 records only nine were found to be before year 2000. This trend implies growing awareness among researcher about considering network level for analysis to get optimum benefit in supply chain.

5. Researchers seemed to prefer "combination" of various entities of analysis for empirical research over single entities. Similar trend is observed in identifying most frequently used element of exchange in SCM and it was traced that researchers preferred "combination" of elements of exchange instead of focusing on single element of exchange.

6. A significant proportion of articles addressed use of performance measurement in their research. Majority of authors employed performance analysis for measuring performance of "combination" of various entities of analysis at "firm" level considering "combination" of elements of exchange in their analysis.

7. It is noteworthy that only six articles out of 87 articles, published before year 2000 considered performance measurement in their theory or framework. Such trend also gives an indication about more and more researchers advocating use of performance measurement in SCM.

Gaps Identified

There exists a huge gap between theory building and theory verification. The rate at which theory building is progressing is far ahead of theory verification. A discipline can only reach maturity stage if rate of theory building and verification is same. Since SCM is growing discipline, there is not much evidence available in supply chain literature that highlights the importance of theory verification in SCM but it can be argued that at some stage in life cycle of a discipline, theory verification should mark the maturity of that discipline.

Among plethora of issues to be addressed in SCM, 115 issues to be specific, only 16 issues spanned more than 50 percent of articles. Such a trend reflects deficiency in treatment of SCM paradigm. Many issues to name a few like Distribution Requirement Planning (DRP), power balance, risk management, supply chain security,

conflict management, strategic alignment, visibility, virtual supply chain etc. have not received sufficient attention in the empirical research. The possible reason for such a scenario could be overemphasis of SCM researchers on core issues like performance measurement, integration, collaboration, relationship management etc. Such core issues are majorly broader in nature with respect to all the levels of management. While issues like DRP and visibility are confined to tactical and operational level. On the other hand, issues like power balance, risk management, supply chain security, conflict management etc. are new to SCM discipline and are catching up with other issues, but slowly. Surprisingly, issue like "strategic alignment" (Which means aligning the supply chain strategy with competitive strategy of the focal firm) has received very scanty attention considering its importance in SCM. Only Quesada et al. (2008) had attempted an empirical investigation into strategic alignment.

Empirical research in SCM is predominately performed in the developed countries of Northern America and Europe while merely 5 percent of the research is performed for developing countries. Countries like India and China are outsourcing hubs for global supply chains of apparel, automobile and electronic consumer goods. Hence, there is higher need of developing and examining the supply chain frameworks for such countries. One of the reasons for lack in empirical research in these countries may be difficulty in carrying out survey and action research or it may be lack of knowledge in SCM. However, these reasons need proper examination and factual support before they can be established.

The existence of performance measures for retailers and distributors in supply chain are almost negligible. It is also observed that only one article measuring performance of retailer and three articles measuring performance of supplier are seen in the sample of articles. The same comment of applicable to performance measures devised for various levels of analysis as very few articles displayed any picture of measurement at dyad (two articles), chain (five articles) or network (13 articles) level.

IMPLICATIONS FOR FUTURE RESEARCH

This chapter presents new avenues of further research in e-collaboration and supply chain management. The research findings and gaps lead to following implications for future research. They are discussed as follows:

Researchers must focus on verifying already existing theories in Supplier relationship management and e-commerce as a huge amount of literature on theory building is accumulated and must get verified. It is also emphasized that large body of Supply Chain Practices needs more standardized terminology and constructs. According to Chen and Paulraj (2004), the existence of clear definitional constructs on which Supply Chain Collaboration research is still lacking. This causes a uneven research field that is open to the danger of a lack of generalization. In this context, the remarkable recommendation of Fabbe-Costes and Jahre (2008, p. 143) that in order to contribute to theory building we need to stabilize the vocabulary, to agree on formal conceptual definitions, and to define their properties clearly before measuring anything.

Traditionally, SCM is an interlinked discipline, with influences from logistics and transportation, operations management and materials and distribution management, marketing, as well as purchasing and IT (Giunipero et al., 2008). It thus addresses plethora of issues and among them some are often visited by empirical researchers while several other not frequently addressed issues like Distribution Resource Planning (DRP), efficiency of supply chain, power balance, risk management, supply chain security, conflict management, strategic alignment, visibility, virtual supply chain, etc. must be given more attention by performing empirical studies on them and hence help in promotion of their importance in Supply Chain paradigm.

Future empirical studies must target inter-organizational level more than intra-firm and intra-functional scope at firm level only. Such studies must at least address "dyad" level with inter-organizational scope and if possible the complete "network" must be under scanner for analysis. The advantage associated with multi-level analysis is that it gives integrated solutions. Simatupang and Sridharan (2008) highlighted that the chain members realize that integrated solutions result in economy of scale that eventually lower costs and enhance revenues (Bowersox, 1990; Buzzell and Ortmeyer, 1995). They also pointed that supply chain collaboration with the design of inter-organizational process improvements coupled with information systems is simply not sufficient enough. Rather, one has to design supply chain collaboration so as incorporate dynamics of collaborative efforts.

Ideally, every practical framework based on empirical study or any other relevant empirical study must involve an element of performance measurement of respective "Entity of analysis" at "network" level considering all the possible "elements of exchange" at various echelons of supply chain. Presently, such approach is lacking the empirical research thus future research efforts in this direction must take aforementioned aspect of performance measurement into consideration. According to Charan et al. (2008), there is an emerging requirement to focus on the performance of the Supply Chain (SC) or network in which company is a partner. Such system can facilitate inter-understanding and integration among the SC members. It is worthwhile to add essential characteristics of performance measurement system given by Morgan (2004) that performance measures must be linked with the strategy of an organization, be part of integrated control system, have internal validity and enable proactive management; and second, the performance measurement system must be dynamic, intra-connectable, focused and usable.

Sachan and Datta (2005) pointed out in their review that most of the multi-national FMCG firms are targeting developing and under developing countries either as new market for their products or for sourcing the raw material due to low cost. Research work in this area is not remarkable, there is a huge scope of research in this area. In our review too same fact is highlighted that very less empirical studies in the area of e-collaboration are published for developing and under developing countries. It is high time for the researchers to start focusing on these avenues of cost reduction and profit making.

CONCLUSION

The chapter reviewed 368 articles on empirical research in e-collaboration and supply chain management, with primary focus of research on content of Supply Chain based e-collaboration in articles. The Chapter started with identifying empirical research articles out of 1,807 research articles and found 368 empirical research articles, followed by classification of each of the selected articles into nine classes. It highlights the growth of empirical research in e-collaboration and supply chain management. Findings of chapter also initiate a debate of theory building vs. theory verification in e-collaboration and supply chain management and also brought inadequately addressed issues into limelight. Classification of articles on basis of entity of analysis, level of analysis and element of exchange is found to be very instrumental in measuring length and breadth of empirical research in Supply Chain based e-collaborations. It was found out that more and more authors are using combination of entity of analysis. But still focus is on firm level rather than network level. In this, another encouraging fact is that most of the authors prefer to consider combination of various elements of exchange in their analysis. It was also

found out that SCM research is still very much confined in developed countries of America and Europe, which is a discouraging. Also, performance measurement in a supply chain seems to be an area of more exploration, especially, measuring performance at network or chain level.

The potential limitation of the study is that it does not attempt to trace out trend using regression techniques neither it endeavors' to test the hypothesis so as to establish a grounded theory, that could lay down a perfect platform for future research. It, however, succeeds in revealing the descriptive statistics behind various classes that addresses content of e-collaboration and supply chain in empirical research. The extension of this study could be statistically testing the figures observed in this chapter and lay down a grounded theory approach for future research in e-collaboration and supply chain.

REFERENCES

Bales, R. R., Maull, R. S., & Radnor, Z. (2004). The development of supply chain management within the aerospace manufacturing sector. *Supply Chain Management: An International Journal*, 9(3), 250–255. doi:10.1108/13598540410544944

Bechtel, C., & Jayaram, J. (1997). Supply chain management: A strategic perspective. *International Journal of Logistics Management*, 8(1), 15–34. doi:10.1108/09574099710805565

Benton, W. C., & Maloni, M. (2005). The influence of power driven buyer seller relationships on supply chain satisfaction. *Journal of Operations Management*, 23(1), 1–22. doi:10.1016/j.jom.2004.09.002

Boger, S., Hobbs, J. E., & Kerr, W. A. (2001). Supply chain relationships in the Polish pork sector. *Supply Chain Management: An International Journal*, 6(2), 74–82. doi:10.1108/13598540110387573

Bowersox, D. J. (1990). The strategic benefits of logistics alliances. *Harvard Business Review*, *68*(4), 36–43.

Brun, A., Caniato, F., Caridi, M., Castelli, C., Miragliotta, G., & Ronchi, S. (2008). Logistics & supply chain management in luxury fashion retail: Empirical investigation of Italian firms. *International Journal of Production Economics*, *114*(2), 554–570. doi:10.1016/j.ijpe.2008.02.003

Burgess, K., Singh, P. J., & Koroglu, R. (2006). Supply chain management: A structured literature review and implications for future research. *International Journal of Operations & Production Management*, *26*(7), 703–729. doi:10.1108/01443570610672202

Buzzell, R. D., & Ortmeyer, G. (1995). Channel partnerships streamline distribution. *Sloan Management Review*, *36*(3), 83–96.

Carter, C. R., & Ellram, L. M. (2003). Thirty-five years of the journal of supply chain management: Where we have been and where we going? *The Journal of Supply Chain Management*, *39*, 27–39. doi:10.1111/j.1745-493X.2003.tb00152.x

Cavinato, J. L. (1992). A total cost/value model for supply chain competitiveness. *Journal of Business Logistics*, *13*(2), 285–301.

Chaffey, D. (2012). *E-business and e-commerce management* (3rd ed.). Upper Saddle River, NJ: Pearson Publication.

Charan, P., Shankar, R., & Baisya, R. K. (2008). Analysis of interactions among the variables of supply chain performance measurement system implementation. *Business Process Management Journal*, *14*(4), 512–529. doi:10.1108/14637150810888055

Chen, I. J., & Paulraj, A. (2004). Towards a theory of supply chain management: The constructs and measurements. *Journal of Operations Management*, *22*(2), 119–150. doi:10.1016/j.jom.2003.12.007

Christopher, M. (2005). *Logistics & supply chain management: Creating value-adding networks*. Upper Saddle River, NJ: Pearson Education Ltd.

Co, H. C., & Barro, F. (2009). Stakeholder theory and dynamics in supply chain collaboration. *International Journal of Operations & Production Management*, *29*(6), 591–611. doi:10.1108/01443570910957573

Cooper, M. C., & Ellram, L. M. (1993). Characteristics of supply chain management & the implications for purchasing & logistics strategy. *The International Journal of Logistics Management*, *4*(2), 13–24. doi:10.1108/09574099310804957

Cooper, M. C., & Gardner, J. T. (1993). Building good relationships – More than just partnering or strategic alliances? *International Journal of Physical Distribution & Logistics Management*, *23*(6), 14–26. doi:10.1108/09600039310044876

Ellram, L. M., & Edis, O. R. V. (1996, September). A case study of successful partnering implementation. *International Journal of Purchasing & Materials Management*, 20-38.

Fabbe-Costes, N., & Jahre, M. (2008). Supply chain integration and performance: A review of the evidence. *International Journal of Logistics Management*, *19*(2), 130–154. doi:10.1108/09574090810895933

Fawcett, S. E., & Magnan, G. M. (2002). The rhetoric and reality of supply chain integration. *Internal Journal of Physical Distribution & Logistics Management*, *32*(5), 339–361. doi:10.1108/09600030210436222

Flynn, B. B., Kakibara, S. S., Schroeder, R. G., Bates, K. A., & Flynn, E. J. (1990). Empirical research methods in operations management. *Journal of Operations Management, 9*(2), 250–284. doi:10.1016/0272-6963(90)90098-X

Giannakis, M., & Croom, S. R. (2004). Towards the development of a supply chain management paradigm: A conceptual framework. *Journal of Supply Chain Management, 40*(2), 27–36. doi:10.1111/j.1745-493X.2004.tb00167.x

Giunipero, L. C., Hooker, R. E., Matthews, S. C., Yoon, T. E., & Brudvig, S. (2008). A decade of SCM literature: Past, present and future implications. *Journal of Supply Chain Management, 44*(1), 66–86. doi:10.1111/j.1745-493X.2008.00073.x

Halldorsson, A., & Arlbjorn, J. S. (2005). Research methodologies in supply chain management – What do we know? In Kotzab, H., Seuring, S., Muller, M., & Reiner, G. (Eds.), *Research Methodologies in Supply Chain Management* (pp. 107–122). Heidelberg, Germany: Physica-Verlag. doi:10.1007/3-7908-1636-1_8

Harland, C. M. (1996). Supply chain management: Relationships, chains and networks. *British Journal of Management, 7*(1), 63–80. doi:10.1111/j.1467-8551.1996.tb00148.x

Kempainen, K., & Vepsalainen, A. P. J. (2003). Trends in industrial supply chains and networks. *Internal Journal of Physical Distribution & Logistics Management, 33*(8), 701–719. doi:10.1108/09600030310502885

Kern, T., & Willcocks, L. (2002). Exploring relationships in information technology outsourcing: The interaction approach. *European Journal of Information Systems, 11*, 3–19. doi:10.1057/palgrave/ejis/3000415

Ketchen, D., & Giunipero, L. (2004). The intersection of strategic management and supply chain management. *Industrial Marketing Management, 33*(1), 51–56. doi:10.1016/j.indmarman.2003.08.010

Knoppen, D., & Christiaanse, E. (2007). Supply chain partnering: A temporal multidisciplinary approach. *Supply Chain Management: An International Journal, 12*(2), 164–171. doi:10.1108/13598540710737343

Kwon, I. G., & Suh, T. (2004). Factors affecting the level of trust and commitment in supply chain relationships. *The Journal of Supply Chain Management, 40*(2), 4–14. doi:10.1111/j.1745-493X.2004.tb00165.x

Langley, J. C. Jr, & Holcomb, M. C. (1992). Creating logistics customer value. *Journal of Business Logistics, 13*(2), 1–27.

Macbeth, K. D., & Ferguson, N. (1991). Strategic aspects of supply chain management. *Integrated Manufacturing Systems, 2*(1), 8–12. doi:10.1108/09576069110002699

Mangan, J., & Christopher, M. (2005). Management development and the supply chain manager of the future. *International Journal of Logistics Management, 16*(2), 178–191. doi:10.1108/09574090510634494

Matthyssens, P., & Van den Bulte, C. (1994). Getting closer and nicer: Partnerships in the supply chain. *Long Range Planning, 27*(1), 72–83. doi:10.1016/0024-6301(94)90008-6

McMullan, A. (1996). Supply chain management practices in Asia Pacific today. *International Journal of Physical Distribution & Logistics Management, 26*(10), 79–95. doi:10.1108/09600039610150479

Morgan, C. (2004). Structure, speed and salience: Performance measurement in the supply chain. *Business Process Management Journal, 10*(5), 522–536. doi:10.1108/14637150410559207

Parry, G., Graves, A., & James-Moore, M. (2006). The threat to core competence posed by developing closer supply chain relationships. *International Journal of Logistics Research and Applications, 9*(3), 295–305. doi:10.1080/13675560600859524

Peck, H., & Juttner, U. (2000). Strategy and relationships: Defining the interface in supply chain contexts. *The International Journal of Logistics Management, 11*(2), 33–44. doi:10.1108/09574090010806146

Quesada, G., Rachamadugu, R., Gonzalez, M., & Martinez, F. L. (2008). Linking order winning and external supply chain integration strategies. *Supply Chain Management: An International Journal, 13*(4), 296–303. doi:10.1108/13598540810882189

Sachan, A., & Datta, S. (2005). Review of supply chain management and logistics research. *International Journal of Physical Distribution & Logistics Management, 35*(9), 664–704. doi:10.1108/09600030510632032

Scott, C., & Westbrook, R. (1991). New strategic tools for supply chain management. *International Journal of Physical Distribution & Logistics Management, 21*(1), 22–23. doi:10.1108/09600039110002225

Simatupang, T. M., & Sridharan, R. (2008). Design for supply chain collaboration. *Business Process Management Journal, 14*(3), 401–418. doi:10.1108/14637150810876698

Soni, G., & Kodali, R. (2011). A critical analysis of supply chain management content in empirical research. *Business Process Management, 17*(2), 238–266. doi:10.1108/14637151111122338

Swaminathan, J., & Tayur, S. (2003). Models for supply chains in e-business. *Management Science, 49*(10). doi:10.1287/mnsc.49.10.1387.17309

Van der Vaart, T., & van Donk, D. P. (2008). A critical review of survey-based research in supply chain integration. *International Journal of Production Economics, 111*(1), 42–55. doi:10.1016/j.ijpe.2006.10.011

Wilding, R., & Humphries, A. S. (2006). Understanding collaborative supply chain relationships through the application of the Williamson organisational failure framework. *International Journal of Physical Distribution & Logistics Management, 36*(4), 309–329. doi:10.1108/09600030610672064

Zheng, J., Harland, C., Lamming, R., Johnsen, T., & Wynstra, F. (2000). Networking activities in supply networks. *Journal of Strategic Marketing, 8*, 161–181.

Chapter 3
Web Applications for the Outsourcing of Logistics Services

Dimitris Folinas
ATEI, Greece

ABSTRACT

This chapter investigates the extent to which the Greek Third-Party Logistics (3PLs) companies use the internet in order to provide information and on-line services to their customers. It is based on the findings of a survey that examined the Web presence of 3PL companies in Greece. Thus, the websites of these companies were contacted and evaluated against a specific questionnaire that consists of two main categories of questions: the scope of logistics services which 3PLs provide, and the Internet practices and technologies that the examined companies use in order to support the identified logistics services. The findings of the survey reveal the effort that 3PL companies in Greece have applied in order to effectively and efficiently support their provided services via the Internet. Furthermore, they support the belief that adaptation and application of the Internet best practices and innovative technologies turns out to be beneficial for all the parties involved in the examined business sector.

INTRODUCTION

Continuous changes (technological, economical, and social) in supply chains have lead to the redesign of the existence logistics processes and the development of new. Logistics processes include the supply of the raw materials and products, their handling and storage for the production planning and the distribution of the final products. According to Christopher (2005) and Blanchard (2007) logistics processes aim to manage effectively the inventory to the right quantity, quality, place and time and with the lower cost using efficiently all the available resources. The above processes can be managed either by the organization or by a third party that provides logistics services based on the outsourcing paradigm (White & James, 1998; Murphy & Wood, 2004; Lazaropoulos, 2009). These companies are the Third Party Logistics providers (or simply 3PLs).

DOI: 10.4018/978-1-4666-3914-0.ch003

The decision for outsourcing or insourcing part or the total of the logistics process is based on specific benefits that the organization can earn. These benefits refer to: 1) Lower cost: an organization that assigns logistics services to a third company achieves savings of resources and release of the assets (the fixed costs are converted to variable costs), 2) Better quality: 3PLs have specialized skills and knowledge; they provide special logistics services possessing the appropriate infrastructure for the execution of logistics processes, and 3) Faster response regarding the provision of the logistics services. Higher level of satisfaction of the customers is the outcome of the above benefits. Furthermore, the organisation becomes more flexible to the special needs of its customers and the new practices and business initiatives of its competitors. Apart from the benefits, outsourcing may cause a number of problems such as the decrease of available working positions and the creation of conflicts in the inner side of the organisation because that the others partners and suppliers may be opposite to this partnership. Additionally, a long partnership may lead to a strong dependency of the organisation by the third party due to gradual loss of knowhow of organization's human resources. Finally, there is a possibility that the third party will not be able to effectively confront with the special needs of the organisation resulting to a lower level of provided services. It is evident that bad services can have a significant effect to the image of the organisation to the market.

According to ICAP (2006, 2009), the demand for outsourcing depends on the following factors:

1. The degree of the familiarity and appreciation of the organisation regarding the benefits of the outsourcing.
2. The complicatedness of the supply chain management in today's globalised business environment.
3. The improved possibilities that the new and innovative information and communication technologies (and especially the internet) can support the information exchange between the companies for a better management and distribution of the inventory.
4. The ability of some of the 3PLs to provide value added services concerning the planning of network distribution, the monitoring of moving products, the provision of the information for the level of the inventory, etc.

Moreover, Aberdeen (2008) research shows that among the top criteria for selecting the right 3PL are data quality, ability to exchange information electronically and ability to provide real time visibility. Gurung (2006) argues that the proliferation of the Internet technologies have provided impetus and challenges to the logistics service providers. However, a number of studies such as the researches by Edwards, Peters and Sharman (2001) and van Hoek (2001) that the Internet still has a limited impact on the way that many firms in the supply chain are operating, as well as, Murphy and Darey (2000) and Lynagh et al. (2001) who point out that mostly the larger members of the supply chain are making significantly greater use of the Internet.

The examination of the adoption level by the 3PLs of the internet practices and technologies is the main objective of this study. Specifically, this study aims to present and analyse the findings of a survey regarding the web presence of the Greek logistics service providers. Specific criteria were used for the identification of the provided logistics services and the assessment of the internet technologies and practices that Greek 3PLs are exploiting in order to support their operation.

During the last decade a number of studies have been conducted regarding the outsourcing of logistics services in Greece (Dinos, 2003; Laios, 2004; Moschuris & Apergi, 2006; Vouxaras & Folinas, 2010). The majority of these studies are concentrated either on presenting case studies and best practices or presenting the findings of national surveys about this sector. This study is focused on the web presence and the internet functionalities of the logistics services business sector. Moreover, this study refers to the web sites evaluation of the examined sector's companies. In the literature there are many researches about other service-oriented business sectors (e.g. hotels: Abdullah et al., 2010; public services: Liu, Wang & Xie, 2010; health services: RochaVictor & Brandão, 2011; agricultural services: Li, 2010; educational services: Sugak, 2011; library services: Jiang, et al., 2006). This is the first study about the 3PLs Web initiatives.

The rest of the paper is organised as follows: the first section presents the options and benefits that service providers can achieve by the usage of web and e-business paradigms in order to provide value added services. The presentation, analysis and discussion of the findings of the research are the objectives of the next section. Finally, the conclusions, as well as, the limitations, recommendations, and the scope for further research into the adoption of internet initiatives within the logistics service providers industry are presented.

3PLS IN THE DIGITAL ERA

During the last two decades, Third Party Logistics companies have provided a number of value added services based on internet technologies in order to achieve a higher level of customers' satisfaction. For example Evangelista and Kilpala (2007) argues that 3PLs are increasingly asked for advanced information services such as real-time tracking and tracing of shipments in addition to basic services such as transportation and warehousing.

These e-services do not refer mainly to the core logistics processes; however, they make the difference and attract new customers (León-Peña, 2008). According to the report of the European Logistics Association (2001) internet has provided a number of services such as:

- Homepage for marketing purposes.
- Tracking and tracing tools.
- Information gathering via internet.
- Procurement, tenders and selling via the internet.
- Order entry.
- Visualisation of processes for better integration of service providers or other production sites.
- Credit management.

Fang and Zhang (2005) identified the following advanced/specialized internet technologies for logistics services:

- I-Mode or similar mobile terminals.
- Electronic maps.
- Positioning systems.
- Web services for tracking, shipping, RFQ and Cargo/Transportation Matching Systems.

The reasons of the application of the above internet practices include: the existence of many reliable and mature technological solutions in the market, the establishment of electronic markets (e-marketplaces) that try to interrelate possible customers to providers and certainly the high number of successful e-commerce and e-business business initiatives (Hultkrantz & Lumsden, 2003).

According to the findings of the 13th Annual Study Third Party Logistics, Results and Findings (2008) the basic IT-based services that the managers of 3PLs are willing to invest are the communication via the web among provider and client, tracking/tracing tools and event management capabilities, barcodes and RFID, and fleet management web applications.

Furthermore a number of other studies/researches that the ICT (and especially the Internet) is a critical success factor of the logistics outsourcing (Rabinovich & Knemeyer, 2006; Xing et al., 2011; Qihai & Yan, 2011). Especially the progress of e-commerce has led to the emergence of new business models for the examined industry. Thus, 3PLs via their websites are able to:

1. Extract specific functionalities and information that refer to the logistics processes. Specifically, many 3PL companies via their web sites extract functionalities from the Business Information Systems (either horizontal or vertical) such as Enterprise Resource Planning (ERP), Warehouse Management Systems (WMS), Transportation Management Systems (TMS), Fleet Management Systems (FMS), etc., providing to the customers access to the business data that are maintained in those systems.

2. Support of e-commerce partnerships. According to Bayles (2002) traditional logistics is being transformed with the advent of electronic commerce. Author also argues that Businesses that outsource e-commerce initiatives can also deploy sites quickly, with minimal capital investment, while maintaining the confidence that customers will receive the level of service they expect. Kull et al. (2007) and Rutner et al. (2003) studied the "last mile" of internet supply chains emphasizing that failure of e-commerce initiatives are due to inadequate logistics support. Regan and Song (2000) proposed five (5) business models that refer to an intermediate business entity, which via an e-marketplace (a typical e-commerce approach / initiative) supports the interaction of 3PLs, carriers, etc., establishing a forum in order to offer more reliable services. These models are the following:

   a. Spot market that allows carriers to inform about their capacity and the quality of services that can offer to the market.
   b. Auction, which supports the management of Request for Quotes (RFQs), and the various auction tasks.

   c. Exchanges that support the above services, as well as, e-services for the support of logistics processes.
   d. Application Service Providers, including companies of the IT industry that provide via the net specialized software applications in order o support the logistics processes and the information exchange between supply chain members.
   e. Purchasing consolidation sites that provide to their members and customers (SME's, VSME's, carriers, etc.) to obtain equipment and supplies via the internet.

3. Support of supply chain partnerships via the:
   a. Deployment, either the inter-enterprise information systems (Supply Chain Management – SCM Systems) for the effective management and optimization of the processes that are executed between the supply chain members. SCM software systems involves automating tasks such as routing, scheduling, load planning, and track and trace (both barcodes and especially RFID are important tools for track and trace), or
   b. Messaging Management Systems that support the interchange of business information (e-documents) for the execution of the real-time transactions (Electronic Data Interchange (EDI) and eXtensible Markup Language (XML)) which are also main e-commerce technologies.

4. Provision of information that produced from the execution logistics processes. Specifically, in the above e-business models a number of content information portals regarding logistics can be added. Usually, these portals are maintained by 3PLs and provide updated, reliable, and useful information about logistics activities.

To conclude with the presentation of the above initiatives it must be emphasised that their aim is the Supply Chain Integration (SCI). Some researchers such as Fabbe-Costes, Jahre and Roussat (2009), as well as, Chow et al., (2007) (using the website analysis) argue that the majority of the LSPs do not consider SCI as part of their job. However, the majority of researchers strongly agree that 3PLs must have the ability to cooperate both vertically with supply chain partners and horizontally with other 3PLs (Fabbe-Costes, Jahre & Roussat, 2009; Mason et al., 2007; Persona et al., 2007).

RESEARCH METHODOLOGY

The main aim of this study is the evaluation of the content and the web services that the Greek 3PLs provide to their customers. Specifically, it aims at first to identify the range of logistics services that the targeting companies provide and second to assess the internet practices and technologies that support the above services.

The method of the Content analysis was selected so as to achieve the above objectives. According to the substantial paper of Kolbe and Burnett (2001) Content analysis is a systematic and objective research technique suitable for making valid and replicable inferences from data to their context. Even if it was first designed for social sciences, it has successfully applied to web site analysis. Nacar and Burnaz (2011) applied it for multinational companies' web sites analysis and Lin and Hwang (2009) used it so as to estimate the quality of online auction sellers. Furthermore, a number of researchers applied Content analysis method for examining web initiatives for supporting logistics and supply chain services. In his work Farrell (2008), studied the role of the Internet in the delivery of export promotion services. Bodkin and Perry (2004) made a comparative analysis of retailers and service providers' web sites. After making a systematic searching it is evident that

there are no studies that apply Content analysis for examining the web presence of 3PLs.

Therefore, a structured questionnaire of closed type questions (see Appendix) has been developed and used for the data collection. The initial list of 3PLs was taken from the online catalog of the e-journal of plant-management online journal (www. plant-management.gr). This catalog consists of 145 companies that operate in this sector. After an initial research only 50 companies (almost 35%) maintain a web site (the above percentage is low and it surely must be the topic for further investigation). The research that follows referred to the above sample. A corresponding number of interviews were arranged with the managers of these companies from May 26th to September 5th. The questionnaire that had been used included 16 questions and it was organized in the following 3 parts:

Part A: This part consists of questions which try to sketch the profile of the examined companies. It includes questions about the name of the company, the city of the company's headquarters and the existence of branches.

Part B: It consists of questions that refer to operational and logistics issues, for example if the companies have privately owned warehouse facilities and fleet of vehicles, what is the geographical scope of services, which logistics services are provided to the market, which are the business domains of the clients of the providers, and which are the mode of transports.

Part C: This part includes questions about the usage of internet practices and technologies by the logistics providers. Managers were asked if their companies via their web sites support one or more logistics services; they were asked to identify the means of communication with their clients and business partners, to name the provided value-added services, and finally the type of information they are provide via their web sites.

FINDINGS

The answers of the above questions are presenting below:

Part A: Company's Profile

According to the responses the majority of the companies are located in Athens (86%) while the rest are located in Thessaloniki and other regions. This was expected because of the population of these cities, the high intensity of commerce activities and certainly because that both of them have the central ports, railway and aviation facilities of the country. The 56% of them has branches in other towns (especially in Thessaloniki and Crete) providing their logistics services to other geographical areas (and especially to North and South Greece respectively). Moreover, most of them (82%) provide logistics services to other countries and especially to the Balkan countries, Italy and Turkey. The above findings justify the expansive strategy of the examined companies and the central role of the Greek companies in the wider area (Figure 1). This is supported by the findings of the ICAP sector report (2009). According to its findings, the overall domestic market has presented a continuous increase during the 1998-2009 with an average rate of 18.7%.

Part B: Operational and Logistics Issues

The majority of the companies of the sample have privately owned warehouse facilities (70%) and privately owned fleet of vehicles (84%) (Figure 2). These results were expected because these two areas are the key outsourcing logistics activities.

Figure 3 presents the logistics services that the 3PL companies provide to their clients.

According to the results the main logistics services that the companies of the sample offer to their clients are: a) Transportation (100%), b) Distribution (96%), c) Warehousing (84%), d)

Figure 1. Profile of the companies (location, branches, and international activities)

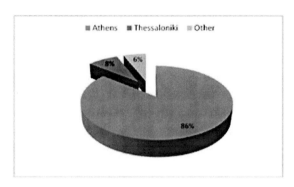

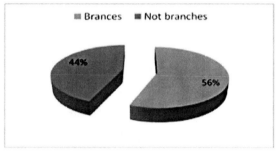

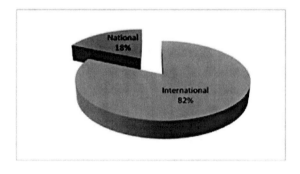

Insurance services (62%), e) Coding / Labeling / Packaging (54%), f) Inventory handling (52%), g) Order handling (46%), h) Customs activities (36%), and j) Cross-docking (22%). The results are slightly different from the findings of the last ICAP sector report (2009) in which the most common logistics service is warehousing, following by the transportation and distribution. On the other hand, the results are aligned with the findings of the 13th Annual Study: "Third Party Logistics, Results, and Findings" (2008) in which the transportation is the first choice (85%), following by the warehousing (72%) and the third is Customs activities (65%).

Figure 2. Warehouse facilities and fleet of vehicles

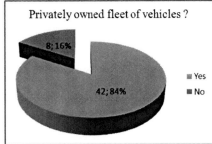

Figure 3. Logistics services

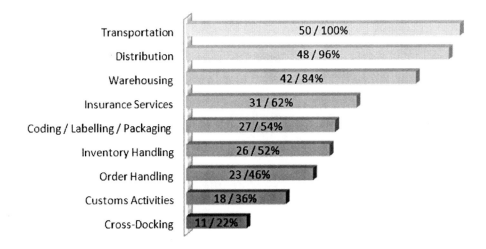

Particularly, regarding the transportation modalities, companies support all modalities and especially road (98%), ship (64%), aviation 58% and rail 24% (Figure 4).

Then, the managers were asked to identify the business sectors of the clients. According to the results (Figure 5), the retail sector is the top answer (94%), electronics (88%), toys (80%), food and beverages (78%), automobile (68%) and chemicals (64%). There is small percentage of 3PLs that provide logistics services to companies that assigned to the providers to carry, handle, and store animals and artworks (22%). The results of the ICAP (2009) are similar; the first sector is food and beverages, the second is electronics and the third is furniture.

Part C: Internet Practices and Technologies

In this survey, managers were asked, at first, if their companies via their web sites support the logistics services. Furthermore, they asked to identify the communication channel with both clients and business partners and to specify the provided value-added services, and finally the type of information. Many logistics providers use the internet as a mean for supporting and improving their logistics and business services in general. Specifically, more than one third (36.67%) uses the internet for the execution of core logistics services while the majority 63.33% uses the internet mainly for supporting and strengthening

Figure 4. Logistics services

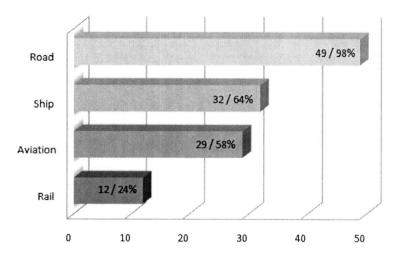

Figure 5. Business sectors of the clients

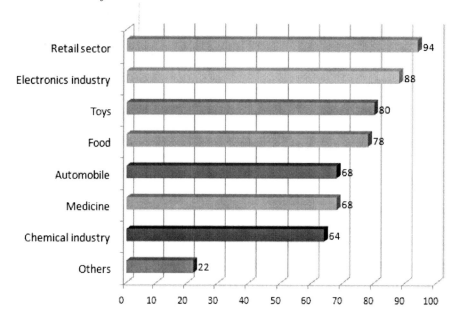

companies' presence in the market (e.g. advertising the provided services). The first group includes logistics service providers that initially asked their clients to fill a form in order to assign specific tasks related to logistics. These tasks, based on the findings (Figure 6), are the following: customs activities (30%), transportation (12%), handling (12%), distribution (10%), inventory handling (8%), and insurance services (4%). For the trans-

portation and distribution providers offer to their clients the capability to monitor the movement of their goods. Moreover, a number of other services were reported -that the initial questionnaire did not include- such as the: Request for Proposals (25%), value for fares (4%), delivery costs (4%) and calculation of transportation and/or distribution costs (4%).

Figure 6. Logistics services via the internet

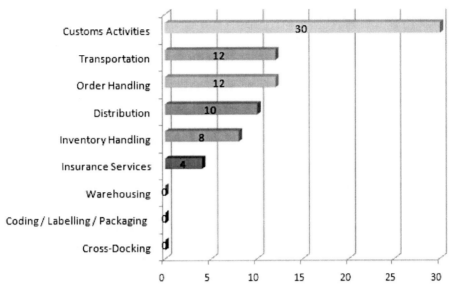

The web sites of the examined 3PLs support all the main communication means such as communication by post, phone, fax, and email (Figure 7). A small number of them give the ability to clients and other partners to communicate via e-forms and to register so as to have access to better services and personalized information.

Then, managers were asked to identify the value-added services that the companies provide to their customers via the web sites. Overall, 3PLs in order to be more competitive and gain more customers they provide e-services based on internet practices and technologies. They are creating more attractive and functional sites providing

Figure 7. Communication means

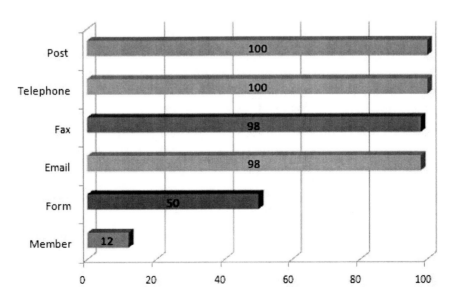

useful services such as: Multilanguage support (74%), news/announcements (38%), useful links (26%), maps (24%), advisory services (16%), search engines (16%), tracking of shipping items (16%), advertisements (10%), frequently asked questions (10%), site statistics (4%), and downloads (2%) (see Figure 8).

The results show, that despite their will, a small part of the 3PLs provides e-services to the market. Nevertheless, the majority of the managers (96.67%) argue that in the near future (2-3 years) their companies will provide the above services.

CONCLUSION

Useful conclusions emerged from the survey. First, even if managers of the Greek Third Party Logistics providers regard very important the communication and cooperation with their clients only 1 to 3 have a web presence; this may be reported because of the traditionally problematic adoption of internet in the targeting country. Secondly, most of the examined companies provide the typical

logistics services such as transportation, warehousing, and distribution. Moreover, they provide their services to both national and international markets owning their owned warehousing facilities and fleet of vehicles. Many of them via their websites give the opportunity to their customers to have access to transportation and warehousing data. These companies, also, by understanding the high competition in the examined market they provide various value added services such as information, news, maps, useful links, tracing and tracking of goods, templates of common transportation documents, etc.

Third, it is well accepted by all managers that the companies of the examined business sector must upgraded the quality of their services to customers. They argue that the adoption of web technologies can give them a critical advantage both on national and international level. Best practices regarding international 3PLs that have been recorded and presented in other countries are far away from the reality that has been recorded in this survey. It is obvious that on one hand, the Greek 3PLs must invest in ICT and especially internet

Figure 8. Value-added e-services

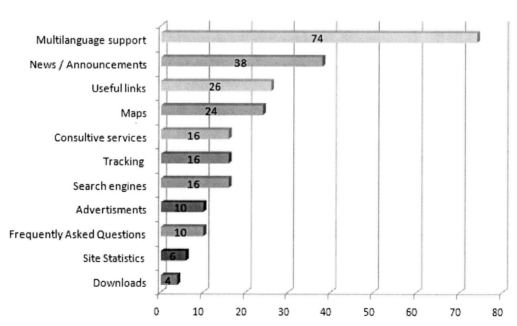

solutions and on the other the Greek software house companies must develop web applications that are focused on the Greek market.

One limitation of this study is that it was not examine the size of the 3PLs; do the bigger players of the sector provide more e-services and web functionalities? Moreover, the size of the clients is not examined. Do the biggest companies in the market require more advanced services?

This research can be extended to assess the critical success factors regarding the adoption of web technologies by the Greek 3PLs. Moreover, the effect of the web sites to the formation of the positive brand perception by the clients can be also examined. Another topic is to identify and categorise the ICT initiatives that the Greek logistics providers have adopted based on the four business models that have presented in a previous section. Finally, the Content analysis of the top logistics services providers in the global market will be a valuable tool for the managers and CEOs of the 3PL companies. The main objective is to motivate managers of the targeting companies to deploy the Internet more fully and effectively. After synthesizing the findings of the researches that indirectly dealt with the same topic in other national or global markets (Fabbe-Costes, Jahre & Roussat, 2009; Mason et al., 2007; Persona et al., 2007) it proved that these are in line with those of this research.

REFERENCES

Abdullah, D., Radzi, S. M., Jamaluddin, M. R., & Patah, M. O. R. A. (2010). Hotel web site evaluation and business travelers' preferences. In *Proceedings of the ICETC 2010 - 2010 2ⁿᵈ International Conference on Education Technology and Computer*, (pp. 3485-3488). ICETC.

Aberdeen Group. (2008). *The changing role of logistics service providers in today's supply chain*. Retrieved from http://www.aberdden.com

Bayles, D. (2002). *E-logistics & e-fulfillment: Beyond the "buy" button*. Paper presented at UNCTAD Workshop 2002. Curaçao, Curaçao.

Blanchard, D. (2007). *Supply chain management - Best practices*. Hoboken, NJ: Wiley & Sons Inc.

Bodkin, C. D., & Perry, M. (2004). Goods retailers and service providers: Comparative analysis of web site marketing communications. *Journal of Retailing and Consumer Services*, *11*(1), 19–29. doi:10.1016/S0969-6989(02)00058-9

Chow, H. K. H., Choy, K. L., Lee, W. B., & Chan, F. T. S. (2007). Integration of web-based and RFID technology in visualizing logistics operations - A case study. *Supply Chain Management: An International Journal*, *12*(3), 221–234. doi:10.1108/13598540710742536

Christopher, M. (2005). *Logistics and supply chain management*. London, UK: Prentice Hall.

Dinos, V. (2003). 3PLs and outsourcing in Greece. *Warehouse. Logistics & Transportation*, *15*, 34–37.

Edwards, P., Peters, M., & Sharman, G. (2002). The effectiveness of information systems in supporting the extended supply chain. *Journal of Business Logistics*, *22*, 1–28. doi:10.1002/j.2158-1592.2001.tb00157.x

European Logistics Association. (2001). *The influence of e-commerce on tomorrows logistics*. Retrieved November 20, 2011, from http://www.elalog.org/publications/tno-ebook.pdf

Evangelista, P., & Kilpala, H. (2007). The perception on ICT use among small logistics service providers: A comparison between Northern and Southern Europe. *European Transport*, *35*, 81–98.

Fabbe-Costes, N., Jahre, M., & Roussat, C. (2009). Supply chain integration: The role of logistics service providers. *International Journal of Productivity and Performance Management*, *58*(1), 71–91. doi:10.1108/17410400910921092

Fang, L., & Zhang, C.-Q. (2005). *The e-logistics framework in e-commerce*. Retrieved September 1, 2011, from: http://delivery.acm. org/10.1145/1090000/1089626/p408-fang. pdf?ip=83.212.54.165&acc=ACTIVE%20 SERVICE&CFID=68228288&CFTOK EN=11031907&__acm__=1330456613_00dd8 1e149cff1801ff348adad525ff5

Farrell, C. (2008). The role of the internet in the delivery of export promotion services: A web site content analysis. *Journal of Global Marketing, 21*(4), 259–269. doi:10.1080/08911760802206094

Gurung, A. (2006). A survey of information technologies in logistics management. In *Proceedings of the 2006 Annual Conference*. Oklahoma City, OK: Decision Sciences Institute.

Hultkrantz, O., & Lumsden, K. (2003). E-commerce and consequences for the logistics Industry. *European Conference of Ministers of Transport Organisation for Economic Co-operation and Development*. Retrieved November 20, 2011, from http://www.oecd.org/dataoecd/3/19/2726935.pdf

ICAP. (2006). *Sector report: Third party logistics*. ICAP.

ICAP. (2009). *Sector report: Third party logistics*. ICAP.

Jiang, Y., Hu, L., Yang, Z., Yan, G., & Shen, X. (2006). Evaluation of cross-strait public library web site. *Journal of Natural Sciences, 11*(5), 1202–1208.

Kull, T. J., Boyer, K., & Calantone, R. (2007). Last-mile supply chain efficiency: An analysis of learning curves in online ordering. *International Journal of Operations & Production Management, 27*, 409–434. doi:10.1108/01443570710736985

Laios, L. (2004). Logistics outsourcing? *Warehouse & Transportation, 21*, 59–62.

Lazaropoulos, H. (2009). *3PLs in Greece*. Retrieved September 1, 2011, from http://www. plant-management.gr

León-Peña, J. (2008). e-Business and the supply chain management. *Business Intelligence Journal*. Retrieved March 1, 2011, from http://www.sayco-corporativo.com/saycoUK/BIJ/journal/Vol1No1/ article_4.pdf

Li, L. (2010). Empirical study on evaluation of agricultural web sites in China. In *Proceedings of the 2010 International Conference on E-Product E-Service and E-Entertainment, ICEEE2010*. ICEEE.

Lin, F.-H., & Hwang, C.-C. (2009). A content analysis of web-site quality of online auction sellers. In *Proceedings of the IADIS International Conference e-Commerce 2009, Part of the IADIS Multi Conference on Computer Science and Information Systems, MCCSIS 2009*, (pp. 105-112). IADIS.

Liu, M., Wang, Z., & Xie, H. (2010). Evaluation of e-government web site. In *Proceedings of the 2010 International Conference on Computer Design and Applications, ICCDA 2010*, (pp. 5432-5434). ICCDA.

Lynag, P., Murphy, P., Poist, R., & Grazer, W. (2001). Web-based informational practices of logistics service providers: An empirical assessment. *Transportation Journal, 40*, 34–45.

Mason, R., Lalwani, C., & Boughton, R. (2007). Combining vertical and horizontal collaboration for transport optimisation. *Supply Chain Management: An International Journal, 12*(3), 187–199. doi:10.1108/13598540710742509

Moschuris, S. J., & Apergi, A. (2006). Transportation outsourcing: A survey of Greek practices. *Paradigm, 10*(1), 1–10.

Murphy, P., & Daley, J. (2000). An empirical study of internet issues among Internet freight forwarders. *Transportation Journal, 39*, 5–14.

Murphy, P., & Wood, D. (2004). *Contemporary logistics*. Upper Saddle River, NJ: Pearson Prentice Hall.

Nacar, R., & Burnaz, S. (2011). A cultural content analysis of multinational companies' web sites. *Qualitative Market Research, 14*(3), 274–288. doi:10.1108/13522751111137505

Persona, A., Regattieri, A., Pham, H., & Battini, D. (2007). Remote control and maintenance outsourcing networks and its applications in supply chain management. *Journal of Operations Management, 25*(6), 1275–1291. doi:10.1016/j.jom.2007.01.018

Qihai, Z., & Yan, L. (2011). Research on logistics distribution mode for e-commerce businesses. *Advanced Materials Research, 181-182*, 3–8. doi:10.4028/www.scientific.net/AMR.181-182.3

Rabinovich, E., & Knemeyer, A. M. (2006). Logistics service providers in internet supply chains. *California Management Review, 48*(4), 84–108. doi:10.2307/41166362

Regan, A., & Song, J. (2000). *An industry in transition: Third party logistics in the information age*. Retrieved November 20, 2011, from http://www.uctc.net/papers/634.pdf

Rocha, Á., Victor, A., & Brandão, P. L. (2011). Quality of health web sites: Dimensions for a wide evaluation. *Lecture Notes in Business Information Processing, 90*, 254–266. doi:10.1007/978-3-642-24511-4_20

Rutner, S. M., Gibson, B. J., & Williams, S. R. (2003). The impacts of the integrated logistics systems on electronic commerce and enterprise resource planning systems. *Transportation Research Part E, Logistics and Transportation Review, 39*(2), 83–93. doi:10.1016/S1366-5545(02)00042-X

Sugak, D. B. (2011). Rankings of a university's web sites on the internet. *Scientific and Technical Information Processing, 38*(1), 17–19. doi:10.3103/S014768821101014X

Van Hoek, R. (2001). E-supply chains-virtually non-existing. *Supply Chain Management International Journal, 6*, 21–28. doi:10.1108/13598540110694653

Vouxaras, N., & Folinas, D. (2010). Logistics outsourcing: Methodology for the selection of the suitable 3PL partner. *Supply Chain & Logistics, 34*, 54–55.

White, R., & James, B. (1998). *The outsourcing manual*. London, UK: Grower House.

Xing, Y., Grant, D. B., McKinnon, A. C., & Fernie, J. (2011). The interface between retailers and logistics service providers in the online market. *European Journal of Marketing, 45*(3), 334–357. doi:10.1108/03090561111107221

ADDITIONAL READING

Delfmann, W., Albers, S., & Gehring, M. (2002). The impact of electronic commerce on logistics service providers. *International Journal of Physical Distribution & Logistics Management, 32*(3), 203–222. doi:10.1108/09600030210426539

Fabbe-Costes, N., Jahre, M., & Roussat, C. (2008). Supply chain integration: The role of logistics service providers. *International Journal of Productivity and Performance Management, 58*(1), 71–91. doi:10.1108/17410400910921092

Lieb, R. C. (1992). The use of third-party logistics services by large American manufacturers. *Journal of Business Logistics, 13*(2), 29–42.

Lieb, R. C., & Butner, K. (2007). The North American third party logistics industry in 2006: The provider CEO perspective. *Transportation Journal, 46*(3), 40–52.

Pan, T., Zheng, L., & Yan, G. (2010). Research of information framework for fourth party logistics. *Journal of Convergence Information Technology, 5*(7).

Płaczek, E. (2010). New challenges for logistics providers in the e-business era. *Electronic Scientific Journal of Logistics, 6*(2). Retrieved July 11, 2011, from http://www.logforum.net/vol6/issue2/no6

Pokharel, S. (2005). Perception on information and communication technology perspectives in logistics - A study or transportation and warehouse sectors in Singapore. *The Journal of Enterprise Information Management, 18*(2), 136–149. doi:10.1108/17410390510579882

Sauvage, T. (2003). The relationship between technology and logistics third-party providers. *International Journal of Physical Distribution & Logistical Management, 33*(3), 236–253. doi:10.1108/09600030310471989

APPENDIX

Table 1. Structured closed-type questions

Questionnaire					
Part A: Company's profile					
Q1	Company Title				
Q2	Web site				
Q3	City	Athens	Thessaloniki	Other	
Q4	Branches	Yes	No		
Q5	Other countries	Yes	No		
Part B: Operational and logistics issues					
Q6	Privately owned warehouse facilities	Yes	No		
Q7	Privately owned warehouse facilities	Yes	No		
Q8	Provided services	Transportation		Warehousing	
		Distribution		Insurance Services	
		Coding/ Labelling/ Packaging		Inventory Handling	
		Order Handling		Customs Activities	
		Cross-Docking		Other	
Q9	Transportation modalities	Rail	Aviation	Ship	Road
Q10	Business sectors	Chemical industry		Medicine	
		Automobile		Food	
		Toys		Electronics industry	
		Retail sector		Other	
Part C: Internet practices and technologies					
Q11	Logistics services via the internet	Customs Activities		Transportation	
		Order Handling		Distribution	
		Inventory Handling		Insurance Services	
		Warehousing		Coding/ Labelling/ Packaging	
		Cross-Docking		Other	
Q12	Communication means	Post		Te;e[jpme	
		Member		Fax	
		Email		Form	

continued on following page

Table 1. Continued

Questionnaire					
Q13	Value-added e-services	Multilanguage support		News/Announcements	
		Useful links		Maps	
		Cunsultive services		Tracking	
		Search engines		Advertisement	
		Frequently Asked Questions		Site Statistics	
		Downloads		Other	
Q14	Future investment in web services	1-2 years		2-3 years	
		More than 3 years		More than 5 years	

Section 2
E–Logistics and E–Supply Chain Management

Chapter 4
Measuring the Impact of Tools on the Leanness of E-Procurement Processes

Carina Nicole Leistner
University of Liverpool, UK

ABSTRACT

The concept of lean thinking is—despite its prominence as waste reducer and value creator—still mainly applied to the manufacturing environment. Whilst investigations on applicability to the service industry are advancing fast, little has been distributed for the area of procurement. This development is opposed by trends of increasing degree of outsourcing and related high portions of procurement of up to 60% of a company's total value creation. The mismatch in terms of lack of strategic attention on lean procurement on the one hand and the responsibility of this function for the majority of a company's value creation on the other, combined with the simultaneous trend of establishing "miracle cures" in the form of e-procurement gave rise to the interest in determining the stake of buy-side systems in the leanness of procurement processes. For this purpose, a case study approach was adopted focusing on the central questions of what lean means for procurement, which measures could portray leanness in this instance, how the stake of buy-side systems can be reflected in the performance indicators with separate consideration of repetitive processes in operational and strategic purchasing, in order to finally attribute a clear enabler role to IT for achieving leanness in operational procurement. This finding has been reached by the means of an objective research approach, relying on quantitative methods such as KPI measurement for data collection and regression analysis for the interpretation of correlation between the variables. As such, this chapter has not only a high value for practitioners by providing a baseline for benchmarking lean performance of e-procurement, by supporting system investment decisions, or by simply facilitating decisions on adapting existing IT solutions. It also proves as enrichment to the existing theoretical body of knowledge filling into the aforesaid gaps of lean procurement and putting—at least for procurement processes—an end to the discussion as to whether ERP systems and lean thinking are reconcilable or not.

DOI: 10.4018/978-1-4666-3914-0.ch004

INTRODUCTION

The concept of lean thinking derives originally from the manufacturing environment. As such, the terminology in general and specifically around the central concept of waste origin is greatly dominated by the context of physical operations like overproduction, unnecessary motion, excessive inventory, and waiting, which according to Abdi et al. (2006) can be applied to the service sector as well. Bowen and Youngdahl (1998) implicitly support this perception by concentrating their research on the similarities between manufacturing and services, thereby emphasizing the lean service characteristics of flow production and just-in-time pull principles, increased customer focus, employee empowerment, value chain orientation for eliminating administrative waste, and reduction of performance tradeoffs between internal efficiency and customer-defined flexibility. Also Seddon and O'Donnavan (2010) characterize, next to the intangible nature of services, the possible presence of customers during service execution and the potential sequential overlapping of services' production and consumption as the only major differences to the manufacturing environment.

In essence all of the afore-quoted authors indicate no objections to the applicability of a lean approach to services and merely suggest minor necessity for adaptation. Therefore, the overall research aspiration towards lean processes in the typically service-oriented function of procurement was deemed sensible. Nevertheless, the lack of a clear meaning of the characteristics implied with lean services hampered the deriving of procurement-related lean indicators, thereby giving rise to the need of a definition. This perceived gap in existing literature is supported by Wilson and Roy (2009) who argue that no harmonized approach exists with regards to the conceptualization of lean procurement as "a philosophy, a work culture, a technique, a management concept, a value, a methodology or an ethos." Nevertheless, critical components arguably include measures such as

standardized transportation, flexibility in specifications, reduction of administrative workload, all kinds of waste elimination, and tighter information sharing with suppliers (Walters-Fuller, 1995, cited by Wilson & Roy, 2009, p. 819). Going even further, tools in e-procurement are said to target specifically at the three latter mentioned factors. Nonetheless the description of critical components to lean procurement is addressed rather vaguely in common literature and latter authors perceive that the attribution of tools to lean procurement is also decided without measures or reasoning in practice. This means that, in order to assess the true contribution of digitalization to lean, both, a clear framework for the measurement of lean procurement, as well as, a dedicated means to deducing the contribution of tools are required. Linked to this perception, Chase (1999, p.2, cited by Bhasin & Burcher, 2006), indicates that an organization or a process is easily referred to as being lean when incorporating only one or two lean elements. Likewise, Womack (2007), 'warns' from a commonly isolated integration of tools as singular 'lean' means "without tackling the difficult task of changing the organization and the fundamental approach to management" despite his general admittance for the value of tools in support of lean.

Research on the general perception of tool contributions to the leanness of information exchange reveals that Puschmann and Alt (2005) report on the contribution of Enterprise Resource Planning (ERP) systems in reducing administrative approval procedures in purchase operations and attribute a high degree of process, product, and inventory savings to electronically enabled Requests for Quotation (RFQ's), auctions, and catalogues. In linking this observation with Wilson and Roy's (2009) interpretation that lean procurement is essentially based on the Total Cost of Ownership (TCO) model and aiming mainly at the reduction of system costs, a clear contribution of tools to leanness could be reasoned for. Tinham (2010) likewise praises transparency of IT as an enabler to lean management in internal as well as externally linked processes and thereby rounds up the arguments in favor of positive tool contributions to lean. On the other hand, Gill (2007) argues that particularly ERP systems are in terms of their inherited design based on long-term planning and data aggregation incompatible with the lean approach and its focus on short-term reactivity. In support of the above, Bradford et al. (2001) indicate that specifically older ERP systems with little adaptability are counterproductive to lean and in general designed to track all activities and material prices, which is argued to be non-value added transactions and therefore a contradiction to lean. As such, it is deduced that no common agreement with regards to a negative or positive implication of digitalization to leanness in procurement can be found. Effectively, this state of discord on the role of IT gave rise to a more detailed investigation based on the above stated research for a definition of lean procurement.

Therefore, this research aimed at measuring the impact of tools on the leanness of procurement processes by answering the question to which extent digitalization contributed to the leanness of operational and strategic procurement processes. Deriving from these findings, it was expected that the role of e-procurement tools to the leanness of a processes was to be expressed as 'facilitating' or 'enabling'. Even though common literature, such as Chan (2000), distinguishes between three roles of IT to business processes, namely initiator, facilitator, and enabler, this study only concentrated on the latter two. This is due to the presumption that the information technology investigated throughout the exemplary case study had been chosen purposefully and in line with the company's strategy, whereas the initiator's role is rather an adaptation of powerful technology without predetermined, problem-oriented vision. A facilitator on the other hand is described as having the capacity to ease up work or workload, thereby, meaning that the solution itself forms an integral part to the operation or product. Lastly,

the enabler role implies that IT is a necessary prerequisite to performing a certain activity. Therefore, the investigation on whether the role of IT, according to the latter distinction, differs for operational and strategic procurement processes finally complemented the research.

LEANING E-PROCUREMENT

According to the reasoning delineated beforehand, five research aspects, relating to a definition of leanness in procurement, the measurement of lean in procurement processes, the ability to quantify a tool's contribution to leanness as well as its dedicated influence measurement along with the determining of differences in terms of lean fostering by IT in operational and strategic procurement, portray research gaps or controversially discussed aspects in existing literature. On the one hand, this is due to the origin of the concept in manufacturing, procurement has mainly received attention in terms of suppliers' lean manufacturing performance in the value chain (Lamming, 1996, p. 183) rather than with regards to the purchasing process flow. On the other hand, the former depth of internal added-value creation and related importance of internal production around 1950, when the Toyota Production System (TPS) was founded as an alternative to Henry Ford's economies of scale for smaller markets, necessitated a strong focus on the manufacturing area in striving for improvement and competitive advantage (Liker, 2004, p. 20). Throughout the last decades, increased competition and price pressure has led to a concentration on core competencies and related swell in outsourcing thereby contributing to the production of complex systems in collaboration with a whole set of organization in the form of a value network (Cagliano et al., 2004). Concurrently, the shift in importance from the secondary sector of manufacturing towards the tertiary sector of services, likewise led to an alternation in business focus. With the stake of the service sector to the total Gross Domestic Product (GDP) throughout Europe amounting to 70.6% by 2006 (World Resources Institute, 2007) and the portion of externally procured value creation consuming easily up to 70% of a company's revenues (Presutti, 2003; Monczka et al., 2009), the shift in importance towards the service sector and service functions, such as procurement, appears quite obvious. With services in general and more specifically the concept of supply chain management, which procurement forms an integral part of, as well as lean thinking concentrating on value creation for the customer through cost-effective processes (Arlbjørn et al, 2011), the extension of Toyota's initial manufacturing philosophy to procurement is reasonably targeted by this publication. Likewise, e-procurement is frequently referred to as adding value in the supply chain (Smart, 2010; Presutti, 2003), even though not necessarily through purposeful adaptation in line with a lean strategy. It has therefore been sought-after examining the exact contribution of digital information exchange in strategic and operational procurement to the leanness of the processes.

Whilst afore-identified gaps in common literature clearly emphasize the value of the research topic on lean procurement and on the standing of buy-side tools in this context, the investigation still relied on the findings of earlier research aspirations to form a reference for the examination. First, in order to determine a holistic definition of lean office processes and more specifically in the areas of procurement, the definition was based upon the proposition of Wincel (2004), who suggests that lean supply chain management as a super-ordinate function to procurement, is the organization of this unit as a profit rather than as cost center. Even though kept short, precise, and finance-related, such presumption directly implies lean key concepts, including customer orientation and value creation. This is due to the central thought of profit generation, which entails a willingness of someone, respectively a client, to pay more for a certain service than the costs consumed by the service generation itself. It appears obvious that in order to be disposed to monetarily remunerate for procurement or other inter-organizational services, its contributions will have to be perceived as adding value. Furthermore, the striving for not only profit generation but rather its maximization gives rise to reflections with regards to the potential for waste reduction, customer-triggered demand –also referred to as pull-principle, as well as considerations in terms of value-stream and its flow. Given the lean characteristics, which can be attributed to the definition of lean procurement as a profit center organization, this meaning has been considered as starting point for the development of a more precise definition of the term.

Secondly, several authors have already determined Key Performance Indicators (KPIs) for the measurement of leanness. Whilst these are partially not even dedicated to the gauging of lean for services, nor specifically for procurement, the applicability of lean thinking to all processes within an organization (Womack & Jones, 2003) reasons in favor of a transferability of manufacturing-oriented KPIs to a procurement environment. In this instance, Hines et al. (2002) argue that KPIs, determined to measure lean progress, are to derive from Critical Success Factors (CSFs). Keeping in mind that lean procurement encompasses its acting as a profit center; this implies entrepreneurial spirit and concurrently allows for the establishing of function-wide CSF's in line with corporate strategy. A matrix for retaining respective influence intensity of each key performance measure to every CSF is therefore suggested. Other authors go even further in presenting dedicated measures for certain processes, such as in-bound and internal logistics according to the generic categories of time, quality, and cost performance (De Toni & Tonchia, 1996) or present a distinct framework for quantifying only the central lean aspect of customer value, comprising "added value, perceived value, and received value" (Setijono & Dahlgaard, 2007). Contrarily to the latter, Bhasin (2008) stresses the necessity for a holistic KPI framework covering all relevant dimensions of "financial and customer led indices, processes, people, and parameters looking at the organization's future prospects," similar to a balanced scorecard.

Another contribution in the area of holistic frameworks, though likewise coined by the manufacturing context, is provided by Singh et al. (2010). The authors aimed at establishing a leanness measure alongside five broad categories consisting of suppliers, investment priorities, lean practices, various waste categories, and customer issues to calculate up to an index for comparability. In line with the research aspirations the above presented literature contributions have formed a starting point for the studies to the extent that: 1) KPI's were developed in line with individual strategic targets (refer to Hines et al, 2002), 2) Cost, quality and time dimensions were covered (refer to De Toni & Tonchia, 1996), and 3) A holistic framework had been provided (Sigh, Garg & Sharma, 2010; Bhasin, 2008) even though admitting for the distinct nature of the study in the area of information technology in procurement.

CASE STUDY ANALYSIS

For the purpose of measuring the impact of tools to the leanness of procurement processes the research has been conducted alongside a typical case study. The company under investigation has recently founded one of the largest indirect procurement organizations in Europe, covering operational purchasing as well as strategic sourcing processes.

Business under Investigation

During the last decade the management of the company decided to centralize its procurement activities for indirect materials within a common shared service center serving internal customers within its business divisions across all European sites. This organization spans six commodities: (1) Facilities Management, (2) Information Technology, (3) Human Resources Services, (4) Investments and Maintenance, (5) Travel, and (6) Product Development.

These material groups imply a largely direct linkage between supplier and (internal) customer via procurement and allow therefore for a pure and simplified measurement of tool influence on leanness compared to multi-stage supply chains, where double-effects, complexity, and other external influences were potentially to impinge on measurement. In addition, the indirect scope without external end-customer triggered demand entails applicability outside the aerospace sector, given that all organizations are likely to procure indirect materials similarly. As such, a high transferability of the research findings to other industries and companies is presumed. Furthermore, the organization has not only announced its emphasis on lean processes and accompanied initiatives such as value stream mapping and continuous improvement, but also undertakes a harmonization of processes throughout the distinct business divisions preceded by benchmarking and the determination of best practices. All of these aspirations have been accompanied by the investigation of the tools questions in both, strategic as well as operational procurement. Thereby, new implementations such as an e- sourcing platform for strategic procurement, were likewise important as enhancements to existing ERP backend or SRM frontend solutions, implied e.g. through the fostering of catalogue managed buying. The case study, hence, allows for comparable measurements for distinct lean indicators alongside increasing degrees of digitalization of a process and generic applicability of the findings has been assured through the scope of procurement with indirect materials being independent of a specific industrial branch.

Business Processes under Investigation

The process in the center of investigation related to the recurring activities conducted, led and directly controlled by the (indirect) procurement function of the company. With on time, on quality, and on cost delivery being the declared focus of procurement operations, the major focus is generally drawn on the material and information flow between (internal) customer and supplier facilitated by the joining link of purchasing. Whilst procurement is generally responsible for the physical material flows coming from the supplier, the latter processes are usually still managed by the suppliers and are only company internally manipulable to the degree of contract and supplier management. On the other hand, procurement directly steers all information related processes and is furthermore in the position to facilitate its digitalization, for instance via buy-side driven systems. In comparison to sell-side one-to-many models, such as e.g. Amazon or other seller managed electronic catalogues, the latter model implies that the product portfolio available for the customer is controlled, maintained, and usually also hosted by the buying organization, thereby allowing for compliance with strict internal security rules, confidentiality, and supplier reduction strategies. Within this scope, the procurement process spans strategy definition with all relevant stakeholders, the management of internal customer requests and conducting of call for tenders, negotiation and supplier selection, ordering of products and services along with its receipt, as well as the monitoring and contract management on dedicated projects. As a supporting sub-process, all activities related to supplier management and development act as a facilitator to each of the aforementioned stages in the procurement process. Within this generic process, the recurring activities are generally distinguished according to their impact on the business, implying either a strategic or operational focus. Strategic procurement activities are

considered as activities ensuring the supply of goods and services crucial for meeting a business' objectives. Operational purchasing by contrary entails a rather limited impact on the overall business performance as well as short-term influence, such as the coverage of low-volume one-time demands. Whilst operational procurement could likewise necessitate a prior sourcing process, for the sake of simplicity this article refers to sourcing process represented only by the sub-activities of managing requests, conducting tenders as well as negotiations along with supplier selection and operational purchasing being restricted to mere ordering.

Ordering Process

With regards to the ordering process three degrees of digitalization can be distinguished applicable to different sorts of demand at the case study company. Manual requisitioning, manual ordering, and e-catalogues represent three ascending degrees in terms of digitalization of information exchange in an operational purchasing process and provided therefore a basis for measurement of changing lean KPI's. Whilst it is targeted at ordering as many goods and services as possible via more automated process types, all three types of processes are still in use at the company in order to cover different demand and approval requirements A request for a specific investment good for instance would still have to follow the manual requisitioning track and c-goods can mostly be acquired via e-catalogues.

Sourcing Process

The degree of digitalization in strategic procurement is represented by the means of information exchange of the activities from call for tender preparation, distribution, Non-Disclosure Agreement (NDA) sending and receipt, to bidding, evaluation, negotiation to award of contract. Previously, important tenders used to be distributed and received only via written means, such as postal mail. Following the introduction of Public Key Infrastructure (PKI) for the decoding of information exchange via the Internet, emails have largely substituted long-winded postal mail. As an even more advanced step towards digitalization, tenders are now managed via an e-sourcing platform, allowing also for individual access control according to each supplier's progress in accepting the NDA and freeing the buyer from administrative tasks such as managing the answering of the technical team to supplier questions, due to information transparency provided by the tool.

As with operational purchasing, afore described stages of digitalization in strategic procurement, restricted to email and e-tendering served as means for examining the changes in KPI results and respective impact on leanness. At the examined company none of the recent CFT's had been distributed via postal mail, therefore restricting the measurement possibility only to the remaining maturity levels of the process.

RESEARCH METHODOLOGY

In order to address the research questions relating to the finding a definition for lean procurement, the determination of lean KPI's, the calculation of tool influence to these measures, as well as the definition of IT's role for leanness for operational and strategic procurement, an appropriate research methodology had to be adopted.

A quantitative approach complemented by supportive, qualitative methods has been deemed particularly suitable for the purpose of this article in order to benefit from the advantages of both quantitative and qualitative research. As a major difference between the two, quantitative research counts on figures, statistics or concrete measurements to derive results whilst qualitative research implies a 'descriptive, non-numerical way to collect and interpret information' (White, 2000, p. 28). It is argued that the scientific nature of

former positivist research approach underlines objectivity and latter qualitative type brings along a more realistic and holistic view for interpretation. A combination of the two methodologies encompasses not only the advantage of more robust and reliable results, but in the event of said case study states also a prerequisite for soundness due to the nature of the respective research questions. More specifically, the research aspects targeting at a definition for lean procurement and the determination of its measurement required a non-numerical approach and focused mainly on descriptive evidence, observation, and supportive interviews to arrive at the findings. The remaining research questions' centering on tool influence measurement, however, explicitly required an application of quantitative means. This has been accounted for by having chosen an experimental approach in measuring KPI's for strategic and operational procurement processes alongside several increasing levels of digitalization. This proceeding states the classical research method in science and aims at investigating whether a change in an independent variable produces an effect in a dependent factor (White, 2000, pp. 55-56).

With the primary research method having been based upon an experiment, comprising the measurement of KPIs in order to undertake regression analyses on the relationship between degree of digitalization and leanness, data collection entailed firstly the determining of a suitable sample. The sample or participants in the frame of this research referred to dedicated operational or strategic procurement process examples, disambiguated according to a unique purchase order number or a sourcing event identification code. The process of determining a suitable sample size and a detailed insight on the chosen sample is provided as part of the next sections. No dedicated account has been given to the data collection methods in the frame of descriptive evidence, observations, and interviews, as those are only supportively drawn on and determined by the role of the researchers to this study, of which one has worked at the case study company with in-depth knowledge on procurement processes.

Sample

For the purpose of determining the data to include in this research, random sampling within distinct groups of the population has been conducted. A population thereby refers to the maximum number of potential participants to the experiment. In the specific case of lean procurement and following a centering around strategic and operational procurement processes at the one of the case study company's divisions, the population was restricted to the sourcing events conducted and Purchase Orders (POs) placed in a period of one week. With regards to the strategic process types, the population was further limited to tenders conducted within a certain commodity per month. This has been done with the aim of avoiding bias emerging through large deviations in tender volumes and resulting differences in processing times. Following the grouping of the raw data per procurement process according to their allocation to either manual requisitioning, non-catalogue facilitated

(manual) ordering, or e-catalogues for operational purchasing and to either e-mail enabled tendering or e-sourcing for strategic procurement, random sampling was applied. This means that every individual event or PO within the population had an equal and independent chance of being selected to the probe (Bui, 2009, pp.142-143) in a method referred to as stratified sampling (White, 2000, p. 65) (see Table 1).

Successive to the determination of population, a statistically significant sample was calculated. Based on an acceptable confidence level of 95%, a confidence interval of 10, referring to the margin of error denoted in percentage points of the result, the sample sizes presented hereunder and calculated with The Survey System (2010) were perceived convincing (see Table 2).

The relationship between overall population per degree of digitalization, subsuming strategic and operational events in one diagram is illustrated in Figure 1.

The discrepancies between appropriate sample and size of population derive from the Gaussian distribution underlying the calculation method for the sample size. Given stratified sampling, the

Table 1. Determination of relevant population size

Process Type	Degree of Digitalization	Population	Restrictions
Operational	E-cat orders	24	limited to one business unit / week
	Manual orders	13	limited to one business unit / week
	Manual requisitioning	5	limited to one business unit / week
Strategic	E-Sourcing	16	limited to one business unit / commodity / month
	E-Mail facilitated	3	limited to one business unit / commodity / month

Table 2. Sample size calculation

Process type	Degree of Digitalization	Population	Confidence Level	Confidence Interval	Calculated Sample Size
Operational	E-cat orders	24	95%	10	19
	Manual orders	13	95%	10	12
	Manual requisitioning	5	95%	10	5
Strategic	E-Sourcing	16	95%	10	14
	E-Mail facilitated	3	95%	10	3

Figure 1. Calculated sample vs. population per degree of digitalization

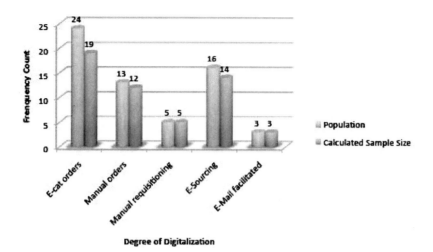

sample to be investigated for this method is by far greater than random sampling across the overall population of events would have suggested (White, 2000, p. 65). In this instance, the overall population across process type and degree of digitalization amounts to 61, potentially resulting in a probe size of 38 opposed to 53 as required with stratified sampling. Nevertheless, the extra effort in investigating roughly 40% more events was perceived indispensable due to high discrepancies in population per event type. Mere random sampling without prior grouping could therefore have led

to the omission of one or the other population group, thereby, disabling comparison in terms of lean performance.

A detailed account of population and sample is provided in appendix 1 and general attributes of the probe are accounted for hereafter.

In terms of spread across commodities as depicted in Table 3 and Figure 2, Facility Management (FM) accounted for the highest portion of orders in operational purchasing by consuming 61% of the sample. Human Resources Services (HR), Information Technologies (IT), as well as

Table 3. Operational procurement sample

Commodity	Sample	Degree of Digitalization	Sample
FM	22	E-Cat	17
		Manual Ordering	3
		Manual requisitioning	2
HR	4	E-Cat	1
		Manual Ordering	2
		Manual requisitioning	1
IT	5	E-Cat	1
		Manual Ordering	2
		Manual requisitioning	2
Invest & Maint	5	Manual Ordering	5

Figure 2. Operational procurement sample: pie chart

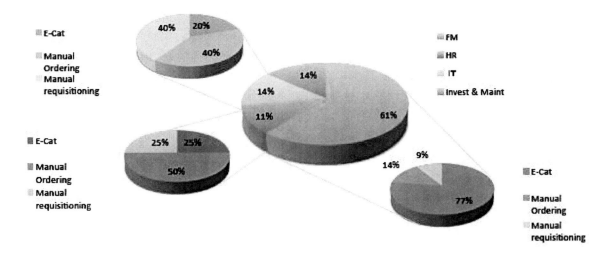

Investment and Maintenance (Invest & Maint) represented each a similar potion of 11% to 14% of the probe.

Interestingly, the majority of orders, namely 77% in the highest represented commodity had been created by e-catalogue orders. It is presumed that this dominance derives mainly from low-volume though high frequency orders such as office consumables. This assumption is underlined by reflecting on the volumes implied with each commodity. Even though representing the greatest stake in terms of overall PO numbers, the ordering volume covered by FM commodity as well as the average PO value is by far the lowest as outlined in absolute figures in Tables 4 and 5 as well as Figure 3.

Further, the commodity of Invest & Maint relied exclusively on manual ordering, potentially explainable through the inability of capital investments to be represented in electronic catalogues at the case study company due to internal process constraints. The total volume covered was thereby the second smallest, though represented through a similar count of PO's as the remaining commodities of IT and HR. Said two latter mentioned applied all three degrees of digitalization

Table 4. Operational procurement sample volume

Commodity	Sample Volume	Degree of Digitalization	Sample Volume
FM	10.190	E-Cat	1.676
		Manual Ordering	8.059
		Manual requisitioning	455
HR	99.626	E-Cat	122
		Manual Ordering	99.386
		Manual requisitioning	119
IT	81.386	E-Cat	11
		Manual Ordering	14.880
		Manual requisitioning	66.495
Invest & Maint	29.435	Manual Ordering	29.435

Table 5. Average PO value per commodity

Commodity	Average PO Value
FM	463
HR	24.907
IT	16.277
Invest & Maint	5.887

with IT mainly following manual ordering and requisitioning processes, and HR benefiting rather from e-catalogues as well as manual ordering and requisitioning in equal portions. Despite e-catalogues covering 25% of allocated PO's, the volume subsumed by these represented less than one percent of the total spend within HR, implying a very low amount of its e-catalogue orders. The ordering volumes handled by IT and HR were once again fairly comparable and the highest amongst the four clusters represented within the sample, with HR providing a slightly higher average PO value than IT. Strikingly, HR as the commodity providing the least number of PO's covered the highest spend in the sample.

In contrary to the plurality of commodities covered within the sample of operational procurement, the sample for strategic sourcing events has purposefully been restricted to the commodity of IT only. Similarly to the prevaillance of the highest form of digitalization (e-catalogue ordering) in operational procurement, the figures related to tendering likewise demonstrated a dominance of e-sourcing over e-mail facilitated requests for proposal by 82% against 18%. This relationship is presented in absolute figures within Table 6 and in percentages in Figure 4.

In terms of sourcing volumes, the e-sourcing events covered almost 98% of the volume, vice versa indicating that e-sourcing was mainly used for large contracts and e-mail facilitated ordering for smaller call for tenders (see Figure 5 and Table 7).

This tendency is also underlined by the average sourcing volume per event type, with e-sourcing covering on average a 10 times higher amount than e-mail RFP's (see Table 8).

By putting the event type per degree of digitalization into relation with respectively average

Figure 3. Operational ordering volume per commodity and degree of digitalization

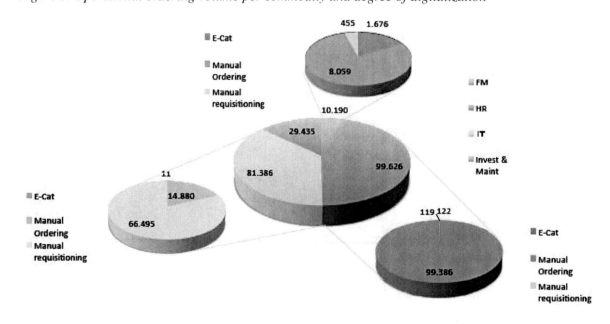

Table 6. Strategic procurement sample

Commodity	Sample	Degree of Digitalization	Sample
		E-Mail facilitated	3
IT	17	E-Sourcing	14

Figure 4. Strategic procurement sample: pie chart

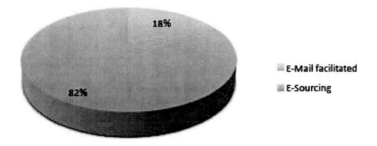

Figure 5. Strategic procurement sample volume

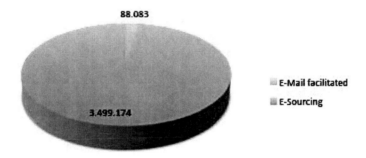

Table 7. Strategic procurement sample volume

Commodity	Sample Volume	Degree of Digitalization	Sample Volume
		E-Mail facilitated	88.083
IT	3.587.257	E-Sourcing	3.499.174

Table 8. Average sourcing volume per degree of digitalization

Degree of Digitalization	Average Sourcing Volume
E-Mail facilitated	29.361
E-Sourcing	249.941

ordering or sourcing volume as presented in Table 10, it can be derived that the events handled via the process entailing highest degree of automation were usually the ones with the greatest number of events in the overall sample. Amongst the sample for strategic procurement, e-sourcing accounted for some 14 events compared to only 3 e-mail tenders. Similarly, 19 e-catalogue orders were incorporated in the sample, compared to 12 manual orders as the next lower level in terms of digitalization, and 5 representing the lowest level of process automation in operational purchasing. It can therefore be argued that the majority of activities is attempted to be covered by a high sophistication of digitalization. The related volume per event thereby develops interestingly into opposite directions. Whilst operative procurement denotes a decreasing average spend with increasing degree of digitalization, the development is vice versa with the strategic process type. Presuming that a high degree of digitalization encompasses a reduction in cycle time, workload, and therefore leaner processes the trend in operational procurement is comprehensible. It can be reasoned that procurement efforts in terms of lengthier, and more complex process are concentrated around a small percentage of non-standard and high volume activities. This presumption, and the surprisingly opposing trend in strategic procurement, had further been investigated on as part of the actual research (see Table 9).

Applicability of Regression Analysis for the Quantitative Approach

In order to pay tribute to the mostly measurement-related questioning of this article, the quantitative approach was combined with data interpretation method of regression analysis. Sykes (2012) describes this as 'a statistical tool for the investigation of relationships between variables' by seeking to establish a causal effect from one variable upon another. Applied to the research problem, the effect of a higher degree of digitalization on the leanness of processes represented the potential causal relationship under investigation. The level of IT involvement and leanness respectively stipulated independent and dependent variable. By establishing a hypothesized relationship between increasing IT usage and rising leanness, the relationship between digitalization and leanness could mathematically be characterized as follows (Sykes, 2012, p. 5):

$$I = \alpha + \beta E + \varepsilon$$

where:

$\alpha =$ a constant amount (achievable leanness without any digitalization in a certain process; constant term of variable E)

$\beta =$ the effect on a lean KPI with incrementally increasing degree of digitalization hypoth-

Table 9. Volumes per level of digitalization contrasted with frequency count in the sample

Process Type	Degree of Digitalization	Total Volume	Sample	Average Volume
	E-Cat	1.809	19	95
	Manual Ordering	151.760	12	12.647
Operational	Manual requisitioning	67.069	5	13.414
	E-Mail facilitated	88.083	3	29.361
Strategic	E-Sourcing	3.499.174	14	249.941

esized to be positive (coefficient of variable E); and

$\varepsilon =$ the "noise" term reflecting other factors that influence leanness.

$I =$ the "dependent" or "endogenous" variable, transferrable to leannness

$E =$ the "independent," "explanatory," or "exogenous" variable; transferrable to degree of digitalization.

Each observable data pair of the sample, determined by I and E is thereby taken into account and determines the calculation of the unobservable factors by a method termed minimum Sum of Squared Errors (SSE). As one of the most important aspect, the research has concentrated on computing R^2, which suggests whether the regression model describes the dependent variable's alternations well or whether the relationship was caused by noise and other variables not under investigation. R^2 is to range between 0 and 1, with a high value implying high suitability of the model in describing the relationship between the variables.

Even though a clear linear relationship between digitalization and leanness was a priori perceived unlikely, Sykes (2012) argues that the method is also applicable to nonlinear correlation. In terms of applying this method to the concrete case study, e-catalogue ordering, as representative for operational procurement, preceded by ERP processing, and formerly even paper-based purchase requisition approval were perceived as three stages of digitalization each having been represented by the afore determined sample size of exemplary activities.

Similarly, the representatives for the strategic procurement side were an e-sourcing process as well as a merely e-mail-enabled distribution of documents. As such, the operational procurement activities were investigated along three and the strategic sourcing process alongside two varying degrees of digitalization, referred to as indepen-dent variable E. Following the determination of the parameters, comprising a pair of distinct measurement of a KPI for a certain process and certain degree of digitalization, each KPI had been depicted in a graph composed of a cohort of parameters and the relationship has been measured by a correlation factor (r) (Watson, 1964). The analysis thereby related to aspects such as the investigation of cycle time of request for proposals or purchase orders, contribution to 'waste' avoidance through measuring communication patterns in counting the number of interfaces for an internal customer, customer orientation, and process cost.

Depending on the intensity of correlation between the extent of tool support and each KPI as well as the number of KPI's influenced positively, a facilitating or enabling value of tools to the leanness of a process was attributed to the related IT system.

Analysis Framework

Despite having analyzed five distinct research questions, all link in to the topic of determining the relationship between buy-side systems in procurement and leanness of its information exchange processes. As such, the analysis of the questions along with its research approach and distinct means will have to be considered as a whole analysis.

Whilst each question has been answered independently, the research methods, findings, and analyses of others likewise led to further angles which were to be incorporated to the response of earlier questions. A sequence in building up the research from question one to five was, though helpful in establishing a clear train of thought, persistently distracted by enrichments from findings to other research questions. For instance, the interpretation of the KPI framework and its limitations provided a means to tracking the leanness of procurement in general and how tool contribution could be determined.

FINDINGS

A Definition for Leanness in Procurement Processes

The first research question under investigation focused on the definition of leanness for office and more specifically for procurement processes. As a starting point for determining a suitable characterization of the concept, the author has concentrated on the implications given by Wincel (2004). Latter author indicates that lean supply chain management and as such also procurement essentially entails its interpretation as profit rather than cost center. Such preliminarily financial consideration automatically entails lean elements of customer orientation and value creation. These key cornerstones of Toyota's philosophy (Womack & Jones, 2003) should be inherited with any strive for profit making, given that the client will only pay for something that is perceived valuable and fulfills conscious or subliminal demand. Procurement's value is thereby typically associated with assuring on time, on quality, and on cost delivery (Wincel, 2004) of goods and services. In addition, other lean aspects of flow of materials and information in a value stream with continuous ambition towards waste reduction support such declared objectives as profit generation. Even further, a reduction of procurement costs by abolishing waste in the intangible and tangible value stream from internal customer to supplier and vice versa at consistent transfer prices influences directly the profit as well as the customer's perception of the service. This double effect is due to the fact that the procurement process itself forms the product delivered to the customer.

Whilst the definition of lean procurement was hence reproducible, the production related 'lean' tools of e.g. poka-yoke, i.e. observable control points in the process (Liker, 2004) or Kanban's to symbolize the pulling of demand by a customer from the latest step in production to the earliest are somewhat out of place for services. However, these visible factors frequently determine whether

a production is considered lean or not, making it difficult for service functions to be reckoned 'lean' at all. Anticipatory to the measurements conducted in the frame of the following research questions, key to the problem of a definition for lean procurement lied in visualizing lean attributes, such as customer orientation, value creation, value stream, flow, and waste reduction rather than its tools as frequently done in the production environment. The results even showed that there might not be such thing as one purely 'lean' state in procurement with the philosophy's principles allowing to be adopted without conducting necessarily a financial transformation to a profit center. The inherited principle of continuous improvement (Womack & Jones, 2003; Liker, 2004) implies an enduring strive for perfection and the possibility to go beyond a profit center organization in becoming leaner and leaner with every increment of improvement. Thereby, opposing developments towards leanness on different KPI's as demonstrated by the increase of cycle time and rising customer orientation in strategic procurement with a higher stage of lean maturity made it hard to determine a level as to when a process can be considered as being truly 'lean'. Certainly, the determining of minimum levels per KPI would not foster a continuous endeavor for perfection. Seeing lean procurement as its transformation towards a profit center rather than a status, provided therefore a good starting point for defining 'leanness' in purchasing, taking additionally into account the underlying concepts of customer orientation, value, value stream, flow, waste reduction as well as continuous improvement through enduring visualization and measurement of lean KPI's. Condensed, the concluded definition reads as follows:

Lean procurement refers to a transformation process of the latter function towards and beyond a profit center by applying, measuring, and continuously improving the lean principles of customer orientation, value creation, value stream management, waste reduction, and pull-triggered flow with regards to the processes administered by purchasing.

Determining KPIs for the Measurement of Leanness in Procurement

Deriving from afore stated definition of lean procurement, the second aspect engaged in determining suitable KPI's for its measurement. As a reminder, the findings of the literature review regarding the aspects to account for when suggesting a measurement framework are the following:

- KPIs are to be developed in line with individual strategic targets (refer to Hines, Silvi and Bartolini, 2002).
- Cost, quality and time dimensions are to be covered (refer to De Toni & Tonchia, 1996).
- A holistic framework is to be provided (refer to Sigh, Garg & Sharma, 2010; Bhasin, 2008) even though admitting for the distinct nature of the study in the area of information technology in procurement.

Given the aspiration of leanness and in accordance with provision one, the objectives to be measured against were to link to the principles of customer orientation, value creation, value stream management, pull-triggered flow, and waste reduction. Value stream management, comprising an analysis and improvement of the value stream and as such streamlining the tasks that add value for the internal customer, can however hardly be measured rather than conducted in the form of an initiative. Latter principle moreover ties in closely with waste reduction and it was therefore refrained from developing a dedicated KPI on this aspect and covering it preferably with measurement of waste reduction. Also, detailed process investigations and related flow charts presented as part of chapter three revealed that all stages of maturity in digitalization and respective operational and strategic procurement processes were initiated by an internal customer's demand and processed with one-piece-flow. As such, the case study under

investigation did not necessitate the development of a KPI for this purpose. This perception is yet dependant on the respective situation under investigation.

Following the two restrictions in terms of value stream management and pull-triggered flow, the objectives to be covered by KPIs related to customer orientation, value creation, and waste reduction along with, of course, profit generation. As the first aspect, customer orientation was surveyed by questioning customers' satisfaction with the information flow related to a specific sourcing event or purchase order on a Likert scale from 1 (not satisfied at all) to 5 (very satisfied). The survey outcomes per event are presented in appendix 2.1. Secondly, value creation was to be translated into a KPI. Based on afore reasoning, the value provided by procurement and delivered to an internal customer relates to on time, on quality, on cost delivery. Given the restriction of this work to information exchange, an obvious measure for this aspect provides cycle time of an operational or strategic sourcing event. In the frame of this case study, the operational cycle time related to the capturing of the demand, its approval, the creation of the purchase order including its validation, as well as the time elapsed from receipt of invoice to its booking. Strategic procurement's cycle time was calculated by the time elapsed for the evaluation of offers and supplier selection depending on the number of RFP rounds. It has neither been accounted for the setting up of an RFP, based on the observation that this investment did not differ with alternating degree of digitalization of the sourcing process, nor for the time given to suppliers for providing a proposal to a CFT, given that this figure was perceived to be greatly influenced by other factors such as complexity of the product or holiday periods. An overview of the measured data on cycle time per event is provided in appendix 2.2. Potentially, typical KPIs measuring the value of procurement with regards to the material flows administered by latter function could e.g. include relation of savings to overall spend or percentage of defects contrasted by delivered pieces. As an answer to the third lean objective, waste reduction was to be captured in the form of a KPI. According to procurement surveys, a major critic from an internal customer point of view entailed the number of interfaces required capturing the demand either in terms of people or with regards to tools. Given that repetitively stating a request in differing formats, either for demand capturing, as an additional input for the purchaser in an oral form, for precisions in a contract or for approving invoices is wasted time, the number of interfaces necessitated per internal customer was established as a KPI. The interface count is hence presented in appendix 2.3. Lastly, profit generation was to be captured as mere cost factor to client business divisions. For this purpose, process cost has been set up, based on the potential assumption that if the service organization was to be organized as profit center, a reduction in process cost would certainly contribute positively. In collaboration with Finance department, a table including standard activities in operational and strategic procurement along with their duration as well as hourly rates per department has been produced. The outcome is presented in Table 10.

Based on this presumption, the cost for each event was calculated as delineated in appendix 2.4, allowing in the case of strategic procurement even for various process KPIs such as cost per

CFT round, invited supplier, or a combination of the two. In contrast to cycle time calculation, which was based on elapsed and as such gross duration, process cost was determined by its net duration.

By measuring the KPI's of customer orientation, cycle time, interface count, and process cost in holistic alignment with the strategic objectives provisions one and three of a suitable KPI framework have been fulfilled. In addition, stated measures likewise covered financial, time-wise, and qualitative dimensions as requested by provision number two. Therefore, the framework was perceived suitable for measuring leanness of information exchange in operative and strategic procurement processes.

Measuring Tool Influence to Lean Procurement

The second aspect requiring numerical recording related to determining the influence of IT systems to lean procurement and thus to afore presented lean KPIs. In the frame of this case study, three maturity levels of digitalization were perceived to be measureable for operational procurement processes comprising e-catalogue ordering as most sophisticated form, manual ordering, and finally manual requisitioning as the type with least IT support. Likewise, strategic procurement

Table 10. Process cost matrix

Activity	Average Time in h	Per	Department	Hourly rate in €
Demand Capturing	0,30		Internal Customers	97,00
Validation	0,10		Finance /Invest Control	78,00
PO Creation	0,50		Procurement	76,00
Sourcing Event Creation	1,00		Legal	81,00
RFP Q&A	1,10	/ supplier or once for e-sourcing	IT	80,00
RFP Analysis 1st round	3,00	/ supplier	IC & Proc	86,50
RFP analysis successive rounds	0,70	/ supplier		
Final Contract	2,00			

distinguished two kind of processes according to their degree of digitalization, with e-sourcing being streamlined on a dedicated tendering portal allowing for the collaboration of internal customer, suppliers, and buyers, and e-mail facilitated RFP's counting more to the traditional way of working. In effect, the distinction between different degrees of digitalization provided two variables. On the one hand, the KPIs delineated beforehand were measured according to each of the sample's PO or sourcing event. On the other, each degree of digitalization was attributed a number of PO's and RFP's thereby allowing for the establishing of a relationship between two variables via linear regression analysis. For this purpose, each PO number and sourcing event were allocated a fictional measure according to the degree of digitalization implied. With the number of measured results per KPI exceeding the available, attributable degree of digitalization categorization, a corridor of closely co-located figures had to be determined. For instance, 17 results for customer orientation on e-catalogue orders were retrieved, since 2 participants out of a total sample of 19 were not available for the survey or not willing to indicate their perception. With e-catalogues stating the highest sophisticated form of digitalization amongst the three investigated operational procurement processes, each result was randomly paired with a the measure for degree of digitalization from a corridor of [3,01; 3,02; 3,03;...3,16; 3,17]. The same was conducted for manual ordering by pairing KPI results with degree of digitalization starting at 2,01 and manual requisitioning commencing at 1,01. In line with this proceeding but paying tribute to only two levels of digitalization for strategic procurement, the values for e-mail facilitated ordering were counted from 1,01 and for e-sourcing from 2,01 in accordance with the number of available KPI results per degree of digitalization. By doing so, a clear pairing of KPI measurement and degree of digitalization was achievable, allowing thus for the application of regression analysis. As a

detailed account of latter method has already been presented as part of afore methodology section, it is refrained from repeating its contribution in further detail. However, the correlation factors of r and R^2 calculated for each correlation indicated the quality of the linear model to describe the relation between the independent and dependent variables of degree of digitalization and each of the four KPI's respectively. The first correlation factor of r was thereby helpful in determining a) the value of the model as well as b) the negatively or positively linear relation between both variables, whilst R^2 additionally projected on the noise and error in the equation. In anticipation to the measurements undertaken hereafter, for each KPI of either customer orientation cycle time, interface count or process cost at least one correlation measurement out of either operational measurements, averaged operational results, or strategic outcomes amounted to a correlation factor $r > |0,75|$. This development is presented as part of Table 11 and implied the suitability of the model. On some measurements, the noise and as such other factors influencing the measurement with $R^2 < 0,5$ was however high and this has therefore been investigated in further detail in the next sections. Overall, the relatively good results of the correlation analysis nevertheless justified that the proceeding on measuring tool influence to the leanness of procurement processes was reasonable and that a clear correlation between leanness and digitalization in procurement exists.

Facilitating or Enabling Role of Tools to Leanness of Operational Procurement

Moreover, this study tries to find the extent that the digitalization contributes to the leanness of processes and according to that, whether information technology can be considered as facilitator or enabler to the leanness of a process. In answering to this, the author has concentrated on operational procurement in the first place.

Table 11. Compilation of correlation factors r and R^2

Correlation	r	R^2
Customer Orientation (Operational)	0,49718365	0,24719158
Averaged Customer Orientation (Operational)	0,99322577	0,9865
Customer Orientation (Strategic)	0,782265939	0,61194
Cycle Time (Operational)	-0,827907	0,68543
Averaged Cycle Time (Operational)	-0,999699955	0,9994
Cycle Time (Strategic)	0,360347055	0,12985
Number of Interfaces for Customer (Operational)	-0,95519108	0,91239
Averaged Number of Interfaces for Customer (Operational)	-0,98866071	0,97745
Number of Interfaces for Customer (Strategic)	-0,930935014	0,86664
Total Process Cost (Operational)	-0,978325099	0,95712
Total Process Cost (Strategic)	-0,236769931	0,05606
Cost per Supplier (Strategic)	0,043127717	0,00186
Cost per Round (Strategic)	-0,769369872	0,59193
Cost per Round and Supplier (Strategic)	-0,32049961	0,10272

At the beginning of the research, the definitions of a facilitating and enabling role are to be recalled as follows: A facilitator, on the one hand, is described as having the capacity to ease up work or workload, thereby, meaning that the solution itself forms an integral part to the operation or product. On the other, an enabler role implies that IT is a necessary prerequisite to performing a certain activity (Chan, 2000), meaning lean procurement in the context of this work.

In transferring this implication to the case study, the fulfilling of four hypotheses related to the influence of digitalization on the KPI framework results was to attribute an enabling role to IT. The hypotheses thereby exemplified a positive correlation to degree of digitalization in influencing leanness and were stated accordingly:

Hypothesis 1: Increasing degree of digitalization and improvement in customer orientation are positively correlated.
Hypothesis 2: Increasing degree of digitalization and decreasing cycle time are positively correlated.
Hypothesis 3: Increasing degree of digitalization and a reduction of interfaces necessitating interference with an internal customer are positively linked.
Hypothesis 4: Increasing degree of digitalization and decrease in internal process cost is positively intertwined.

For each pretension a linear regression model had been created according to afore stated proceeding. Thereby, the calculation as well as graphical illustration of the regression relied mainly on a separate consideration of each KPI result. Nevertheless, high dispersion amongst results gave rise to re-calculating the model with average results per degree of digitalization in order to illustrate a clear linear correlation (see Figure 6).

Hypothesis 1: Increasing degree of digitalization and improvement in customer orientation are positively correlated.

The regression model established for the testing of hypothesis 1 reveals a positive linear correlation between degree of digitalization and customer orientation. However, the correlation factor is rather low due to the dispersion of results. Therefore a retesting with simple average values

Figure 6. Linear regression for customer orientation (operational)

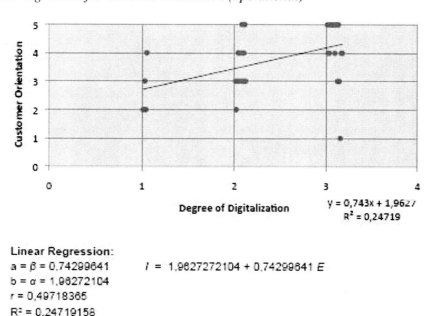

Linear Regression:
a = β = 0,74299641   *I* = 1,9827272104 + 0,74299641 *E*
b = α = 1,98272104
r = 0,49718365
R² = 0,24719158
y = ax+b; *I* = α +β*E*

for KPI results and univocal figures rather than a corridor for degree of digitalization had been conducted in Figure 7.

By doing so, the influence of dispersion was eliminated and high value in terms of correlation factor and accordingly low influence of other factors to the model could be derived. Based on these findings, hypothesis one has been considered to be true.

Hypothesis 2: Increasing degree of digitalization and decreasing cycle time are positively correlated.

For the purpose of testing hypothesis 2 in a regression model, a slight alternation was required. In order to allow for its measurement, the pretension was to be reworded towards a negative correlation between increasing degree of digitalization and cycle time. The measurement thereby revealed a clear negative correlation between independent and dependent variable, despite wide dispersion of results (Figure 8).

Averaging the results according to the same method conducted for the regression on customer orientation revealed an even more striking negative correlation with very little noise (Figure 9). Alike hypothesis 1, pretension 2 was hence considered valid.

Hypothesis 3: Increasing degree of digitalization and a reduction of interfaces necessitating interference with an internal customer are positively linked.

In line with afore statement, the positive connection between increasing degree of digitalization and decreasing number of interfaces for an internal customer was at first to be transferred to its matching negative correlation. The linear regression itself once again revealed a clear negative linear relationship between the two variables, reaching even without averaging a comparatively low rate of noise though high reliability of the model (Figure 10).

Figure 7. Linear regression for averaged customer orientation (operational)

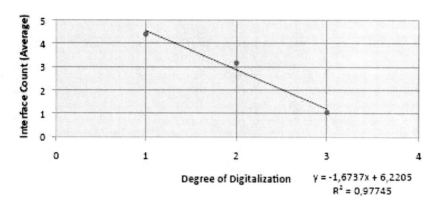

Averaged (Operational)	
Degree of Digitalization	Interface Count
3	1,052631579
2	3,166666667
1	4,4

Linear Regression:

$a = \beta = -1,6737$ $I = 6,2205 - 1,6737\ E$

$b = \alpha = 6,2205$

$r = -0,9886607103$

$R^2 = 0,97745$

$y = ax+b;\ I\ =\ \alpha + \beta E$

With some KPI measurement being nevertheless dispersed, averaging the results led to minor improvement in both correlation factors (Figure 11). Therefore, hypothesis 3 is also correct.

Hypothesis 4: Increasing degree of digitalization and decrease in internal process cost is positively intertwined

For hypothesis 4, the positive formulation was once again to be transferred into its negative correlation. More precisely, the regression model investigated the negative correlation between increasing degree of digitalization and process cost. The measurement resulted in the best linear relation with separate results' consideration and proved that the claim is true (Figure 12).

Given that all four hypotheses were tested to be valid for operational procurement processes, a clear enabling role was to be attributed to IT in determining the leanness of ordering processes.

According to the same test scenario as for operational procurement, the investigation on whether strategic procurement process follow the same logic and IT systems were also to be considered as enablers to leanness was targeted with the last research aspect.

Hypothesis 1: Increasing degree of digitalization and improvement in customer orientation are positively correlated.

As with operational procurement, the results on hypothesis 1 demonstrated a clear positive linear

Figure 8. Linear regression for cycle time (operational)

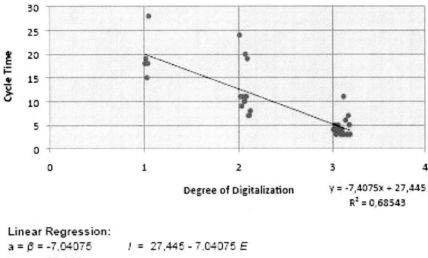

Linear Regression:
a = β = -7,04075 $l = 27,445 - 7,04075\ E$
b = α = 27,445
r = -0,8279089996
R^2 = 0,68543
y = ax+b; $l = α + βE$

Figure 9. Linear regression for averaged cycle time (operational)

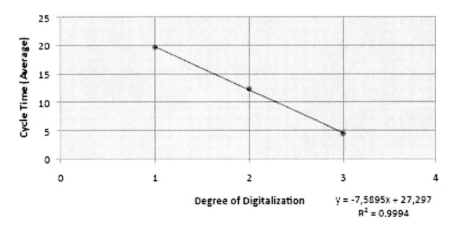

Averaged (Operational)	
Degree of Digitalization	Cycle Time
3	4,421052632
2	12,33333333
1	19,6

Linear Regression:
a = β = -7,5895 $l = 27,297 - 7,5895\ E$
b = α = 27,297
r = -0,999699955
R^2 = 0,9994
y = ax+b; $l = α + βE$

Figure 10. Linear regression for number of interfaces (operational)

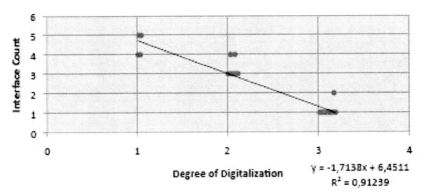

Linear Regression:
a = β = -1,7138   / = 6,4511 - 1,7138 E
b = α = 6,4511
r = -0,9551910804
R² = 0,91239
y = ax+b; / = α +βE

Figure 11. Linear regression for averaged number of interfaces (operational)

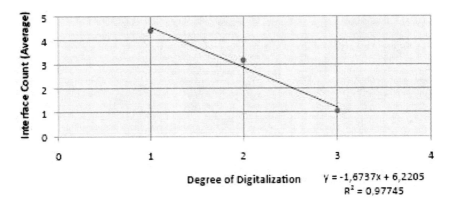

Averaged (Operational)	
Degree of Digitalization	Interface Count
3	1,052631579
2	3,166666667
1	4,4

Linear Regression:
a = β = -1,6737   / = 6,2205 - 1,6737 E
b = α = 6,2205
r = -0,9886607103
R² = 0,97745
y = ax+b; / = α +βE

Figure 12. Linear regression of total process cost (operational)

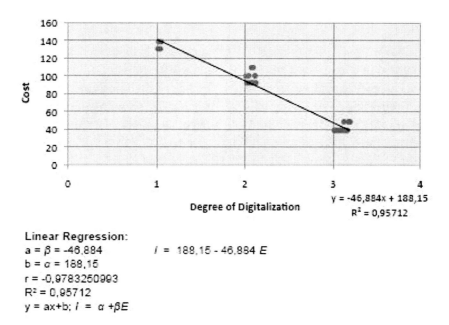

Linear Regression:
a = β = -46,884   / = 188,15 - 46,884 E
b = α = 188,15
r = -0,9783250993
R² = 0,95712
y = ax+b; / = α +βE

correlation. Despite some dispersion of results, noise was not to be diminished by averaging the measurements, given that a correlation between two points would always reveal a 100% linear linkage. In line with operational procurement's finding, hypothesis 1 hence also held true for strategic sourcing (Figure 13).

Figure 13. Linear regression for customer orientation (strategic)

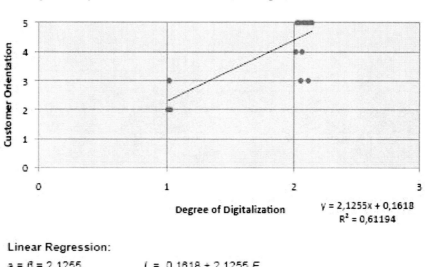

Linear Regression:
a = β = 2,1255   / = 0,1618 + 2,1255 E
b = α = 0,1618
r = 0,7822659394
R² = 0,61194
y = ax+b; / = α +βE

Hypothesis 2: Increasing degree of digitalization and decreasing cycle time are positively correlated.

Unlike the suggestion of hypothesis 2 and the findings for operational procurement, no negative correlation between increasing degree of digitalization and cycle time of CFT's could be measured. By contrary, a slightly positive linkage was found between the two variables implying an increasing evaluation length with increasing degree of digitalization. This finding is however accompanied by a great error rate, indicating the influence of further factors on the correlation. In recalling on the sample analysis performed beforehand, it could be derived that the average RFP volume associated with e-sourcing of ten times the factor of e-mail facilitated tendering could well have had an influence on this development. For the time being and for strategic procurement, hypothesis 3 was therefore to be rejected (Figure 14).

Hypothesis 3: Increasing degree of digitalization and a reduction of interfaces necessitating interference with an internal customer are positively linked.

Unlike hypothesis 2, hypothesis 3 related to a decreasing number of interfaces with increasing degree of digitalization revealed a high correlation factor. As with operational purchasing, this hypothesis is hence also valid for strategic procurement (Figure 15).

Hypothesis 4: Increasing degree of digitalization and decrease in internal process cost is positively intertwined.

With regards to process costs as incorporated in hypothesis 4, several results were tested, given the ability to distinguish between total cost (cf. Figure 16), cost per invited supplier (cf. Figure 17), cost per RFP round (cf. Figure 18), and cost per supplier and RFP round (cf. Figure 19).

Thereby, all measurements implied a similar trend even though the negative linkage between increasing degree of digitalization cost per round provided the strongest linear regression. The re-

Figure 14. Linear regression for cycle time (strategic)

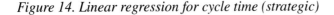

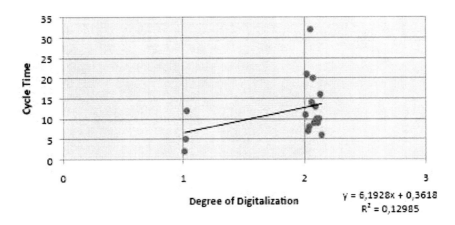

Linear Regression:
$a = \beta = 6,1928$ $l = 0,3618 + 6,1928\ E$
$b = \alpha = 0,3618$
$r = 0,3603470549$
$R^2 = 0,12985$
$y = ax+b;\ l = \alpha + \beta E$

Figure 15. Linear regression for number of interfaces (strategic)

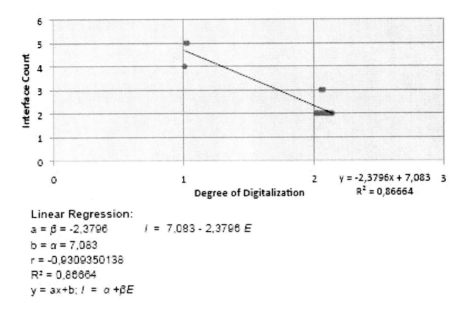

Linear Regression:
a = β = -2,3796   I = 7,083 - 2,3796 E
b = α = 7,083
r = -0,9309350138
R² = 0,86664
y = ax+b; I = α +βE

Figure 16. Linear regression for total process cost (strategic)

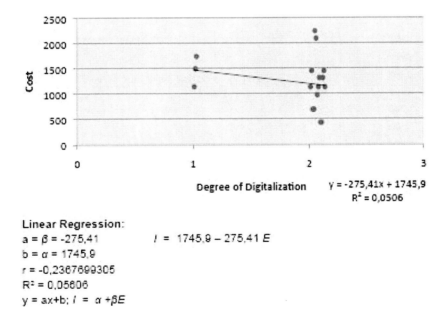

Linear Regression:
a = β = -275,41   I = 1745,9 – 275,41 E
b = α = 1745,9
r = -0,2367699305
R² = 0,05806
y = ax+b; I = α +βE

maining cost factors were mainly influenced by other aspects as indicated by a high level or error or did not correspond with the degree of digitalization at all (refer to cost per supplier). As such, the hypothesis four had to be rejected for strategic procurement and rephrased as follows:

Hypothesis 4.1: Increasing degree of digitalization and decrease in internal process cost per RFP round is positively intertwined.

Latter claim was then cautiously considered as valid.

Figure 17. Linear regression for cost per supplier (strategic)

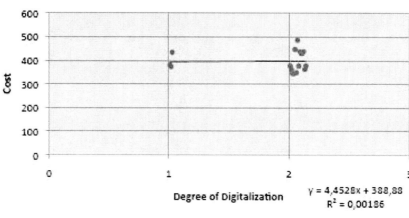

Linear Regression:
a = β = 4,4528   I = 388,88 + 4,4528 E
b = α = 388,88
R = 0,04312771731
R² = 0,00186
y = ax+b; I = α +βE

Figure 18. Linear regression for cost per round (strategic)

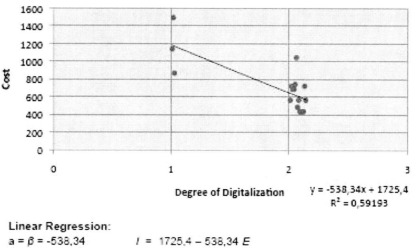

Linear Regression:
a = β = -538,34   I = 1725,4 – 538,34 E
b = α = 1725,4
r = -0,769369872
R² = 0,59193
y = ax+b; I = α +βE

Based on the rejection of Hypothesis 2 as well as the rephrasing and cautious acceptance of Hypothesis 4.1, the role of IT to the leanness of strategic procurement did not seem as strong as for operational purchasing. The results indicated that the systems have more of a facilitating but not enabling influence on leanness.

Figure 19. Linear regression for cost per round and supplier (strategic)

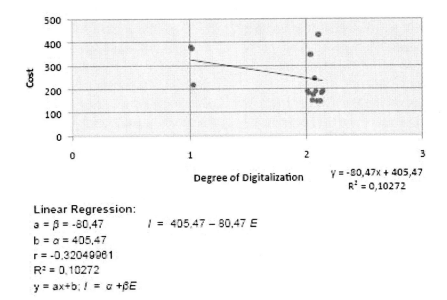

CONCLUSION

As a general summary, this research has concentrated on investigating the correlation between digitalization of information processes in operational and strategic procurement via buy-side systems and its leanness via a typical case study approach. The intension was thereby to derive whether an adoption of IT systems allegorizes a prerequisite for obtaining lean processes. The research was complemented by the actual measurement of assumed correlation alongside a distinct contemplation for operational and strategic procurement processes.

The key findings therefore comprised the following:

- Lean procurement relates to a transformation of the processes hosted by latter function towards profit thinking, thereby applying, measuring, and continuously improving the principles of customer orientation, value creation, value stream management, pull-triggered one-piece flow, and waste reduction. In contrast to the ex-

istence of visible lean tools for production, it is rather the repetitive measurement of KPIs, which allows for determining whether a procurement process can be perceived as having improved in terms of lean performance. As such, a predefined state of what constitutes leanness in procurement is non-existent.

- The measurements revealed that increasing digitalization in operational procurement is a clear enabler to lean processes.

- In strategic procurement, IT systems had less, even though an overall positive, influence on the leanness of processes. Digitalization is therefore considered as facilitator to lean sourcing activities.

As the actual research aspiration, this study aimed at extending the existing body of knowledge on the stake of buy-side IT tools to the leanness of procurement processes. Thereby all of the above stated key findings provide answers to identified gaps in current literature and hence contributed to enlarging common knowledge on the subject. Most remarkably, the study aided in disproving the perception that the lean approach and ERP systems are not reconcilable (Gill, 2007; Mayfield & Toney, 2001) with quantitative evidence, which was so far rejected with only general comments praising the transparency of IT as enabler to lean management (Tinham, 2010).

Even though extending the existing body of knowledge and allowing for practical recommendations, the study still has its limitations. Whilst a typical case study has been chosen, the individual peculiarities per process certainly differ across organizations. As such, in case of reproducing the study particularly with regards to less standardizable, strategic procurement processes, adaptations will be required. Regarding the particular case study, one of the limitations relates moreover to the contradictory measurement of 'cycle time' for strategic procurement, which was perceived to be greatly influenced by the tender volume and related complexity of the RFP evaluation. In order to reassess the true role of IT systems for this perimeter, it would therefore be helpful to measure with a set of data with low variations in tendering volume.

As another limitation, the regression analysis has only been conducted with three or respectively two maturity stages. Watson (1964), however, argues that the more data sets are available, the higher the reliability of the found correlation. Lastly, the KPI measurements concentrated exclusively on improvements in terms of leanness without accounting for the capital expenditure and related need for Return On Investment (ROI) implied with the incorporation of more sophisticated IT tools. It has been refrained from including this aspect for the research as the solutions are already in use at the company, thereby implying a positive expected ROI for the company. Companies considering a new implementation of these systems are however clearly recommended to account for investment costs.

In line with the limitations of the study, areas for further research can be formulated. This implies on the one hand the repetition of the study with a sample comprising similar tendering volumes for e-mail facilitated sourcing and e-sourcing to avoid 'noise' in the regression mainly decisive on the KPI for cycle time. On the other hand, freeing up the measurements from differing volumes associated with the sample for operational procurement could additionally provide a clear account as to whether the positive influence of increasing digitalization to leanness despite high R^2 values is amplified by decreasing ordering volumes. As another aspect to include for further research, it is suggested to extend the framework by further KPI's for making it more robust and enabling for benchmarking with other indirect procurement organizations. A longer-term aspiration moreover relates to broadening the data set for degree of digitalization, presupposing however the implementation of new process technology in this particular area.

ACKNOWLEDGMENT

This article would not have been accomplished without the support and guidance of Dr. Dimitris K. Folinas. Dimitris, your supervision during the past months and particularly in stressful times was extraordinary and went clearly beyond expectations, for that I would like to express my sincere gratitude.

REFERENCES

Abdi, F., Shavarini, S. K., & Hoseini, S. M. S. (2006). Glean lean: How to use lean approach in service industries? *Journal of Service Research*, 6, 191–206. Retrieved from http://web.ebscohost.com.ezproxy.liv.ac.uk/ehost/pdfviewer/pdfviewer?hid=18&sid=855e0e21-c986-4197-95a2-32f406d7d4a7%40sessionmgr11&vid=2

Arlbjørn, J. S., Freytag, P. V., & de Haas, H. (2011). Service supply chain management: A survey of lean application in the municipal sector. *International Journal of Physical Distribution & Logistics Management, 4*(3), 277–295. Retrieved from http://www.emeraldinsight.com.ezproxy. liv.ac.uk/journals.htm?issn=0960-0035&volume=41&issue=3&articleid=1917332&show=pdf doi:10.1108/09600031111123796

Bhasin, S. (2008). Lean and performance measurement. *Journal of Manufacturing Technology Management, 19*(5), 670–684. Retrieved from http://www.emeraldinsight.com.ezproxy.liv. ac.uk/journals.htm?issn=1741-038X&volume=19&issue=5&articleid=1728408&show=pdf doi:10.1108/17410380810877311

Bhasin, S., & Burcher, P. (2006). Lean viewed as a philosophy. *Journal of Manufacturing Technology Management, 17*(1), 56–72. Retrieved from http://www.emeraldinsight.com.ezproxy. liv.ac.uk/journals.htm?issn=1741-038X&volume=17&issue=1&articleid=1532807&show=pdf doi:10.1108/17410380610639506

Bowen, D. E., & Youngdahl, W. E. (1998). Lean service: In defense of a production-line approach. *International Journal of Service Industry Management, 9*(3), 207–225. Retrieved from http://www.emeraldinsight.com. ezproxy.liv.ac.uk/Insight/viewPDF.jsp?contentType=Article&Filename=html/Output/Published/EmeraldFullTextArticle/Pdf/0850090301.pdf doi:10.1108/09564239810223510

Bradford, M., Mayfield, T., & Toney, C. (2001). Does ERP fit in a lean world? *Strategic Finance, 82*(11), 28-34. Retrieved from http://ehis.ebscohost.com.ezproxy.liv.ac.uk/eds/pdfviewer/pdfviewer?vid=10&hid=6&sid=6cb9fd95-fa0b-417e-9ac6-0034b265e2c9%40sessionmgr11

Bui, Y. N. (2009). *How to write a master thesis.* London, UK: Sage Publications Ltd.

Cagliano, R., Caniato, F., & Spina, G. (2004). Lean, agile and traditional supply: How do they impact manufacturing performance? *Journal of Purchasing and Supply Management, 10*(4-5), 151–164. Retrieved from http://www.sciencedirect.com.ezproxy.liv.ac.uk/science?_ob=MImg&_imagekey=B7579-4FBHW7M-1-1&_cdi=12893&_user=822084&_pii=S147840920500004X&_origin=search&_zone=rslt_list_item&_coverDate=07%2F01%2F2004&_sk=999899995&wchp=dGLzVzb-zSkWB&md5=52954d872906932ed6c3352fbcc7b261&ie=/sdarticle.pdf doi:10.1016/j.pursup.2004.11.001

Chan, S. L. (2000). Information technology in business processes. *Business Process Management Journal, 6*(3), 224–237. Retrieved from http://www.emeraldinsight.com.ezproxy.liv. ac.uk/journals.htm?issn=1463-7154&volume=6&issue=3&articleid=843451&show=pdf&PHPSESSID=3df7d1voc136p4s47cfvd73ig3 doi:10.1108/14637150010325444

De Toni, A., & Tonchia, S. (1996). Lean organization, management by process and performance measurement. *International Journal of Operations & Production Management, 16*(2), 221–236. Retrieved from http://www.emeraldinsight. com.ezproxy.liv.ac.uk/journals.htm?issn=0144-3577&volume=16&issue=2&articleid=848951&show=pdf&PHPSESSID=p4b9p490euietmkqiqgvdt5l44 doi:10.1108/01443579610109947

Gill, R. (2007). Lean manufacturing and ERP systems: Different by design. *Ceramic Industry, 157*(8), 19-20. Retrieved from http://web.ebscohost.com.ezproxy.liv.ac.uk/ehost/pdfviewer/pdfviewer?vid=2&hid=5&sid=95dd27a9-43b5-4713-b92c-d09eacf666f3%40sessionmgr13

Hines, P., Silvi, R., & Bartolini, M. (2002). *Lean profit potential*. Cardiff, UK: Lean Enterprise Research Centre. Retrieved from http://www.constructingexcellence.biz/pdf/document/Lean-profit.pdf

Lamming, R. (1996). Squaring lean supply with supply chain management. *International Journal of Operations & Production Management, 16*(2), 183–196. Retrieved from http://www.emeraldinsight.com.ezproxy.liv.ac.uk/journals.htm?issn=0144-3577&volume=16&issue=2&articleid=848948&show=pdf doi:10.1108/01443579610109910

Liker, J. K. (2004). *The Toyota way: 14 management principles from the world's greatest manufacturer*. New York, NY: McGraw- Hill.

Monczka, R. M., Handfield, R. B., Giunipero, L. C., & Pattercon, J. L. (2009). *Purchasing & supply chain management* (4th ed.). Mason, GA: South-West Cengage Learning.

Presutti, W. D. (2003). Supply management and e-procurement: Creating value added in the supply chain. *Industrial Marketing Management, 32*, 219–226. Retrieved from http://www.sciencedirect.com.ezproxy.liv.ac.uk/science?_ob=MImg&_imagekey=B6V69-46NX5XJ-5-6&_cdi=5809&_user=822084&_pii=S0019850102002651&_origin=&_coverDate=04%2F30%2F2003&_sk=999679996&view=c&wchp=dGLbVlW-zSkWl&md5=31b671e27f110bb99a241c7a7e1aa9db&ie=/sdarticle.pdf doi:10.1016/S0019-8501(02)00265-1

Puschmann, T., & Alt, R. (2005). Successful use of e-procurement in supply chains. *Supply Chain Management: An International Journal, 10*(2), 122 – 133. Retrieved from http://www.emeraldinsight.com.ezproxy.liv.ac.uk/journals.htm?issn=1359-8546&volume=10&issue=2&articleid=1464663&show=pdf

Seddon, J., & O'Donavan, B. (2010). Rethinking lean service. *Management Services, 54*(1), 34-37. Retrieved from http://web.ebscohost.com.ezproxy.liv.ac.uk/ehost/pdfviewer/pdfviewer?hid=18&sid=4d80a25b-7da8-47cf-89f7-bcf273aba0d5%40sessionmgr12&vid=3

Setijono, D., & Dahlgaard, J. J. (2007). Customer value as a key performance indicator (KPI) and a key improvement indicator (KII). *Measuring Business Excellence, 11*(2), 44-61. Retrieved from http://www.emeraldinsight.com.ezproxy.liv.ac.uk/journals.htm?issn=1368-3047&volume=11&issue=2&articleid=1610500&show=pdf

Singh, B., Garg, S. K., & Sharma, S. K. (2010). Development of index for measuring leanness: Study of an Indian auto component industry. *Measuring Business Excellence, 14*(2), 46-53. Retrieved from http://www.emeraldinsight.com.ezproxy.liv.ac.uk/journals.htm?issn=1368-3047&volume=14&issue=2&articleid=1863916&show=pdf

Smart, A. (2010). Exploring the business case for e-procurement. *International Journal of Physical Distribution & Logistics Management, 40*(3), 181–201. Retrieved from http://www.emeraldinsight.com.ezproxy.liv.ac.uk/journals.htm?issn=0960-0035&volume=40&issue=3&articleid=1852848&show=pdf doi:10.1108/09600031011035083

Survey System. (2010). *Sample size calculator*. Retrieved from http://www.surveysystem.com/sscalc.htm

Sykes, A. O. (2012). *An introduction to regression analysis*. Retrieved from http://www.law.uchicago.edu/files/files/20.Sykes_.Regression.pdf

Tinham, B. (2010). Driving up efficiency: Lean processes and IT. *Works Management, 63*(4), 34-37. Retrieved from http://ehis.ebscohost.com.ezproxy.liv.ac.uk/eds/pdfviewer/pdfviewer?vid=9&hid=6&sid=6cb9fd95-fa0b-417e-9ac6-0034b265e2c9%40sessionmgr11

Watson, G. S. (1964). Smooth regression analysis. *Sankhyā: The Indian Journal of Statistics, Series A, 26*(4), 359-372. Retrieved from http://www.jstor.org.ezproxy.liv.ac.uk/stable/pdfplus/25049340.pdf?acceptTC=true

White, B. (2000). *Dissertation skills for business and management students.* Andover, MI: Cengage Learning.

Wilson, M. M. J., & Roy, R. M. (2009). Enabling lean procurement: A consolidation model for small- and medium-sized enterprises. *Journal of Manufacturing Technology Management, 20*(6), 817–833. Retrieved from http://www.emeraldinsight.com.ezproxy.liv.ac.uk/journals.htm?issn=1741-038X&volume=20&issue=6&articleid=1801230&show=pdf doi:10.1108/17410380910975096

Wincel, J. P. (2004). *Lean supply chain management: A handbook for strategic procurement.* New York, NY: Productivity Press.

Womack, J. P. (2007). Moving beyond the tool age (lean management). *IET Manufacturing Engineer, 86*(4), 4-5. Retrieved from http://web.ebscohost.com.ezproxy.liv.ac.uk/ehost/pdfviewer/pdfviewer?hid=18&sid=ab420297-1492-4a61-953f-1df158c7a222%40sessionmgr11&vid=2

Womack, J. P., & Jones, D. T. (2003). *Lean thinking.* New York, NY: Free Press.

World Resources Institute. (2007). *GDP: Percent GDP from services 2006 for Europe.* Retrieved from http://earthtrends.wri.org/searchable_db/index.php?step=countries&ccID%5B%5D=2&theme=5&variable_ID=216&action=select_years

ADDITIONAL READING

Charlton, C. (2008, April). Reducing waste with ERP software. *Manufacturers' Monthly*, 22. Retrieved from http://ehis.ebscohost.com.ezproxy.liv.ac.uk/eds/pdfviewer/pdfviewer?vid=4&hid=122&sid=f358f9ad-f6e5-40a5-98d2-50f9b1e15fc4%40sessionmgr113

Eisenhardt, K. M. (1989). Building theories from case study research. *Academy of Management Review, 14*(4), 532–550. Retrieved from http://www.jstor.org.ezproxy.liv.ac.uk/stable/pdfplus/258557.pdf?acceptTC=true

Hanna, J. (2007). *Bringing "lean" principles to service industry.* Retrieved from http://hbswk.hbs.edu/item/5741.html

Kleinbaum, D. G., Kupper, L. L., Nizam, A., & Muller, K. E. (2008). *Applied regression analysis and other multivariable methods* (4th ed.). Belmont, CA: Thomson Higher Education.

Laudon, K. C., & Traver, C. G. (2009). *E-commerce: Business, technology, society* (5th ed.). Upper Saddle River, NJ: Pearson Prentice Hall.

Neef, D. (2001). *E-procurement: From strategy to implementation.* Upper Saddle River, NJ: Prentice Hall.

Spear, S., & Bowen, H. K. (1999). Decoding the DNA of the Toyota production system. *Harvard Business Review, 77*(5), 96–106. Retrieved from http://web.ebscohost.com.ezproxy.liv.ac.uk/ehost/pdf?vid=2&hid=5&sid=09fcf8ef-43c5-463d-85fc-57bc75021b51%40sessionmgr4

APPENDIX 1: DATA POPULATION AND SAMPLE

Table 12.

Process Type	Degree of Digitalization	Population Event Number	Selected for Sample	Volume in €	Commodity
Operational	E-Cat	8110057196	x	402,72	FM
Operational	E-Cat	8110057197	x	7,43	FM
Operational	E-Cat	8110057251	x	29,55	FM
Operational	E-Cat	8110057290	x	323,82	FM
Operational	E-Cat	8110057308	x	29,22	FM
Operational	E-Cat	8110057396	x	159,18	FM
Operational	E-Cat	8110057400	x	36,72	FM
Operational	E-Cat	8110057415	x	38,83	FM
Operational	E-Cat	8110057429	x	127,80	FM
Operational	E-Cat	8110057444	x	82,05	FM
Operational	E-Cat	8110057478	x	25,47	FM
Operational	E-Cat	8110057528	x	271,76	FM
Operational	E-Cat	8110057532	x	2,50	FM
Operational	E-Cat	8110057534	x	10,22	FM
Operational	E-Cat	8110057583	x	18,50	FM
Operational	E-Cat	8110057585	x	26,31	FM
Operational	E-Cat	8110057591	x	84,13	FM
Operational	E-Cat	8110057652	x	121,61	HR
Operational	E-Cat	8110057653	x	11,31	IT
Operational	E-Cat	8110057654	-	74,12	HR
Operational	E-Cat	8110057668	-	100,56	FM
Operational	E-Cat	8110057687	-	361,18	FM
Operational	E-Cat	8110057701	-	119,91	FM
Operational	E-Cat	8110057818	-	13,05	FM
Operational	Manual Ordering	8110036091	x	10.000,00	Invest & Maint
Operational	Manual Ordering	8110044573	x	1.319,31	Invest & Maint
Operational	Manual Ordering	8110045653	x	363,25	Invest & Maint
Operational	Manual Ordering	8110046925	x	8.000,00	IT
Operational	Manual Ordering	8110047948	x	7.761,60	FM
Operational	Manual Ordering	8110053843	x	461,00	Invest & Maint
Operational	Manual Ordering	8110056247	x	96.000,00	HR
Operational	Manual Ordering	8110056596	x	120,74	FM
Operational	Manual Ordering	8110057163	x	17.291,75	Invest & Maint
Operational	Manual Ordering	8110057217	x	177,02	FM

continued on following page

Table 12. Continued

Process Type	Degree of Digitalization	Population Event Number	Selected for Sample	Volume in €	Commodity
Operational	Manual Ordering	8110057228	x	6.879,58	IT
Operational	Manual Ordering	8110057319	x	3.385,70	HR
Operational	Manual Ordering	8110057412	-	124,96	FM
Operational	Manual Requisitioning	4670045667	x	119,00	HR
Operational	Manual Requisitioning	4670045677	x	1.695,00	IT
Operational	Manual Requisitioning	4670045712	x	177,02	FM
Operational	Manual Requisitioning	4670045629	x	277,55	FM
Operational	Manual Requisitioning	4670045645	x	64.800,00	IT
Strategic	E-Sourcing	SP10742059	x	299.458,00	IT
Strategic	E-Sourcing	SP12727876	x	368.422,00	IT
Strategic	E-Sourcing	SP15151147	x	23.808,00	IT
Strategic	E-Sourcing	SP15359848	x	23.900,00	IT
Strategic	E-Sourcing	SP10635983	x	871.000,00	IT
Strategic	E-Sourcing	SP15380320	x	235.700,00	IT
Strategic	E-Sourcing	SP15582623	x	499.846,00	IT
Strategic	E-Sourcing	SP15734174	x	139.120,00	IT
Strategic	E-Sourcing	SP18347824	x	440.930,00	IT
Strategic	E-Sourcing	SP20931209	x	178.230,00	IT
Strategic	E-Sourcing	SP23241808	x	76.500,00	IT
Strategic	E-Sourcing	SP22757521	x	124.000,00	IT
Strategic	E-Sourcing	SP17743458	x	192.140,00	IT
Strategic	E-Sourcing	SP18208524	x	26.120,00	IT
Strategic	E-Sourcing	SP18670839	-	14.400,00	IT
Strategic	E-Sourcing	SP18604831	-	20.250,00	IT
Strategic	E-Mail facilitated	IM.RFP.10.00023	x	7.217,00	IT
Strategic	E-Mail facilitated	IMA.RFP.F.10.0136	x	19.866,00	IT
Strategic	E-Mail facilitated	IMA.RFP.F.10.0059	x	61.000,00	IT

APPENDIX 2: KPI MEASUREMENT

Table 13. Customer orientation

Process Type	Degree of Digitalization	Sample Event Number	Volume in €	Commodity	Customer Orientation (Results of Survey from 1-5)
Operational	E-Cat	8110057196	402,72	FM	5
Operational	E-Cat	8110057197	7,43	FM	4
Operational	E-Cat	8110057251	29,55	FM	4
Operational	E-Cat	8110057290	323,82	FM	5
Operational	E-Cat	8110057308	29,22	FM	5
Operational	E-Cat	8110057396	159,18	FM	5
Operational	E-Cat	8110057400	36,72	FM	5
Operational	E-Cat	8110057415	38,83	FM	5
Operational	E-Cat	8110057429	127,80	FM	4
Operational	E-Cat	8110057444	82,05	FM	5
Operational	E-Cat	8110057478	25,47	FM	5
Operational	E-Cat	8110057528	271,76	FM	3
Operational	E-Cat	8110057532	2,50	FM	N/A
Operational	E-Cat	8110057534	10,22	FM	5
Operational	E-Cat	8110057583	18,50	FM	3
Operational	E-Cat	8110057585	26,31	FM	N/A
Operational	E-Cat	8110057591	84,13	FM	1
Operational	E-Cat	8110057652	121,61	HR	4
Operational	E-Cat	8110057653	11,31	IT	4
Operational	Manual Ordering	8110036091	10.000,00	Invest & Maint	3
Operational	Manual Ordering	8110044573	1.319,31	Invest & Maint	2
Operational	Manual Ordering	8110045653	363,25	Invest & Maint	3
Operational	Manual Ordering	8110046925	8.000,00	IT	4
Operational	Manual Ordering	8110047948	7.761,60	FM	4
Operational	Manual Ordering	8110053843	461,00	Invest & Maint	3
Operational	Manual Ordering	8110056247	96.000,00	HR	4
Operational	Manual Ordering	8110056596	120,74	FM	5
Operational	Manual Ordering	8110057163	17.291,75	Invest & Maint	3
Operational	Manual Ordering	8110057217	177,02	FM	4
Operational	Manual Ordering	8110057228	6.879,58	IT	5
Operational	Manual Ordering	8110057319	3.385,70	HR	3

continued on following page

Table 13. Continued

Process Type	Degree of Digitalization	Sample Event Number	Volume in €	Commodity	Customer Orientation (Results of Survey from 1-5)
Operational	Manual requisitioning	4670045667	119,00	HR	2
Operational	Manual requisitioning	4670045677	1.695,00	IT	2
Operational	Manual requisitioning	4670045712	177,02	FM	3
Operational	Manual requisitioning	4670045629	277,55	FM	2
Operational	Manual requisitioning	4670045645	64.800,00	IT	4
Strategic	E-Sourcing	SP10742059	299.458,00	IT	4
Strategic	E-Sourcing	SP12727876	368.422,00	IT	5
Strategic	E-Sourcing	SP15151147	23.808,00	IT	5
Strategic	E-Sourcing	SP15359848	23.900,00	IT	5
Strategic	E-Sourcing	SP10635983	871.000,00	IT	3
Strategic	E-Sourcing	SP15380320	235.700,00	IT	4
Strategic	E-Sourcing	SP15582623	499.846,00	IT	5
Strategic	E-Sourcing	SP15734174	139.120,00	IT	5
Strategic	E-Sourcing	SP18347824	440.930,00	IT	5
Strategic	E-Sourcing	SP20931209	178.230,00	IT	5
Strategic	E-Sourcing	SP23241808	76.500,00	IT	3
Strategic	E-Sourcing	SP22757521	124.000,00	IT	5
Strategic	E-Sourcing	SP17743458	192.140,00	IT	5
Strategic	E-Sourcing	SP18208524	26.120,00	IT	5
Strategic	E-Mail facilitated	IM.RFP.10.00023	7.217,00	IT	2
Strategic	E-Mail facilitated	IMA.RFP.F.10.0136	19.866,00	IT	3
Strategic	E-Mail facilitated	IMA.RFP.F.10.0059	61.000,00	IT	2

Table 14. Cycle time

Process Type	Degree of Digitalization	Sample Event Number	Volume in €	Commodity	Cycle Time			
					Total	Creation up to Approval of SC	PO Creation	Invoice Receipt to Booking
Operational	E-Cat	8110057196	402,72	FM	*4*	1		3
Operational	E-Cat	8110057197	7,43	FM	*4*	1		3
Operational	E-Cat	8110057251	29,55	FM	*5*	1		4
Operational	E-Cat	8110057290	323,82	FM	*3*	1		2
Operational	E-Cat	8110057308	29,22	FM	*4*	1		3
Operational	E-Cat	8110057396	159,18	FM	*5*	1		4
Operational	E-Cat	8110057400	36,72	FM	*4*	1		3
Operational	E-Cat	8110057415	38,83	FM	*4*	1		3
Operational	E-Cat	8110057429	127,80	FM	*3*	1		2
Operational	E-Cat	8110057444	82,05	FM	*4*	1		3
Operational	E-Cat	8110057478	25,47	FM	*3*	1		2
Operational	E-Cat	8110057528	271,76	FM	*11*	3		8
Operational	E-Cat	8110057532	2,50	FM	*3*	1		2
Operational	E-Cat	8110057534	10,22	FM	*6*	1		5
Operational	E-Cat	8110057583	18,50	FM	*3*	1		2
Operational	E-Cat	8110057585	26,31	FM	*3*	1		2
Operational	E-Cat	8110057591	84,13	FM	*7*	1		6
Operational	E-Cat	8110057652	121,61	HR	*5*	2		3
Operational	E-Cat	8110057653	11,31	IT	*3*	1		2
Operational	Manual Ordering	8110036091	10.000,00	Invest & Maint	*24*	2	15	7
Operational	Manual Ordering	8110044573	1.319,31	Invest & Maint	*11*	2	5	4
Operational	Manual Ordering	8110045653	363,25	Invest & Maint	*9*	1	4	4
Operational	Manual Ordering	8110046925	8.000,00	IT	*11*	4	3	4
Operational	Manual Ordering	8110047948	7.761,60	FM	*11*	4	3	4
Operational	Manual Ordering	8110053843	461,00	Invest & Maint	*10*	2	5	3
Operational	Manual Ordering	8110056247	96.000,00	HR	*20*	8	6	6
Operational	Manual Ordering	8110057163	17.291,75	Invest & Maint	*19*	6	5	8
Operational	Manual Ordering	8110057217	177,02	FM	*7*	2	1	4
Operational	Manual Ordering	8110057228	6.879,58	IT	*7*	3	2	2
Operational	Manual Ordering	8110057319	3.385,70	HR	*8*	3	2	3

continued on following page

Table 14. Continued

Process Type	Degree of Digitalization	Sample Event Number	Volume in €	Commodity	Cycle Time			
					Total	Creation up to Approval of SC	PO Creation	Invoice Receipt to Booking
Operational	Manual requisitioning	4670045667	119,00	HR	*18*	10	4	4
Operational	Manual requisitioning	4670045677	1.695,00	IT	*19*	11	4	4
Operational	Manual requisitioning	4670045712	177,02	FM	*15*	7	5	3
Operational	Manual requisitioning	4670045629	277,55	FM	*18*	10	5	3
Operational	Manual requisitioning	4670045645	64.800,00	IT	*28*	15	11	2
						Evaluation & Nego 1st round	Evaluation & Nego 2nd round	Evaluation & Nego 3rd round
Strategic	E-Sourcing	SP10742059	299.458,00	IT	*11*	8	3	
Strategic	E-Sourcing	SP12727876	368.422,00	IT	*21*	10	11	
Strategic	E-Sourcing	SP15151147	23.808,00	IT	*7*	7		
Strategic	E-Sourcing	SP15359848	23.900,00	IT	*8*	8		
Strategic	E-Sourcing	SP10635983	871.000,00	IT	*32*	14	12	1+5=6
Strategic	E-Sourcing	SP15380320	235.700,00	IT	*14*	12	2	
Strategic	E-Sourcing	SP15582623	499.846,00	IT	*20*	13	5+2=7	
Strategic	E-Sourcing	SP15734174	139.120,00	IT	*9*	8	1	
Strategic	E-Sourcing	SP18347824	440.930,00	IT	*13*	9	3	1
Strategic	E-Sourcing	SP20931209	178.230,00	IT	*10*	10		
Strategic	E-Sourcing	SP23241808	76.500,00	IT	*9*	9		
Strategic	E-Sourcing	SP22757521	124.000,00	IT	*10*	5	4	1
Strategic	E-Sourcing	SP17743458	192.140,00	IT	*16*	10	6	
Strategic	E-Sourcing	SP18208524	26.120,00	IT	*6*	5	1	
Strategic	E-Mail facilitated	IM.RFP.10.00023	7.217,00	IT	*2*	2		
Strategic	E-Mail facilitated	IMA. RFP.F.10.0136	19.866,00	IT	*5*	5		
Strategic	E-Mail facilitated	IMA. RFP.F.10.0059	61.000,00	IT	*12*	6	6	

Table 15. Interface count

Process Type	Degree of Digitalization	Sample Event Number	Volume in €	Commodity	Interface Count	
					Count	Explanation
Operational	E-Cat	8110057196	402,72	FM	1	Buy-side system
Operational	E-Cat	8110057197	7,43	FM	1	Buy-side system
Operational	E-Cat	8110057251	29,55	FM	1	Buy-side system
Operational	E-Cat	8110057290	323,82	FM	1	Buy-side system
Operational	E-Cat	8110057308	29,22	FM	1	Buy-side system
Operational	E-Cat	8110057396	159,18	FM	1	Buy-side system
Operational	E-Cat	8110057400	36,72	FM	1	Buy-side system
Operational	E-Cat	8110057415	38,83	FM	1	Buy-side system
Operational	E-Cat	8110057429	127,80	FM	1	Buy-side system
Operational	E-Cat	8110057444	82,05	FM	1	Buy-side system
Operational	E-Cat	8110057478	25,47	FM	1	Buy-side system
Operational	E-Cat	8110057528	271,76	FM	1	Buy-side system
Operational	E-Cat	8110057532	2,50	FM	1	Buy-side system
Operational	E-Cat	8110057534	10,22	FM	1	Buy-side system
Operational	E-Cat	8110057583	18,50	FM	1	Buy-side system
Operational	E-Cat	8110057585	26,31	FM	1	Buy-side system
Operational	E-Cat	8110057591	84,13	FM	2	Buy-side system / Accounting
Operational	E-Cat	8110057652	121,61	HR	1	Buy-side system
Operational	E-Cat	8110057653	11,31	IT	1	Buy-side system
Operational	Manual Ordering	8110036091	10.000,00	Invest & Maint	3	Buy-side system / Purchaser / Accounting
Operational	Manual Ordering	8110044573	1.319,31	Invest & Maint	3	Buy-side system / Purchaser / Accounting
Operational	Manual Ordering	8110045653	363,25	Invest & Maint	3	Buy-side system / Purchaser / Accounting
Operational	Manual Ordering	8110046925	8.000,00	IT	4	Buy-side system / Purchaser/ Accounting (2 separate invoices)
Operational	Manual Ordering	8110047948	7.761,60	FM	3	Buy-side system / Purchaser / Accounting
Operational	Manual Ordering	8110053843	461,00	Invest & Maint	3	Buy-side system / Purchaser / Accounting
Operational	Manual Ordering	8110056247	96.000,00	HR	3	Buy-side system / Purchaser / Accounting
Operational	Manual Ordering	8110056596	120,74	FM	3	Buy-side system / Purchaser / Accounting
Operational	Manual Ordering	8110057163	17.291,75	Invest & Maint	4	Buy-side system / Purchaser/ Accounting (2 separate invoices)
Operational	Manual Ordering	8110057217	177,02	FM	3	Buy-side system / Purchaser / Accounting

continued on following page

Table 15. Continued

Process Type	Degree of Digitalization	Sample Event Number	Volume in €	Commodity	Interface Count	
					Count	Explanation
Operational	Manual Ordering	8110057228	6.879,58	IT	3	Buy-side system / Purchaser / Accounting
Operational	Manual Ordering	8110057319	3.385,70	HR	3	Buy-side system / Purchaser / Accounting
Operational	Manual requisitioning	4670045667	119,00	HR	4	Request Capturing (Word) / Accounting / Invest Control / Purchaser
Operational	Manual requisitioning	4670045677	1.695,00	IT	5	Request Capturing (Word) / Accounting / Invest Control / IT / Purchaser
Operational	Manual requisitioning	4670045712	177,02	FM	4	Request Capturing (Word) / Accounting / Invest Control / Purchaser
Operational	Manual requisitioning	4670045629	277,55	FM	4	Request Capturing (Word) / Accounting / Invest Control / Purchaser
Operational	Manual requisitioning	4670045645	64.800,00	IT	5	Request Capturing (Word) / Accounting / Invest Control / IT / Purchaser
Strategic	E-Sourcing	SP10742059	299.458,00	IT	2	e-Sourcing / Purchaser
Strategic	E-Sourcing	SP12727876	368.422,00	IT	2	e-Sourcing / Purchaser
Strategic	E-Sourcing	SP15151147	23.808,00	IT	2	e-Sourcing / Purchaser
Strategic	E-Sourcing	SP15359848	23.900,00	IT	2	e-Sourcing / Purchaser
Strategic	E-Sourcing	SP10635983	871.000,00	IT	3	e-Sourcing / Purchaser / Legal
Strategic	E-Sourcing	SP15380320	235.700,00	IT	2	e-Sourcing / Purchaser
Strategic	E-Sourcing	SP15582623	499.846,00	IT	3	e-Sourcing / Purchaser / Legal
Strategic	E-Sourcing	SP15734174	139.120,00	IT	2	e-Sourcing / Purchaser
Strategic	E-Sourcing	SP18347824	440.930,00	IT	2	e-Sourcing / Purchaser
Strategic	E-Sourcing	SP20931209	178.230,00	IT	2	e-Sourcing / Purchaser
Strategic	E-Sourcing	SP23241808	76.500,00	IT	2	e-Sourcing / Purchaser
Strategic	E-Sourcing	SP22757521	124.000,00	IT	2	e-Sourcing / Purchaser
Strategic	E-Sourcing	SP17743458	192.140,00	IT	2	e-Sourcing / Purchaser
Strategic	E-Sourcing	SP18208524	26.120,00	IT	2	e-Sourcing / Purchaser
Strategic	E-Mail facilitated	IM.RFP.10.00023	7.217,00	IT	4	3 Suppliers / Purchaser via Email
Strategic	E-Mail facilitated	IMA. RFP.F.10.0136	19.866,00	IT	5	4 Suppliers / Purchaser via Email
Strategic	E-Mail facilitated	IMA. RFP.F.10.0059	61.000,00	IT	5	4 Suppliers / Purchaser via Email

Table 16. Process cost (based on interviews with Finance)

Activity	Average Time in H	Per	Department	Hourly Rate in €
Demand Capturing	0,30		Internal Customers	97,00
Validation	0,10		Finance /Invest Control	78,00
PO Creation	0,50		Procurement	76,00
Sourcing Event Creation	1,00		Legal	81,00
RFP Q&A	1,10	/ supplier or once for e-Sourcing	IT	80,00
RFP Analysis 1st round	3,00	/ supplier	IC & Proc	86,50
RFP analysis successive rounds	0,70	/ supplier		
Final Contract	2,00			

Table 17. Process cost determination

Process Type	Degree of Digitalization	Sample Event Number	Volume in €	Commodity	Process Cost	
					Explanation	Calculated Cost
Operational	E-Cat	8110057196	402,72	FM	IC creation & validation	38,8
Operational	E-Cat	8110057197	7,43	FM	IC creation & validation	38,8
Operational	E-Cat	8110057251	29,55	FM	IC creation & validation	38,8
Operational	E-Cat	8110057290	323,82	FM	IC creation & validation	38,8
Operational	E-Cat	8110057308	29,22	FM	IC creation & validation	38,8
Operational	E-Cat	8110057396	159,18	FM	IC creation & validation	38,8
Operational	E-Cat	8110057400	36,72	FM	IC creation & validation	38,8
Operational	E-Cat	8110057415	38,83	FM	IC creation & validation	38,8
Operational	E-Cat	8110057429	127,80	FM	IC creation & validation	38,8
Operational	E-Cat	8110057444	82,05	FM	IC creation & validation	38,8
Operational	E-Cat	8110057478	25,47	FM	IC creation & validation	38,8
Operational	E-Cat	8110057528	271,76	FM	IC creation & validation / 2nd IC validation	48,5
Operational	E-Cat	8110057532	2,50	FM	IC creation & validation	38,8
Operational	E-Cat	8110057534	10,22	FM	IC creation & validation	38,8
Operational	E-Cat	8110057583	18,50	FM	IC creation & validation	38,8
Operational	E-Cat	8110057585	26,31	FM	IC creation & validation	38,8
Operational	E-Cat	8110057591	84,13	FM	IC creation & validation / validation invoice	48,5
Operational	E-Cat	8110057652	121,61	HR	IC creation & validation / 2nd IC validation	48,5
Operational	E-Cat	8110057653	11,31	IT	IC creation & validation / validation invoice	48,5

continued on following page

Table 17. Continued

Process Type	Degree of Digitalization	Sample Event Number	Volume in €	Commodity	Process Cost	
					Explanation	Calculated Cost
Operational	Manual Ordering	8110036091	10.000,00	Invest & Maint	IC creation & validation / Finance validation / Procurement PO Creation/ Approval Procurement (2)	99,8
Operational	Manual Ordering	8110044573	1.319,31	Invest & Maint	IC creation & validation / Finance validation / Procurement PO Creation / Approval Procurement (1)	92,2
Operational	Manual Ordering	8110045653	363,25	Invest & Maint	IC creation & validation / Finance validation / Procurement PO Creation / Approval Procurement (1)	92,2
Operational	Manual Ordering	8110046925	8.000,00	IT	IC creation & validation / Finance validation / IT validation/ Procurement PO Creation / Approval Procurement (1)	100,2
Operational	Manual Ordering	8110047948	7.761,60	FM	IC creation & validation / Finance validation / Procurement PO Creation / Approval Procurement (1)	92,2
Operational	Manual Ordering	8110053843	461,00	Invest & Maint	IC creation & validation / Finance validation / Procurement PO Creation / Approval Procurement (1)	92,2
Operational	Manual Ordering	8110056247	96.000,00	HR	IC creation & validation / 2nd IC validation / Finance validation / Procurement PO Creation / Approval Procurement (2)	109,5
Operational	Manual Ordering	8110056596	120,74	FM	IC creation & validation / Finance validation / Procurement PO Creation / Approval Procurement (1)	92,2
Operational	Manual Ordering	8110057163	17.291,75	Invest & Maint	IC creation & validation / 2nd IC validation / Finance validation / Procurement PO Creation / Approval Procurement (2)	109,5
Operational	Manual Ordering	8110057217	177,02	FM	IC creation & validation / Finance validation / Procurement PO Creation / Approval Procurement (1)	92,2
Operational	Manual Ordering	8110057228	6.879,58	IT	IC creation & validation/ Finance validation / IT validation/ Procurement PO Creation / Approval Procurement (1)	100,2

continued on following page

Table 17. Continued

Process Type	Degree of Digitalization	Sample Event Number	Volume in €	Commodity	Process Cost	
					Explanation	Calculated Cost
Operational	Manual Ordering	8110057319	3.385,70	HR	IC creation & validation / Finance validation / Procurement PO Creation / Approval Procurement (1)	92,2
Operational	Manual requisitioning	4670045667	119,00	HR	IC creation & validation / Finance validation / Invest Control validation / Procurement demand capturing / Procurement PO Creation / Approval Procurement (2)	130,4
Operational	Manual requisitioning	4670045677	1.695,00	IT	IC creation & validation / Finance validation / Invest Control validation / IT validation / Procurement demand capturing / Procurement PO Creation / Approval Procurement (2)	138,4
Operational	Manual requisitioning	4670045712	177,02	FM	IC creation & validation / Finance validation / Invest Control validation / Procurement demand capturing / Procurement PO Creation / Approval Procurement (2)	130,4
Operational	Manual requisitioning	4670045629	277,55	FM	IC creation & validation / Finance validation / Invest Control validation / Procurement demand capturing / Procurement PO Creation / Approval Procurement (2)	130,4
Operational	Manual requisitioning	4670045645	64.800,00	IT	IC creation & validation / Finance validation / Invest Control validation / IT validation / Procurement demand capturing / Procurement PO Creation / Approval Procurement (2)	138,4

Table 18.

Process Type	Degree of Digitalization	Sample Event Number	Volume in €	Commodity	Explanation	Calculated Cost	Average Cost per Round	Average Cost per Supplier	Average Cost per Round and Supplier
Strategic	E-Sourcing	SP10742059	299.458,00	IT	2 Rounds with Buyer / IC involvement / 3 suppliers	1.131,30	565,65	377,10	188,55
Strategic	E-Sourcing	SP12727876	368.422,00	IT	2 Rounds with Buyer / IC involvement / 4 suppliers	1.451,35	725,68	362,84	181,42
Strategic	E-Sourcing	SP15151147	23.808,00	IT	1 Round with Buyer / IC involvement / 2 suppliers	690,15	690,15	345,08	345,08
Strategic	E-Sourcing	SP15359848	23.900,00	IT	1 Round with Buyer / IC involvement / 2 suppliers	690,15	690,15	345,08	345,08
Strategic	E-Sourcing	SP10635983	871.000,00	IT	3 Rounds with Buyer / IC / Legal involvement / 5 suppliers	2.236,15	745,38	447,23	149,08
Strategic	E-Sourcing	SP15380320	235.700,00	IT	2 Rounds with Buyer / IC involvement / 6 suppliers	2.091,45	1.045,73	348,58	174,29
Strategic	E-Sourcing	SP15582623	499.846,00	IT	2 Rounds with Buyer / IC / Legal involvement / 2 suppliers	973,25	486,63	486,63	243,31
Strategic	E-Sourcing	SP15734174	139.120,00	IT	2 Rounds with Buyer / IC involvement / 3 suppliers	1.131,30	565,65	377,10	188,55
Strategic	E-Sourcing	SP18347824	440.930,00	IT	3 Rounds with Buyer / IC involvement / 3 suppliers	1.312,95	437,65	437,65	145,88
Strategic	E-Sourcing	SP20931209	178.230,00	IT	1 Round with Buyer / IC involvement / 1 supplier	430,65	430,65	430,65	430,65
Strategic	E-Sourcing	SP23241808	76.500,00	IT	1 Round with Buyer / IC involvement / 1 supplier	430,65	430,65	430,65	430,65
Strategic	E-Sourcing	SP22757521	124.000,00	IT	3 Rounds with Buyer / IC involvement / 3 suppliers	1.312,95	437,65	437,65	145,88
Strategic	E-Sourcing	SP17743458	192.140,00	IT	2 Rounds with Buyer / IC involvement / 4 suppliers	1.451,35	725,68	362,84	181,42

continued on following page

Table 18. Continued

Process Type	Degree of Digitalization	Sample Event Number	Volume in €	Commodity	Explanation	Calculated Cost	Average Cost per Round	Average Cost per Supplier	Average Cost per Round and Supplier
Strategic	E-Sourcing	SP18208524	26.120,00	IT	2 Rounds with Buyer / IC involvement / 3 suppliers	1.131,30	565,65	377,10	188,55
Strategic	E-Mail facilitated	IM.RFP.10.00023	7.217,00	IT	1 Round with Buyer / IC involvement / 3 suppliers	1.139,95	1.139,95	379,98	379,98
Strategic	E-Mail facilitated	IMA. RFP.F.10.0136	19.866,00	IT	1 Round with Buyer / IC involvement / 4 suppliers	1.494,60	1.494,60	373,65	373,65
Strategic	E-Mail facilitated	IMA. RFP.F.10.0059	61.000,00	IT	2 Rounds with Buyer / IC involvement / 4 suppliers	1.736,80	868,40	434,20	217,10

Chapter 5

A Hybrid E–Auction/Negotiation Model as a Tool for 4PL to Improve the Transport Provider Selection Process

Eleni Maria Papadopoulou
ATEI of Thessaloniki, Greece

Athanasios Kelemis
ATEI of Thessaloniki, Greece

ABSTRACT

The evolution of e-business has enabled the development of e-marketplaces facilitating the transactions among existing and potential supply chain members on an integrated platform. E-auctions are already considered a critical process for the selection of transport providers, but have not yet been systematically integrated in the 4PL concept. Specifically, a 4PL provider must add value to the e-auction process by assessing, in prior, the capabilities of potential transport providers through an e-negotiation process in order to justify its administrative role. The aim of this chapter is to present a hybrid e-auction-negotiation model, managed by a 4PL provider aiming to improve the transport provider selection process.

INTRODUCTION

Since the evolution of e-business, significant progress has been made in the field, covering all sections of electronic activity among consumers, business and government (Kourgiantakis et al., 2006), also affecting the functions of supply chains accordingly (Jin and Wu, 2006).

The need for e-marketplaces emerged in the late 1990's, as this e-business model promises to enhance the process of information sharing. It also facilitates the transactions among existing and potential supply chain members on an integrated platform, the development of vendor managed inventory schemes and in general, it leverages the operations of collaborative mechanisms (Daniel and White, 2005).

DOI: 10.4018/978-1-4666-3914-0.ch005

Concerning transportation, it refers to the physical flow of goods from an origin to a redefined destination (Lai et al., 2004). Particularly, it constitutes an information intensive sector that continuously evolves in an attempt to follow the market trends. Therefore, the traditional communication means, such as phone and fax, are being gradually substituted by updated e-transportation tools, with main reference to bulletin boards, e-auctions, electronic Request for Quote (e-RFQ), horizontal and vertical portals, public and private exchange marketplaces, as well as collaborative communities (Nair, 2005). The requirements of each marketplace depend on the mode of transport, the number of modes and the types of goods (Kameshwaran and Narahari, 2001).

One of the trends in supply chain is considered to be the 4PL provider. The term was introduced by Accenture with the following definition (Bedeman and Gattorna, 2003):

A supply chain integrator that assembles and manages the resources, capabilities and technology of its own organization with those of complementary service providers to deliver a comprehensive supply chain solution.

This chapter focuses on the utility of e-auctions in the transportation process, as an alternative of the traditional and time consuming RFQ process, within the concept of 4PL dominance. The first section of literature review refers to the traditional RFQ process, the auction types and e-auction administration, also presenting the benefits and drawbacks of e-auctions. Additionally, the characteristics of negotiations and e-negotiations are displayed, as they hold a prominent position in the negotiation process among the 4PL provider and the logistics service providers, based on specific criteria. The second section of the chapter presents the proposed framework that refers to the establishment of an auction process by a 4PL provider. The paper concludes with the presentation of the described process.

LITERATURE REVIEW

A comprehensive literature review was conducted, aiming to provide the framework on which the conceptual process is based. The literature provides details regarding the RFQ, e-auction, and negotiation process, so that the authors further use this information in order to construct the proposed model.

The RFQ Process

The RFQ process prerequisites the requested characteristics to be specified by the buyer, such as the type of product or service, the quality specifications, the quantity demanded, the terms and time of delivery and payment, etc., so that detailed information can be provided by the suppliers. Once the supplier responds, the buyer has to compare the proposals and decide to whom to award the contract. The time consuming and costly nature (Teich et al., 2004) of the process can be counterbalanced by an updated procedure, where RFQs can be implemented in an RFQ venue, created by an independent party. Clients electronically disseminate their shipping needs on site, without mentioning a price limit. This technique, processed either as an open request or as a closed tender, replaces the manual (fax, email) mechanism and condenses the RFQ cycle time (Kameshwaran and Narahari, 2001).

The E-Auction Process

E-Auction Types

Auctions can be distinguished in forward and reverse. A more analytical classification is provided below.

Forward Auctions

English auctions and sealed-bid auctions belong into the category of forward auctions.

The *English auctions* are regarded as open auctions where the auctioneer announces the minimum payable amount for the negotiated product and bidders compete each other by raising the price, till the bidder with the highest bid wins (Kourgiantakis et al., 2006). In *sealed-bid auctions* (Vickrey auction), each bidder submits a bid only once and sealed. The two most common types of sealed-bid auctions are the first and second price auctions. In the first case, the winner is the bidder with the highest bid for the amount of her bid. In the second case, the winner is the bidder of the highest bid, but for a bid equal to the second highest one (Kourgiantakis et al., 2006; Nair, 2005). An example of forward auctions is https://negotiations-live.p.agentrics.com/.

Reverse E-Auctions

Reverse e-auctions are held in e-marketplaces and have been broadly adopted by the vast majority of them. Their main feature is that the price descends until the agreement is reached (Giampietro and Emiliani, 2007; Martinelli and Marchi, 2007), thus resulting in dynamic pricing, provided that the seller is able to reduce his profit margin without suffering from loss. (Smeltzer and Carr, 2003).

E-auctions resemble traditional bidding with the difference that the interested buyer invites prequalified (Loesch and Lambert, 2007) suppliers to participate in the auction by submitting their bids online, in real time (Hur et al., 2007). Some representative websites can be regarded "uship. com," "anyvan.com," "shiply.com," etc. The most popularly used categories of reverse e-auctions are presented below:

The *Dutch auction* is signified as a descending auction, as the auctioneers continuously reduce the price, till a bidder agrees on the proposed rate and purchases the product (Hur, et al, 2006; Kourgiantakis et al., 2006).

Reverse E-Auction Types

A basic distinction among auction types is based on the number of items being auctioned, i.e. as single- unit or multi-unit auctions (Heavey et al., 2006). In the case of *combinatorial auctions* the bidders have preferences for bundles of items and the competition is leveraged to the level of product/services combination into a single bid package (Krajewska and Kopfer, 2006; Nair, 2005; Schoenherr, 2008; Teich et al., 2004).

In *multidimensional auctions*, buyers are interested not solely in price, but also regarding other dimensions such as quality, delivery time and warranty terms. Such features must be incorporated into the offer, in order to affect buyers' final partner selection. In case the feature of quantity is added to the buyers' selection criteria, the auction type is renamed to *multiple issue auctions*, where the buyer can set a price for the aggregated quantity or different prices for different quantities. The auction owner is in charge of the determination of product quantity to be accepted from the bidders, for the specification of the auction issues / attributes and additionally, for the size of the bid decrement (Teich et al., 2004). Next, supplier competition can be held either on an open-cry or a sealed-bid basis. Multi-issue auction can also appear as *multi-attribute* auction in literature, both negotiating the price, quantity and qualitative attributes (Bichler et al., 2003). This type of auction proves to be advantageous for all parties, due to increased speed of negotiation and market transparency (Bichler and Kalagnanam, 2005), despite the difficulty of deciding on the different scoring functions and parameter deployment (Bichler, 2000).

Multi-stage auctions require multiple stages to complete (Bichler, 2000).

In *Combined value auctions*, an order can consist of manifold items, allowing the logistics provider to submit a combined value for the entire supply chain. In this case, the creation of trust and confidence among the participating members is of pivotal importance, and therefore, the identification of few reliable "partners" is reinforced in order to nominate them with exclusive rights to bid in the auction (Ledyard et al., 2000).

In *sequential auctions*, the bidding process concludes in more than one round. Provisional winners are announced at the end of each round, which while proceeding to the next round have to bid even more dynamically to remain in the bidding process. The cost savings achieved by this auction type can be significant, as bidders concentrate on their competitive advantage. In the final round the total acquisition cost does not decline by a percentage of at least x% from the previous round (Ledyard et al., 2000).

E-Auction Administration

The above-mentioned auction types can be further categorized in the "e-environment," according to their administrative nature. *Full-service e-auctions* are provided by specialized, software owning third parties, thoroughly managing the auction process. Their activity portfolio includes spend analysis, opportunity assessment, supplier identification and prequalification, Request for Quote preparation, supplier training, bidding execution and post-bid analysis (Hur et al., 2007). In *Self-service e-auctions*, buyers are responsible to undertake the entire process, from market analysis, supplier identification, Request for Bids preparation, supplier training to bidding execution, also including the development or licensing of e-auction software (Hur et al., 2007). In *Polymorphic combinations* (hybrids) of full- and self-service auctions, the buyer may rely on the technical expertise of third-party service providers, whereas the buyer undertakes part of specific tasks (Hur, *2007*).

Reverse E-Auctions Prerequisites

The size of an organization may be a determinant of the adoption of e-auctions mechanism. Large organizations have the potential to harvest the advantages offered by the e-auctions, contrary to the small ones. The purchasing firm must establish the suitable IT infrastructure and its personnel must have analytical skills and be familiar with the relevant technology. Moreover, the participation degree of suppliers is an important issue, as a considerable number of suppliers must be willing to participate, in order for an e-auction to be considered successful. This major economic and technological obstacle can be overcome through the cooperation with larger corporations, possessing the appropriate technological platform and know-how, managing to attract more potential suppliers via large volumes of requests (Schoenherr, 2008). Finally, apart from the number of the participating suppliers, the auction performance also depends on the preparation time and the switching costs (Martinelli and Marchi, 2007).

E-Auction Benefits and Drawbacks

Regarding their perceived benefits, numerous studies have been carried out emphasizing their positive impact on the involved parties. E-auctions are considered to benefit both customers and suppliers in that they reduce operating or customer acquisition costs (Emiliani and Stec, 2004), focus on total cost (Emiliani and Stec, 2004), view market prices to validate their competitiveness (Emiliani, 2000), end with lowered inventory costs (Hartley et al., 2004), reduce transaction costs (Emiliani and Stec, 2004), save time (Emiliani and Stec, 2004; Manciagli, 2001), reduce the bid cycle time (Emiliani and Stec, 2004), access to new markets (Emiliani and Stec, 2004), lead to potential increase in sales (Emiliani and Stec, 2004), improve customer service/customer satisfaction (Emiliani and Stec, 2004), share critical information (Emiliani and Stec, 2004), facilitate process efficiencies (Emiliani and Stec, 2004), reduce geographic boundaries/(Carter et al., 2004; Hartley et al., 2006), reduce excess inventory (Carter et al., 2004; Smeltzer and Carr, 2003), improve supplier communication (Emiliani and

Stec, 2004), reduced purchase prices (Carter et al., 2004; Gang et al., 2005; Smeltzer and Carr, 2003), increase price visibility (Smeltzer and Carr, 2002), shorten order-cycle times (Hartley et al., 2004), enable prompt information flow (Wu and Feng, 2005), leverage dynamic, real time competition (Hartley et al., 2004; Hartley et al., 2006), enable access to a large pool of potential suppliers (Carter et al., 2004), focus on strategic sourcing rather than on processing transactions (Avery, 2000).

On the contrary, e-auctions have also revealed significant drawbacks, such as price-only bidding (Emiliani and Stec, 2005; Smeltzer and Carr, 2003), buyers' manipulative process to profit at the suppliers' expense (Hartley et al., 2004; Smeltzer and Carr, 2003), unrealistic price offers, in order not to lose business (Smeltzer and Carr, 2003), damaged long-term relationship (Giampietro and Emiliani, 2007; Schoenherr and Mabert, 2007), destroyed trust (Schoenherr and Mabert, 2007), arms-length relationships, lack of loyalty (Tassabehji et al., 2006), reduced investment for customers (Giampietro and Emiliani, 2007), aggressive expansion of buyer power (Giampietro and Emiliani, 2007), one-way transparency, in favour of the buyer (Giampietro and Emiliani, 2007), information asymmetry (Tassabehji et al., 2006), possible cooperation with unqualified suppliers (Emiliani and Stec, 2005), retaliation from incumbent suppliers (Giampietro and Emiliani, 2007), less capital reinvestment for innovation and process improvements (Hahn et al., 1986), emphasis on purchase price, disregard of quality features (Hartley et al., 2004) etc.

The Negotiation Process

The Importance of Negotiation

The auction process must not be strictly separated from the negotiation process, particularly in cases where qualitative features are embedded in the outcome. Auctions are competition oriented and

mainly focus on the outcome, by determining the final value. On the other hand, negotiations create the value for the auctioned objects, and mainly refer to more complex projects (Kersten et al., 2000). Furthermore, they account for multiple attributes of a deal such as quality, delivery time or terms of payment (Bichler, 2000).

Kersten et al (2000) have categorized negotiations into integrative, distributive and mixed negotiations. In *integrative* negotiations, both parties' interests merge in order to create value, exchange relevant information, and promote learning and problem solving. These value added characteristics derive from discussion between the parties. In *distributive* negotiations, only one party can be declared as winner. In a purely competitive atmosphere, each party tries to increase its benefits from the strict exchange of offers and counter-offers. *Mixed* negotiations are a more realistic scenario combining characteristics from both integrative (explore options, trust the negotiator) and distributive (commitment to firm position) negotiations (Kersten et al., 2000).

The influence of information systems on negotiation process is significant. Electronic negotiation tables, decision and negotiation support systems, artificial negotiating software agents (Kaihara, 2001), as well as, software platforms for bidding and auctioning add value to the process, reinforcing electronic communication with an auction-centric perspective. Within this concept, new negotiation protocols have been introduced, including auction protocols with combinatorial bids on product bundles, supply curve bids in a volume discount auction, multi-attribute auctions, iterative double auctions, automated negotiations among software agents and protocols supporting bi- and multilateral negotiations among human negotiators.

Different negotiation structures are defined based on the above mentioned protocols, referring to unstructured negotiations (face to face negotiations), semi-structured negotiations (negotiations supported by Negotiation Support Systems) and structured negotiations (auctions) (Bichler et al., 2003).

The authors further discuss the evolution from traditional negotiations to e-negotiations to be facilitated via electronic media. They distinguished three types of e-negotiation, namely *unsupported* e- negotiations, characterized by the absence of information systems in the process, *supported* e-negotiations, where people and information systems coexist and share tasks and *automated* e-negotiations, executed by software agents that control the entire process, without human mediation.

CONCEPTUAL FRAMEWORK

The Managerial Problem: Selection of the Appropriate Transport Provider

Freight transportation is considered a complex area, taking into consideration the pluralism of heterogeneous agents (Wycisk, McKelvey and Huelsmann, 2008), the pluralism of physical, information and communication structures, as well as, the difference in dynamics (Nilsson and Waidringer, 2006). The pluralism of functions, the capital intensive nature of investments, internationalization, political/regulatory, economical, social changes along with the necessity for service quality (total delivery time) and reliability, also accompanied by distribution network design (Crainic and Laporte, 1997), and cultural differences, represent additional components of complexity.

For all these reasons, the transport provider selection is critical for the success of the entire supply chain. It depends on multiple characteristics, such as quality, transit time, price (Loesch and Lambert, 2007), response time, familiarity with the shipper's operations, equipment availability and suitability, non-transportation services (collecting payment, delivery beyond the dock,

mid-route stop-offs), pick up performance, hub performance, technological advancements, billing accuracy, visibility systems availability (track and trace systems), claims ratio and payment (Sheffi, 2004), flexibility of contractual terms (Van der Putten et al., 2006), financial stability, geographic coverage (Chen, 2003), Cargo Handling Capacity/Capability (Volume, Special, Hazardous), routing, sailing frequency (WCL Consulting, 2006), clear rates and charges, consistent follow up of shipments, etc. (Papadopoulou et al., 2010).

The Proposed Solution: The Design and Adoption of a Hybrid E-Auction/Negotiation Model by 4PLs

Combinations and hybrid forms of auctions- negotiations exist, exploiting the advantages of the two systems. Multiple types of combinations can be applied, such as the reduction of the supplier base through auctions, so that bilateral, real time negotiations can be realized. Another combination could refer to the negotiation phase coming first in order to establish the issues/attributes and the initial bids of the auction that will follow.

A hybrid auction/negotiation form combines the flexibility of the negotiation with the competitiveness of the auction. The auction owner is responsible to evaluate the bidders prior to the auction process, in order to separate the qualified from the non conforming ones, based on the bidder attributes. The auction process follows in an automatic, manual or pause mode (Kersten et al., 2000).

The aim of this chapter is to provide the framework for a hybrid e-auction/negotiation model to assist the decision of transportation partner selection by a 4PL provider. The web environment, in which the 4PL provider operates, provides the opportunity of streamlining the logistics activities between transport/ 3pl providers and customers on a macro basis, as well as, matching demand and supply in real time (Lau and Goh, 2002). Moreover, the 4PL provides one-stop-shop services, in an environment of increasing complexity and competitiveness (Van der Putten et al., 2006), strengthening their relationship with customers and providers, adding value to all chain members (Ho et al., 2003).

The 4PL must conduct the negotiation process in order to identify and categorise the best-of-breed supply chain partners from transport providers, to technology developers, customs brokers and insurance companies, thereby enhancing the on-line trade process (Khalifa et al., 2003).

On the other hand, the 4PL must cater for the promotion of knowledge management, thus creating on-line support mechanisms for those buyers that are not aware of the auction process. Both buyers' and suppliers' concerns must be addressed prior to the auction and the rules must be completely understood. However, in case the provision of assistance during the auction is imminent, the fourth party must have settled a reliable mechanism (instant messaging tool or a discussion board), so that the participants place their concerns (Schoenherr and Mabert, 2007).

Furthermore, the establishment of published rules, procedures and secure auction protocols will encourage information sharing and thus, enhancing collaboration among parties.

The 4PL must obtain feedback from the parties involved, in order to continuously improve both the negotiation and the auction process. Feedback is also required after the task execution by the auction winner, so that statistics which are kept will help the 4PL in partner re-evaluation process.

The 4PL is responsible to create an atmosphere of fairness, trust and equity among the auction partners. Since buyers and suppliers meet only virtually in the marketplace, and no prior relationship has been evolved, the auctioneer (4PL) must establish penalties to the non conforming transport providers, having either monetary or promotional expressions. Monetary penalties can refer to certain amounts of refund payable to the buyer, covering the relevant loss caused by the delay. The promotional penalty can have the meaning of exclusion from a subsequent auction.

The issue of price visibility is of major importance. The 4PL provider has already agreed on certain tariffs with its network partners for a predefined shipment volume. The auction mechanism resembles the spot rate acquaintance, where freight rates are provided for a specific shipment on a specific sailing, which is higher than a contract rate.

The problem is twofold, though. A distinction has to be made between Category A, consisting of the clients that purchase rates through the traditional way, using the RFQ system and Category B, representing those that are more familiar with the benefits that IT has to offer and prefer to by-pass the traditional process and participate in an e-auction. Since the negotiation process between the 4PL provider and its partners has been granted, emphasis must be given to the on-going process. In case the traditional RFQ process is followed, the interaction with the 4PL provider is essential. The 4PL provider must forward the client's RFQ to the chain partners and wait for their response. Afterwards, the 4PL has to revert to the client providing multiple prices, sailing schedules and routing options as received from the carriers and intermediaries. In a door-to-door multimodal request, the fourth party has to elaborate all relevant quotes and provide the clients with the most suitable solution, in terms of price, transit time, and safety. Further to the client's confirmation regarding the selected partner, the 4PL sends the relevant booking order to the transport providers, so that the task execution begins. This process cannot be considered as value added, as it just describes the typical tasks of a freight forwarding company. Furthermore, it is time consuming and does not reflect the intermediary's (4PL) technological expertise. Additionally, in the RFQ process, the participating transport providers do not have the opportunity for dynamic pricing or reducing the price based on the market trend, since they are not aware of the competitive rate quotes.

As a result, the 4PL provider must intermediate in order to communicate the client's attitude regarding pricing.

In the auction process the clients interact directly with the transport providers in an e-marketplace created by the 4PL provider. The existence of the fourth party is clearly supportive, allowing the auction to be executed autonomously among the concerned parties. Further to the bidding process and the consequent, based on predefined rules, winner—partner selection, the coordinated booking order must be conducted electronically, also containing all data needed for the issuance of Bill of Lading. This process justifies the selection of a 4PL provider as an intermediary, seeing that it adds value to the whole supply chain partner selection process through direct interaction.

Agent based automation has to be considered by the 4PL provider, within the time saving concept. Auction protocols would be suitable for both negotiation and auction process. In the first case, multi-issue and multi-item negotiation models can be regarded as enablers for mutually beneficial agreements, beyond price competition. In the auction process, the 4PL provider will act as the auctioneer (Van der Putten et al., 2006).

The ultimate goal is to attract clients to participate in all on-line, electronic events, organized by the fourth party, on a single integrative e-platform. In order for this achievement to be realized, certain motives should be appointed related with specified benefits, as mentioned in literature review.

In order for the fourth party to operate in a total quality framework, properly exploiting the advantages of feedback receipt, statistical information must be kept in electronic files, providing detailed information about transit time, rates, without revealing actual data. Performance mechanisms, such as the use of close-of-auction price reductions, must be also introduced (Hur et al., 2007).

The pricing mechanisms that will be embodied into the auction process must be carefully selected, in order to achieve optimized results. A point that has to be reconsidered is the settlement of a maximum price that the client is willing to pay. The client has to conduct an extended market research, in order to be able to determine a specific amount, and this is due to the existence of multiple price parameters that constitute the freight rate. These include cargo's classification, volumetric weight, applicable surcharges, such as Fuel Costs (Bunker Adjustment Factor), Currency Fluctuation, Terminal Handling Charges, Hazardous Cargo, Unusual Size Cargo, etc. The freight rate also depends on whether the cargo completes a full container/truck (FCL, FTL etc), or Less than Container/ Truck Load (LCL, LTL, etc). Seasonability and demand factors also affect the rate fluctuation (WCL Consulting, 2006). Consequently, as it is time consuming for the client to determine the upper price limit, the 4PL provider must reconcile this process, based on its expertise.

Another aspect that has to be taken into consideration is the fact that the fourth party needs to promote the on-line function, in order to reduce the transaction processes and cycle time, and thus has to proceed with a price promotional strategy. A percentage discount, resulting from reduction of operational expenses, can be applied to the rate when the shipment is booked through an e-auction.

The issue of the stopping rule is considered as critical to the auction performance, in terms of both final acquisition cost and process completion time, as it affects the bidder information.

The issue of bid visibility is of major importance and has to be further discussed. Information sharing is critical in collaborative relationship, so that continuous improvement is facilitated. Competitive reasons, though, may impose the anonymity of logistics providers that participate in the e-auction and consequently preclude open bidding. A feedback procedure is considered to be pivotal disclosing freight rate and transit time, which can be presented in the form of ranking instead of open bidding, without revealing the corresponding bidder, after having checked the relevant legislation and secure that price disclosure is allowed (Hartley et al., 2006).

The notion of trust is manifold in the overall auction process. Due to intermediary's anonymity, it is reasonable on the buyers' behalf to display hesitation towards the outcomes. Trust cannot be secured, though, merely through the existence of a personal relationship. The online auction site, associated institutions and system functionality, among other features, can be considered as objects of trust. Furthermore, the sharing of common values and goals, accompanied by the seller's good reputation reinforce trust (Bailey and Francis, 2008). The relationship between dispute resolution and trust can be also regarded as an important issue. The existence of an online arbitrator to cope with a risen dispute provides protection to the transacting parties (Bewsell et al., 2005). Additional trust-building mechanisms would be the minimization of information asymmetry regarding the product's/ service's specifications. Under-investment in capacity, misallocation of inventory, transportation and management resources, increased prices and penalties resulting from line shut-downs and reduced customer services, are only examples of the inefficiencies caused by information asymmetry (Atallah et al., 2003). Imminent is also considered the statement of explicit process terms and conditions (Nair, 2005), along with the clarity and completeness of the winning criteria (Tassabehji et al., 2006).

The above mentioned affairs have been embedded in the e-auction process presented in Figure 1, describing the integrated process of negotiation-auction held under the 4PL provider.

FUTURE RESEARCH DIRECTIONS

The procedure of rate and contract negotiation is already embedded in the process of transportation partner selection. The procedure of e-auctions, though, has not yet been incorporated in the logistics sector, under the guidance of 4PL. In an attempt to provide a framework considering how an e-auction platform could be introduced into the Greek designed and operate, the current chapter is developed. The next step is to investigate the opinion of both transport providers (carriers, freight forwarders and NVOCCs) and importers/exporters against this proposal, and identify the perceived benefits and areas for improvement, so that the relevant adjustments can be made.

CONCLUSION

The construction of such a hybrid e-auction/ negotiation process mainly consists of three steps/phases. In the phase of *Negotiation,* the auction owner, in this case the 4PL provider evaluates the participating transport providers in prior to the auction process, in order to classify them according to qualitative characteristics, such as transit time, etc. The 4PL provider can entice a considerable number of logistics providers, due to the volume of the handling shipments. The second phase refers to the *RFQ Process,* where the fourth party can provide its technological and logistical expertise to companies that do not have the economic and technological opportunity to incorporate the e-auction process in their operations. As an independent party, the 4PL will provide the users with an RFQ venue, so that the clients disseminate their needs on site, in the form of a closed tender, without mentioning a price limit. Besides the RFQ process, the clients will have the opportunity to select the e-auction process, on the same platform. Therefore, in the third phase, the 4PL, as a software owning third-party, will provide full service e-auctions, including spend analysis, opportunity assessment, supplier identification and prequalification, RFQ preparation, supplier training, bidding execution and post-bid analysis.

Since the 4PL provides integrative supply chain solutions, the type of auction organised will be a *combined value multi-attribute auction,* taking into consideration price, quantity and qualitative attributes, along the existence of manifold items, such as transit time, frequency of sailings, track

Figure 1. The hybrid e-auction/negotiation model

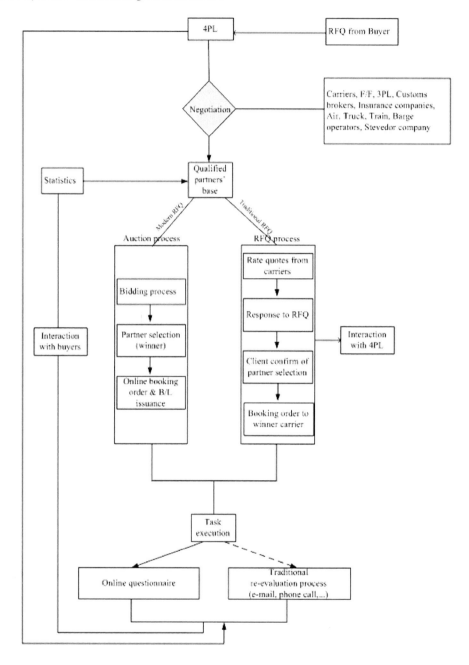

and trace process etc, thus allowing the logistics provider to submit a combined value for the entire supply chain. The advantages of speed and market transparency that accompany the multi-attribute auction type are facilitated by the prerequisites of trust and confidence in the combined value

auction, providing a framework of few reliable "partners," nominated with exclusive rights to bid in the auction.

The chapter examined the utility a hybrid auction/negotiation model could provide to a fourth party logistics provider. An extensive literature review was conducted that revealed the different reverse e-auction types, as well as their benefits and drawbacks for both buyers and suppliers of services. The notion of negotiation has also been analysed and finally combined with the e-auction process, in order to contribute to the improvement transportation process, through the model construction.

REFERENCES

Atallah, M. J., Elmongui, H. G., Deshpande, V., & Schwarz, L. B. (2003). Secure supply-chain protocols. In *Proceedings of IEEE International Conference on E-Commerce*, (pp. 293–302). Newport Beach, CA: IEEE Press.

Avery, S. (2000). E-procurement: A wealth of information for buyers. *Purchasing, 129*(5), 111.

Bailey, K., & Francis, M. (2008). Managing information flows for improved value chain performance. *International Journal of Production Economics, 111*(1), 2–12. doi:10.1016/j.ijpe.2006.11.017

Bewsell, G., Jamieson, R., Gardiner, A., & Bunker, D. (2005). An investigation of dispute resolution mechanisms on power and trust: A domain study of online trust in e-auctions. *Lecture Notes in Computer Science, 3592*, 288–298. doi:10.1007/11537878_29

Bichler, M. (2000). A roadmap to auction-based negotiation protocols for electronic commerce. In *Proceedings of the 33rd Hawaii International Conference on System Sciences,* (pp. 1857-1866). Hawaii, HI: IEEE.

Bichler, M., & Kalagnanam, J. (2005). Configurable offers and winner determination in multi-attribute auctions. *European Journal of Operational Research, 160*(2), 380–394. doi:10.1016/j.ejor.2003.07.014

Bichler, M., Kersten, G., & Strecker, S. (2003). Towards a structured design of electronic negotiations. *Group Decision and Negotiation, 12*(4), 311–335. doi:10.1023/A:1024867820235

Carter, C. R., Kaufmann, L., Beall, S., Carter, P. L., Hendrick, T. E., & Petersen, K. J. (2004). Reverse auctions – Grounded theory from the buyer and supplier perspective. *Transportation Research Part E, Logistics and Transportation Review, 40*(3), 183–270. doi:10.1016/j.tre.2003.08.004

Chen, X. (2003). *Transportation service procurement using combinatorial auctions.* (Master Thesis). MIT. Cambridge, MA.

Consulting, W. C. L. (2006). *Global supply chain overview (consumer goods), ocean carriers.* Retrieved November 16, 2011, from http://www.wclconsulting.com

Daniel, E. M., & White, A. (2005). The future of inter-organisational system linkages: Findings of an international delphi study. *European Journal of Information Systems, 14*(2), 188–203. doi:10.1057/palgrave.ejis.3000529

Emiliani, M., & Stec, D. (2004). Aerospace parts supplier's reaction to online reverse auctions. *Supply Chain Management, 9*(2), 139–153. doi:10.1108/13598540410527042

Emiliani, M. L. (2000). Insight from industry: Business-to-business online reverse auctions: Key issues for purchasing process improvement. *Supply Chain Management: An International Journal, 5*(4), 176–186. doi:10.1108/13598540010347299

Emiliani, M. L., & Stec, D. J. (2005). Wood pallet suppliers' reaction to online reverse auctions. *Supply Chain Management: An International Journal, 10*(4), 278–288. doi:10.1108/13598540510612758

Giampietro, C., & Emiliani, M. L. (2007). Coercion and reverse auctions. *Supply Chain Management: An International Journal, 12*(2), 75–84. doi:10.1108/13598540710737253

Hahn, C., Kim, K., & Kim, J. (1986). Costs of competition: Implications for purchasing strategy. *International Journal of Purchasing and Materials Management, 22*(3), 2–7.

Hartley, J. L., Lane, M. D., & Duplaga, E. A. (2006). Exploring the barriers to the adoption of e-auctions for sourcing. *International Journal of Operations & Production Management, 26*(2), 202–221. doi:10.1108/01443570610641675

Hartley, J. L., Lane, M. D., & Hong, Y. (2004). An exploration of the adoption of e-auctions in supply management. *Proceedings of IEEE Transactions on Engineering Management, 51*(2), 153–161. doi:10.1109/TEM.2004.826010

Heavey, C., Byrne, P. J., Liston, P., & Byrne, J. (2006). Operational design in VO supply networks creation network- centric collaboration and supporting fireworks. In Camarinha-Matos, L. M., Afsarmanesh, H., & Ollus, M. (Eds.), *Handbook of Network-Centric Collaboration and Supporting Frameworks* (pp. 381–388). Boston, MA: Springer. doi:10.1007/978-0-387-38269-2_40

Ho, D. C. K., Au, K. F., & Newton, E. (2003). The process and consequences of supply chain virtualization. *Industrial Management & Data Systems, 103*(6), 423–433. doi:10.1108/02635570310479990

Hur, D., Mabert, V. A., & Hartley, J. L. (2007). Getting the most out of reverse e-auction investment. *Omega, 35*(4), 403–416. doi:10.1016/j.omega.2005.08.003

Jin, M., & Wu, S. D. (2006). Supplier coalitions in on-line reverse auctions: Validity requirements and profit distribution scheme. *International Journal of Production Economics, 100*(2), 183–194. doi:10.1016/j.ijpe.2004.10.017

Kaihara, T. (2001). Supply chain management with economics. *International Journal of Production Economics, 73*(1), 5–14. doi:10.1016/S0925-5273(01)00092-5

Kameshwaran, S., & Narahari, Y. (2001). *Auction algorithms for achieving efficiencies in logistics marketplaces.* Paper presented at the International Conference on Energy, Automation and Information Technology. Kharaghpur, India.

Kersten, G. E., Noronha, S. J., & Teich, J. (2000). *Are all e-commerce negotiations auctions?* Paper presented at the Fourth International Conference on the Design of Cooperative Systems. Sophia-Antipolis, France.

Khalifa, M., Banerjee, P., & Ma, L. (2003). Strategies for successfully deploying e-markets: Lessons from the China context. In *Proceedings of the 36th Hawaii International Conference on System Sciences (HICSS 2003).* Hawaii, HI: IEEE.

Kourgiantakis, M., Mandalianos, I., Migdalas, A., & Pardalos, P. M. (2006). Optimization in e-commerce. In Resende, M. G. C., & Pardalos, P. M. (Eds.), *Handbook of Optimization in Telecommunications* (pp. 1077–1050). New York, NY: Springer. doi:10.1007/978-0-387-30165-5_35

Krajewska, M. A., & Kopfer, H. (2006). Collaborating freight forwarding enterprises, request allocation and profit sharing. *OR-Spektrum, 28*(3), 301–317. doi:10.1007/s00291-005-0031-2

Lai, K. H., Ngai, E. W. T., & Cheng, T. C. E. (2004). An empirical study of supply chain performance in transport logistics. *International Journal of Production Economics, 87*(3), 321–331. doi:10.1016/j.ijpe.2003.08.002

Lau, H. C., & Goh, Y. G. (2002). An intelligent brokering system to support multi-agent web-based 4th-party logistics. In *Proceedings of the 14th IEEE International Conference on Tools with Artificial Intelligence,* (pp. 154-161). IEEE Press.

Ledyard, J. O., Olson, M., Porter, D., Swanson, J. A., & Torma, D. P. (2002). The first use of a combined value auction for transportation services. *Interfaces, 32*(5), 4–12. doi:10.1287/inte.32.5.4.30

Loesch, A., & Lambert, J. S. (2007). Information behaviour in e-reverse auctions: Purchasing in the context of the automobile industry. *Journal of Enterprise Information Management, 20*(4), 447–464. doi:10.1108/17410390710772713

Manciagli, D. (2001). A supplier's view. *Purchasing, 130*(12), 26–28.

Martinelli, E., & Marchi, G. (2007). Enabling and inhibiting factors in adoption of electronic-reverse auctions: A longitudinal case study in grocery retailing. *International Review of Retail, Distribution and Consumer Research, 17*(3), 203–218. doi:10.1080/09593960701368721

Nair, A. (2005). Emerging internet-enabled auction mechanisms in supply chain. *Supply Chain Management: An International Journal, 10*(3), 162–168. doi:10.1108/13598540510606214

Papadopoulou, E. M., Panousopoulou, P., & Manthou, V. (2010). Performance indicators in the freight transportation sector- The case of the Greek market. In *Proceedings of the 12 WCTR.* Lisbon, Portugal: WCTR.

Schoenherr, T. (2008). Diffusion of online reverse auctions for B2B procurement: An exploratory study. *International Journal of Operations & Production Management, 28*(3), 259–278. doi:10.1108/01443570810856189

Schoenherr, T., & Mabert, V. A. (2007). Online reverse auctions: Common myths versus evolving reality. *Business Horizons, 50*(5), 373–384. doi:10.1016/j.bushor.2007.03.003

Sheffi, Y. (2004). Combinatorial auctions in the procurement of transportation services. *Interfaces, 34*(4), 245–252. doi:10.1287/inte.1040.0075

Smeltzer, L. R., & Carr, A. (2002). Reverse auctions in industrial marketing and buying. *Business Horizons, 45*(2), 47–52. doi:10.1016/S0007-6813(02)00187-8

Smeltzer, L. R., & Carr, A. S. (2003). Electronic reverse auctions promises, risks and conditions for success. *Industrial Marketing Management, 32*(6), 481–488. doi:10.1016/S0019-8501(02)00257-2

Tassabehji, R., Taylor, W. A., Beach, R., & Wood, A. (2006). Reverse e-auctions and supplier-buyer relationships: An exploratory study. *International Journal of Operations & Production Management, 26*(2), 166–184. doi:10.1108/01443570610641657

Teich, J. E., Wallenius, H., Wallenius, J., & Koppius, O. R. (2004). Emerging multiple issue e-auctions. *European Journal of Operational Research, 159*(1), 1–16. doi:10.1016/j.ejor.2003.05.001

Van der Putten, S., Robu, V., Poutré, H. L., Jorritsma, A., & Gal, M. (2006). Automating supply chain negotiations using autonomous agents: A case study in transportation logistics. In *Proceedings of the 5th International Conference on Autonomous Agents and Multi Agent Systems,* (pp. 1506-1513). ACM Press.

Wu, G., & Feng, Y. (2005). Study on workflow-based open competitive bidding e-procurement mechanism. *Services Systems and Services Management, 1*(1), 791–796.

ADDITIONAL READING

Bakos, J. Y. (1991). A strategic analysis of electronic marketplace. *Management Information Systems Quarterly, 15*(3), 295–310. doi:10.2307/249641

Bandyopadhyay, S., Barron, J. M., & Chaturvedi, A. R. (2002). Competition among sellers in online exchanges. *Information Systems Research, 16*(1), 47–60. doi:10.1287/isre.1050.0043

Beall, S., Carter, C., Carter, P. L., Germer, T., Hendrick, T., Jap, S., et al. (2003). *The role of reverse auctions in strategic sourcing.* Tempe, AZ: CAPS Research Focus Study.

De Smet, Y. (2006). *A multicriteria perspective on reverse auctions*. (PhD Dissertation). Université Libre de Bruxelles. Brussels, Belgium.

Fitzgerald, K. R. (2000). Big buyers jump on the Internet. *Purchasing, 128*(4), 7–16.

Hartley, J. (2004). An exploration of the adoption of e-auctions in supply management. *Proceedings of IEEE Transactions on Engineering Management, 51*(2), 153–161. doi:10.1109/TEM.2004.826010

Hur, D., Mabert, V. A., & Hartley, J. L. (2007). Getting the most out of reverse e-auction investment. *Omega, 35*(4), 403–416. doi:10.1016/j.omega.2005.08.003

Jap, S. (2000). Going, going, gone. *Harvard Business Review, 78*(60), 3.

Kumar, S., & Maher, M. (2008). Are the temptations of online reverse auctions appropriate? *Supply Chain Management: An International Journal, 13*(4), 304–316. doi:10.1108/13598540810882198

Mabert, V. A., & Skeels, J. A. (2002). Internet reverse auctions: Valuable tool in experienced hands. *Business Horizons, 45*(4), 70–76. doi:10.1016/S0007-6813(02)00229-X

Plouffe, C. R., Hulland, J. S., & Vandenbosch, M. (2001). Research report: Richness versus parsimony in modeling technology adoption decisions - Understanding merchant adoption of a smart card-based payment system. *Information Systems Research, 12*(2), 208–222. doi:10.1287/isre.12.2.208.9697

Sashi, C., & O'Leary, B. (2002). The role of internet auctions in the expansion of B2B markets. *Industrial Marketing Management, 31*(2), 103–110. doi:10.1016/S0019-8501(01)00189-4

Simpson, J. T., & Mayo, D. T. (1997). Relationship management: A call for fewer influence attempts. *Journal of Business Research, 39*, 209–218. doi:10.1016/S0148-2963(96)00205-6

Smart, A., & Harrison, A. (2003). Online reverse auctions and their role in buyer-supplier relationships. *Journal of Purchasing and Supply Management, 9*(5/6), 257–269. doi:10.1016/j.pursup.2003.09.005

Teich, J. E., Wallenius, H., Wallenius, J., & Zaitsev, A. (2006). A multi-attribute e-auction mechanism for procurement: Theoretical foundations. *European Journal of Operational Research, 175*(1), 90–100. doi:10.1016/j.ejor.2005.04.023

Wagner, S. M., & Schwab, A. P. (2004). Setting the stage for succesful electronic reverse auctions. *Journal of Purchasing and Supply Management, 10*(1), 11–26. doi:10.1016/j.pursup.2003.11.001

Wyld, D. C., & Settoon, R. P. (2003). When should you bring the tool out of the shed? How and when reverse auctions fit as part of a corporate e-procurement strategy. *Proceedings of the Academy of Strategic E-Commerce, 2*(2), 23–28.

KEY TERMS AND DEFINITIONS

3PL: They constitute external companies that undertake the execution of logistics functions that were traditionally performed within an organization, by encompassing the entire logistics process or selected activities within that process.

4PL Provider: A logistics broker that intermediates and integrates all supply chain stakeholders, in an attempt to provide value added services, through exploitation of its own and its partners' competencies and technological advancements.

Freight Forwarder: Freight forwarders represent key logistical intermediaries that arrange for freight transport architecture from a point of origin to a point of destination.

Reverse E-Auctions: In reverse auctions, the suppliers compete through the provision of decreased transportation prices, in order to be nominated with the relevant task from the buyer.

Transportation Partner Selection: The process during which the interested parties identify the potential transportation partners, establish objective selection criteria, adopt the appropriate methodology for the selection process, form a partnership and monitor the partners' performance against predefined measures.

Transport Providers: Entities, such as carriers, freight forwarders and/ or 3PLs that undertake the execution of transportation services, thus contributing to the overall supply chain efficiency.

Chapter 6
The Use of Cloud Computing in Shipping Logistics

Kamalendu Pal
City University London, UK

Bill Karakostas
City University London, UK

ABSTRACT

The aim of this chapter is to showcase the potential of new, Cloud-based, Information and Communication Technology (ICT) platforms for transport logistics chain management. The related literature is analysed from five perspectives. First, by examining supply chain issues relating to integration of core processes across organizational boundaries, through improved communication, partnerships, and cooperation. Second, from a strategy and planning perspective, by examining supply chain management as an IT platform dependent business practice. Third, by considering implementation issues using agent, as well as Web service technologies. Fourth, by considering the impact of new trends in service computing built around technologies, such as Semantic Web services and Service Oriented Architecture (SOA), on transport logistics. Finally, the chapter proposes a Cloud-based SOA software platform as an enabler for lowering transaction costs and enhancing business opportunities through service virtualization in shipping transport logistics. The operational aspects of shipping transport logistics management are illustrated using a business case that shows the opportunities for increased collaboration through Cloud-based virtualized services.

INTRODUCTION

This chapter explains why Cloud computing creates many opportunities and value-enhancing capabilities for supply chain logistics organisations. In particular, this chapter proposes a systematic approach for identifying and modelling services in shipping transport logistics and provides examples of how such services can execute in a Cloud-based infrastructure.

In general, a logistics chain can be considered to constitute five interdependent types of actors: suppliers, manufacturers, distributors, retailers, and customers. The actors and their objectives are

DOI: 10.4018/978-1-4666-3914-0.ch006

illustrated in Figure 1. Suppliers are responsible for supplying resources to this chain of activities. The strategic procurement decisions at corporate and functional level include supplier evaluation, optimal use of the supplier base through the management of supplier relationships, purchase order processing, buying, and payment, as well as the management of quality control processes. The role of manufacturers is the transformation of raw materials into finished goods. Modern manufacturing includes all intermediate processes required for the production and integration of a product's components. Some of the important activities in manufacturing include forecasting, engineering, service level optimization, replenishment planning, inventory deployment, and quality control processes (Chopra & Meindl, 2012; Lysons & Gillingham, 2003; Mathe & Shapiro, 1993). The responsibilities of distributors are to minimize the cost of labour, space and equipment

in the warehouse, while meeting deadlines. The responsibilities of distributors include receiving, putting away, storing, picking, and shipping the goods. A retailer purchases goods or products in large quantities from manufacturers or through wholesalers, and then sells them on to consumers. Retailing can be done in either physical locations or online. Retailing includes subordinate services, such as delivery. Developing and maintaining a customer service policy is an important aspect of these interconnected activities.

The objective of transport logistics is to move goods from pick-up to deliver-to locations within specified times as dictated by the customer service policy. Transport logistics activities includes network design and optimization, shipment management, fleet and container management, carrier management, and freight management. In this view of supply chains, customers order from retailers, who, in turn, order from distributors, who,

Figure 1. A simplified supply logistics chain

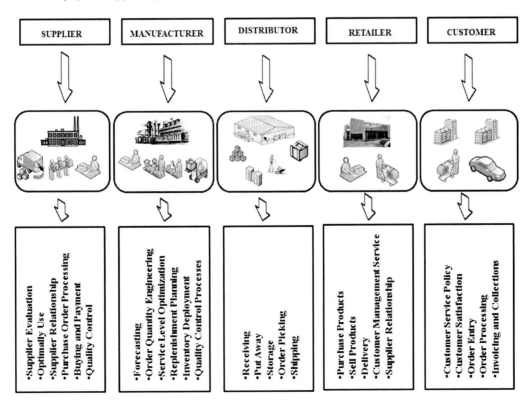

in turn, order from manufacturers, who, in turn, order from suppliers. In other words, one can consider a supply chain as a 'network of networks.'

In addition, the supply logistics chain includes a communications infrastructure. In order to achieve collaboration, organisations need to orchestrate supply chain operations with external partners—beyond the corporate boundaries. A supply chain can be therefore, viewed also as an extended enterprise beginning with the final customer and ending with the suppliers. This concept implies a mutual dependency between the actors based on shared responsibility to pool core competencies and to utilise business knowledge from each network participant.

This chapter argues that visibility of the provided supply chain services is a critical prerequisite for such collaboration. The chapter therefore introduces a systematic approach for identifying and modeling such services, using shipping transport logistics as a case study. Finally, it argues that for effective orchestration and coordination, services need to be virtualised as parts of a Cloud approach. The remaining of the chapter is structured as follows. Section 2 presents the main organisation, business and process requirements for collaboration in transport logistics, and a survey of technologies for process integration such

as software agents, web services and semantic web services. Section 3 introduces a software platform that virtualises shipping transport logistic services by migrating them to the cloud. The use of this platform for the discovery and modelling of services in service transport domain is explained by an example in Section 5. Finally, the chapter concludes with the future directions for research and with a set of recommendations on how transportation chains can coordinate to deliver values to their stakeholders.

BACKGROUND

Modern transport logistics can be understood as the integration of goods flow and information flow in a supply chain. Information plays an important role in the integration of logistics processes. Figure 2 shows the complex flows of goods and information amongst participants in a shipping transport logistics chain.

This complexity is caused by increased globalization of manufacturing, more demanding customer requirements, and technological developments that have resulted in unprecedented levels of complexity and dynamism in the product development process. Organizations therefore

Figure 2. Actors and relationships in transport logistics

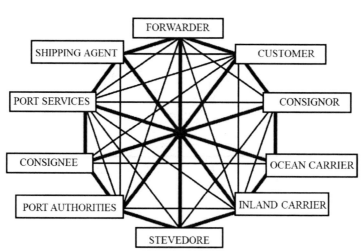

need to orchestrate supply chain operations with external partners—beyond the corporate physical boundary. As argued in the previous section, the new generation supply chains can be considered as a network of networks, or as extended enterprises beginning with the end customer and ending with the suppliers. This concept implies a mutual dependency between the actors based on shared responsibility and the pooling of core competencies.

A growing number of manufacturers and retailers have adopted a management strategy based on shared responsibility. In particular, for these companies logistics has become an integral part of their products, and as important as the product itself (Sheffi, 1990). Moreover, the worldwide trend in globalization has led many companies to outsource their logistics function to Third Party Logistics (3PL) companies (McKinnon, 1999), so as to focus on their core competencies.

Logistics companies nowadays have a more responsible role than in the past, as they coordinate and accelerate physical and information flows in the different tiers of the supply chain (Cooper, Lambert and Page, 1998). Indeed, in keeping up with rapid market changes, the whole logistics system has become more efficient and flexible. This in turn has forced 3PL companies to look for accurate and real-time information on the status of the entire shipment process to improve their customer satisfaction levels (Stough, 2001).

Transport logistic chains can be understood from different perspectives:

- From a business relationship perspective, as shown in the diagram of Figure, 2 three types of business relationships can be identified: business to business (B2B), business to administration (B2A), and administration to administration (A2A).
- A different perspective of the transport business domain is geographical coverage. Some business relationships are geographically confined to a single area or region, while others are location independent. For example, port authority services are defined in the region where the port is based, while a carrier offers businesses in one or more shipping lines and a forwarder can provide an even broader geographical coverage (for example worldwide freight forwarding services).
- Finally, a business service perspective provides an alternative view of transport logistics chains. A business service is a set of resource entitlement grants, based on a temporal or fixed duration based on standard, unilaterally defined or multi lateral defined contracts. In a business service there are at least two different party roles involved, namely provider(s) and consumer(s).

B2B services are defined by a set of interactions that take place between consumer and provider, and include selection of provider based on selection criteria, as well as contractual agreements that are usually long running and repeat. B2B might involve an intermediary that stands between the actual consumer and provider and becomes in effect a surrogate consumer/provider. The freight forwarder participant shown in Figure 2 for example, acts an intermediary between shipper and carrier.

Relationships with service provider partners require ongoing attention. Processes must be in place for partners to share information, so that problems in the service chain can be solved quickly, even when they result from complex interactions of infrastructure components owned by different players. Problem-tracking and customer relationship (CRM) systems, for example, must be able to exchange problem-tracking information as well as customer account information. Procedures and technical interfaces between partner systems must be therefore properly designed and maintained.

Information and Communication Technology (ICT) is of critical importance in developing logistics services in a supply chain context. In this context, Sauvage (2003) found that in a highly competitive business characterised by time compression, technological effort becomes a critical variable and a significant tool for differentiation of logistics services. The improving role of ICT has a knock on effect to the evolution of the competitive market of 3PL business (Regan and Song, 2001). The following three general trends are apparent as a result of the impact of ICT and web technologies on the logistic service business (Evangelista, 2002).

- **New E-Services:** One of the apparent effects of the increasing adoption of ICT in the logistics service business is the integration of tradition services (e.g. transportation and warehousing) with information-based services (e.g. tracking and tracing, booking, freight rate computation, routing and scheduling). Despite the fact that logistics companies may not be considered leaders in the field of technological innovation (Tilanus, 1997), over the last few years, such companies have made remarkable achievements in the adoption of new technologies, particularly those linked to the Internet and web-based system for facilitating integration and collaboration (Lynagh, Murphy, Poist, and Grazer, 2001). In recent years, the important transport and logistics service companies are able to provide a variety of information via the Internet and to secure transactions online with customers (Ellinger, Lynch, Andzulis and Smith, 2003).
- **New Functions:** The Internet and web-based technology has opened up promising channels for the development of new roles in the supply chain, the so-called *infomediaries* or online freight e-marketplaces. The aim of these web-based intermediaries is to give added value to transport and logistics businesses through greater efficiency

and information transparency. They run Internet portals which bring together buyers and sellers of transport and logistics services (Gudmundsson and Walczuch, 1999). With the rapid development of web technologies, the Internet has become ubiquitous and instantaneously accessible. The proliferation of the Internet makes it most cost effective means of driving supply chain integration and information sharing.

- **New Alliances:** Another feature emerging alongside the Internet and e-business is the creation of a new category of service provider called Fourth Party Logistics (4PL). A 4PL is a supply chain integrator who inter-connects and manages the resources, capabilities and technology of its organisation with those of complementary service providers to deliver a comprehensive supply chain solution (Bade, Mueller, and Youd, 1999). These 4PL companies help clients to outsource the business management processes of the entire logistic chain to a single company. In order to do this, often 4PL companies form alliance with management consulting firms, financial service companies and technology service companies. Beyond the emergence of 4PLs, there is an ongoing trend in the logistics service industry to form alliances with firms operating in other industries (Eyefortransport, 2001).

For nearly four-decades, organizations have been buying business software and Electronic Data Interchange (EDI) enablement technology to help them connect to their business partners. However, these technologies, which began their life before the Internet was born and well before business outsourcing and globalization became all-defining mega trends, have proven inadequate in giving companies visibility and control over the hundreds of vital business processes that characterise the new era of transport logistics.

New technologies, namely software agents and web services (both traditional and semantic ones), reviewed in the following sections, promise more effective means to achieve business process integration and traceability. These technologies are complimentary and can be used in combination for improved effectiveness.

Logistics Integration with Agents

The application of software agent systems in the field of logistics has received a great deal of exposure over the last few decades in both industry and in the academic world. It appears that software agent systems (also known as multi-agent systems) would underpin enterprise integration technologies. Although there are many definitions of agents (Jennings, Sycara, and Wooldridge, 1998), one common characteristic of all agent approaches is autonomy. Agents can autonomously act as proxies for their human counterparts. A multi-agent system consists of a number of agents that interact with each other in order to accomplish a pre-defined goal.

Recent developments in agent technologies have indicated that rule concepts play an important role in modelling agents' interaction (Torre, Boella, and Verhagen, 2008). While the main objective is to design systems of autonomous agents, it is also essential that agent systems may exhibit global desirable properties. Like in human societies, such characters are ensured if the interaction of artificial software agents, too, uses organisational models whose objective is to guide agent behaviour through rule-based systems in supporting coordination, cooperation, and decision-making. In order to prove the validity of software agents it is of major importance to achieve a clear view of the application environment and to develop appropriate methods for agent-oriented modelling.

One of the most important advantages of multi-agent systems refers to their ability to decompose complex problems into more simple manageable sub-problems. According to (Bodea and Mogo, 2007), this idea can be used in many real-world areas, which includes the business problems of managing contractual agreements, service discovery, service analysis, process optimization analysis, and so on. In order to understand a business problem, agents need to understand its constituent environment consisting of objects and their interaction. One way to model this environment is use the concept of ontology which is a model of concepts and their relationships. Recent research (Genong et al., 2009) describes how agents can interact and communicate with their community by using ontologies as the communication languages.

Another important characteristic of software agents is their mobility capabilities. Such ability of software agent has been used in manufacturing companies, where agents are used to collect data over the web and to transform such data into knowledge, and help corporate decision-making processes. In addition, this mechanism facilitates the use of business intelligence and collaboration among enterprises, through appropriate communication channels. For example, researchers (Lau & Goh, 2002) report an approach by which an e-Market Place allows intelligent third-party logistics (3PL) agents to bid for customers' job requests. The intelligence lies on the e-Market Place ability to optimally decide which agents bids should be satisfied, based on a set of predefined business characteristics (pricing, preferences and fairness). Kwon, *et al* (2005) as reported in Fink *et al* (2005) combine case-based reasoning within a multi-agent framework for solving operations management problems within supply chains. Finally, Huang *et al* (2009), propose a multi agent based model for intra-organizational logistics management.

Logistics Integration with Web Services

With the advent of current information and communication technologies, the Internet has become ubiquitous and readily accessible. Together with the huge growth of online information sources, the web services model is a desirable approach to connect remote software applications and information sources, by using appropriate computer networking protocols.

A 'web service' can be described as a specific function that is delivered over the web to provide information or services to users. It can create dynamic responses and is different from conventional web sites, which presents only static information. A simple web service can be said to have the following characteristics:

Web services are modular, self-describing applications that can be published, located and invoked from just about any-where on the Web or a local network. The provider and the consumer of the XML web service do not have to worry about operating system, language, environment, or component model used to create or access the XML Web service, as they are based on ubiquitous and open Internet standards, such as XML, HTTP, and SMTP (Cauldwell, Chawla, & Chopra, 2010).

Web services usually encapsulate their implementation, i.e. do not expose it to the users. Changing the implementation of one web service function does not require changes of the invoking function.

Many languages have been proposed to facilitate the development and reuse of web services. Examples include Web Services Description Language (WSDL) and Web Service Flow Language (WSFL). As shown in Figures 3 and 4, the basic web service architecture consists of specifications (SOAP, WSDL, and UDDI) that support the interaction of a web service request with a web service provider and the potential discovery of the web service description.

One related idea of the web services model is the Service-Oriented Architecture (SOA). SOA is a model in which information sources and software functionality are delivered as individual distinct service units, which are distributed over a network and combined to create business applications to solve complex problems. SOA provides interoperability among information sources and systems, which are converted into

Figure 3. The three pillars of web services

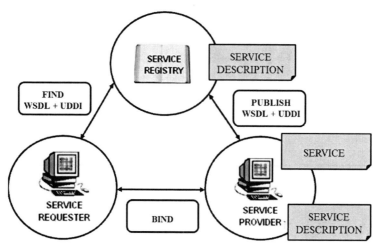

Figure 4. Levels of service oriented architecture

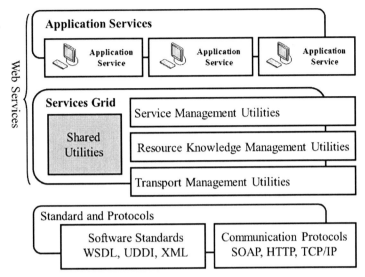

modular and flexible service components that can be requested through a standard protocol, as shown in Figure 4.

Web services can be located, invoked, and combined to provide complex business related services. Multi-agent systems are closely related to web service technology because they represent interoperable, portable and distributed business solutions. Agents and web services can be combined in different ways: agents can use web services, web services can be realized as agents, or agents can be composed of, deployed as, and dynamically extended by web services (Martin, et al. 2005).

However, if agents are not implemented with semantic (knowledge) capabilities, they fail to adapt to the continuously changing business environment. According to (Weiming, et al. 2007), the failure is related to the fact that they function based on predefined models of their environment that lack adaptability. On the other hand, traditional web-based technologies, including web services, cannot fulfill the needs of virtual enterprises applications, because they do not offer the possibility to automatically discover new services at run time. In addition, traditional web service description provides only software levels

description of their capabilities and not a semantic one. The semantically enabled web services model permits for highly dynamic provision of information technology services. Rather than establishing a long-term relationship with specific service providers, client organisations using web services negotiate and procure services in real time from a dynamic market composed of companies offering those services.

There have been several academic research works reported (Ji *et al*, 2004; Yogbin & Quofeg, 2010) in recent years for transportation system based on web services for 3PL and 4PL companies. Moreover, technologies supporting fourth party logistics information service platforms based on Web service have been proposed. Almeida et al (2011) propose a web-based software architecture for transportation and logistics management. Ji *et al* (2004) address the cross-platform and interoperability of a freight transportation system. Shen *et al* (2008) propose a web environment where each logistics company packages its business as web services. The use of Key Performance Indicators (KPIs) is proposed to make the choice of Web service more accurate and be in line with the targets of logistics activities.

Logistics Integration with Semantic Web Services

Several architectures for web service compositions have been proposed, however almost all of these solutions suffer from different disadvantages. One of the main disadvantages is attributed to the insufficiency of syntactic only description of these web services. In order to overcome this limitation, an enhanced semantic description is essential. The traditional ways for describing web service functionality do not have enough semantic information to be used in the composition. In order to achieve a complete web service description the use of ontologies is required. Such type of semantic annotated web services is called semantic web services (Mcilraith, Son and Zeng 2001). A semantic web service is therefore, the combination of semantic web and web services. The main application of the semantic web services is to achieve the automated service discovery and combination through semantic information. While WSDL (Booth and Canyang 2007) provides a syntactic description containing information regarding the structure of the input and output parameters, semantics provide a description of what the web service actually does. The semantic web and web services are two core technologies, and languages such as OWL-S (a service description language) serves as the bridge between them.

Several approaches use the semantic web services technology for logistics coordination and integration by using ontologies for services semantic matching and integration. Salomie *et al* (2008) propose a semantically enhanced broker that acts a logistics provider by planning, executing, and monitoring logistic chains, including upstream and downstream traceability, according to the requested parameters and quality of service. Fagui *et al* (2008) propose a logistics service platform which can discover, combine services and track the goods status automatically so that the quality of logistics service is greatly improved. Meanwhile, the process of services searching,

matching, composition, and calling are all achieved by information system efficiently. Hoxha *et al.* (2010), propose the semantic representation of logistic services in a framework that enables automated and intelligent techniques for discovery, ranking, execution, and efficient composition of services into more complex and flexible logistics processes. Zhang *et al.* (2008), report a detailed analysis to determine the integrated applications' pattern for modelling business processes within enterprises. They also provide the detailed description of ontology for modelling business processes within enterprises.

MAIN FOCUS OF THE CHAPTER

As argued in the previous sections, over the past years, Internet-based business service solutions have been creating an opportunity to facilitate business strategies and operations by outsourcing and leveraging logistics functions. In particular, Cloud computing offers the promise of advantages and value-added capabilities that supply chain logistics organisation require in order to remain competitive in the market place. The term, Cloud computing was first introduced in 2007. It describes a concept for the provision of resources, which are available to service customers by Internet-based interfaces. According to the United States National Institute of Standards and Technology (NIST), Cloud computing is defined as "a model for enabling ubiquitous, convenient, on-demand network access to a shared pool of configurable computing resources (e.g., networks, servers, storage, applications, and services) that can be rapidly provided and released with minimal management effort or service provider interface" (Mell & Grace, 2011). However, there are also contradicting viewpoints regarding Cloud computing viability (Dillon, Wu & Chang, 2010; Vouk, 2008; Kshetri, 2010). In this section, we introduce the basic concepts of Cloud computing in order to understand the potential of Cloud computing and its functionality in supply chain logistics. Cloud services exhibit five essential characteristics that demonstrate their relation to, and differences from, traditional computing approaches as shown in Figure 5:

- **On-Demand Self-Service:** This refers to provision of computing service facilities (e.g. server time, network storage), that can be accessed without any human intervention with a service provider.
- **Broad Network Access:** This characteristic refers to Cloud computing ability to provide service access over the network. It can be accessed through standard mechanisms that promote use by heterogeneous platforms (e.g. laptops, mobile phones, and so on).
- **Resource Pooling:** Resource pooling means that the computing resources in the Cloud are shared. This means that multiple clients may be using the same set of resources at the same time. It helps to provide physical and virtual resources dynamically assigned and reassigned according to customer demand. There is a degree of

location independence in that the customer generally has no control or knowledge over the exact location of the provided resources.

- **Rapid Elasticity:** In simple, it means that capabilities can be rapidly and elastically provisioned, in some cases automatically. This characteristic helps to quickly scale out services. To the customer of this type service, the capabilities available for provisioning often appear to be unlimited and can be purchased in any quantity at any time. The purpose of resource pooling is to avoid the capital expenditure required for the establishment of network and computing infrastructure. The reason these expenses are so high is because firms must account for spikes in demand for their services. By outsourcing to a cloud, their demand becomes "cushioned" by the cloud provider's sheer size and computing capacity.
- **Measured Service:** The cloud service providers can automatically control and optimize resource usage by leveraging a meter-

Figure 5. Main characteristics of cloud computing

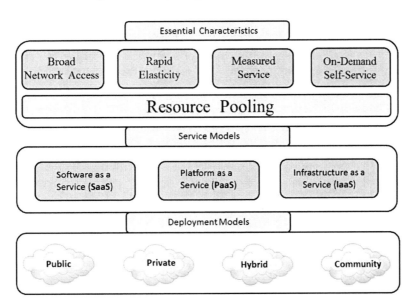

ing capability at some level of abstraction appropriate to the type of service (e.g., storage, processing, bandwidth, or active user accounts). Resource usage can be monitored, controlled, and reported—providing transparency for both the provider and consumer of the service. Cloud service provider can essentially act like other utility services (e.g., gas, electricity, water) – for example measuring the amount of service provided and reacting accordingly (both in terms of billing the client, and updating hardware and software as appropriate).

Cloud Service Models

Computer enabled service practices often change due to the enhancement of information and communication technologies, just like fashion changes over a time in consumer industries. Computing is being transformed to a model consisting of commoditized services, through a "cloud" from which users can access applications anywhere in the world on demand (Buyya, Yeo, Venugopal, Broberg, & Brandic, 2009).

Cloud computing users have access to three types of services (Mell & Grace, 2011; Zhang, Cheng & Boutaba, 2010), as follows:

- **Software as a Service (SaaS):** It focuses on providing users to run existing on-demand online applications accessed over the Internet. For example, warehouse management systems, and transportation management systems are typical applications.
- **Platform as a Service (Paas):** It allows users to create their own applications using supplier-specific tools and languages. Typical examples of this category are Google App Engine, and Microsoft Windows Azure.
- **Infrastructure as a Service (IaaS):** It provides users to run any applications of their own choice on cloud hardware (e.g.

network, memory, and storage facilities). Prominent examples of this category are AmazonEC2, GoGrid, and Flexiscale.

Clouds computing architectures can take four forms: private cloud, public cloud, hybrid cloud, and community cloud. Private clouds are built within an organization's own data center and are designed to provide and distribute virtual application, infrastructure, and communication services for internal business users. In contrast, public clouds extend the data center's capabilities by enabling the provision of the third-party providers over a communication network. A hybrid cloud system uses a combination of private and public clouds. Finally, community cloud service shares it infrastructure by a number of organizations with common interests and aims.

Application of Cloud Computing to Transport Logistics

Cloud has recently started to move from its original purpose as a vehicle for sharing computing resources to a platform for collaboration. For example, Cloud as a technology for supply chain management has started to emerge in many industries (Gardner, 2009).

Karakostas and Katsoulakos (2011) report an application of collaborative Cloud to a shipping logistics business to government (B2G) scenario, realising the concept of Single Window (UN/CEFACT, 2004). In this application, resources are totally virtualized both in terms of ownership, content, as well as in terms of location. This facility can provide a gain in productivity by eliminating labour consuming bureaucratic procedures.

Another real-world application of cloud on logistics has been reported in (Kshetri, 2010). This pilot implementation is IBM's pilot project, known as Yun (Chinese for 'cloud'). This project allows businesses to select and implement cloud services, while the platform dynamically allocates storage, server, and network resources without human input. One of the China's largest retailers with more than 10 million customers, the Wang Fu Jing department store, is reported to have deployed Cloud computing in order to share corporate information with its network of retail stores.

Another relevant work includes the Logistics Mall project (Gsell & Nagel, 2012) in Germany. This is a large research project partly funded by the Fraunhofer Society and the German Federal State North Rhine-Westphalis. The Logistic Mall aims at offering logistics applications and IT services as well as logistics process as tradable goods in a Cloud.

Cloud Computing in Shipping Logistics

This chapter therefore presents the case for applying Cloud computing in transport logistics process coordination. As explained in earlier sections, shipping transport (business) services are offered, bided for, contracted, outsourced and regulated. The system complexity arises from the tight interdependencies amongst the services in transport execution chains. Being able to coordinate services during transport execution is a prerequisite for collaboration. This involves the services of multiple participants in more complex and dynamic patterns than the typical 'publish-discover-consume' service. Hence, we argue that the highest leverage from employing an SOA approach will not come from creating and deploying standalone services, but from understanding transport chain as a community of participants, and supporting it with service enabled collaborative processes, on a Cloud infrastructure.

As said earlier Cloud is a multi-faceted concept with more than 20 definitions of it in existence (Vaquero *et al*, 2009). In this chapter, we propose a minimal definition for Cloud consisting only of the essential characteristics of service scalability, and virtualization.

By employing such principles, technology connects shippers, suppliers, and logistics partners through a Cloud-based, centralized data network, making end-to-end global supply chain visibility a reality. Companies with these capabilities are putting themselves in a different league than their less tech-savvy competitors. Cloud-based supply chain visibility technology provides an alternative to the old paradigm of constrained supply chain management systems. The new Cloud-enabled systems enable fundamental and strategic improvements in operations with the following main impacts:

- Reducing transportation spending.
- Meeting regulatory compliance requirements.
- Streamlining import/Customs processes.
- Tracking actual landed costs.

On a Cloud platform, web service chaining approaches, and both automatic and semi-automatic web service composition, can be used. In order to facilitate the composition process, web services can be managed by intelligent agents (as explained in Section 2). Both RESTful and SOAP-based web services can be employed (OASIS 2005). Using multiple intelligent agents, each following its own goal during the composition process, the composition effort can be distributed and the performance bottlenecks avoided. Web-services can be annotated using the OWL-S semantic language in order to specify their purpose (Section 2.2).

The first step is to identify services, the requirements they are intended to fulfil, and the anticipated dependencies between them. Methods such as IBM's SOMA (Arsanjan, 2004) can be employed for this purpose.

High-level business process functionality in the transport chain can be externalised as large-grained services for procuring, planning, executing and monitoring transportation chains. Finer grained services - can then by identified by examining the message exchanges between participants in transport chains. These services can be implemented by wrapping adaptors around, or by componetising legacy functionality (current IT systems used for transport planning, execution and monitoring).

Techniques such as goal-service modelling (Bieberstein *et al*, 2008) will filter through the candidate services that have been identified, by selecting those that support directly goals of the transportation chain.

New services can be discovered using a middle-out view consisting of goal-service modeling to validate and unearth other services, by either top-down or bottom-up service identification approaches. It ties services to goals and sub-goals, key performance indicators, and metrics.

- Specifying services including the functional capabilities they provide, what capabilities consumers are expected to provide, the protocols or rules for using them, and the service information exchanged between consumers and providers.
- Defining service consumers and providers, what requisition and services they consume and provide, how they are connected and how the service functional capabilities are used by consumers and implemented by providers in a manner consistent with both the service specification protocols and fulfilled requirements (see Figure 6).

Simple services a one-way interaction provided by a participant on a port represented as a UML interface. The participant receives operations on this port and may provide results to the caller (see Table 1).

SOLUTIONS AND RECOMMENDATIONS

As explained in the introductory section of this Chapter, transport logistics domain is by its nature geographically distributed. Business operations and relationships are geographically defined, in terms for example, of shipping lines or corridors operated by carriers. Intermediaries such as freight forwarders connect shippers with customers in-

Figure 6. Modelling transport services with SOAML

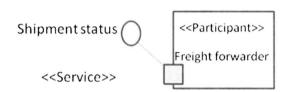

dependently from their locations by combining the services of possibly multiple carriers. Third and fourth party logistic (3PL and 4PL) service providers have decoupled the service consumers (shippers) and providers (carriers), but they have effectively created new points of centralisation in the transportation chains (see Figure 7).

Consider for example the following scenario:

Carrier C1 uses Freight Forwarder 1 (FF1) to organise the complete door-to-door transport. FF1 uses another Freight Forwarder (FF2) and one Transport Service Provider (TSP-C) to organise transport from origin to destination (Location O to Location D). FF2 uses two Transport Service Providers (TSP-A and TSP-B) to deliver the appropriate service...

Assuming that an SOA infrastructure is in place to support the above transport chain, the number of fixed service interfaces and contracts can grow very large. The main coordinator of the transportation chain (FF1 in the above example) will be responsible for managing not only its direct contracts with its sub-contractors (FF2 and TSP-C), but also to at least be aware of contracts established at other tiers of the chain (e.g. between FF2 and TSP-A) in order to maintain a complete overview of the status of the transport chain's performance during execution.

We propose that such fixed and inflexible service connections can be virtualised through a Cloud infrastructure (see Figure 8).

As SOA virtualises the service implementation through an interface (such as WSDL), the Cloud

Table 1. Some typical service types in transport logistics

Service Name	Service Type	Provider	Consumer(s)	Intermediary	Simple/Complex
Ship arrival and departing notifications	B2A	Port authority	Carrier	'Single Window' system	Simple
Cargo declaration	B2A	Customs	Shipper	'Single Window' system	Complex
Cargo customs clearance service	B2B	Handling agent	Shipper	Customs	Complex
Stevedoring services	B2B	Stevedore	Carrier	-	Simple
Cargo consolidation service	B2B	Freight forwarder	Shipper	-	Simple

Figure 7. Multi-party services

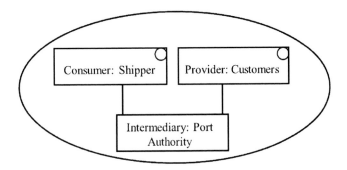

Figure 8. Virtualising the service on the cloud

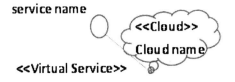

virtualises the service provider, thus freeing the service consumer from having to establish dedicated service connections ('clients') to every service provider. Figure 7 illustrates this idea by making available service interfaces on the Cloud. Consumers connect to services through this interface, with the Cloud implementing the service and acting therefore as both a broker and a service provider. A Service Contract defines the terms, conditions, interfaces and choreography that interacting participants must agree to (directly or indirectly) for the service to be enacted—the full specification of a service which includes all the information, choreography and any other "terms and conditions" of the service.

This approach represents a win-win situation for both providers and consumers. It frees consumers from the need to support dedicated clients for each current and potential provider, and it frees providers from the need to host and support the implementation of their services.

For example, port arrival/departure notification services are currently provided by some ports, allowing ships to submit their reports online. Thus, a carrier who wants to take advantage of such services is forced to provide and maintain separate clients for each of the ports visited by its ships. A Cloud-virtualised notification service would allow the decoupling of carrier/port with the former having to maintain only a single client to the virtual service and the latter freed from the responsibility of having to provide and support an infrastructure for the notification service.

FUTURE RESEARCH DIRECTIONS

Cloud computing is an emerging and disruptive technology for the transport logistics sector. Schuldt *et al* (2011) propose that logistics planning and control as a promising application for clouds. However, they argue that two prerequisites must be met for Cloud-based logistics control. Firstly, the platform-as-a-service layer (see Section 3) must provide synchronisation of the physically distributed real-world material flows and the data flows in the cloud. Secondly, appropriate and scalable control software must be implemented on the software-as-a-service (defined in Section 3) layer. Clearly, typical Cloud concerns such as issues of security and confidentiality apply also to the transport logistics domain. There are also other technical and business obstacles that need to be tackled and further research is required across several areas of Cloud computing.

CONCLUSION

This chapter has argued that the Cloud can provide the next enabler for collaboration in transport logistics, currently realised by technologies such as portals and electronic exchanges, and more recently by SOA. Exchanges have reduced the cost of getting consumers and providers together, and SOA has reduced, to an extent, the cost of their technical interoperability and integration. The Cloud will take things one step further, by abstracting not only services but also their provision infrastructures, as shown in Figure 9. Thus, we expect the transport service aggregator of the future to be a Cloud operator that will offer to transport service providers a platform for their services, and to consumers a virtual environment in which they can access services.

Figure 9. The vision of a cloud oriented transport logistics sector

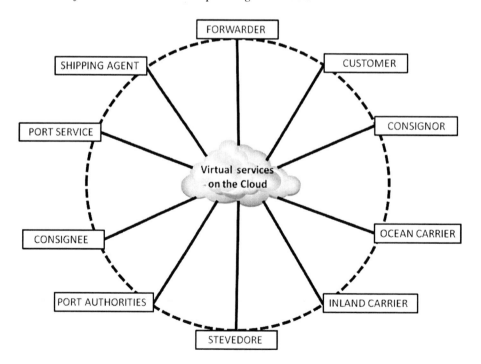

REFERENCES

Arsanjan, A. (2004). Service-oriented modeling and architecture: How to identify, specify, and realize services for your SOA. *IBM Developer Works*. Retrieved from http://www.ibm.com/developerworks/library/ws-soa-design1/

Bade, D., Mueller, J., & Youd, B. (1999). *Technology in the next level of supply chain outsourcing: Leveraging the capabilities of fourth party logistics*. Retrieved from http://bade.ascet.com

Bieberstein, N., Jones, K., Laird, R. G., & Mitra, T. (2008). *Executing SOA: A methodology for service modeling and design*. New York, NY: IBM Press.

Bodea, C., & Mogos, R. (2007). An electronic market space architecture based on intelligent agents and data mining technologies. *Informatica Economica Journal*, *11*(4), 115–118.

Booth, D., & Canyang, L. (2007). *Web services description language (WSDL) version 2.0 part 0: Primer*. Retrieved from http://www.w3.org/TR/2007/REC-wsdl20-primer-20070626

Buyya, R., Yeo, C. S., Venugopal, S., Broberg, J., & Brandic, I. (2009). Cloud computing and emerging IT platforms: Vision, hype, and reality for delivering computing as the 5th utility. *Future Generation Computer Systems*, *25*(6), 599–616. doi:10.1016/j.future.2008.12.001

Cauldwell, P., Chawala, R., & Chopra, V. (2001). *Professional XML web services*. Wrox Press.

Chopra, S., & Meindl, P. (2012). *Supply chain management*. London, UK: Pearson Education Limited.

Dillon, T., Wu, C., & Chang, E. (2010). Cloud computing: Issues and challenges. In *Proceedings of the 24th IEEE International Conference on Advanced Information Networking and Applications*, (pp. 27-33). IEEE Press.

Ellinger, A. E., Lynch, D. F., Andzulis, J. K., & Smith, R. J. (2003). B-to-B e-commerce: A content analytical assessment of motor carrier websites. *Journal of Business Logistics*, *24*(1), 119–220. doi:10.1002/j.2158-1592.2003.tb00037.x

Evangelista, P. (2002). Information and communication technology key factor in logistics and freight transport. In Ferrara, G., & Morvill, A. (Eds.), *Training in Logistics and Freight Transport Industry: The Experience of the European Project ADAPT-FIT* (pp. 15–36). London, UK: Ashgate Ltd.

Fagui, L., Kun, L., & Yang, Z. (2008). *Semantic web services and its application in third-party logistics*. Paper presented at the 2008 International Workshop on Education Technology and Training & 2008 International Workshop on Geoscience and Remote Sensing. New York, NY.

Gardner, D. (2009, August 25). How the cloud aids supply chain recalls cloud computing uniquely enables product and food recall processes across supply chains. *Cloud Computing Journal*.

Genong, Y., Liping, D., Wenli, Y., Peisheng, Z., & Peng, Y. (2009). Multi-agent systems for distributed geospatial modeling, simulation and computing. In *Handbook of Research on Geoinformatics* (pp. 196–205). Hershey, PA: IGI Global.

Gsell, H., & Nagel, R. (2012). *Application integration in the logistics mall*. Washington, DC: Society for Design and Process Science.

Gudmundsson, S. V., & Walczuch, R. (1999). The development of electronic markets in logistics. *The International Journal of Logistics Management*, *10*(2), 99–113. doi:10.1108/09574099910806021

Hoxha, J., Scheuermann, A., & Bloehdorn, S. (2010). An approach to formal and semantic representation of logistics services. In *Proceedings of the ECAI 2010 Workshop on Artificial Intelligence and Logistics*, (pp. 73-78). ECAI.

Jennings, N., Sycara, K., & Wooldridge, M. (1998). A roadmap of agent research and development. *Journal of Autonomous Agents and Multi-agent Systems, 1*(1), 7–36. doi:10.1023/A:1010090405266

Ji, C., Li, M., & Li, L. (2004). Freight transportation system based onweb service. In *Proceedings of the IEEE International Conference on Services Computing (SCC 2004)*. IEEE Press.

Karakostas, B., & Katsoulakos, T. (2011). A collaborative resource-based cloud architecture for freight logistics. *CLOSER*, 141-144.

Kshetri, N. (2010). Cloud computing in developing economics. *IEEE Computer, 43*(10), 47–55. doi:10.1109/MC.2010.212

Lynagh, P. M., Murphy, P. R., Poist, R. F., & Grazer, W. R. (2001). Web-based informational practices of logistics service providers: an empirical assessment. *Transportation Journal, 40*(4), 34–45.

Lysons, K., & Gillingham, M. (2003). *Purchasing and supply chain management*. London, UK: Pearson Education Limited.

Martin, D., Burstein, M., McIlraith, S., Paolucci, M., & Sycara, K. (2005). OWL-S and agent-based systems. In *Extending Web Services Technologies: The Use of Multi-Agent Approaches* (pp. 53–77). New York, NY: Springer.

Mathe, H., & Shapiro, R. (1993). *Integrating service strategy in the manufacturing company*. London, UK: Chapman & Hall.

Mcilraith, S., & Son, C. T. (2002). Adapting golog for composition of semantic web services. In *Proceedings of the 8th International Conference on Principles and Knowledge Representation and Reasoning (KR-02)*, (pp. 482-496). San Francisco, CA: Morgan Kaufmann.

McKinnon, A. (1999). The outsourcing of logistical activities. In Walter, D. (Ed.), *Global Logistics and Distribution Planning* (pp. 215–234). London, UK: Kogan Page.

Mell, P., & Grace, T. (2011). *A NIST definition of cloud computing*. Retrieved November 1, 2011, from http://csrc.nist.gov/publications/nistpubs/800-145/SP800-145.pdf

Regan, A. C., & Song, J. (2001). An industry in transition: Third party logistics in the information age. In *Proceedings of the 80th Annual Meeting of the Transportation Research Board*. Washington, DC: IEEE.

Salomie, I., Dinsoreanu, M., Pop, C. B., & Suciu, S. L. (2008). Logistic chain generation with traceability features using web services composition. In *Proceedings of the 2008 IEEE International Conference on Automation, Quality and Testing. Robotics*. IEEE Press: *1*, 393–397.

Sauvage, T. (2003). The relationship between technology and logistics third-party providers. *International Journal of Physical Distribution and Logistics Management, 33*(3), 236–253. doi:10.1108/09600030310471989

Schuldt, A., Hribernik, K. A., Gehrke, J. D., Thoben, K.-D., & Herzog, O. (2011). Towards fourth-party logistics providers: A business model for cloud-based autonomous logistics. In *Proceedings of CLOSER 2011*. CLOSER.

Sheffi, Y. (1990). Third party logistics: Present and future prospects. *Journal of Business Logistics, 11*(2), 27–39.

Stough, R. R. (2001). New technologies in logistics management. In Brewer, (Eds.), *Handbook of Logistics and Supply Chain Management* (p. 517). London, UK: Elsevier Science Limited.

Tilanus, B. (1997). *Information systems in logistics and transportation*. London, UK: Pergamon.

Torre, L., Boella, G., & Verhagen (Eds.). (2008). Normative multi-agent systems. *Journal of Autonomous Agents and Multi-Agent Systems, 17*(1).

Vouk, M. (2008). Cloud computing – Issues, research and implementations. *Journal of Computing and Information Technology, 16*(4), 235–246.

Weiming, S., Qi, H., Shuying, W., Yinsheng, L., & Hamada, G. (2007). An agent-based service-oriented integration architecture for collaborative intelligent manufacturing. *Robotics and Computer-integrated Manufacturing, 23*, 315–325. doi:10.1016/j.rcim.2006.02.009

Yongbin, H., & Qifeng, W. (2010). Study on the forth party logistics information service platform based on web services. In *Proceedings of the International Conference on Innovative Computing and Communication and 2010 Asia-Pacific Conference on Information Technology and Ocean Integration Architecture for Collaborative Intelligent Manufacturing. Robotics and Computer-integrated Manufacturing*, IEEE, *23*, 315–325.

Zhang, K., Xu, R., Zhang, Y., Sai, Y., & Wang, X. (2008). An ontology supported semantic web service composition method in enterprise. In *Proceedings of the IEEE International Multi-Symposiums on Computer and Computational*, (pp. 222-227). IEEE Press.

Zhang, Q., Cheng, L., & Boutaba, R. (2010). Cloud computing: State-of-the-art and research challenges. *Journal of Internet Services and Applications, 1*(1), 7–18. doi:10.1007/s13174-010-0007-6

ADDITIONAL READING

Ajzen, I., & Fishbein, M. (1975). *Belief, attitude, intention and behavior: An introduction to theory and research*. Reading, MA: Addison-Wesley Publishing Company.

Armbrust, M., Fox, A., Griffith, R., Joseph, A. D., Katz, R., & Konwinski, A. (2010). A view of cloud computing. *Communications of the ACM, 53*(4), 50–58. doi:10.1145/1721654.1721672

Benlian, A., & Hess, T. (2011). Opportunities and risks of software-as-a-service: Findings from a survey of IT executives. *Decision Support Systems, 52*(1), 232–246. doi:10.1016/j.dss.2011.07.007

Cardinal. (2011). *About cardinal*. Retrieved November 25, 2011, http://www.cardlog.com/about-cardinal

Coper, M. C., Lambert, D. M., & Pagh, J. D. (1998). What should be the transportation provider's role in supply chain management? In *Proceedings of the 8th World Conference on Transport Research*. IEEE.

Cutlip, R. (2004). *Ontology-based web services for business integration*. Retrieved March 15, 2007, from http://www.alphaworks.ibm.com/tech/owsbi

Dillman, D. A. (2000). *Mail and internet surveys: The total design method*. New York, NY: John Wiley & Sons.

Dillon, T., Wu, C., & Chang, E. (2010). Cloud computing: Issues and challenges. In *Proceedings of the 24th IEEE International Conference on Advanced Information Networking and Applications*, (pp. 27-33). IEEE Press.

Dumitru, R., Holger, L., & Keller, U. (Eds.). (2006, October 21). *D2v1.3: Web service modeling ontology (WSMO)*. Retrieved March 15, 2007, from http://www.wsmo.org/TR/d2/v1.3/

Farrell, J., & Lausen, H. (Eds.). (2006). *Semantic annotations for WSDL and XML schema (SAWSDL)*. Retrieved March 15, 2007, from http://www.w3.org/TR/ sawsdl/

Ginsburg, S. (2011). *Jaguar freight receives Descartes excellence and innovation award: Leader recognized for cutting-edge transportation management system (TMS) applications.* Retrieved November 20, 2011, from http://www.marketwatch.com/story/jaguar-freight-receives-descartes-excellence-and-innovation-award-2011-11-16

Han, Y. (2010). On the clouds: A new way of computing. *Information Technology & Libraries, 29*(2), 87–92.

Heflin, J., & Hendler, J. (2001). A portrait of the semantic web in action. *IEEE Intelligent Systems, 16*(2), 54–59. doi:10.1109/5254.920600

Helo, P., & Szekely, B. (2005). Logistics information systems: An analysis of software solutions for supply chain co-ordination. *Industrial Management & Data Systems, 105*(1), 5–18. doi:10.1108/02635570510575153

Holcomb, M. C., Ponomarov, S. Y., & Manrodt, K. B. (2011). The relationship of supply chain visibility to frm performance. *Supply Chain Forum: An International Journal, 12*(2).

Imrc. (2008). *Electronic logistics marketplaces research report.* Cardiff, UK: Cardiff University Innovative Manufacturing Research Centre.

Jeffery, K., & Neidecker-Lutz, B. (Eds.). (2010). *The future of cloud computing opportunities for European cloud computing beyond 2010: Expert group report public version 1.0.* Retrieved from http://cordis.europa.eu/fp7/ict/ssai/docs/cloud-report-final.pdf

Jones, S. D. (2011). Cloud computing is changing how businesses work, KPMG finds. *The Wall Street Journal.*

Juretic, J. (2011). *ebuilder talks to global logistics media.* Retrieved November 1, 2011, http://www.youtube.com/watch?v=ycaOSMhCPXM

Koomneef, R. (2011). *Global e-commerce in the cloud.* Retrieved October 1, 2011, from http://blog.moduslink.com/bid/64259/Global-e-Commerce-in-the-Cloud

KPMG. (2011). *Embracing the cloud: Global forces shaping the service provider market.* Retrieved from http://www.kpmg.com/Global/en/IssuesAndInsights/ArticlesPublications/Documents/embracing-cloud.pdf

Kreger, H. (2001, May). *Web services conceptual architecture (WSCA 1.0).* New York, NY: IBM Software Group.

Marston, S., Li, Z., Bandyopadhyay, S., Zhang, J., & Ghalsasi, A. (2011). Cloud computing — The business perspective. *Decision Support Systems, 51*, 176–189. doi:10.1016/j.dss.2010.12.006

Martin, D., Burstein, M., Hobbs, J., Lassila, O., McDermott, D., McIlraith, S., et al. (2007). *OWL-S: Semantic markup for web services.* Retrieved March, 16 2007, from http://www.ai.sri.com/daml/services/owl-s/1.2/overview/

Martin, J. A. (2010). *Should you move your small business to the cloud?* Retrieved November 1, 2011, http://www.pcworld.com/businesscenter/article/188173/should_you_move_your_small_business_to_the_cloud.html

McAfee, A. (2011, November). What every CEO needs to know about the cloud. *Harvard Business Review*, 124–132.

McKendrick, J. (2011). *Cloud computing set to 'skyrocket,' driven by economy: Survey.* Retrieved from http://www.forbes.com/fdc/welcome_mjx.shtml

Mell, P., & Grace, T. (2011). *A NIST definition of cloud computing.* Retrieved November 1, 2011, from http://csrc.nist.gov/publications/nistpubs/800-145/SP800-145.pdf

Microsoft. (2011). *Learn more about the benefits of cloud computing*. Retrieved December 3, 2011, from http://www.microsoft.com/en-in/server-cloud/readynow/default.aspx?resourceId=Private_Cloud

Nguyen, A. (2011). *Cloud servics air transport industry plans private cloud*. Retrieved November 1, 2011, from http://www.computerworld.com/s/article/355807/Air_Transport_Industry_Plans_Private_Cloud

Novak, D. (2011). *How cloud computing helps 3PLs differentiate to gain a competitive advantage*. Retrieved from November 1, 2011, http://www.supplychainbrain.com/content/headline-news/single-article/article/how-cloud-computing-helps-3pls-differentiate-to-gain-a-competitive-advantage/

Pallos, M. S. (2001, December). Service-oriented architecture: A primer. *EAI Journal*, 32-35.

Poozhikunnel, J. (2007). *Building an enterprise service bus to support service-oriented architecture*. Retrieved August 19, 2007, from http://www.15seconds.com/issue/050519.htm

PRNewswire. (2011). *Cardinal hosted logistics™ receives TMWSuite 2011 technology award*. Retrieved November 25, 2011, from http://www.prnewswire.com/news-releases/cardinal-hosted-logistics-receives-tmwsuite-2011-technology-award-130657243.html

RedPrairie. (2011). Business software and service companies: RJW Transport doubles warehousing revenue with RedPrairie's on-demand WMS. *Journal of Transportation*, 92-93.

Reuters. (2011). *Cloud computing disappoints early adopters: Survey*. Retrieved October 10, 2011, from http://www.rawstory.com/rs/2011/10/04/cloud-computing-disappoints-early-adopters-survey/

Rust, R. T., & Kannan, P. K. (2003). E-service: A new paradigm for business. *Communications of the ACM*, *46*(6). doi:10.1145/777313.777336

Schramm, T., Wright, J., Seng, D., & Jones, D. (2010). *Supply chain executives should evaluate what cloud computing can mean for their operations: Asking the right questions is a good place to start*. Retrieved October 1, 2011, from http://www.accenture.com/SiteCollectionDocuments/PDF/10-2460-Supply_Chain_Cloud_PoV_vfinal.pdf

Sleeper, B. (2003). *Toward the service-oriented enterprise*. Retrieved March 15, 2007, from http://www.Webservicespro.com/Webservicespro-69-20030903TowardstheServiceOrientedEnterprise.pdf

Srinivasan, K., Kekre, S., & Mukhopadhyay, T. (1994). Impact of electronic data interchange technology on JIT Shipments. *Management Science*, *40*, 1291–1304. doi:10.1287/mnsc.40.10.1291

SupplyChainBrain. (2011). *The cloud could be answer you need, but there are questions to ask first*. Retrieved December 13, 2011, from http://www.supplychainbrain.com/content/nc/technology-solutions/cloud-saas-on-demand-systems/single-article-page/article/the-cloud-could-be-answer-you-need-but-there-are-question-to-ask-first/

W3C. (2004). *Web services architecture*. Retrieved March 15, 2007, from http://www.w3.org/TR/ws-arch/Watson, S. T. (2011). *Catch a cloud*. Retrieved November 20, 2011, http://www.buffalonews.com/incoming/article640773.ece

Weinhardt, C., Anandasivam, A., Blau, B., Borissov, N., Meinl, T., Michalk, W., & Stößer, J. (2009). Cloud computing: Classification, business models, and research directions. *Business & Information Systems Engineering*, *1*(5), 391–399. doi:10.1007/s12599-009-0071-2

KEY TERMS AND DEFINITIONS

Cloud Computing: The application of principles of elasticity, on demand distributed computation units as the computing platform.

E-Logistics: The use of electronic (e-business) technologies for the management of transport operations.

Logistics Collaboration Platform: An electronic platform used by transport logistic participants to carry out collaborative processes.

Semantic Web Service: A service whose interface and properties are described in terms of a semantic formalism such as an ontology.

Service Oriented Architecture (SOA): A modeling paradigm for architecting software systems in terms of collaborating web services.

Transport Logistics: In general, logistics is the planning, organisation, management, execution, and control of moving goods between a source and a destination. Transport logistics focuses on the actual transport operations.

UDDI: A standard for web-based, electronic directories that contain detailed information about businesses, the services they provide (including web services), and the means for utilizing these services.

Virtual Service: A service whose address and port have been virtualized (i.e. located on the 'Cloud').

Chapter 7
A Web Application for Supply Chain Traceability

Ioannis Manikas
University of Greenwich, UK

ABSTRACT

The efficiency of a traceability system depends on the ability to identify uniquely each unit that is produced and distributed in a way that enables the continuous tracking from the primary production to the retail point of sale. An efficient traceability system must follow some rules that define which data must be gathered and stored in each stage of the supply chain. This is achieved by standardization of the gathered data and typification of the messages that enable storing and communication of the data. This chapter presents a Web-platform that will be able to support efficiently food traceability by monitoring and administering the data gathered and recorded in a central database. This application will be user friendly and provide the ability to keep, display, and communicate information through widely implemented technologies, such as the Internet and electronic mail services.

INTRODUCTION

During the past decade, the credibility of Food Industry safety schemes was heavily challenged after a number of food crises, such as Bovine Spongiform Encephalopathy (BSE) and foot-and-mouth disease. The necessity of sufficient traceability systems to tackle such crises brought into light the need for reassessing and updating traceability systems currently implemented in the food sector. Thus, the successful control of the physical flow of the products along the supply chain and product safety assurance depends on the existence of an efficient traceability system (Giraud and Halawany, 2006). This system must be able to identify each and every single unit produced and distributed from farm to fork. Apart from tackling food borne crises, a traceability system shall be able to meet the differentiated and dynamic demands for transparency information by consumers and government as well as by the supply chain actors (Triekenens, 2012).

According to the definitions at Article 3 of the E.C. General Food Law Regulation 178/2002, traceability in the food sector is defined as the ability to trace and follow a food, feed, food pro-

DOI: 10.4018/978-1-4666-3914-0.ch007

ducing animal or substance through all stages of production and distribution (European Union, 2002). Stages of production and distribution refer to any stage including import, from and including the primary production of food, up to and including its sale or supply to the final consumer and, where relevant to food safety, the production, manufacture and distribution of feed (Herdon et al, 2006). This is the newest general regulation on the hygiene of foodstuffs, where hygiene rules will apply from farm to fork. Primary responsibility is taken by the food business: Hazard Analysis and Critical Control Point (HACCP) and more recently ISO 22000 (Arvanitoyannis et al., 2005). The E.U. directive 178/2002 regarding the establishment of the European Food Safety Agency (EFSA) set the foundations towards more strict traceability requirements in food sector and paved the way for further legal requirements at a national level assuring information flow transparency and efficient traceability in the Food Industry of each country-member of the E.U. According to the E.U. directive 178/2002, which took effect on January 1st 2005, "...food business shall have in-place systems and procedures to identify the other businesses to which their products have been supplied. This information shall be made available to the competent authorities on demand."

This Regulation does not lay a specific methodology to be followed by all food business operators. Instead, food companies are free to choose those mechanisms that fit their needs and ensure efficient traceability for their products. According to ISO Quality Standards, traceability is defined as: "the ability to trace the history, application or location of an entity by means of recorded information" (ISO 8402:1994). Moreover, the same institution introduced at the beginning of 2006, two new standards that define the requirements for a traceability system within a food safety management system and the data that needs to be retained (ISO 22000:2005 - Food Safety Management Systems - Requirements, and ISO 22519 - Traceability System in the Agriculture

Food Chain - General Principles for Design and Development). ISO 22000:2005, gives the basic requirements for a food safety management system to ensure safe food supply chains. ISO 22000 incorporates the principles of the CAC 's Hazard Analysis and Critical Control Point (HACCP) system for food hygiene.

The effectiveness of a traceability system lies on the ability to collect information related to product quality and consumer safety (Resende-Filho and Buhr, 2008; Sasazaki et al., 2004). There is a wide range of traceability systems currently used in food chains; from paper- based to IT enabled (Food Standards Agency, 2002). IT enabled systems have been developed and introduced over the last years in the food sector, based on technologies implemented in more sophisticated industries, such as pharmaceuticals (Wilson and Clarke, 1998). Bar code and Radio Frequency Identification (RFID) technologies have been implemented in food chains, reducing errors associated with manual data handling, and make the tracking more feasible (Karkkainen, 2003; Salin, 1998). The development of software systems and databases (data pools) increases the effectiveness in collecting, transmitting and analyzing larger volumes of safety and quality related data (Food Standards Agency, 2002; Wilson and Clarke., 1998).

REVIEW OF LITERATURE ON TRACEABILITY SUPPORT SYSTEMS

Traceability Support in Agrifood SMEs

In the agrifood sector most software that support traceability have been own developed by the companies and often are supported by record and data that are maintained in printed form. Most SMEs do not have the possibility of adopting complicated technologies as that of ERP systems. Van der Vorst et al (2004) propose the solution of central database that will serve mainly the small producers, in which they can access through a personal computer and an Internet connection. By the same research it was proved that the differences in traceability systems are not presented in country level but in supply chain level.

One of the main factors recognized that prevent effective traceability along the fresh produce supply chain is that most agrifood trading and retailing SMEs are unable to manage such systems. The weakness of supporting and managing traceability systems from SMEs mainly derives from the high cost of consolidation and management of a great volume of required information and is recognized by Daives (2004) and also reported by Kelepouris et al (2007). Still, the existing legislation does not place detailed requirements regarding supply chain traceability; neither is given a standard model to follow in product coding. According to Triekenens (2012), traceability management solutions should always be accompanied by matching governance mechanisms and quality and safety standards.

The traceable unit depends from the packing process, the lack of which makes traceability rather difficult to achieve. According to Garcia et al (2003), in many cases the produced quantities are often very low for backing up the cost of an investment on a system that will assure efficient traceability. Van Dorp (2004) was led to similar conclusions through his research in which a line of constraining factors are determined regarding the implementation of IT systems for supporting traceability. Van Dorp reports that software houses seldom develop individual applications for traceability management and usually agrifood companies ensure traceability of their products by combining printed record keeping procedures with electronic data bases.

Factors Affecting Traceability

A relative unity of opinions was identified between authors regarding the factors that affect traceability in the agrifood supply chain. The distinctive structure of each agrifood supply chain, the position that each company holds in it as well as the relations between supply chain members, are commonly recognized as the main factors that affect traceability effectiveness, so much in business-to-business as in door-to-door level. The existence within an agrifood company of systems aiming in managing transactions, quality and production processes, along with their supportive technologies, also plays an important role for achieving efficient traceability. Finally, the existing product packaging methods and materials also affect substantially the choice of a suitable traceability system and its efficiency.

The stricter requirements for traceability force the agrifood industry stakeholders to assemble and maintain more information than they use to until now. This volume of data should be filed and stored in such way and means that allow easy access and precise retraction. In case that a problem occurs, errors or inaccuracies in the retraction and process of data may cause from false recall to shutdown. Data should be assembled and stored in real time, following the product physical flow, in door-to-door level as much as along the supply chain. The companies should keep the cost of this process in low level in order to avoid an increase in the product retail price.

ICT vs. Paper-Based Systems

According to Schwagele (2005), agrifood stakeholders should avoid printed record keeping or manual data entry but should apply integrated traceability systems that allow product follow-up at all stages of production, storage and trading, systems that will be capable to correspond immediately in queries emanated from consumers or stakeholders. Such integrated systems were developed and imported in the agrifood sector based on technologies that already been used in more sophisticated industries, such as pharmaceutical, automobile industry etc. The import of technologies as the bar-codes and Radio Frequency

Identification (RFID) in the agrifood sector has decreased the rates of error related to data management and human intervention and increased traceability effectiveness (Salin 1998; Karkkainen, 2003). The development of IT solutions increases the effectiveness of collection, distribution and analysis of bigger volume of data related with product quality and consumer safety (Wilson and Clarke, 1998; Food Standards Agency, 2002).

Contrary to Schwagele (2005), Knight et al (2002) support that a traceability system should be always adapted on the abilities of each company, in terms of investment and application of new technologies, as long as this will cover legislation requirements. This argument is also supported by the report of Food Standards Agency (FSA) according to which even large companies of the sector follow printed record keeping procedures in order to support traceability of their products. Karlsen et al (2011) stresses out the important of human motivation for the successful implementation of a traceability system; during their research on developing a traceability system for the fish industry, it became clear that human behaviour towards the acceptance of the system was strongly affected by at least three factors: 1) their day-to-day routines and the possibility to work with other activities, 2) identification of necessary investment to be able to trace the products and 3) motivation.

According to the Japanese Committee that published the Governing Directives of Traceability Systems Development in March 2003, it is not mandatory that a traceability system should be based on information technology tools. The effectiveness of a traceability system is based on the ability of quality and safety related data collection. A great variety of traceability systems is implemented in food supply chains, from less evolved systems based on printed record keeping, up to systems that are based entirely on IT solutions. What is important is that a traceability system should follow already applied practices and correspond with the culture of the company (Food Standards Agency, 2002). Traceability support is achieved through systems that monitor product and data flows.

System Structure

A traceability system is structured by two main entities: products and activities such as supply, sale, and distribution that describe product flow (Figure 1). A group of features is defined for each entity, such as type, quantity, duration, and each

Figure 1. Typical traceability system entity structure (source: Moe, 1998)

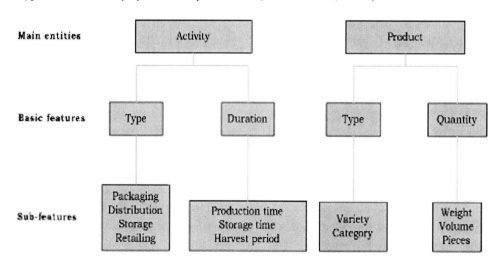

feature is described by sub-features (Moe, 1998). Moreover, a traceability system is characterized by two basic elements: the product routes and the extent of traceability. The product routes describe the path and the means with that the products are recognized along the stages of production, distribution and retailing. The extent of traceability is determined by the type and the number of sub-features selected for describing the entities features (Moe, 1998).

According to Kelepouris et al (2005) each traceability system should meet a line of requirements. Firstly, all tracked products in the supply chain should be recognized uniquely. In addition, the way a product is identified should be the same for all members of the supply chain. In opposite case, data synchronization would be essential, and this would lead to increase of cost and low quality of data. The level of recognition determines traceability accuracy and resolution (Jansen-Vullers et al, 2003). The highest level of analysis in the chain is that of single item identification. In this case the cost and the complexity of information management are significantly increased.

A lower level of accuracy is that of the identification of boxes, pallets or lots, that is a much more cost saving.

Traceability Application and Benefits

Rabade and Alfaro (2006) conducted empirical case research on the effect of different forms of relations between customer-supplier in the implementation of traceability systems. The research was taken place in the Spanish fresh produce industry. After a thorough review of literature and the empirical study, Rabade and Alfaro (2006) concluded that traceability is mainly a mechanism that promotes competitiveness. This comes in contrast with the definition given by the European Commission as well as with the outcomes of other researchers that do support that traceability is mainly a mechanism that allows the effective detection of origin of products and their compo-

nents in the event of a food crisis (Hobbs, 2006; Knight et al, 2002; European Commission, 2000).

Moe (1998) suggested the two main contexts in which traceability can be used and in which it covers the fundamental concepts included in advanced traceability systems related to products and their processing: a) Product; in which it relates material, processing history, distribution, and location, and b) Data; in which it relates calculations and data generated through the quality loop. Full traceability requires information for the total product's lifecycle. In cases of supply chains where food products are subject to alteration operations, such as slaughtering and chopping in meat industry or milking and pasteurization in dairy industry, full traceability requires information about animal breeding procedures, batch dispersion, bill of materials and distribution information. On the contrary, in cases of non-processed products, such as fresh produce, full traceability requires only farming and distribution information. Distribution information includes lot and packaging information.

Verdenius (2006) approaches the definition of a traceability system by defining three main orientations. These are the position, state, and quality. The position is reported in the dimension of logistics processes in the physical flow of products, defining the place, the time, and the logistics state in which the product is found. The state is reported in the dimension of processes realised in the physical flow of product, defining conditions, and stages of treatment during production and distribution. Quality is reported in the dimension of quality of product while this is moved along the supply chain. Quality is particularly significant for a fresh produce traceability system, because in this sector quality is found in dynamic state and is altered constantly while the product is moved along the supply chain. Golan et al (2004) agree with the above stressing that in case of development of a traceability system for fresh produce it is of fundamental importance to define the qualitative features and the corresponding indicators that will monitor the changes in produce quality from the early stages of the supply chain. Wognum et al (2011) introduce the environmental impact of the manufacturing and distribution processes monitored by a traceability system as a product quality dimension, just as technical product characteristics. Data regarding the environmental impact can be sourced by the implementation of Life Cycle Assessment; LCA may add to the transparency of the supply chain by providing information to consumers and other relevant stakeholders on the environmental impact of a specific product (Roy, 2009).

According to Verdenius (2006), there are three basic operations accomplished by a traceability system; these are the identification, the registration and elaboration of data. Identification refers to the connection of physical product with the information that is reported in this product and is useful for its identification and distinction from other similar products. Registration allows access - via the primary information required for product identification - in secondary information regarding the product, such as production or processing stage, supply chain stage etc. Data elaboration depends from the objectives of each traceability system. As minimal objective of such system can be defined the evaluation of crises and the control of problematic products. Finally, Verdenius (2006) demonstrates a model of traceability systems development constituted by seven steps (Figure 2). This model is analyzed in detail in related literature (Scheer, 2006; Hulzebos and Koenderink, 2006; Koenderink and Hulzebos, 2006; Klafft, 2006).

OPERATIONAL MODEL VALIDATION

Technological Background

In most food manufacturing sectors it is rather convenient to include traceability related procedures and record keeping in a wider system that support business transactions and logistics

Figure 2. A model for traceability system development (source: Verdenius, 2006)

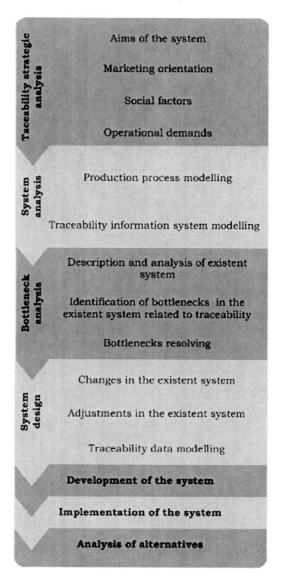

procedures. In the Fresh Produce sector, few or no automated integrated information gathering systems, based on bar codes and radio frequency identifiers exist on the market. Several technologies are not compatible from an electronic and computer point of view. (Terzi, 2004) This necessitates the purchase of various scanners by the various stakeholders in the chain, i.e. producers, distributors, and retailers. Furthermore, a large technological structure is often required. Salin

(1998), Karkkainen (2003), and Roussos (2006), emphasize the benefits from the implementation of Bar code and Radio Frequency Identification (RFID) technologies in food chains. At the same time, Regattieri et al., (2007) argued that some RFID properties limit traceability systems due of their costs, while (Feder, 2004; Fordice, 2004) pointed out the difficulties of management. Also, Wilson and Clarke (1998) and Food Standards Agency (2002) indicates that the development of software systems and databases (data pools) increases the efficiency in collecting, transmitting, and analyzing larger volumes of safety and quality related data. Most fresh produce stakeholders operate under tight profit margins, thus they are reluctant to invest in technologies as mentioned above and most of the product is traded loose. Emerging technologies such as the RFID tags are being implemented for tracing products of animal origin (Wang and Wang, 2006), but their cost prevent them to be adopted by the fresh produce sector, for implementing traceability in retail unit level (Panella, 2001). For this reason, a traceability model must be developed per se, and not as a part of a transactions support system.

Conceptual Framework

The proposed application aims to link primary production with the rest of the supply chain effectively and with low cost. Based on thorough review of the related literature, a plethora of physical labelling schemes already exist, depending on the level of the supply chain, the investment capacities, and the type of supply chain relations (conformity with sectoral standards such as EurepGAP, suppliers-buyers requirements, etc.). Moreover, it is generally recognized that the companies operate at the supply chain base (SMEs, producers, packers) are not willing to invest in novel technologies, that would be required if a new physical labeling system had been proposed. Thus, a decision was taken to develop an application that does not introduce a new means of physical labeling but will attempt to

unify the existing labeling systems. The integration of the existing labeling systems is achieved under a virtual labeling system that operates as an "umbrella" for the physical labeling systems implemented in different levels of the supply chain and follows the produce along the supply chain. This application focuses on the activities taking place along the supply chain without connecting them with specific stakeholders operate within it. This happens because there is no clear segregation of operations and processes realized in each supply chain level, i.e. all supply chain operations such as sorting, storing, and packaging can be performed either in the field, in the packhouse facilities, by a 3PL provider or by the retailer.

The Reference Model

A number of reference models have been proposed in order to support traceability. Bevilacqua et al. (2008) propose several models of traceability processes for a supply chain of vegetable products and to set up a computerized system for managing product traceability. Bertolini et al., (2006) designed a tool that aimed at detecting the possible critical points of its traceability system. Salomie et al. (2008) designed a broker-based service-oriented model that captures the main elements necessary to follow a product throughout its lifecycle, from manufacturing to the end consumer. Regattieri et al. (2006), provide with a general framework for the identification of fundamental mainstays and functionalities in an effective traceability system.

An emerging trend is the use of Cloud computing and Software-as-a-Service (SaaS) model in supporting supply chain management and, among others, traceability support. Cloud computing and the Software-as-a-Service (SaaS) models aim to offer a practical solution for traceability support, especially for the stakeholder operating in the supply chain base, such as the farmers and agricultural cooperatives. The evolution of cloud computing over the past few years is potentially one of the major advances in the history of computing (Marston et al, 2011). Cloud computing is changing the way industries and enterprises do their businesses in that dynamically scalable and virtualized resources are provided as a service over the Internet. This model creates a brand new opportunity for enterprises (Xu, 2012).Cloud computing is currently promoted as a means for efficient supply chain collaboration and information visibility (Jun and Wei, 2011).

Our model is based on the traceability data pool model described in the literature (CPTTF, 2004). The Traceability Data Pool (TDP) model describes a central repository of traceability data maintained for the fresh produce industry. The TDP builds upon the product identification data communicated by SC members. In case of a food safety incident initiated e.g. at retail store level, the retailer will quickly search the TDP via an Internet browser. Search criteria will include SSCC number and lot number (if the supplier pallet tag is available), or the case level human-readable information. The TDP search will return the supplier contact info along with the retailer's purchase order number and related SKU numbers. Additionally, this data will be used to search their internal database for other store level deliveries. The supplier will also be contacted and provided

with relevant traceability information to initiate internal traceability procedures (see Figure 3).

The data pool model is reported in the work of Wilson and Clarke (1998) who propose a similar web application to support traceability in the agrifood supply chain. This application is also referenced in the work of van Dorp (2004), as a practical solution for supporting traceability in the fresh produce supply chain. One of the main differences between the application reported in the literature and the one proposed in this paper is the design of traceability data entry module. In the first case, data entry is taking place through masks (user interface) that were customized according to the needs of each type of company participated in the supply chain, whereas in the latter, the data entry forms are activity oriented and not related to specific types of companies. This makes the system more flexible, as the same activity can be realised in various levels of the supply chain from different stakeholders respectively. The standard, activity oriented data entry forms facilitate supply chain members that operate under different collaboration schemes to utilize the application, e.g. a production data entry form can be filled by an agronomist based at the cooperative's offices on the behalf of the grower.

Figure 3. Traceability data pool model

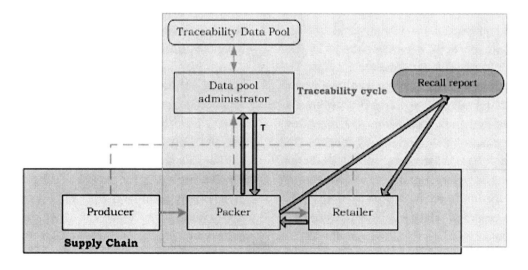

Another difference concerns the labeling algorithm. In the application reported in literature, the administrator provides the users with access codes that allow them to access the system and a key each time they use the corresponding forms (masks) for data entry. In the proposed application, each crop is tagged with a unique virtual label (Traceable Crop Unit) that follows the produce along the supply chain and enables to trace back to the field.

Definition of Traceable Unit

According to Council Directive 89/396EEC of 14 June 1989 on indications or marks identifying the lot to which a foodstuff belongs: "lot is a batch of sales units of a foodstuff produced, manufactured or packaged under practically the same conditions" (CIES, 2004). In Draft International Standard ISO/DIS 22005, lot is defined as "a set of units of a product which have been produced and/or processed or packaged under similar circumstances". Also, in the same ISO standard, it is noted that the lot is determined by parameters established beforehand by the organization (SC stakeholder). The lack of a standardized lot hinders traceability system standardization. In food manufacturing sectors, complicated product recipes and multiple raw materials make lot definition a difficult task. On the other hand the harvested produce moves across the supply chain, from the grower to the consumer. Although some basic processes occur, regarding post harvest handling and sometimes ripening control, the products are not processed, but remained fresh. As mentioned in the last paragraph, the *traceable unit* in this particular application coincides with a single crop, this is the total quantity of the produce received the same field treatments. A similar approach of lot definition is reported in literature, by Golan et al (2004). According to Golan (2004):

Lots can vary depending on the needs of the shipper and grower. At one end of the spectrum, a lot could be one grower's entire production of a particular crop over the length of a season. But identifying lots by smaller production units can be an important business tool..... On the other hand, there are diminishing benefits to precision. No one traces apples back to a particular tree. So far, there is no reason to do so. The costs would be high, and the benefits, compared to just being able to trace back to an orchard block (or part of one), would appear to be negligible, if not zero. Most things that would affect apples would generally affect more than one tree. So if an apple from a particular block had a problem, the entire block would be treated to be sure the problem was resolved.

This is supported by the Handbook for Introduction of Food Traceability Systems (2007) of the Food Marketing Research and Information Center in Japan, in which it is stated that

...As for farm products, products cultivated in a cultivated field or lot in the same conditions, cultivated with the same standard or method by farmers or by the farming group, of the same variety, and being harvested on the same day or in the same period, could be identified as part of one lot.

User Groups

The main user groups for this application are the registers and the administrators. The administrators are responsible for processing the registers' applications and activate their account and allow access into the system. The registers can be further divided into three sub-groups; producers, SC stakeholders, and the consumers. In an activity oriented traceability application, it was necessary to separate the producers from the rest of the supply chain stakeholders, as they perform specific pre-harvest activities, different from the group of activities commonly performed by the rest of the SC stakeholders.

The producers and SC stakeholders are responsible to record all information on performing activities in the respective forms provided in the application. The type of forms visible to each register depends of the account type, thus the system will allow access to a "producer" account type to forms regarding pre-harvest activities such as treatment with pesticides and herbicides, fertilizing etc, while a SC stakeholder have access to data entry forms strictly related to post harvest activities, such as packing, storing, grading, and quality control. If a producer wants to utilize post harvest related activity forms, it is necessary to sign out from the system and sign in again as a SC stakeholder.

In order to benefit from the traceability application, the consumer should firstly sign in by providing with name, address, and contact information, in order to avoid misusing incidents and anonymous complaints. The consumer triggers traceability process, by submitting queries for purchased produce or report spoilage or poisoning incidents. In order for the system to process the query, the consumer should provide through the respective form with all necessary information, such as produce type, purchase date, consumption date, and full address of the retailer. Moreover, a free text section will be provided for the consumer to describe textural or color degradation or report poisoning incident.

Tracking or tracing process may be triggered by a SC stakeholder of a producer as well, by submitting query on a specific traceable crop unit ID upstream or downstream the supply chain.

WEB APPLICATION DEVELOPMENT

User Requirements

The operational model described in Section 3 was implemented into a web application that covers the following requirements:

- Allow real time data entry.
- Connect pre-harvest field treatments with post-harvest and logistics activities into a single supply chain monitoring system.
- Unify physical labeling under a virtual produce code corresponding to a single crop (Traceable Crop Unit).
- Allow the SC stakeholder to manage and process directly all queries and complaints submitted in the system without the intervention of the administrator or a third party.

Application Architecture

The proposed traceability application software is developed using Microsoft.NET framework and it is based on 3-tier architecture. It is a client-server architecture in which the users interface, the business rules, data storage, and data access are developed and maintained as independent modules, most often on separate platforms. The user interface runs on a desktop PC or workstation and uses a standard graphical user interface. Business rules consist of one or more separate modules running on a workstation or application server, and an RDBMS on a database server contains the computer data storage logic. The middle tier may be multi-tiered itself (in which case the overall architecture is called an "n-tier architecture"). The different modules of this web application are described in Section 5.5.

For the efficient development of the traceability application, the following tools were selected:

- Development platform Microsoft.NET
- System development software Microsoft Visual Studio.Net 2003 (Johnson et al, 2003)
- eXtensible Markup Language
- Development Programming language Visual Basic.Net
- RDBMS Microsoft SQL Server 2005 (Rankins et al, 2006; Petkovic, 2005)

eXtensible Markup Language Implementation

Bevilacqua et al. (2008), points out that in a traceability system the need to share information requires the use of a standardized language. There have been introduced several standard systems but the most promising is GS1 (GS1 Official Website, 2006), which it is considered as the most robust lot identification system in the world. Moreover, Folinas et al. (2003) indicates that there is a need for common business vocabularies that describe the structure and the semantics of the traceability data. These vocabularies allow users to document these requirements (existing or proposed) in a neutral format that will act as a standard. In essence, a standard is just an agreed-upon set of elements, attributes, structure, semantics, and processes with which information can be used, exchanged, or presented, in order to support the traceability process.

All the above can be easily represented in eXtensible Markup Language (XML) Schemas technology, which is the W3 Consortium standard (W3C Specification). XML Schemas can be used to encode traceability information needed, to provide adequate technology for specifying standards and assuring that various documents prepared are valid. The last mentioned is very important due to the fact that in most other data formats, errors are not usually detected until something goes wrong leading to low information quality, which in turn leads to poor decision quality in food-crisis situations.

Due to its nature, XML is data-centric, unlike document-centric typed or electronic reports as pdfs or html pages, allowing information to be structured in a way that makes it readily accessible for the final users. As Laurent notes (1999), it represents not only the information to be presented, but also the metadata encapsulating its meaning, and the structure of the information to be presented. Another main characteristic is that XML is designed with the Internet in mind. Indeed, one of the main goals in the initial design of XML was to be a web-enabled version of SGML, so as to take advantage of the simple and open transport layers that the Internet provides, such as email (SMTP), Web (HTTP), file transfer (FTP), and other mechanisms. It can even take advantage of some of the native security features such as SSL, which are present on the web.

Application Modules

The proposed traceability application software consists of four (4) modules based on the proposed generic traceability framework, as it is depicted in Figure 4. Screenshots from all modules are given in Appendix.

Figure 4. Application main modules

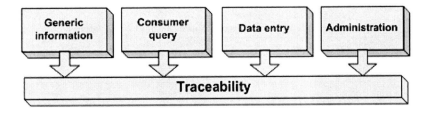

The main operations of each module are given in Table 1.

The information module includes the home page, including information for the consumers, the objectives of the application, the funding scheme, and user guidelines. The most important element in this module is the area where the results from the consumer complaints assessment are reported. The traceability mechanism is triggered by consumer (or SC stakeholders) complaints regarding produce related incidents (e.g. food poisoning, spoiled produce, quality degradation). The complaint is communicated downwards the supply chain and the assessment outcomes and corrective actions are posted in the relevant information page. Moreover, there is a contact page where the consumers and other users of the application may address their queries to the system administrators.

The data entry module is the main interactive point of the application. The registers (producers, SC stakeholders) log in to the application and enter product and actions related data, through a respective control panel. The registration procedure is given. The producer control panel provides with information concerning pre-harvest conditions for each crop, such as crop type and variety, plottage in hectares or number of trees, plant treatment information etc. The producer control panel is

given. The SC stakeholder control panel provides with information on supply chain activities, such as warehousing, packing, and distribution, while the register can also access pre-harvest produce information by selecting a specific virtual crop unit ID. In case a SC stakeholder selects "send" action, all the necessary information regarding pre-harvest crop treatments will be sent to the next level of the supply chain.

Consumer may submit a query regarding purchased produce, by using the respective form provided in the consumer's control panel. In order to trigger traceability process, consumer must enter information regarding produce physical labeling (if exist), trade name and address of retailer, produce type, purchase date, and consuming date. If the retailer is not registered in the system, the consumer is notified that "the retailer is not registered in the system." If the retailer is registered in the system's database, the system connects queried produce with the respective virtual label and initiates traceability process downward the supply chain, notifying the consumer that his query is being assessed. The query is being communicated to the stakeholders that handled produce matched with the virtual label. The decision for recall and production of the notification report is taken by the SC stakeholders involved in produce handling, from field to fork.

Table 1. Web application modules and operations

Web Application Modules	Basic Operations
Information module	Information on the application operations, aims and objectives Information on query/ complaints processing Administrator contact Reporting results from query processing
Traceability data entry module	Registering information regarding all pre-harvest and logistics activities taking place from farm to fork.
Consumer query module	Query/complaint submission Query processing and management from members of the supply chain
Administration module	Database management Registered users information management System parameters management

The administrator can operate the application control panel, add, and update the data base support tables, regarding information as:

- Pre-harvest action types (fertilization, irrigation)
- User state types (active, inactive)
- "Producer" types (farmers, cooperatives)
- SC stakeholder types (packhouse, cooperative, wholesaler, distribution centre, retailer)
- Affection types
- Agrochemical types and trade names
- Producer state types (active, inactive)
- SC stakeholder state types (active, inactive)

CONCLUSION

The efficiency of a traceability system depends on the ability to identify uniquely each unit that is produced and distributed, in a way that enables the continuous tracking, from the primary production to the retail point of sale. An efficient traceability system must follow some rules that define which data must be gathered and stored in each stage of the supply chain. This is achieved by standardization of the gathered data and typification of the messages that enable storing and communication of the data. The proposed web-platform will be able to support efficiently food traceability by monitoring and administering the data gathered and recorded in a central database. This application will be user friendly and provide with the ability to keep, display, and communicate information through widely implemented technologies, such as the Internet, and electronic mail services.

For the fresh produce supply chain stakeholders, the proposed web application is a practical solution for supporting farm to fork traceability. It does not require any investment on sophisticated technology and integrates the existing physical labeling schemes. In order to achieve total traceability, it is essential that all actors participating in the supply chain must registrate and utilize the application by consistent and real time data entries. The main advantages of this web application for SC stakeholders are summarized below:

- It is a low cost practical solution for farm to fork fresh produce traceability.
- It integrates data communication and continuous information flow between supply chain actors.
- It ensures information flow transparency.
- The data entry forms are designed according to standard forms used in quality and safety assurance schemes, such as Agro and HACCP.
- Data can be extracted by databases that support quality and safety assurance schemes, such as Agro and HACCP.
- All physical labeling schemes are integrated under a single virtual codification system.
- Produce physical flow is monitored in real time.
- All information is stored in real time.

For the consumers, this application provides with the ability to communicate food related queries and complaints to SC stakeholders and to receive direct reply. The main advantages of this web application for the consumers are summarized below:

- Ability to address queries directly to SC stakeholders.
- Direct feedback concerning fresh produce related incidents.
- Access to information concerning all stages of the supply chain, from farm to fork.

REFERENCES

Arvanitoyannis, I. S., Choreftaki, S., & Tserkezou, P. (2005). An update of EU legislation (directives and regulations) on food-related issues (safety, hygiene, packaging, technology, GMOs, additives, radiation, labelling): Presentation and comments. *International Journal of Food Science & Technology, 40*(10), 1021–1112. doi:10.1111/j.1365-2621.2005.01113.x

Bertolini, M., Bevilacqua, M., & Massini, R. (2006). FMECA approach to product traceability in the food industry. *Food Control, 17*(2), 137–145. doi:10.1016/j.foodcont.2004.09.013

Bevilacqua, M., Ciarapica, F., & Giacchetta, G. (2008). Business process reengineering of a supply chain and a traceability system: A case study. *Journal of Food Engineering, 93*, 13–22. doi:10.1016/j.jfoodeng.2008.12.020

CIES. (2004). *Implementing traceability in the food supply chain committee on the guidelines for introduction of food traceability systems: Handbook for introduction of food traceability systems* (2nd ed.). Tokyo, Japan: Food Marketing Research and Information Center.

CPTTF CPMA/PMA. (2004). *Traceability best practices: Fresh produce industry (North America)*. Traceability Task Force.

Daives, C. (2004). *Preparing for new EU traceability laws*. Supply Chain Europe.

European Commission. (2000). *White paper on food safety*. Brussels, Belgium: European Commission.

European Union. (2002). Regulation (EC) No 178/2002 of the European parliament and of the council. *Official Journal of the European Communities*. Brussels, Belgium: European Union.

Feder, B. J. (2004, December 28). Wal-Mart edict on radio tags hits snag. *The Denver Post*, p. 6C.

Folinas, D., Vlachopoulou, M., Manthou, V., & Manos, B. (2003). A web-based integration of data and processes in agribusiness supply chain. In *Proceedings of the EFITA 2003 Conference*, (vol. 1, pp. 143-150). EFITA.

Food Standards Agency. (2002). *Traceability in the food chain: A preliminary study*. Food Chain Strategy Division.

Fordice, R. (2004). Under control. *Meat Processing, 11*, 34–40.

GS1. (2006). *Official website*. Retrieved from http://www.gs1.org

Garcia, M., Skinner, C., Poole, N., Escribano, J. B., Boente, I., & Bandeiras, P. … Messaho, D. (2003). *Benchmarking safety and quality management practices in the Mediterranean fresh produce export sector*. Working Paper. London, UK: Imperial College.

Giraud, G., & Halawany, R. (2006). Consumers perception of food traceability in Europe. In *Proceedings of the 98th EAAE Seminar: Marketing Dynamics within the Global Trading System*, (p. 7). Chania, Greece: EAAE.

Golan, E., Krissoff, B., Kuchler, F., Calvin, L., Nelson, K., & Price, G. (2004). *Traceability in the U.S. food supply: Economic theory and industry studies. Agricultural Economic Report, No 830*. Washington, DC: U.S. Department of Agriculture.

Herdon, M., Rózsa, T., & Füzesi, I. (2006). *Food traceability solutions in information systems*. Paper presented at the Conference HAICTA 2006: International Conference on: Information Systems in Sustainable Agriculture, Agroenvironment and Food Technology. New York, NY.

Hobbs, J. E. (2006). Liability and traceability in agri-food supply chains. In Onderstejn, C. J. M., Wijnands, J. H. M., Huirne, R. B. M., & van Kooten, O. (Eds.), *Quantifying the Agri-Food Supply Chain* (pp. 87–102). Berlin, Germany: Springer. doi:10.1007/1-4020-4693-6_7

Hulzebos, L., & Koenderink, N. (2006). Modeling food supply chain for tracking and tracing. In Smith, I., & Furness, A. (Eds.), *Improving Traceability in Food Processing and Distribution* (pp. 67–87). New York, NY: Woodhead Publishing. doi:10.1533/9781845691233.2.67

Jansen-Vullers, M. H., van Dorp, C. A., & Beulens, A. J. M. (2003). Managing traceability information in manufacture. *International Journal of Information Management, 23,* 395–413. doi:10.1016/S0268-4012(03)00066-5

Johnson, B., Skibo, C., & Young, M. (2003). *Inside Microsoft visual studio. NET 2003*. Redmond, WA: Microsoft Press.

Jun, C., & Wei, M. Y. (2011). The research of supply chain information collaboration based on cloud computing. *Procedia Environmental Sciences, 10,* 875–880. doi:10.1016/j.proenv.2011.09.140

Karkkainen, M. (2003). Increasing efficiency in the supply chain for short shelf life goods using RFID tagging. *International Journal of Retail and Distribution Management, 31,* 529–536. doi:10.1108/09590550310497058

Karlsen, K. M., Sørensen, C. F., Forås, F., & Olsen, P. (2011). Critical criteria when implementing electronic chain traceability in a fish supply chain. *Food Control, 22,* 1339–1347. doi:10.1016/j.foodcont.2011.02.010

Kelepouris, T., Pramatari, K., & Doukidis, G. (2007). RFID-enabled traceability in the food supply chain. *Industrial Management & Data Systems, 107,* 183–200. doi:10.1108/02635570710723804

Klafft, M. (2006). Including process information in traceability. In Smith, I., & Furness, A. (Eds.), *Improving Traceability in Food Processing and Distribution* (pp. 107–127). New York, NY: Woodhead Publishing. doi:10.1533/9781845691233.2.107

Knight, C., Stanley, R., & Jones, L. (2002). Agriculture in the food supply chain: an overview. *Key Topics in Food Science and Technology, 5,* 91–96.

Koenderink, N., & Hulzebos, L. (2006). Dealing with bottlenecks in traceability systems. In Smith, I., & Furness, A. (Eds.), *Improving Traceability in Food Processing and Distribution* (pp. 88–107). New York, NY: Woodhead Publishing. doi:10.1533/9781845691233.2.88

Laurent, S. (Ed.). (1999). *XML™: A primer* (2nd ed.). New York, NY: MIS Press.

Marston, S., Li, Z., Bandyopadhyay, S., Zhang, J., & Ghalsasi, A. (2011). Cloud computing - The business perspective. *Decision Support Systems, 51,* 176–189. doi:10.1016/j.dss.2010.12.006

Moe, T. (1998). Perspectives on traceability in food manufacture. *Trends in Food Science & Technology, 5,* 211–214. doi:10.1016/S0924-2244(98)00037-5

Panella, L. (2001). *Guidelines for redesigning the supply chain: Classification -electronic identification - traceability: Multi-regional operating programme services for trade valorisation of southern Italian agricultural products*. Rome, Italy: Ismea.

Petkovic, D. (2005). *Microsoft SQL server 2005: A beginner's guide*. New York, NY: McGraw-Hill.

Rabade, L. A., & Alfaro, J. A. (2006). Buyer-supplier relationship's influence on traceability implementation in the vegetable industry. *Journal of Purchasing and Supply Management, 12,* 39–50. doi:10.1016/j.pursup.2006.02.003

Rankins, R., Bertucci, P., Gallelli, C., & Silverstein, A. T. (2006). *Microsoft SQL server 2005 unleashed*. New York, NY: Sams Publishing.

Regattieri, A., Gamberi, M., & Manzini, G. (2006). Traceability of food products: General framework and experimental evidence. *Journal of Food Engineering, 81,* 347–356. doi:10.1016/j.jfoodeng.2006.10.032

Resende-Filho, M. A., & Buhr, B. L. (2008). A principal-agent model for evaluating the economic value of traceability system: A case study with injection: Site lesion control in fed castle. *American Journal of Agricultural Economics*, *90*(4), 1091–1102. doi:10.1111/j.1467-8276.2008.01150.x

Roussos, G. (2006). Enabling RFID in retail. *IEEE Computer*, *39*(3), 25–30. doi:10.1109/MC.2006.88

Roy, P., Nei, D., Orikasa, T., Xu, Q., Okadome, H., Nakamura, N., & Shiina, T. (2009). A review of life cycle assessment (LCA) on some food products. *Journal of Food Engineering*, *90*(1), 1–10. doi:10.1016/j.jfoodeng.2008.06.016

Salin, V. (1998). Information technology in agri-food supply chains. *International Food and Agribusiness Review*, *1*, 329–334. doi:10.1016/S1096-7508(99)80003-2

Salomie, J., Dinsoreanu, M., Bianca Pop, C., & Liviu Suciu, S. (2008). Model and SOA solutions for traceability in logistic chains. In *Proceedings of iiWAS2008*, (pp. 339-344). Linz, Austria: iiWAS.

Sasazaki, S., Itoh, K., Arimitsu, S., Imada, T., Takasuga, A., & Nagaishi, H. (2004). Development of breed identification markers derived from AFLP in beef cattle. *Meat Science*, *67*, 275–280. doi:10.1016/j.meatsci.2003.10.016

Scheer, F. P. (2006). Optimizing supply chains using traceability systems. In Smith, I., & Furness, A. (Eds.), *Improving Traceability in Food Processing and Distribution* (pp. 52–64). New York, NY: Woodhead Publishing. doi:10.1533/9781845691233.1.52

Schwagele, F. (2005). Traceability from a European perspective. *Meat Science*, *71*, 164–173. doi:10.1016/j.meatsci.2005.03.002

Terzi, S., Cassina, J., & Panetto, H. (2004). Development of a metamodel to foster interoperability along the product lifecycle traceability. In *Proceedings of INTEROP 2004*. INTEROP.

Trienekens, J. H., Wognum, P. M., Beulens, A. J. M., & van der Vorst, J. G. A. J. (2012). Transparency in complex dynamic food supply chains. *Advanced Engineering Informatics*, *26*, 55–65. doi:10.1016/j.aei.2011.07.007

Van der Vorst, J. G. A. J. (2004). *Performance levels in food traceability and the impact on chain design: Results of an international benchmark study*. Paper presented at the 6th International Conference on Chain and Network Management in Agribusiness and the Food Industry. Ede, The Netherlands.

Van Dorp, C. A. (2004). *Reference-data modelling for tracking and tracing*. (Ph.D. Thesis). Wageningen University. Wageningen, The Netherlands.

Verdenius, F. (2006). Using traceability systems to optimise business performance. In Smith, I., & Furness, A. (Eds.), *Improving Traceability in Food Processing and Distribution* (pp. 26–51). New York, NY: Woodhead Publishing. doi:10.1533/9781845691233.1.26

Wang, N., Zhang, N., & Wang, M. (2006). Wireless sensors in agriculture and food industry-Recent development and future perspective. *Computers and Electronics in Agriculture*, *50*, 1–14. doi:10.1016/j.compag.2005.09.003

Wilson, T. P., & Clarke, W. R. (1998). Food safety and traceability in the agricultural supply chain: Using the internet to deliver traceability. *Supply Chain Management*, *3*, 127–133. doi:10.1108/13598549810230831

Wognum, P. M., Bremmers, H., Trienekens, J. H., van der Vorst, J. G. A. J., & Bloemhof, J. M. (2011). Systems for sustainability and transparency of food supply chains – Current status and challenges. *Advanced Engineering Informatics*, *25*, 65–76. doi:10.1016/j.aei.2010.06.001

Xu, X. (2012). From cloud computing to cloud manufacturing. *Robotics and Computer-integrated Manufacturing*, *28*, 75–86. doi:10.1016/j.rcim.2011.07.002

APPENDIX

Screenshots of the System Modules

Figure 5. Registration interface

Figure 6. Producer control panel

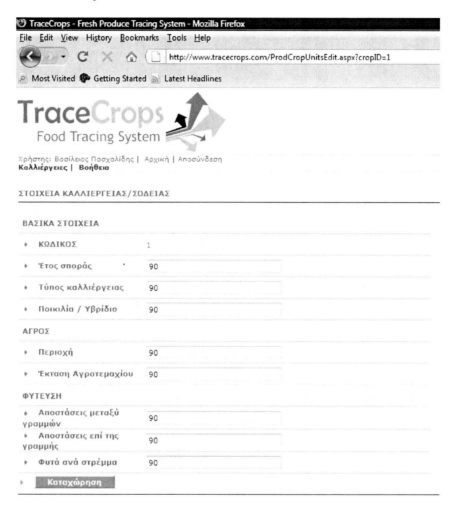

Figure 7. Information module

Figure 8. Consumer control panel

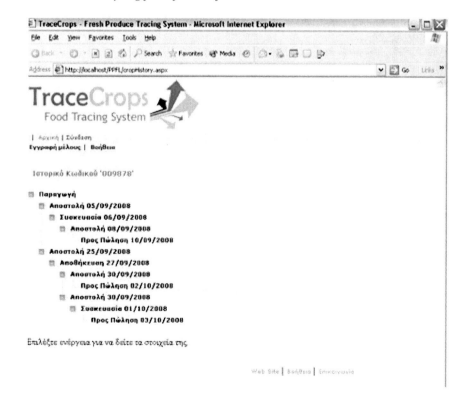

Figure 9. Produce traceability log from field to fork

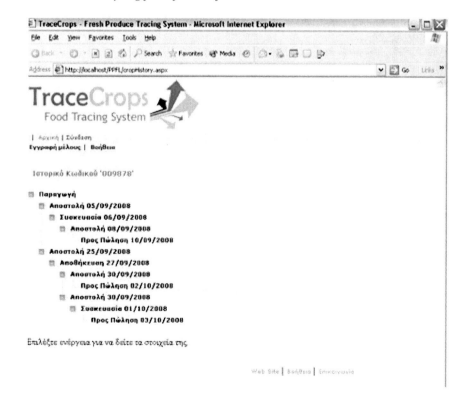

Chapter 8
E–Enterprise:
Organisational Issues of CRM, SRM, and ERP Systems Integration

Constantinos J. Stefanou
Alexander Technological Institute of Thessaloniki, Greece

ABSTRACT

This chapter provides a framework and discusses the integration of Customer Relationship Management (CRM) and Supplier Relationship Management (SRM) systems in e-ERP environments in supply chains. Currently, the economic environment enterprises are operating in is extremely competitive and influenced greatly by Information and Communication Technologies (ICT). ICT can be an enabler of business performance but also an obstacle if these technologies are not managed carefully. Enterprises are implementing integrated CRM and SRM software in order to remain competitive, but high rates of failure indicate that the implementation of these solutions is not straightforward. In this chapter, organizational issues concerning the integration of CRM, SRM, and ERP software in supply chains are discussed. This chapter aims at informing managers, scholars, students, and researchers of the issues involved, and identifying critical factors of success for enterprises adopting and implementing integrated CRM/SRM solutions.

INTRODUCTION

CRM systems aim at improving the relationship between enterprises and customers while SRM systems manage the relationships between the enterprise and its suppliers. A far as CRM is concerned, it is widely accepted that acquiring, satisfying and retaining customers can increase revenue growth (Stefanou et al., 2003). Although multiple interpretations of the CRM term exist (see

e.g. Papoutsakis and Stefanou, 2012) this chapter takes the view that CRM is a business philosophy developed around the relationship management and customer-centric enterprise concepts. It is comprised of a set of tools, techniques, methods and approaches assisted by information and communication technology aiming at managing and understanding customer activities and responding efficiently to customer requirements in order to enhance the competitive advantage of the enter-

DOI: 10.4018/978-1-4666-3914-0.ch008

prise. On the other side of the supply chain, SRM can be also viewed as a business philosophy supporting the decision making concerning suppliers' selection and relationship management aiming at improving business process efficiency, facilitating procurement, product design and development, cost reduction across the supply chain and enhancing performance. It is true that enterprises have historically been interested in forging lasting relationships with their partners. However, only during the last two decades enterprises have acknowledged the importance of CRM software systems in developing a customer–centric business model (see e.g. Choy et al., 2003). Until recently at least, the required attention was not given to the opposite end of their logistics operations, that is, the software applications concerning the relationship between the enterprise and its suppliers.

However, after the prevalence of the e-business model, defined as "the use of electronically enabled communication networks that allow business enterprises to transmit and receive information" (Fingar et al., 2000) this attitude has changed as the significance of the suppliers for the success of a supply chain was eventually documented. It became apparent that the value chain should respond quickly to competitive pressures not only by managing separately the relationships with customers and suppliers but also by coordinating and matching effectively these relationships in order to reduce costs, improve operational effectiveness and enhance the performance of the value chain.

The objective of the chapter is to identify and discuss critical organizational issues concerning the implementation of integrated CRM and SRM systems in e-business environments running ERP systems. The chapter aims at informing scholars, students and researchers having an interest in the area of business integrated e-CRM, e-SRM and e-ERP software. In the field of practice, it will provide managers with information and knowledge required in making decisions regarding the acquisition and implementation of such systems.

The chapter is organized as follows: Next section discusses CRM and SRM systems and their relation to e-ERP systems. The following section provides a literature review on CRM/SRM and e-ERP organizational issues concerning the implementation of integrated software. The final two sections provide suggestions for future research and concluding remarks.

BACKGROUND

Customer Relationship Management is a general industry term for methodologies, software, and Internet capabilities used by enterprises to systematically manage customer relationships. CRM is primarily a business philosophy emphasizing the importance for the adopting organization of customer acquisition, satisfaction and retention to sustain its competitive standing (Stefanou et al, 2003; Sarmaniotis and Stefanou, 2005). Nevertheless, modern CRM systems are based on information and web-technologies and in most cases CRM systems are software off-the-shelf packages developed by vendors such as Siebel (Oracle) and SAP.

Supplier Relationship Management as defined by the Gartner Group is the "practices needed to establish the business rules, and the understanding needed for interacting with suppliers of products and services of varied criticality to the profitability of the enterprise" (Hope-Ross and Spencer, 2001). Accenture gives the following definition: "Supplier Relationship Management is the systematic management of supplier relationships to optimize value through cost reduction, innovation, risk mitigation and growth throughout the relationship life cycle" (Brimacombe et al., 2011)

Therefore, SRM, similarly to CRM, is a general industry term describing the management of relationships that exist or should exist between an organization and its suppliers aiming at cost reductions and revenue growth by improving multi-enterprise business processes across the supply chain and facilitating supplier's selection, efficient procurement and rapid product cycles. SRM is first a business philosophy and then a technological issue that organizations need to take care of. As such, SRM has been historically practiced by enterprises, although only recently software vendors and business managers have focused systematically on SRM and its integration with the IT infrastructure. SRM systems are important as they lead to cost reductions, increase responsiveness to customer demands and requirements and reduce cycle times (Choy et al., 2003).

It should be noted that both CRM and SRM systems rely heavily on data produced by the transactional systems of the organization, usually a standard ERP system and other legacy transactional information systems. CRM software is often regarded as the stand alone front-office system having limited interaction with the transactional systems of the organization such as the Enterprise Resource Planning (ERP) and Supply Chain Management (SCM) systems (Stefanou and Athanasaki, 2012).

ERP systems are modular and customizable software packages providing support to integrated business processes across organizational functions such as production, sales, distribution, finance and logistics. The package can be extended to support additional applications, such as a supply chain management system, provided by the same or a third party vendor. It has been reported that ERP systems extended by SCM systems impact positively on business process performance (Wieder et al, 2006). Several other advantages arising from the integration of ERP and SCM systems have been also reported, such as improved operations, efficient inventory tracking and picking, reduced lead time and inventory levels optimization (Bose et al, 2008). ERP + E-Business = A New Vision of Enterprise System Betty Wang and Fui Hoon (Fiona) Nah University of Nebraska-Lincoln, USA.

By definitions and by their respective functions, traditional ERP systems take care of internal value chain (i.e., within a company) whereas e-businesses establish the value chain across the market and the industries. More and more companies construct their systems' architectures by integrating ERP systems with e-business. They use Web-based interface (corporate portals) without side entities plus add-on modules such as CRM, SCM, etc. in the integration.

However, due to the complexity and integrative nature of the ERP software, its implementation is not straightforward, let alone its integration with other add-on enterprise applications. A number of organizational, technological and human factors need to be carefully considered and managed if the system is to be successful (Stefanou, 2001b). Although recently ERP systems have been enhanced to include CRM and SRM functionality, dedicated CRM and SRM systems still offer greater value in addressing crucial issues concerning customers and suppliers that enterprises need to pay attention to (Kumar & Thapliyal, 2010; Himanshu, 2011). Respectively, CRM software has been augmented in an effort to include basic but nevertheless elementary ERP operating effectiveness (Athanasaki & Stefanou, 2012). There is certainly a need for enterprises to integrate their front and back-office systems in order to implement effectively their customer-centric strategies (Schumbert and Williams, 2009). Table 1 summarizes the basic functionality of CRM, ERP and SRM systems.

The emergence of the e-business phenomenon changed considerably the way enterprises transmit and receive information and communicate with their customers, suppliers, and partners. E-business, beyond the web-based applications, includes also other means of real-time business communication such as mobile phones and tablets. It has also forced vendors to provide on-line real-time capabilities to their products in order to facilitate the formation of alliances with customers, suppliers and partners over the internet (see e.g.

Table 1. CRM, ERP, and SRM systems basic functionality

CRM	ERP	SRM
Customer contact management	Business process and operations monitoring	Supplier contact management
Customer activity monitoring	Order fulfillment management	Supplier activity scheduling
Pre sales activities	Sales and operation planning	Monitoring supplier activities
Sales force automation	Inventory control	Purchase orders processing
Quoting and sales order process	Financials	Purchases/Supplier analytics
Sales forecasting	Controlling/Costing	Purchases reporting
Sales reporting	Workflow management	
Sales/Customer analytics	Project management	
Marketing campaign automation	Materials Requirements Planning	
Call center	Production planning	
Service center	Financial and MIS reporting	

Markus et al., 2000) or through other channels. Thus, vendors added value to their systems by considerably extending their functionality. For example, e-business enabled CRM (e-CRM) provides online capabilities for marketing operations such as campaigns, promotions and advertising, mobile sales and real-time monitoring of customers. e-SRM facilitates e-procurement and automated purchasing, web-based purchases bidding and e-procurement among others. As far as the e-ERP system is concerned, its functionality has been extended to support processes such as real-time scheduling and just-in-time inventory, continuous monitoring and auditing, real-time point-of-sale inventory management and real-time invoicing and payment. Table 2 summarizes the

extended functionality of e-CRM, e-ERP and e-SRM systems.

ORGANIZATIONAL ISSUES OF E-CRM, E-SRM, AND E-ERP INTEGRATION

Although e-CRM, e-SRM, and e-ERP systems have been enriched by additional features and increased functionality compared to the non web-enabled Enterprise Systems (ES), it is their seamless integration within the e-business environment that sustains the competitive advantage of a supply chain. The successful integration of these systems in an e-business environment is of

Table 2. e-CRM, e-ERP, and e-SRM systems extended functionality

e-CRM	e-ERP	e-SRM
Tablets, smart phones, and PDAs mobility access customer management	Real-time order processing	Tablets, smart phones, and PDAs mobility access supplier management
Mobile sales	Real-time scheduling and just-in-time inventory	Mobile procurement
e-sales, automated sales order	Real-time build-to-order coordination	e-procurement and automated purchasing
Real-time monitoring of customer and market trends	Web-based Business-to-Business (B2B) interaction	Real-time monitoring of suppliers and raw products market conditions
Chapterless ordering processing	Continuous monitoring and auditing	Real-time supplier commitments monitoring
Real-time customer orders	Real-time product configuration	Web-based purchases bidding
Web 2.0 applications management	Real-time point-of-sale inventory management	Web-based Business-to-Supplier (B2S) interaction
Web-based Business-to-Customer (B2C) interaction	On-line invoicing and payment	Web-based purchase system measurement tools
Web–based sales system measurement tools		e-sourcing and e-catalog
e-service		e-reverse auctions
e-campaigns and promotions		orders

paramount importance for today's supply chains operating in an extremely competitive environment but most integration projects do not deliver up to expectations at the best (Papoutsakis and Stefanou, 2012). According to Power (2005), the integration of supply chain processes can provide an effective means to reduce costs and improve customer service levels.

Today's information intensive business environment has radically transformed the traditional business model. Enterprises recognize that they cannot compete in isolation to their suppliers and customers and instead they need to optimize their supply chains in order to remain competitive (Sharif and Irani, 2005). Information and communication technologies play a crucial role in facilitating organizations achieve supply chain optimization by offering the tools needed to interconnect business systems. This goal is greatly facilitated in the case the transactional information system (e.g. an ERP system) of the organization is not only integrated with the internal business processes but also externally to encompass the overall business and trading environment (Sharif and Irani, 2005). Therefore, Business to Business (B2B) and Business to Consumer (B2C) applications as well as CRM, SRM and supply chain management systems need to be integrated with the core ERP systems in order to expand it across and outside the organization. Other researchers take a similar view. Power mentions that ERP and CRM, as well as other business application such as order management, demand planning and date warehouse systems are included among the effective applications of IT leading to integration of supply chain activities by allowing better information flow throughout the supply chain (Power, 2005). According to Christopher (2000), the use of information technology to share data between buyers and suppliers creates an information-based virtual supply chain. However, little can be achieved in terms of attaining and sustaining a supply chain completive advantage if the degree of

information systems integration across and outside the organization boundaries is low as inefficiencies arise leading to an increase in costs and lead times and a decrease in customer service levels.

Thus, the integration concept refers both to the integration of the intra-organizational systems but also to the integration of back and front-end company systems with the e-business infrastructure of the enterprise. As it has been mentioned above, e-business refers not only to the web-enabled platforms of doing business but also to all means available today for real-time communication, such as tablets, PDAs, and smart phones. The importance of social networks in conducting business is growing and it has to be taken into account when designing the integration of web-enabled enterprise systems. Web 2.0 and social networking applications have facilitated the notion of the internet as a secure and accepted platform for business computing, even for critical integrated enterprise systems on which all or most of the organizational core functions depend upon. Specifically for ERP, it has been argued that emerging Web 2.0 technologies such as wiki and social tagging systems may be used to enhance the quality and reduce the risk and cost of ERP implementations (Wu and Lao, 2009). These technologies can provide, for example, a repository system, collaborative documentation and knowledge databases supporting ERP implementations.

Taking the above into consideration, a conceptual framework of the extended enterprise is depicted in Figure 1.

Several success factors for integrating standard enterprise systems, such as CRM and ERP, have been proposed in the literature (see e.g. Athanasaki & Stefanou, 2012). Factors frequently cited are, among others, top management support and clarity of responsibilities concerning the integration project for ensuring efficient processes, users' integration expertise, qualified project team and effective coordination between project team and

Figure 1. e-Enterprise framework

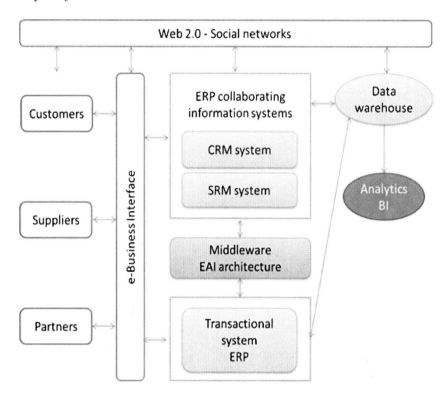

ERP/CRM staff (Themistocleous et al., 2009; Gericke et al., 2010).

However, the extended enterprise has not been studied extensively and certainly not by employing a holistic approach which seems plausible for its nature and characteristics. Although technical, human, managerial, social and environmental factors are important for the success of ES integration, the remaining of this section will focus on the organizational issues which are often ignored (Stefanou, 2001) aiming at highlighting factors having an impact on ES integration success especially in e-business environments.

BPR and Alignment of Multi-Business Processes

Discuss solutions and recommendations in dealing with the issues, controversies, or problems presented in the preceding section.

The implementation of an integrated e-business Information System is a huge project and so complex that many failures are reported frequently in the literature. Enterprises usually underestimate the change management dimension and the efforts they have to make towards streamlining their business processes in nearly every aspect of their organizational and functional units. This is because, usually, enterprises have to adapt to a great extend to the integrated company wide information systems, e.g. the ERP system, by reengineering their business processes in order to make them more competitive and not vice-versa (Stefanou, 2001). ERP implementations are generally associated with and frequently require extended business process reengineering (Davenport, 2000; Al-Mashari and Zairi, 2000). A web-enabled ERP system (e-ERP) not only extends beyond functional enterprise boundaries redefining business processes but also develops processes that span multiple enterprises (Kumar

& Thapliyal, 2010). Thus, Business Process Re-engineering (BPR) is of paramount importance not only in streamlining the enterprise business processes but also in aligning them with those of customers, suppliers and other partners in the supply chain in the effort to reduce costs and improve efficiency.

Organizational Culture Change and Learning Readiness

In connecting distinct platforms, applications and data formats across the value chain, enterprises have to overcome various obstacles such as user resistance to change (Ash and Burn, 2001) and reluctance for establishing a company culture open to sharing business processes and to collaboration. Extant research has shown that organizations in e-business environments recognize facilitators in aspects of e-business change management such as cultural readiness, knowledge, and learning capabilities and relationship building. The degree that all these enablers are incorporated in the implementation process varies significantly and influences the success of e-ERP projects (Ash and Burn, 2001). Cultural issues, time availability for training employees on integration technologies and resistance to change have also been identified as factors affecting the effectiveness of Enterprise Application Integration technologies (Themistocleous and Irani, 2003)

Collaboration between Partners

Integration requires full cooperation between industry partners in order to align business processes, exchange information, and facilitate communication. Enterprise systems flexibility is also required in order for enterprises to adapt quickly to new business needs along the value chain. For this to be successful, the participation of all partners is required in the decision making process (Sharma et al., 2011)

Trust and Information Sharing

Information sharing between partners in the value chain is of paramount importance in synchronizing decisions resource planning and actions that enable operational effectiveness. The cultivation of relationships improving collaboration (Gunasekaran et al, 2004) requires trust between the partners (Stefanou, 2001) and full commitment for successful relationship management. An infrastructure enabling effective information flows and streamlined logistics has also been considered crucial for the success of ERP and SCM integration projects (Power, 2005).

Integration Motivation, Vision, Objectives, and Strategy

The motivation for integration and a clearly defined strategy and set of goals are fundamental for achieving organizational structures supporting the integration project (Athanasaki and Stefanou, 2012). The justification for investment in ERP/CRM/SRM integration and the support of a systematic application integration process are based on clearly defined objectives and strategy and an appropriate set of policies, methods and tools (Gericke et al., 2010; Kamal et al., 2009).

Effective External Communication

Internal communication refers to communication between all functional departments of an organization in order to ensure minimum resistance to change, clarity of business goals and strong support and commitment (Al Mamari and Nunes, 2008). External communication refers to the communication between an enterprise and its suppliers, customers and partners outside the enterprise boundaries for determining business requirements, needs, and opportunities and for taking decisions (Athanasaki & Stefanou, 2012). In supply chains internal communication has to be accompanied with effective external communication between enterprises and their partners (Al Mamari and Nunes, 2008; Cybulski and Lukaitis, 2005; Goodman and Truss, 2004).

FUTURE TRENDS AND RESEARCH OPPORTUNITIES

Despite the importance of integrated e-CRM/e-SRM systems and e-ERP systems for modern enterprises, research on the subject is rather limited. This chapter intended to shed light to the organizational dimension of ES integration which is often ignored despite its importance for the effective implementation of integrated software in supply chains. remaining of this section will focus on the organizational issues which are often ignored aiming at highlighting factors having an impact on ES integration success especially in e-business environments.

Other dimensions, such as the technological, human, and environmental dimensions should be explored in a more systematic way. Empirical research is also important to validate and generalize the findings of the extant literature on ES integration in e-business environments. Developments such as Web.2.0 applications have been recently exploited for business purposes. Social media networks are powerful and their analysis should be an integral part of future e-CRM and e-SRM research. The same holds true for Business Intelligence (BI) and risk management which are crucial for sustaining the competitive advantage of the enterprises and especially of supply chains and alliances.

CONCLUSION

The chapter presented a discussion concerning the organizational issues involved in implementing integrated e-business software aiming at highlighting the factors that seem to have an impact on ES integration success in e-business environments.

It also provided a conceptual framework of the e-Enterprise which can be useful in addressing future research issues and presented a summary of benefits arising by employing e-CRM, e-SRM and e-ERP systems. Enterprises, in their effort to remain competitive, implement integrated, company-wide business software critical for their operations in a continuous globalized and competitive environment. However, the implementation of this type of software is not always a risk free investment. The implementation task becomes even more daunting in extended enterprises operating in supply chains. Today, the backbone of e-business is the integration of CRM, SRM, SCM and ERP software. The extent to which these applications are integrated is of paramount importance to supply chains because seamless integration makes reliable real-time information available for decision making, streamline business processes across the supply chain, reduce costs and increase customer service level and the supply chain's revenue growth. Certain factors, such as willingness for information sharing, trust among partners and collaborative and open organizational culture were highlighted aiming at informing the academics with an interest in Enterprise Systems (ES) integration as well as managers wishing to undertake ES integration projects.

REFERENCES

Al-Mamari, S., & Nunes, M. (2008). Readiness for CRM use in developing countries: Case of Oman. In *Proceedings of the IADIS International Conference - Information Systems*, (pp. 1-12). Algarve, Portugal: IADIS.

Al-Mashari, M., & Zairi, M. (2000). Supply-chain re-engineering using enterprise resource planning (ERP) systems: An analysis of a SAP R/3 implementation case. *International Journal of Physical Distribution & Logistics Management*, *30*(3-4), 296–313. doi:10.1108/09600030010326064

Ash, C., & Burn, J. M. (2001a). Managing information technology in a global economy. In Khosrow-Pour, M. (Ed.), *Information Resources Management Association*. Hershey, PA: IGI Global.

Ash, C. G., & Burn, J. M. (2001b). E-ERP: A comprehensive approach to e-business. In Khosrow-Pour, M. (Ed.), *Managing Information Technology in a Global Economy*. Hershey, PA: IGI Global.

Athanasaki, M. T., & Stefanou, C. J. (2012). Critical success factors for implementing integrated ERP/CRM systems. In *Proceedings of the International Conference on Contemporary Marketing Issues*, (pp. 357-364). Thessaloniki, Greece: IEEE.

Bose, I., Pal, R., & Ye, A. (2008). ERP and SCM systems integration: The case of a valve manufacturer in China. *Information & Management*, *45*(4), 233–241. doi:10.1016/j.im.2008.02.006

Brimacombe, A., Cotter, B. C., & Timmermans, K. (2011). *Supplier relationships: Cracking the value code*. Accenture.

Choy, K. L., Lee, W. B., & Lob, V. (2003). Design of a case based intelligent supplier relationship management system—The integration of supplier rating system and product coding system. *Expert Systems with Applications*, *25*, 87–100. doi:10.1016/S0957-4174(03)00009-5

Christopher, M. (2000). The agile supply chain – Competing in volatile markets. *Industrial Marketing Management*, *29*(1), 37–44. doi:10.1016/S0019-8501(99)00110-8

Cybulski, J., & Lukaitis, S. (2005). The impact of communications and understanding on the strategic alignment model. In *Proceedings of the 16th Australasian Conference on Information Systems*. Sydney, Australia: IEEE.

Fingar, P., Kumar, H., & Tarun, S. (2000). *Enterprise e-commerce: The software component breakthrough for business-to-business commerce*. Meghan-Kiffer Press.

Gericke, A., Klesse, M., Winter, R., & Wortmann, F. (2010). Success factors of application integration: An exploratory analysis. *Communications of the Association for Information Systems*, *27*(37), 678–694.

Goodman, J., & Truss, C. (2004). The medium and the message: Communicating effectively during a major change initiative. *Journal of Change Management*, *4*(3), 217–228. doi:10.1080/1469701042000255392

Gunasekaran, A., Patel, C., & McGaughey, R. E. (2004). A framework for supply chain performance measurement. *International Journal of Production Economics*, *87*, 333–347. doi:10.1016/j.ijpe.2003.08.003

Hendricks, K. B., Singhal, V. R., & Stratman, J. K. (2007). The impact of enterprise systems on corporate performance: A study of ERP, SCM, and CRM system implementations. *Journal of Operations Management*, *25*, 65–82. doi:10.1016/j.jom.2006.02.002

Hope-Ross, D., & Spencer, C. (2001). *SRM is not yet a suite spot*. Washington, DC: Gartner Group.

Kamal, M. M., Themistocleous, M., & Morabito, V. (2009). Justifying the decisions for EAI adoption in LGAs: A validated proposition of factors, adoption lifecycle phases, mapping and prioritisation of factor. In *Proceedings of the 42nd Hawaii International Conference on System Sciences*, (pp. 1-10). Hawaii, HI: IEEE.

Kumar, P., & Thapliyal, M. P. (2010). Integration of e-business with ERP systems. *International Journal of Computer Science & Communication*, *1*(2), 13–17.

Markus, M. L., Axline, S., Petrie, D., & Tanis, C. (2000). Learning from adopters experiences with ERP: Problems encountered and success achieved. *Journal of Information Technology, 15*(4), 245–265. doi:10.1080/02683960010008944

Morgan, R. M., & Hunt, S. D. (1994). The commitment-trust theory of relationship marketing. *Journal of Marketing, 58,* 20–36. doi:10.2307/1252308

Papoutsakis, E., & Stefanou, C. J. (2012). The evaluation process of CRM systems: A review of the literature. In *Proceedings of the International Conference on Contemporary Marketing Issues,* (pp. 377-383). Thessaloniki, Greece: IEEE.

Power, D. (2005). Supply chain management integration and implementation: A literature review. *Supply Chain Management: An International Journal, 10*(4), 252–263. doi:10.1108/13598540510612721

Sarmaniotis, C., & Stefanou, C. J. (2005). A framework of CRM development phases and key success factors. In *Proceedings of the 2nd International Conference on Enterprise Systems and Accounting,* (pp. 477-495). Thessaloniki, Greece: IEEE.

Schubert, P., & Williams, S. P. (2009). An extended framework for comparing expectations and realized benefits of enterprise systems implementations. In *Proceedings of the 15th Americas Conference on Information Systems.* San Francisco, CA: IEEE.

Sharif, A. M., & Irani, Z. (2005). Emergence of ERPII characteristics within an ERP integration context. In *Proceedings of the Eleventh Americas Conference on Information Systems,* (pp. 1-9). Omaha, NE: IEEE.

Sharma, H., Lavania, D., & Gupta, N. (2011). ERP + e-business = an emerging relationship. *International Journal of Managing Value and Supply Chains, 2*(2).

Sharma, S. K., & Kitchens, F. (2003). Assessing technology integration. In *Proceedings of the 7th Pacific Asia Conference on Information Systems.* Adelaide, Australia: IEEE.

Stefanou, C. J. (2001a). Organizational key success factors for implementing SCM/ERP systems to support decision making. *Journal of Decision Systems, 10*(1), 49–64. doi:10.3166/jds.10.49-64

Stefanou, C. J. (2001b). A framework for the ex-ante evaluation of ERP software. *European Journal of Information Systems, 10,* 204–212. doi:10.1057/palgrave.ejis.3000407

Stefanou, C. J., & Athanasaki, M. T. (2012). The adoption and selection process of CRM software: A review of the literature. In *Proceedings of the International Conference on Contemporary Marketing Issues,* (pp. 390-399). Thessaloniki, Greece: IEEE.

Stefanou, C. J., Sarmaniotis, C., & Stafyla, A. (2003). CRM and customer-centric knowledge management: An empirical research. *Business Process Management Journal, 9*(5), 617–634. doi:10.1108/14637150310496721

Themistocleous, M., & Irani, Z. (2003). Integrating cross-enterprise systems: An innovative framework for the introduction of enterprise application integration. In *Proceedings of the Eleventh European Conference on Information Systems.* Naples, Italy: IEEE.

Themistocleous, M., Mantzana, V., & Morabito, V. (2009). Achieving knowledge management integration through EAI: A case study from healthcare sector. *International Journal of Technology Management, 47*(1/2/3), 114–126.

Wieder, B., Booth, P., Matolcsy, Z. P., & Ossimitz, M. (2006). The impact of ERP systems on firm and business process performance. *Journal of Enterprise Information Management, 19*(1), 13–29. doi:10.1108/17410390610636850

Chapter 9
Monitoring and Warning Mechanisms of Supply Coordination in Assembly System under Delivery Uncertainty

Guo Li
Beijing Institute of Technology, China

Xiang Zhang
Beijing Institute of Technology, China

Zhaohua Wang
Beijing Institute of Technology, China

ABSTRACT

As supply uncertainty increases in recent years, it is of great importance to manage multiple suppliers, monitor, and warn the supply process of problems to achieve supply coordination in the assembly system in case of supply risks. This chapter analyzes the uncertainty factors and emergence mechanism of supply uncertainty in the assembly system. To achieve supply coordination, the monitoring operation mode under uncertain delivery in the assembly system is constructed. Under this circumstance, suppliers can be classified into four categories, and monitoring tactics are provided for supply coordination. Additionally, case-based reasoning is presented to monitor and warn the supply process with detailed steps and methodology, which are conducive to finding similar cases to provide warning insights and suggestions.

DOI: 10.4018/978-1-4666-3914-0.ch009

INTRODUCTION

In a common JIT assembly system, if one of the suppliers does not deliver its components on time or in incorrect quantity, the manufacturer cannot assemble the product on time or in less quantity than original target, which will not only damage the interests of other suppliers but also jeopardize the interests of enterprises and reduce the competitiveness of the supply chain. Obviously the delivery of a certain components is disrupted or postponed, the manufacturer's production will be greatly affected, followed by the penalty cost increased dramatically (Tomlin, 2005, 2009).According to Frank et al. (2008) statistics, dissatisfaction that upstream enterprises can't provide components for the downstream enterprises on time or in insufficient quantity in China had reached 18.35%, and 2.33% of them was very disappointed. While dissatisfaction that the downstream enterprises cannot provide accurate information for the upstream enterprises had accounted for 10.47%, and 1.60% of them was very dissatisfied. In order to achieve the predetermined goal of the assemble system and ensure each supplier coordination in delivery time and delivery quantity, supply process in assembly system should be monitored and warned, which can contribute to taking effective measures timely when there are deviations during the supply process.

In recent years, the uncertainty of assembly system in upstream supply chain increased significantly due to influence of natural disasters, strikes, terrorist attacks and political instability and other factors. Especially after U.S. 9/11 incident, the supply uncertainty and its associated potential losses are becoming much larger. Some studies suggest that the frequency of disaster events is increasing year by year, and its harms are gradually rising up. Natural disasters and unexpected social events often cause the supply process of assembly system unstable and even interrupted, which eventually leads to enterprise's production shutdown, loss of market share and other serious consequences. In

2000, Philips Semiconductor Factory's fire leads to Ericsson's supply disruptions of the chip, which caused the loss of 1.8 billion Ericsson and 4% of market share loss (Norman and Jansson, 2004). In July 2010, Hitachi's unexpected shortage of car engine control part resulted in Nissan's plant shutdown for 3 days in Japan, and the production of 1.5 million cars affected. In March 2011, Japan 9 earthquakes in northeast region devastated the area of industrial enterprises. Car production of three major Japanese automakers, Toyota, Honda, and Nissan, are affected by the disruption of supply chain and some joint ventures in China also had different levels of supply disruptions. Generally, after investigation of 800 companies' disruption cases, Hendricks and Singhal (2003, 2005a, 2005b) find that firms that experienced supply glitches suffer from declining operational performance and eroding shareholder value (e.g. the abnormal return on stock of such firms is negative 40% over three years).

Supply chain risk management has emerged as an important source of competitive advantage and an effective method of reducing vulnerability in a supply chain (Lin and Zhou, 2011).Therefore, the field of supply chain risk has attracted more and more attention from both practitioners and researchers over the past decade (Sawik, 2011). Research addresses the two risk levels: operational risks or disruption risks. Operational risks with high likelihood and low impact refer to inherent uncertainties arising from the problems of coordinating supply and demand such as uncertain customer demand, uncertain supply, and uncertain cost. Disruption risks with high impact and low probability refer to the major disruptions to normal activities caused by natural and man-made disasters such as earthquakes, floods, fires or equipment breakdowns, labor strikes, terrorist attacks, etc (Sawik, 2011b). The issue of linking risk assessment with risk mitigation for low-probability high-consequence events such as disruptions of supplies is discussed by Kleindorfer and Saad (2005), Cohen and Kunreuther (2007), and Hallikas (2004). In Kleindorfer and Saad (2005) a set of 10 principles is formulated for specifying sources of risk, assessment and mitigation of risk. Following Paul Kleindorfer's framework for risk analysis, Knemeyer et al. (2009) consider a proactive planning for catastrophic events in supply chains. The proposed proactive planning process involves four critical steps: identification of key supply chain locations and threats, estimation of probabilities and loss for each location, evaluation of alternative countermeasures for each location, and selection of countermeasures for each location.

In addition to high-impact, low-likelihood disruption risks, supply chains are more vulnerable to high-likelihood and low-impact delay risks (Oke and Gopalakrishnan, 2009). Despite the random nature of components' delivery, research seldom considers uncertainty and risk. For example, Kasilingam and Lee (1996) developed chance constrained programming models with stochastic demand and Wu and Olson (2008) considered expected losses from quality acceptance inspection or late delivery. Following the same decision framework, Ruiz-Torres and Farzad (2007) consider unequal failure probabilities for all the suppliers. Berger and Zeng (2006) study the optimal supply size under a number of scenarios that are determined by various financial loss functions, the operating cost functions and the probabilities of all the suppliers being down.

In spite of the importance of monitoring and warning the risky assembly system, the principle and mechanism are not sufficiently addressed in the literature (Zhang et al., 2011), in particular for JIT assembly system, see Blackhurst et al., 2008). The majority of literature concerned with risky supply chain is mathematical programming models with either single objective, e.g. Kasilingam and Lee (1996), Basnet and Leung (2005) or multiple objectives, e.g. Wu and Olson (2008), Xia and Wu (2007), Demirtas and Ustun (2008), Ustun and Demirtas (2008).

In the past literature about early monitoring and warning of the supply chain, the research

mainly focused on inventory control, quality control, financial control and integration control monitoring system of supply chain (Beamon & Ware, 1998; Bi, 1999; Xu & Zhang, 2001; Zhang, 2002; Robb, 2003; Seferlis & Giannelos, 2004; Perea et al, 2004). However, few scholars make comprehensive researches on the monitoring and warning of management process in supply chain. The typical Collaborative Planning Forecasting and Replenishment (CPFR) and the corresponding information management platform are also mainly based on joint management of business processes and co-sharing of demand forecasting information to realize the monitoring and management of inventory between the links of the supply chain. But the above methods can't realize the monitoring of the logistics, other information flow and capital flow operation between the upstream and downstream enterprises in supply chain, not to mention the early warning and emergency response capabilities, and providing decision support and emergency response programs for the emergence in special circumstances.

However, there may be unexpected problems in the supplier's production and supply process, for example there may be something unexpected with the supply of the supplier, or the interruption occurs during the supplier's production process. These unexpected problems may break the existing synergies, so it is necessary for the manufacturer as a key enterprise to further coordinate the assembly system to achieve new synergies. In order to timely indentify the supplier's problem, it's essential to monitor and warn in the supplier's production process. In this regard, Dong et al. (2006) based on difference between production status and monitoring requirements of all kinds of materials required by the leader enterprise of the alliance and the member enterprises in an agile supply chain. The control method of production process based on multiple monitoring modes was provided. However, the paper did not design an effective process monitoring and warning mechanism of coordination in assembly system based on multiple suppliers and single manufacturer. Thus it is very necessary and of practical significance for assembly system consisting of multiple supplier and single manufacturer to establish monitoring and warning mechanism of coordination.

To address these gaps in the current literature, we investigate the interaction between emergence mechanism of supply uncertainty and monitoring and warning mechanism of supply coordination in an assembly system. We address the following questions:

- Why does supply uncertainty emerge in the assembly system? What is the consequence of uncertainty in the assembly system?
- How can the manufacturer monitor the supply process in the assembly system? What are the monitoring tactics?
- Which technology can be used to monitor and warning the uncertainty of supply process?

In answering these questions, we limit our consideration within delivery uncertainty in the assembly system and the paper is organized as follows. In section 2 we analyze the emergence mechanism and consequence of supply uncertainty in the assembly system. Section 3 provides the monitoring mode of supply coordination in the assembly system under uncertain delivery. The monitoring mechanism and tactics of supply coordination are presented in section 4. And finally section 5 explains how case based reasoning can be used in monitoring and warning the supply process.

THE EMERGENCE MECHANISM OF SUPPLY UNCERTAINTY IN ASSEMBLY SYSTEM

In an assembly system consisting of multiple suppliers and single manufacturer, the key emphasis of the whole supply operation is stressed on two-dimension coordination between different suppliers, and each supplier and manufacturer. However, the difficulty lies in supply coordination between different suppliers.

The assembly system consisting of multiple suppliers and single manufacturer pursues to satisfy the demand side in the fast, punctual, reliable time and low cost through the method including responding positively to meeting the practical requirements and creating potential demand actively. Resources of supply system should be integrated and collaboratively optimized to improve two-dimensional coordination of operational activities between the suppliers, and each supplier and manufacturer. On one hand, the horizontal coordination, which belongs to inner supply system, requires the integrations of each supplier to realize synchronized collaborative delivery. On the other hand, the vertical coordination needs integrating supply side and demand side including all suppliers and the manufacturer, see Figure 1.

During collaborative operation process of assembly system with multiple suppliers and a single manufacturer, there are many factors leading to uncertainty of assembly system, including customer demand for quantity and variety, production and processing (including production quantity, mechanical failure and transport reliability), manufacturing process time (including machine downtime, production processes and rework time), transport process, distribution performance, the quality of purchased materials and so on. Beside these, other interactions between the above factors increase the difficulty of coordination in assembly system. In general, assembly system suffers not only risks from the upstream supply chain, but also from downstream supply chain. Besides, information magnification from the sides intensifies uncertainty of assembly system. In order to illustrate the emergence mechanism of uncertainty in assembly system more clearly, the conceptual model was constructed, see Figure 2. As shown in Figure 2, the assembly system has been greatly influenced by uncertainty factors and itself

Figure 1. Assembly system consisting of multiple suppliers and single manufacturer

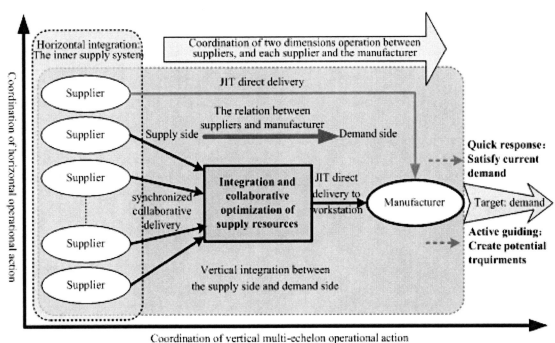

Figure 2. The conceptual model of emergence mechanism of uncertainty in assembly system

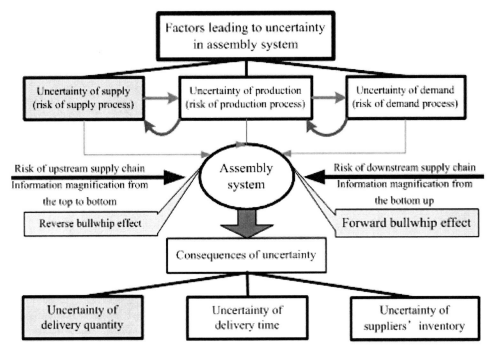

constraints in the collaborative operation process. As a result, the consequence is uncertainty of delivery quantity, delivery time, and supplier's inventory.

Therefore, to reduce these uncertainty which influences assembly system with multiple suppliers and single manufacturer, managers need to understand the source and influence of the uncertainty in assembly system, analyze the mechanism of the uncertainty, and then find the corresponding controlling mechanism.

Analysis of Uncertainty Factors

As for assembly system consisting of multiple suppliers and single manufacturer, the source of uncertainty emergence mainly lies in three aspects, namely supply process, production process, and demand process. These three sources of uncertainty make assembly system respond to customer slowly and decrease service level, resulting in inventory and warehousing fee increase, etc. Therefore, the above three uncertainty sources are the most basic factors, which determine the performance of assembly system.

The Supply Process

The uncertainty of supply process is that the suppliers are unable to provide a specified quality or quality of goods and services in agreed time and place due to the suppliers themselves or irresistible forces. As a result, the manufacturer can't assemble the components according to production plan to meet customer's demand. These factors include the fluctuating purchase price, uncertainty of supplier quantity (the quantity is not tested or partially checked), uncertainty of supply quality (quality is not examined), and random lead time.

Supply uncertainty directly affects the performance of assembly system. Although the suppliers have strict quality control in the production process, some components may become waste products due to characteristics of production

processing craft, especially in some accidental events such as fire and machines' out of control, etc., and eventually supplier can't deliver a sufficient number of components within the stipulated time. Beside, although suppliers and manufacturers negotiate a fixed lead time, there are many reasons caused that it is hard for the supplier to provide components on time in guarantee period. For example, the occurrence of natural disasters, poor production management, and the delayed delivery of supplier in higher level can also cause delay in delivery.

The Production Process

The uncertainty of production process mainly originates from manufacturing and assembling process, which may be caused by machinery breakdown, mismatching of suppliers' delivery, or the delay and disruption of the whole manufacturing resulting from other irresistible external environment changes. The uncertainty of production process often affects both upstream supply system and downstream distribution system. For example, temporary power failure, fires, strike in manufacturer's production workshop, production planning and improper management can also cause uncertainty in production process.

The Demand Process

The uncertainty of demand process is mainly caused by customer's frequent revision on the order and the irregular purchase resulting in demand instability. The demand uncertainty will not only affect the manufacturer's production planning, scheduling, control problem, but also indirectly affect delivery quality, time and supplier's inventory status.

For example, the volatility of customer preferences will cause irregular purchase inclination. It is very difficult to predict customers' demand, and the following factors exacerbate the uncertainty of customer demand: (1) Product life cycle continues shortening. On the one hand the market demand for product is changing, and on the other hand the technology offers the possibility for product updating, which cause customers' historical data of demand unacquirable or inaccurate. Let's take cars for example; product life cycle is 12 years in the 1970s, 4 years in the 1980s, and just for 18 months in 1990s. Electronic product life cycle is much shorter, and now the computer is almost out of date when approaching market. (2) Product varieties and competitive products increase, and market competition becomes increasingly fierce. The increasing products' varieties make it more and more difficult to predict the demand for a particular product. According to the Japanese Toyota Motor Corporation statistics, it produces 364,000 cars in three months with a total of 4 basic models and 32,100 different types. The average output number of each type is 11, where the most is 17, and the least is 6. Now many companies have begun pursuing "single production" (One of a kind production). It is obviously that compared with the uncertainty of supply process and the production process, the uncertainty of demand process mainly originates from the customers, and is relatively difficult to control.

Internal Characteristic of Assembly System

The internal characteristic of assembly system consisting of multiple suppliers and single manufacturer is an important factor, which exacerbates the uncertainty, and its influence is reflected in the following two aspects: one is the complexity of network structure and the other is the complexity of individual interactions in assembly system.

Complex Network Structure of Assembly System in Series-Parallel Connection

From the Figure 1, assembly system is the network system composed of multiple suppliers and single manufacturer, and each supplier has

its own supplier. Therefore, assembly system is a complex series-parallel network structure composed of multi-stage multiple suppliers and manufacturers, which exacerbates the uncertainty of assembly system.

As for the complex series-parallel assembly system, the uncertainty of assembly system can be measured through the reliability of a series of serial and parallel tasks. The reliability of raw materials at each level constitutes the reliability of the lower parts, and the reliability of parts at each level constitutes the reliability of each component. Finally the reliability of the components at each level constitutes the reliability of the entire product. For example, in a three-tier assembly system shown in Figure 3, the reliability of each node in the third tier has an impact on the node in the second tier, and eventually affects the node in the first tier. As a result, if the reliability of each node, which composed the assembly network, is

$$P_{ij}(i = 0,1,2,\cdots,n; j = 0,1,2,\cdots,k_i)$$

The entire reliability of assembly system is the multiple of the reliability of each node, that is

Figure 3. Network structure of a three-echelon assembly system

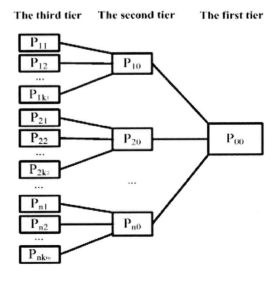

$$P = \prod_{i=0}^{n}\prod_{j=0}^{k_i} P_{ij}$$

So any echelon node will influence the reliability of assembly system. In assembly system as illustrated in Figure 3, the manufacturer's suppliers can be defined as first-tier supplier, and the first-level supplier's suppliers can be defined as second-level supplier, and so on. Then these different echelons constitute the supply chain system vertical hierarchy, while the suppliers at the same echelon constitute the horizontal hierarchy. Therefore, the uncertainty of the supply process will increase with the number of vertical hierarchy and the horizontal hierarchy in assembly system, just as the reverse bullwhip effect illustrated in Figure 2. For example, in a certain echelon any supplier's fault such as the quality of material, delay of delivery time, or breakdown of the production machinery will affect performance of the whole assembly system.

In summary, the regular operation of the upstream node enterprises is essential basis and condition of downstream business operation, such as car manufacturers. If fasteners supplier in the second tier can't delivery on time, it will affect chassis assembly in the first tier, which thus affect the whole production schedule. As a result, the uncertainty of the supply chain transfers along the supply chain from the initial material suppliers to each echelon step by step, which directly affects production process, the delivery time, and customer satisfaction. Ultimately the customer may turn to the other competitors.

The Interaction between the Different Node Enterprises in Assembly System

Each node enterprise in assembly system is the independent or semi-independent economic entity and these node enterprises have the relation of supply and demand in many properties such as competition, corporation or alliance, etc.

Every nodal enterprise of the supply chain system is the independent or semi-independent economic entity; these nodal enterprises have the competition, cooperation, dynamic and other of supply and demand relationship. The complexity of these node enterprises can be expressed in the two aspects such as entity dispersion and value difference.

The entity constituting a specific assembly system is usually dispersed geographically and the distribution range may be a region, a city or a country, etc. Entities can be classified as separate entities, semi-autonomous entities and dependent entities according to difference of the authority in management and decision-making.

Each node enterprise has its own objectives, business strategy, internal structure and survival power as to the value difference of enterprise. The goal of each enterprise is to enhance its competitiveness and gain profit through continuously improving their adaptation.

Each subject has subjective initiative, individual rationality and enterprise value orientation, and therefore various direct and coordinative measures in centralized organization used to coordinate the node enterprises in assembly system are not effective. Thus a new coordinative means is required.

For the dependent entities and semi-autonomous entities in internal node enterprises, the management complexity relates to enterprise culture orientation, each entity's function division, related rights and obligations, performance evaluation standards and other factors. For example, every department in the enterprise can accomplish their tasks independently, and performance of each department is individually evaluated. Therefore, in this structure, each entity just used to concern part of the efficiency in this enterprise, and not want to consider overall effectiveness of the whole enterprise.

For the independent entities outside the enterprise, the management complexity relates to the entities organizational structure, enterprise culture, information infrastructure and other factors. For example, each autonomous entity seeking for their own interests do not want to share some important information with other entities, and sacrifice their own interests to obtain the best interests of the whole supply chain.

Whether mutual information flow, logistics and cash flow are unblocked or not will have a direct impact on the difficulty of supply chain management and decision-making. For example, the fluency of information flow has a direct impact on collaborative operational efficiency of assembly system. Information asymmetry or information unequal asymmetry will make the originally controlled uncertainty out of control and enhance assembly system dependence on inventory. Millstein (1994) and Beamon (1998) have pointed out that asymmetric information, unequal symmetric information and decentralized decision-making amplified the uncertainty of supply chain. As a result, inventory level of each node enterprises in the supply chain is abnormal and unbalanced, which was a disaster for the entire supply chain coordination. In addition, actual operation of the capital flows also affects coordination efficiency of the supply chain. In supply chain, upstream and downstream node enterprises adopt inbound settlement, outbound settlement and pay-on-produce settlement currently. Among these settlements, pay-on-produce settlement transforms the cost of components into the upstream enterprises, strengthens its capital cost, make it hard to control the inventory in the downstream enterprises, and finally increase the uncertainty of supplier. While inbound settlement increases the costs and risks of downstream enterprises, for example, when a components fail to be delivered on time, even though other parts of suppliers delivery on time, the manufacturer eventually still cannot assemble the products on time. The inventory cost and opportunity cost of other surplus components delivered by other suppliers is undertaken by the manufacturer, which also harm the manufacturer's interests and increase the manufacturer's uncertainty.

In summary, in supply chain node enterprises carry out self-isolation of resources (including physical resources and information resources) for their own interests. The cooperation between enterprises is only temporary co-operation on trade, which artificially increases the information barriers and communication obstacles between enterprises. Node enterprises have to establish inventory to cope with any accidents, resulting in difficulties of coordinating inventory and aggravating the uncertainty of the assembly system.

The Consequence of Uncertainty in Assembly System

Due to the interaction of uncertainty sources and internal characteristic assembly system, there are many uncertainties in the coordination operation, which ultimately leads to inefficiency of the work, decline of revenue and low service level in the assembly system. The supply chain uncertainty's effects on supplier delivery mainly are: (1) the delivery quantity uncertainty, (2) the delivery time uncertainty, (3) the supplier inventory uncertainty.

Uncertainty of the Delivery Quantity

Uncertainty of supplier's delivery quantity is mainly caused by uncertainty sources in supply process. Uncertainty of supplier's delivery quantity is mainly caused by the following three aspects: emergencies in supply process, constraints of supplier's capacity and the characteristics of components production and processing.

The emergencies in supply process mainly refer to the events that affect supplier's regular production, which happens accidently. These emergencies in supply process may include the natural disaster, social events or other abnormal factors that influence supplier's regular production. The suppliers influenced by emergencies may be the manufacturer's first-echelon supplier, second-echelon supplier and even multi-echelon supplier. The occurrence of emergencies will eventually lead to uncertainty of delivery quantity. For example, a catastrophic fire occurred on February 3, 1997 in Aisin Seiki, which was Japan's largest auto manufacturer Toyota's subsidiary supplier. Aisin Seiki provided main brake cylinders for several kinds of Toyota models, and is the only supplier of brake proportion metering valves. After the fire the stock of important components required by Toyota just could be used for a half day, soon the Toyota production line stopped and the fire also affected the regular production of other suppliers. Obviously emergencies in supply process can result in disruption or partial disruption of supplier production and it is the important source that causes the uncertainty of supplier delivery.

Constraints of the supplier's capacity refer to limited supply quantity due to excessive demand or limited capacity. As a result, suppliers deliver in accordance with a random percentage of orders. In Chinese thermal power industry when the summer peak comes, the supply of coal-fired power plant becomes a thornier problem. Because of the limited capacity, upstream suppliers of the coal-fired power plant often deliver the coal according to a certain percentage of the downstream coal-fired power plants' orders. Therefore, the coal deliveries are often uncertain.

Uncertainty of supplier's delivery quantity caused by the characteristics of components production and processing indicates that though quality of components is strictly controlled final production quantity of qualified products is uncertain due to the elaborate and complex process of product processing. Such as in industry of electronic chip and liquid crystal display, the average effective outputs often less than 50%. Thus, the uncertainty of delivery quantity caused by the characteristics of components production and processing is common related industry.

Uncertainty of the Delivery Time

Among logistics, capital flow and information flow in supply chain, logistics is the bottleneck of supply chain management, which is constrained by physical distribution limited by time and space. In the process of physical distribution, supply delay mainly originates from the three crossing areas: supply process of raw materials, production process, and transportation process.

In the supply process of raw materials, the supply uncertainty transfers from the initial suppliers of raw material to lower the echelon step by step along the supply chain, which directly affects the assembly process of production and delivery time, leading to customer dissatisfaction. Supply delay of raw material will lead to delivery delays, and even customers' returns and turning to its competitors.

Supply uncertainty has particularly serious effect on enterprise whose product lifecycle is short and adaption is frequent. For example, a home appliance manufacturer received a batch of product order several years ago, and the manufacture produced and deliver batch-by-batch, but the last batch of products failed to be delivered on time for some reason. At this time, the products in the market are being replaced by new products. Therefore, the buyer refused the products, which brought great economic losses to manufacturer.

In the production process, under the premise of ensuring the supply of raw materials, the key factor affecting uncertainty of the delivery time is the uncertainty of production equipment downtime. The higher the equipment availability probability is, the less the average downtime and the smaller the production process uncertainty are. But the essential reason of the logistics distribution process delay is the complexity of the assembly system structure, and of course the occasional factors in transportation process are also the reason for delay.

Uncertainty of the Supplier's Inventory

Each node enterprise in assembly system determines its own purchasing plan, inventory level and production plan according to demand information of downstream node enterprise, and then the deviation of demand information enlarges step by step along the direction of information flow. The results of accumulated deviation are as follows: the demand information got by the material suppliers in the source of supply chain is large differently from the actual demand information of the market, and the total deviation of demand information in both ends of the supply chain is much greater than the magnitude of two nodes in the supply chain. Because of this effect, in order to ensure the timely supply of materials, the upstream suppliers would maintain more inventory than the next echelon to prevent the material demand fluctuations—this is the typical positive bullwhip effect caused by demand uncertainty, as shown in Figure 2.

In addition, the uncertainty caused by gradual amplification of demand information deviation also affects enterprise's lead time at each echelon. When the market demand changes smoothly or has occasional small fluctuation, manufacturers have to prepare more components' inventory to meet the occasional fluctuations. Besides suppliers have to prepare more raw materials inventory to meet the changing needs of the manufacturer. The suppliers' suppliers need much more raw materials inventory to meet the downstream demand, and then the lead time is also extended forward.

After a multi-echelon amplification of information, the original material suppliers need to have more inventory than the actual market demand and the longer stock time, which also means the inventory cost and the occupation of capital opportunity cost is greater. In order to ensure their business reputation, the supplier has to afford this additional inventory costs. Because assembly system with multiple suppliers and single manufacturer is a complex series-parallel network system, the more obvious the amplification of cumulative deviation is, the greater the inventory cost of the corresponding upstream supplier is.

The research shows that the bullwhip effect caused by demand amplification exists in industries of automobile, daily necessities, computer, papermaking and other processing industries. For example, logistics manager in Procter and Gamble has checked the order of one of their most popu-lar products - baby diapers, and found that retail sales have some fluctuations compared with the orders. But the P&G's own suppliers, such as 3M Company's orders have more amazing fluctuation deviation compared with the sales. Although the baby diapers are functional products, and the consumption is relatively stable and the demand is predictable, the order in delivery process is increasing among different members step by step to the upstream supply chain.

MONITORING OPERATION MODE OF SUPPLY COORDINATION IN ASSEMBLY SYSTEM UNDER UNCERTAIN DELIVERY

Monitoring Operation Process of Supply Coordination in Assembly System under Uncertain Delivery

Monitoring of supply coordination in assembly system under uncertain delivery is a very complex problem. The inventory information can be monitored to control the production process. Mastering suppliers' production status, forecasting and monitoring supply capacity and delivery time, and ensuring timely supply enable that the enterprise dynamically tracks the market changes and implementation of orders, and then makes the necessary adjustments and decision-making timely.

In the supply process of assembly system with multiple suppliers and single manufacturer, manufacturer's purchasing and supply services are entrusted to professional organization, such as their professional procurement departments or Supply-hub managed by third party logistics. In practical operation of the assembly system the manufacturer often outsource procurement and supply activities to third party logistics, and the third party logistics take charge of Supply-hub for the two sides. Thus, Supply-hub can be regarded as a subordinate entity or semi-autonomous entity of the manufacturer. This paper constructs monitoring operation process of supply coordination in assembly system under uncertain delivery, as shown in Figure 4. The basic operation process is as follows:

The manufacturer determines its production plan according to downstream customer orders and demand forecasting, then generates procurement plan of purchased parts, production plan of self-made parts, and weekly, daily requirement plan of the total materials after running MRP, which will be released on the monitoring platform of coordination in assembly system.

Each component supplier knows the manufacturer's purchasing plan and confirms the purchasing orders from this coordination monitoring platform then check their components' inventory dynamically in Supply Hub and finally sends their delivery plan to the coordination monitoring platform sharing with the third party logistics. Each component supplier can realize coordination design, synchronous manufacturing, and collaborative supply according to the coordination monitoring platform.

According to weekly and daily requirement plan released on the coordination monitoring platform, the third party logistics will deliver the components to manufacturer's workstation in JIT, and send the dynamic inventory information of all components on the coordination monitoring platform, which supports supplier's inquiry of inventory status.

The manufacturer can classify all suppliers into different groups by importance, and correspondingly adopt different monitoring grade, such as monitoring final product, monitoring inventory and monitoring work procedure, etc. (Dong et al., 2006). According to information shared from the coordination monitoring platform, the manufacturer can carry out these deferent monitoring grades with different groups of suppliers. If suppliers' delivery is uncertain, the relevant information will be sent to the coordination monitoring platform, the manufacturer will take relevant measures

Figure 4. Monitoring operation process of supply coordination in assembly system under uncertain delivery

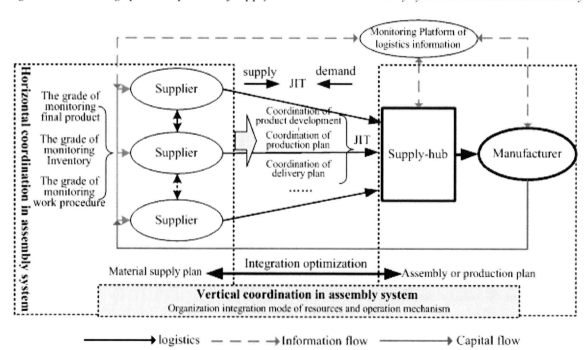

and implement the corresponding coordination monitoring and warning.

In the operation process of coordination, logistics, information flow, capital flow and business flow in assembly system from component suppliers, Supply Hub operators to the manufacturer can be integrated through Supply Hub and coordination monitoring platform. The operator can monitor logistics and capital flow based information flow obtained from monitoring platform. Therefore, Coordination of two dimensions activities between suppliers, and each supplier and the manufacturer can be achieved.

Monitoring Mode of Collaborative Supply Process in Assembly System under Uncertain Delivery

In general, supplier production process includes activities of processing and assembly. The purpose of monitoring collaborative supply process is to ensure the stability of supply, and the supply stability will require supplier production should be stable. However, the contingency in suppliers' production and the fluctuations in supply process of raw materials will damage the stability more or less. To reduce the losses caused by the abnormal events, the appropriate treatment and prevention should be prepared when the accidents happen or are likely to happen. In assembly system, components provided by different suppliers are of different importance to manufactures. Therefore, in the process of collaborative supply the manufacturer actually takes different mode of monitoring different types of suppliers through the logistics information monitoring platform based on Supply Hub. In the operation process of collaborative supply, the manufacturer can adopt the following controlling mechanisms according to different types of suppliers under uncertain delivery.

The mode of monitoring final product. The mode of monitoring final product means to monitor the completion of the supplier production and the storage of finished products, which can be done

by comparing supplier's production plan with its actual completion. The grade of monitoring final product is the simplest monitoring, so it can be used for all suppliers to monitor supply process. Its advantage is simple, and the manufacturer just needs to monitor the completion of suppliers' production. If the manufacturer knows suppliers' production plan in advance and suppliers have the storage of finished products, whether the problems of suppliers' production exist or not can be obtained by comparing the storage time with the scheduled time. If there are problems, the manufacturer can send alarm information to suppliers, and suppliers can take some measures to remedy the situation. The disadvantage is that it can just be used to monitor suppliers simply, but cannot monitor the suppliers dynamically. When the problems are found at the moment of inbound storage, the accident has occurred. If measures cannot be taken to remedy, it will cause losses to assembly system. Therefore, this monitoring mode is most applicable to monitoring non-key suppliers.

The mode of monitoring inventory. The mode of monitoring inventory refers to monitoring storage status of suppliers' raw materials or semi-finished products. If the supplier provides components for the manufacturer, the inbound and outbound inventory information of raw materials, semi-finished products and assembly components can monitored. If the supplier provides the main components for the manufacturer, its production process can monitored by setting up several monitoring points. The supplier's final completion time can be predicted from the information acquired by monitoring. If the prediction is that there may be some problems with the supplier's final completion time, alarm information can be sent to the supplier and remind the supplier to solve this problem. Its advantages are as follows: compared to the grade of monitoring final product, this mode can find and solve the problems ahead of time, and the operation is relatively simple. The disadvantage is that the forecasting accuracy is also limited due to the limited intensity of monitoring. Therefore, this monitoring mode is suitable for monitoring sub-key suppliers.

The mode of monitoring work procedure. The mode of monitoring work procedure means dynamically monitoring each supplier's work procedure in its production process. The implementation of this monitoring model requires that supplier should provide its detailed production plan for the manufacturer. The manufacturer establishes a database according to the completion time of each work stage promised by supplier and regards it as the basis for the implementation of monitoring work procedure. If manufacturer finds that supplier's completion time of the procedure is not the same as the schedule, it will send warning to the supplier, and the supplier will be able to solve the problem immediately. Its advantage is that due to the strict control, manufactures and suppliers can find the problem of production in time, which reduces losses to the minimum. The disadvantage of this monitoring is too complicated. Therefore, this monitoring mode can be used to monitor important key suppliers.

MONITORING MECHANISM OF SUPPLY COORDINATION IN ASSEMBLY SYSTEM UNDER UNCERTAIN DELIVERY

According to the above definition of different monitoring modes, different grades of monitoring modes can be adopted to different importance of materials in the manufacturer's bill of material. And which mode to adopt is determined by the importance of suppliers' components. Therefore, suppliers that participate in collaborative supply need to be classified and managed.

Supplier Classification under Uncertain Delivery

In order to coordinate assembly system under uncertain delivery, the manufacturer is required to classify and manage the suppliers. Not all suppliers that participate in supply coordination will have the phenomenon of supply uncertainty, which includes uncertainty of delivery quantity, uncertainty of delivery time and uncertainty of suppliers' inventory. In the supply process of components ordered by the manufacturer, the suppliers who have supply uncertainty are few. Therefore, the manufacturer can reduce and even eliminate the supply uncertainty phenomenon of few suppliers by the classified management, which can reduce assembly system's losses caused by supply non-coordination.

From the aspect of manufacturer, suppliers who participate in supply coordination can be two-dimensionally divided into four quadrants according to the importance of supplier to purchaser and the importance of purchaser to supplier, see Figure 5.

Type of Commercial Suppliers

For manufacturers, commercial suppliers mean that suppliers are not very important to purchasing business, and can be selected and substituted easily by others. The components provided by commercial supplier generally are of little value and great substitutability. In reality, commercial suppliers account for a larger proportion of the suppliers who provided components to manufactures. When the supply uncertainty happens to this kind of supplier, the manufacture can find the appropriate substitute quickly in the market. Therefore, the phenomenon of supply uncertainty happening to the commercial suppliers has little effect on supply coordination.

Figure 5. Classification of suppliers under uncertain delivery

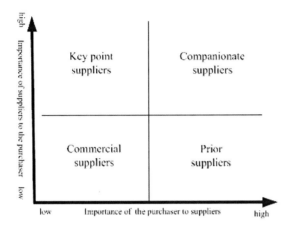

Type of Prior Suppliers

Prior suppliers imply that the manufacturer believes procurement of some suppliers is not very important to them, but the supplier argues the manufacturer's procurement is very important to them. In this case, the procurement is very beneficial for manufacturers and suppliers generally will not be allowed out of stock. The components provided by prior suppliers are of little value and great substitutability. Compared with commercial suppliers, the supply uncertainty phenomenon happening to priority-based supplier is much less; therefore, prior suppliers will seldom have the phenomenon of supply uncertainty.

Type of Key Point Suppliers

Key point supplier means that suppliers believe that manufacturer's purchasing does not matter to them, but the manufactures hold that their purchasing is very important to them. In general, the components provided by key point suppliers are generally of great value and little substitutability, and suppliers are more easily out of stock. In reality, the key point suppliers account for a smaller proportion of the suppliers. But key point suppliers have greater supply uncertainty. Their shortages or delivery delays will cause great losses to the manufacture. Therefore, key point suppliers are the key monitoring objects in assembly system.

Type of Companionate Suppliers

Companionate suppliers are suppliers that believe the procurement is very important to them, and the manufactures also believe the procurement is very important to them. In general, the components offered by companionate supplier are of great value and little substitutability, but suppliers are unlikely to be out of stock. In reality, the number of partner-type supplier is a little more than key point suppliers. Companionate suppliers have little supply uncertainty, so companionate suppliers are the sub-key monitoring objects of supply coordination.

In the operation process of supply coordination, different suppliers are monitored with different grades. So according to the classification of suppliers under uncertain delivery, and combining with the characteristics of purchased components (value, importance and supply risk), the relationship diagram between purchased parts and supplier type is given, as shown in Figure 6 (Dong et al., 2006). The important products in short supply and the non-important products in short supply are more likely to have supply uncertainty, and the suppliers of important products in short supply are mostly key point suppliers and companionate suppliers respectively. The suppliers of non-important products in short supply are mostly key-point suppliers. Thus, for manufactures (purchasers), the key point suppliers and companionate suppliers should be the key monitoring object of supply coordination.

Supply Chain Collaboration Supply Monitoring Mechanism under Uncertain Delivery Condition

From the above analysis, different supplier is of different importance to the manufacturer, and the possibility of uncertainty which happens to different suppliers is not exactly the same. So under this

Figure 6. The relationship diagram between purchased parts and supplier's type

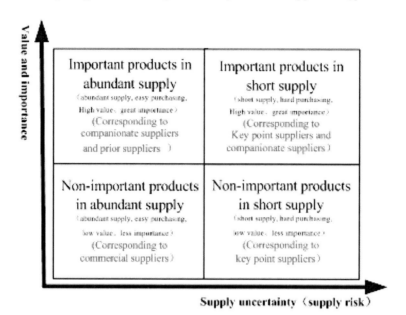

uncertain delivery, assembly system with multiple suppliers and single manufacturer needs to adopt different monitoring modes to different types of suppliers (See, Figure 7), specifically, are:

- Components provided by commercial suppliers or prior suppliers have many supply source, strong substitutability, and less supply risk, so the mode of monitoring fi-

nal product can be applied to monitor commercial suppliers and prior suppliers.

- Components provided by companionate suppliers are of great value, less supply sources and may have more supply risk, so the mode of monitoring inventory should be used to monitor companionate suppliers.
- Components provided by key point suppliers are of high-value, less supply sourc-

Figure 7. Monitoring mechanism based on different grades of suppliers

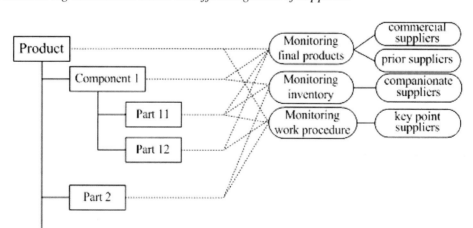

es, and in weak substitutability and great risks. Therefore, mode of monitoring work procedure should be adopted to monitor the key point suppliers.

In monitoring process of supply coordination, we can use the layered network diagram of monitoring supply coordination in assembly system to express various complex supply relationships according to the BOM layer relationship in each node and the monitoring mode of each node, as illustrated in Figure 8.

The top layer is the assembly system based on BOM, which expresses the suppliers participating in the supply coordination clearly. The second layer is network of monitoring the final products, which regards commercial suppliers and prior suppliers as monitoring objects. The third layer is network of monitoring inventory, which takes companionate suppliers as monitoring objects. The last layer is network of monitoring work

procedure, which regards key point suppliers as monitoring objects. In the network system of supply coordination based on BOM in assembly system illustrated in Figure 8, each supplier's monitoring mode can also be expressed clearly. The shadow rectangle nodes represent the final product manufacturers. The rectangular nodes represent the suppliers of monitoring final products. The triangular nodes represent the suppliers of monitoring inventory, and the oval-shaped nodes represent the suppliers of monitoring work procedure.

In the process of monitoring supply coordination, the importance of monitoring grades can be arranged to descending order as follows: the mode of monitoring work procedure, the mode of monitoring inventory and the mode of monitoring final product. Monitoring nodes of high grades are composed of the nodes which monitoring grades are lower. As illustrated in Figure 8, in the first layer of assembly system based on BOM, the

Figure 8. Layered network diagram of monitoring supply coordination in assembly system

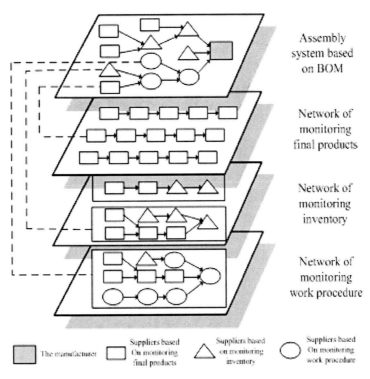

monitoring grade of upper echelon of the terminal manufacturer are respectively monitoring inventory, monitoring inventory, and monitoring work procedure. When we carry forward the upper supply echelon, the upper-echelon' monitoring grade is not higher than the next-echelon monitoring grade. For example, if monitoring grade in this echelon is monitoring final products, the highest monitoring grade in upper echelon is monitoring final products.

The hierarchical relationship of this monitoring mode is more in line with reality, because when there are great uncertainties in supply source, the suppliers close to the final product assembly also have a lot of uncertainty, therefore the closer to the assembly manufacturer, the higher monitoring mode the suppliers need. If there are great uncertainties on the final product assembly, the suppliers in the supply source may not have great uncertainty, because the uncertainty of suppliers close to final assembly may caused by other processes, and therefore, the upstream upper echelon is not higher than the downstream lower monitoring grades.

In summary, as for the problems we study in this paper, the key suppliers of the manufacturer account for very little percentage of the total number of suppliers, but the components provided by key suppliers are key components for assembling. Therefore the grade of monitoring work procedure should be used. If some unexpected accidents happen to a certain key point supplier in the production process, they should be monitored and warned in time, and appropriate measures could be taken. The manufacturer try to help key point suppliers to avoid the losses caused by their shortage or delivery delay, and ensure coordination operation of assembly system is not affected and customers' service level can be achieved.

SUPPLY PROCESS MONITORING AND WARNING MODEL OF COORDINATION IN ASSEMBLY SYSTEM BASED ON CASE BASED REASONING

As the important products in short supply and the non-important products in short supply provided by key point suppliers are of great uncertainty and of weak substitutability. When the components provided by key point suppliers are out of stock, the manufactures' assembly will not be possible, which results in huge losses of the whole assembly system. For example, on March 17, 2000, the NO.22 chip factory of New Mexico Philips caught fires. This factory is an important part of Ericsson's assembly system, and provides many kinds of important parts of the chip. In the first few days after the fire, as easily believed that this is just a small event in security of the supplier, Ericsson did not realize fire's possible effect on mobile phone manufactures. In Early April, as Ericsson did not have a selectable alternative supplier, and many important chips supplied by that factory are disrupted. Several weeks later, when the factory resumed production, Ericsson had lost 4 billion in sales, and the market share had declined from 12% to 9%. It can be seen that the burst fire happening to the upstream major chip supplier makes huge losses to the downstream manufacturer Ericsson. If Ericsson took effective measures to monitor and warn the supplier's production and supply process when the fire happened or after it happened, the losses suffered by Ericsson will be greatly reduced.

Therefore, grade of monitoring work procedure should be applied to monitoring and warning the supply coordination process of key point manufacturer. When something happens to the production of key point suppliers, the manufacture should take appropriate remedial measures based on the specific case of monitoring and warning to avoid or reduce the loss of components uncertainty in assembly system. Based on this, this paper will use the Case-Based Reasoning (CBR) approach to monitor and warn supply coordination process of key point suppliers and establish the appropriate early warning models.

The Monitoring and Warning Model of Supply Coordination Based on CBR

Case-Based Reasoning and Reasoning Process

With the rapid development of computer science and information technology, human beings face exponential growth in knowledge and information, which makes the traditional rule-based reasoning (Rule-Based Reasoning (RBR)) system in insurmountable difficulties at the acquisition of knowledge and rules. The case-based reasoning references the way of people's dealing with problems, avoids this bottleneck, and use the previously accumulated knowledge and experience to solve the problem directly, which cause concerns of experts and scholars and has becoming a hot research field of artificial intelligence.

CBR is an important and effective reasoning technology in artificial intelligence, and the core idea is: when solve the same or slightly change problems, the experience and knowledge is applied to reasoning and making decision without having to start all over again. The reasoning is as follows:

- Input the requirements, initial conditions, and other relevant information of the problem to be solved.
- According to the requirements of new issues and initial conditions, retrieve a set of cases similar to new problems in the case library.
- Find the most similar cases from similar instances or combine multiple instances to solute the new problem.

- If satisfied, it will be stored in case library as a new case; or analysis the reason for failure and act accordingly.

The Monitoring and Warning Framework of Supply Coordination in Assembly System-Based CBR

CBR method is actually based on the classification of suppliers. By searching the feature of emergency that happens to key point suppliers, it find the same or similar cases and extract the corresponding feature and output the results of early warning, which provides decision support for the coordination of supply process in assembly system quickly. Figure 9 describes the conceptual monitoring and warning framework of supply coordination in assembly system (Naken, 2001).

In assembly system based CBR there are five basic activities in this process (Naken, 2001).

- **Matching:** Retrieving the most appropriate case from a collection of past cases is a search-and-match problem in which the emergency feature is used as a search criterion. The matching rule may be a straight match or it may be modified to improve the match (i.e. the different emergency may be included to influence the match result).
- **Retrieval:** The retrieval task in CBR deals with searching past cases to find the best match between the new case and individual past case using the emergency feature as matching criteria. For key point suppliers, as the supply uncertainty are more likely happen to them, so there are more emergency cases in the case library. Thus, a partially matched case that has highest match score is retrieved.
- **Adoption/Adaptation:** This function is responsible for applying the information retrieved from the past cases to the new case. If the related feature of retrieval case is consistent with the new emergency, this

Figure 9. The monitoring and warning framework of supply coordination

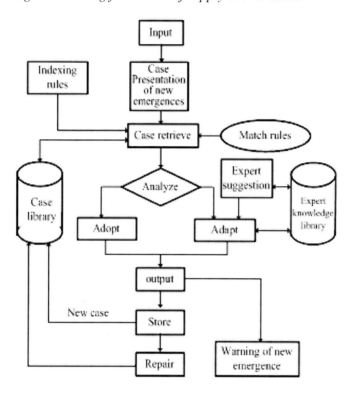

case is adopted. However, in most of the artificial intelligence issues, the retrieval information is not consistent with the new emergency; therefore, it must be adapted to suit the new case, which is actually an adaptation process of a new instance.

- **Storage:** Store the adapted representative new emergency case into the case library.
- **Repair:** Maintenance and update the case library, in case the abnormal scheme matching and retrieval results happen because of the integration of new case.

The Benefits of Warning of Supply Coordination in Assembly System Based on CBR

CBR method can be applied to monitoring and warning supply coordination of assembly system. Its main goal is to find the case which is most similar to the emergency of key point suppliers,

then output the corresponding processing results of warning and countermeasures. Case library actually means the original emergence database. The advantages of this method on supply coordination monitoring and warning are:

- CBR parallels actual human decision-making process. When a new emergence is presented, similar emergences from the past are used as the basis for solving the new emergence.
- CBR is an artificial intelligence with self-organizing learning, and can add some representative examples to the case library automatically.
- Creating a case-based system is usually more rapid than creating a traditional knowledge based system.
- CBR use computer technology as the support. It is a kind of approximate rapid warning methods and takes little time to

solve new problems, so its handling of warning emergency is quick, which is benefit for assembly system to take effective measures to remedy, reduce, or eliminate losses caused by uncertainty of the key point suppliers.

- CBR provides better explanation and justification. CBR can easily justify a solution by pointing to similar solutions and describing the rules that are generated through the reasoning process.
- CBR does not require a large number of past data to be able to solve a new problem.

The Key Technology of Monitoring and Warning Supply Coordination Based on CBR

CBR-based monitoring and warning model of supply coordination is mainly based on case library and consisted of these five aspects case, such as library's organization, case index, case initialization, case search and retrieval, and case adaptation. For the monitoring and warning of supply coordination in this paper, the difficulty is the establishment of case index and case retrieving in the case library.

The Establishment of the Case Index

The establishment of the case index is the basis and prerequisite condition for effective case retrieval. If the index definition is too wide, more cases may be retrieved. On the contrary, if the definition is too narrow, the similar cases may not be retrieved.

Since in operation process of supply coordination, there are many sporadic factors leading to uncertainty of key point suppliers and their performance at different stages is different. Thus, relational database can be used to store case, which is described in Table 1.

Search and Retrieval of Case

The most critical work in monitoring and warning mode of supply coordination based on CBR is to search the best matching case, and thus obtain the current emergency's warning source, warning signs, warning grade and other disposal strategies, thereby reducing and eliminating the key point suppliers' delivery uncertainty which influences the whole assembly system. Therefore, after determining presentation of case index, whether the retrieval method is appropriate or not is very important to monitoring and warning mode of supply coordination. In general, there are three main methods for case retrieval: the first is the most adjacent method, that is, definite and calculate the similarity between cases (or matching), and the case of largest similarity is the matching case. The second is the inductive method, which extracts characteristics difference between cases and forms a hierarchy similar to the differentiating network, use the decision tree as search strategy to retrieve. The inductive method is suitable for the cases which are independent of each other. The third is the knowledge guided method. This method precedes the indexing and controlling by a set of rules, and determines which characteristic is the most important in indexing according to the known knowledge, and organize and retrieve according to these features.

However, according to characteristics of monitoring and warning of supply coordination, the most adjacent method is the most suitable for solving the overall similarity of this case. The specific algorithm can be described as follows:

1. Divide the indexes described in the case characteristics in Table 1 into quantitative indexes and qualitative indexes, and calculate the deviation from each index and the corresponding indexes in the existing case library.

Table 1. Date field description of emergency of key point suppliers

No.	Field Name	Emergence Instruction
1	Case ID	
2	Case type	Include natural disasters, production accidents, political unrest, upstream suppliers default, transport disruption, abnormal fluctuation in the market, etc.
3	Case consequence	The effects on delivery time, quality, goal of revenue, and other aspects
4	Case warning level (emergence severity)	Divided into five levels: 5 (lightest), 4 (lighter), 3 (general), 2 (serious), 1 (particularly serious)
5	Occurrence time	
6	Occurrence place	
7	Reason	
8	Case description	
9	Case features	Level 1 early-warning index 1 (index 1, value 1, weight 1; index2, value2, weight 2; …, index m, value m, weight m) Level 2 early-warning index 2 (index 1, value 1, weight 1; index2, value2, weight 2; …, index m, value m, weight m) …… Level n early-warning index n (index 1, value 1, weight 1; index2, value2, weight 2; …, index m, value m, weight m)
10	Affected work procedure	Include supply, production, distribution, etc.
11	Directly affected subject	Suppliers, manufacturers, logistics providers, etc.
12	Response	
13	Details response	Include file labels, file name, etc.
14	Parties	Man participating in handling emergence or detailedly understanding the internal information.
15	Other instruction	

Quantitative indexes need to be normalized and dimensionless, while the qualitative indexes can be transformed into quantitative indexes using fuzzy evaluation method and then can be normalized and dimensionless. This paper use extreme value method of dimensionless indexes. If $x_i(t_j)$ is the described index for the feature of emergency, set

$$R = \max_i \left\{ x_i(t_j) \right\} (i = 1, 2, \cdots, n;\ j = 1, 2, \cdots m)$$

$$r = \min_i \left\{ x_i(t_j) \right\} (i = 1, 2, \cdots, n;\ j = 1, 2, \cdots m)$$

The dimensionless function of positive index is:

$$x_i^*(t_j) = \frac{x_i - r}{R - r}$$

The dimensionless function of inverse indicator is:

$$x_i^*(t_j) = \frac{R - x_i}{R - r}$$

and $x_i^*(t_j)$ is the dimensionless observations.

2. Use the AHP method to solve the wight of each attribute indexes of the emergency. Different attribute indexes have different impacts on the key point suppliers of supply uncertainty; hence weights should be given differently.

3. According to deviation between the new emergency and the existing cases in the case library and the indexing weights, the integrated deviation can be calculated between new emergency and the existing case in the case library.

Let the distance between the new emergency cases and known cases is $x_i^*(t_j)$, the formula is:

$$d_s = \frac{\sum_{i=1}^{n}[w_i \times S(f_i^*, f_i^k)]}{\sum_{i=1}^{n} w_i}$$

In the formula, * means the target case, k is the number of source case in the case library, $S(f_i^1, f_i^k)$ means the similarity of the target and source characteristic in the i th characteristic, and w_i is the weight of the i th characteristic.

If integrated deviation between new emergency and some existing case is greater than the pre-determined threshold, then the retrieved results of case library can be used as early warning basis of new emergency. If the integrated deviation is less than the pre-determined threshold, then consult experts and get the early-warning result and add the modified case into the case library.

FINDINGS AND RESEARCH CONTRIBUTION

Base on vast investigation of automobile industry in China such as Jiangling engine company, Shen Long automobile company, General Motors' corporation in China, Dongfeng Automobile company, etc., and analysis of supply uncertainty and classification of suppliers in assembly system, this study provide the first warning and monitoring mechanisms of supply coordination in assembly system under delivery uncertainty. Although the findings in these aspects are mainly through investigation of Chinese automobile industry, these findings are found in compliance with other industries such as Nokia in the electronics manufacturing industry (Tang, 2006). Therefore, the main findings and contributions can be concluded as follows.

First, the uncertainty factors in assembly system are given and emergence mechanism of supply uncertainty in the assembly system is also proposed. The uncertainty of supply process in the assembly system originates from supply process uncertainty, production process uncertainty and demand process uncertainty. And the uncertainty of supply coordination increased with the characteristics of the assembly system (i.e. the network of complex assembly system based on series-parallel structure and interactions between node enterprises). Taking these reasons, monitoring mode of uncertainty in assembly system with multiple suppliers and single manufacturer can be divided into grade monitoring final products, grade of monitoring inventory and grade of monitoring work procedure.

Second, the monitoring operation mode of supply coordination is first provided in assembly system under uncertain delivery. In the supply process of assembly system with multiple suppliers and single manufacturer, manufacturer's purchasing and supply services are entrusted to professional organization, such as their professional procurement departments or Supply-hub managed by third party logistics. In the practical operation of the assembly system manufacturers often outsource procurement and supply activities to third party logistics, and the third party logistics take charge of Supply-hub for the two sides. Thus, Supply-hub can be regarded as the subordinate entity or the semi-autonomous entity of manufacturer. This paper constructs monitoring operation process of supply coordination in assembly system under uncertain delivery.

Third, the suppliers are first classified into four categories according the supply risk and value of component, and monitoring tactics for supply coordination are also provided. In the assembly system based on multiple suppliers and single manufacturer, not all suppliers will have the phenomenon of supply uncertainty. In the supply process, the suppliers that have the uncertainty phenomenon are few, so the manufacturer (the purchaser) can be divided into four categories based on the importance of suppliers to purchasers and purchasers to suppliers, which are key point suppliers, companionate suppliers, commercial suppliers, and prior suppliers.

Key point suppliers generally provide the important products in short supply and the non-important products in short supply, while companionate suppliers supply the non-important products in short supply and the general important products. The prior suppliers provide the important products in abundant supply, while commercial suppliers offer the non-important products in abundant supply. Therefore, according to the importance of the different types of suppliers, the key point suppliers should be under grade of monitoring work procedure, while companionate suppliers are under grade of monitoring inventory. And the other two types of supplier can be taken the grade of monitoring final products. As the key point suppliers are more likely to be uncertain, and in case of supply disruption, the components are non-substitutable, so the stock out of components provided by key point suppliers will bring great losses to the assembly system.

Fourth, case based reasoning is used to monitor and warn the supply process in assembly system. Monitoring and warning model of supply coordination based on CBR has the advantages of less time on warning process, better prediction accuracy, easier to maintain the case library and so on. The key process of monitoring and warning model of supply coordination lies in the establishment of case index and case retrieving. The case indexes can be established by storing the case related characteristics' data fields in the relational data tables, and retrieving of case through the most adjacent method. After retrieving the case library, if the integrated deviation between new emergency and some existing case is greater than the pre-determined threshold, then the search matches and the early warning results retrieved in case library can be used as early warning basis of new emergency. If the integrated deviation is less than the pre-determined threshold, then consult experts, and get the early warning result and add the modified case into the case library.

CONCLUSION

Currently due to frequent natural disasters and social events, the uncertainty of assembly system increases. For assembly system, how to reduce and eliminate negative impacts of supply uncertainty, production uncertainty and demand uncertainty is a real problem need to be solved in great need. Based on this, this paper proposes monitoring and warning mechanism of supply coordination under uncertain delivery, analyzes the problems of supply coordination and draws the following conclusions:

First, the uncertainty of supply process in assembly originates from supply process uncertainty, production process uncertainty and demand process uncertainty. And the uncertainty of supply coordination increased with the characteristics of the assembly system (i.e. the network of complex assembly system based on series-parallel structure and interactions between node enterprises).

Second, in the assembly system based on multiple suppliers and single manufacturer, not all suppliers will have the phenomenon of supply uncertainty. In the supply process, the suppliers that have the uncertainty phenomenon are few, so the manufacturer (the purchaser) can be divided into four categories based on the importance of suppliers to purchasers and purchasers to suppliers.

Third, monitoring and warning model of supply coordination based on CBR has the advantages of less time on warning process, better prediction accuracy, easier to maintain the case library and so on.

There are also several limitations in this study. The factors of supply uncertainty are just analyzed in assembly system, as supply chain is a very complex network. Second, the suppliers can be categorized in other principles in place of supply risks, value, and importance. Third, although the warning and monitoring model is constructed based on CBR, the more suitable and reliable model should be explored. One future research direction is to include more reliable and advanced method into this model, which we expect will further complicate the analysis and make the characterization of model more challenging and interesting.

ACKNOWLEDGMENT

This research was supported by the National Natural Science Foundation of China (No.71102174, 71072035, 60979010), Program for New Century Excellent Talents in University, China (No.NCET-10-0048, NCET-10-0043), Beijing Natural Science Foundation, China (No.9123028, 9102016), Beijing Philosophy and Social Science Foundation, China (No.11JGC106), Key Project Cultivation Fund of the Scientific and Technical Innovation Program in Beijing Institute of technology, China (No.2011DX01001), Excellent Young Teacher in Beijing institute of Technology, China (No.2010YC1307), and Basic Research in Beijing institute of Technology, China (No.20102142013).

REFERENCES

Basnet, C., & Leung, J. M. Y. (2005). Inventory lot-sizing with supplier selection. *Computers & Operations Research*, *32*, 1–14. doi:10.1016/S0305-0548(03)00199-0

Beamon, B. M., & Ware, T. M. (1998). A process quality model for the analysis, improvement and control of supply chain systems. *International Journal of Physical Distribution & Logistics Management*, *28*(9/10), 704–715. doi:10.1108/09600039810248127

Berger, P. D., & Zeng, A. Z. (2006). Single versus multiple sourcing in the presence of risks. *The Journal of the Operational Research Society*, *57*(3), 250–261. doi:10.1057/palgrave.jors.2601982

Blackhurst, J. V., Scheibe, K. P., & Johnson, D. J. (2008). Supplier risk assessment and monitoring for the automotive industry. *International Journal of Physical Distribution & Logistics Management*, *38*(2), 143–165. doi:10.1108/09600030810861215

Cohen, M. A., & Kunreuther, H. (2007). Operations risk management: Overview of Paul Kleindorfer's contributions. *Production and Operations Management*, *16*(5), 525–541. doi:10.1111/j.1937-5956.2007.tb00278.x

Demirtas, E. A., & Ustun, O. (2008). An integrated multi objective decision making process for supplier selection and order allocation. *Omega: The International Journal of Management Science*, *36*, 76–90. doi:10.1016/j.omega.2005.11.003

Dong, T. Y., Zhang, L., Tong, R. F., & Dong, J. X. (2006). Production procedure control in agile supply chain management based on multiple monitoring modes. *Computer Integrated Manufacturing Systems*, *12*(1), 117–126.

Frank, S., Ma, S. H., & Michael, B. (2008). *Internationalization of logistics systems: How Chinese and German companies enter foreign markets.* Berlin, Germany: Springer.

Hallikas, J., Karvonen, I., Pulkkinen, U., Virolainen, V.-M., & Tuominen, M. (2004). Risk management processes in supplier networks. *International Journal of Production Economics, 90*, 47–58. doi:10.1016/j.ijpe.2004.02.007

Hendricks, K. B., & Singhal, V. R. (2003). The effect of supply chain glitches on shareholder wealth. *Journal of Management, 21*, 501–522.

Hendricks, K. B., & Singhal, V. R. (2005a). Association between supply chain glitches and operating performance. *Management Science, 51*(5), 695–711. doi:10.1287/mnsc.1040.0353

Hendricks, K. B., & Singhal, V. R. (2005b). An empirical analysis of the effect of supply chain disruptions on long-run stock price performance and equity risk of the firm. *Production and Operations Management, 14*(1), 35–52. doi:10.1111/j.1937-5956.2005.tb00008.x

Kasilingam, R. G., & Lee, C. P. (1996). Selection of vendors-a mixed-integer programming approach. *Computers & Industrial Engineering, 31*, 347–350. doi:10.1016/0360-8352(96)00148-9

Kleindorfer, P. R., & Saad, G. H. (2005). Managing disruption risks in supply chains. *Production and Operations Management, 14*(1), 53–68. doi:10.1111/j.1937-5956.2005.tb00009.x

Knemeyer, A. M., Zinn, W., & Eroglu, C. (2009). Proactive planning for catastrophic events in supply chains. *Journal of Operations Management, 27*(2), 141–153. doi:10.1016/j.jom.2008.06.002

Lin, Y., & Zhou, L. (2011). The impacts of product design changes on supply chain risk: A case study. *International Journal of Physical Distribution & Logistics Management, 41*(2), 162–186. doi:10.1108/09600031111118549

Norrman, A., & Jansson, U. (2004). Ericsson's proactive risk management approach after a serious sub-supplier accident. *International Journal of Physical Distribution and Logistics Management, 34*(5), 434–456. doi:10.1108/09600030410545463

Oke, A., & Gopalakrishnan, M. (2009). Managing disruptions in supply chains: A case study of a retail supply chain. *International Journal of Production Economics, 118*, 168–174. doi:10.1016/j.ijpe.2008.08.045

Perea, E., & Zabala, E. (2005). Measurement campaign and assessment of the quality of supply in Res and Dg facilities in Spain. In *Proceedings of the 18th International Conference on Electricity Distribution.* IEEE.

Ruiz-Torres, A. J., & Farzad, M. (2007). The optimal number of suppliers considering the costs of individual supplier failures. *Omega: The International Journal of Management Science, 35*(1), 104–115. doi:10.1016/j.omega.2005.04.005

Sawik, T. (2011a). Selection of supply portfolio under disruption risks. *Omega: The International Journal of Management Science, 39*, 194–208. doi:10.1016/j.omega.2010.06.007

Sawik, T. (2011b). Selection of a dynamic supply portfolio in make-to-order environment with risks. *Computers & Operations Research, 38*, 782–796. doi:10.1016/j.cor.2010.09.011

Seferlis, P., & Giannelos, N. F. (2004). A two-layered optimization-based control strategy for multi-echelon supply chain networks. *Computers & Chemical Engineering, 28*, 799–809. doi:10.1016/j.compchemeng.2004.02.022

Tang, C. S. (2006). Perspectives in supply chain risk management. *International Journal of Production Economics, 103*, 451–488. doi:10.1016/j.ijpe.2005.12.006

Tomlin, B. (2009). Impact of supply learning when suppliers are unreliable. *Manufacturing & Service Operations Management, 11*(2), 192–209. doi:10.1287/msom.1070.0206

Tomlin, B., & Wang, Y. (2005). On the value of mix flexibility and dual sourcing in unreliable newsvendor networks. *Manufacturing & Service Operations Management, 7*(1), 37–57. doi:10.1287/msom.1040.0063

Ustun, O., & Demirtas, E. A. (2008). An integrated multi-objective decision making process for multi-period lot sizing with supplier selection. *Omega: The International Journal of Management Science, 36*, 509–521. doi:10.1016/j.omega.2006.12.004

Wongvasu, N. (2001). Methodologies for providing rapid and effective response to request for quotation (RFQ) of mass customization products. (Dissertation). Northeastem University. Boston, MA.

Wu, D., & Olson, D. L. (2008). Supply chain risk, simulation, and vendor selection. *International Journal of Production Economics, 114*, 646–655. doi:10.1016/j.ijpe.2008.02.013

Xia, W., & Wu, Z. (2007). Supplier selection with multiple criteria in volume discount environments. *Omega: The International Journal of Management Science, 35*, 494–504. doi:10.1016/j.omega.2005.09.002

Xiao, Y. M., & Wang, X. Y. (2008). Early-warning analysis on stability of supply chain based on entropy theory. *Journal of Industrial Engineering and Engineering Management, 3*, 57–63.

Xu, Y. T., & Zhang, S. L. (2001). The supervision and control system research of SCM based on process enterprise. *Basic Automation, 8*(4), 12–14.

Zhang, K., Chai, Y., Yang, S. X., & Weng, D. L. (2011). Pre-warning analysis and application in traceability systems for food production supply chains. *Expert Systems with Applications, 38*(3), 2500–2507. doi:10.1016/j.eswa.2010.08.039

Zhang, Y. (2002). The characteristic analysis of finance supervision in supply chain management. *Shanghai Accounting, 11*, 31–32.

Chapter 10
The Strategic Contribution of ERP Systems to the Formulation of Non–Financial Key Performance Measures (KPIs) in Logistics Activities:
An Exploratory Study in Northern Greece

Fotios Misopoulos
City College, Thessaloniki, Greece

Sophia P. Asprodini
City College, Thessaloniki, Greece

ABSTRACT

The purpose of this chapter is the thorough observation of supply chains within the broader geographical area of Northern Greece in order to recognize whether organizations formulate and use KPIs in order to evaluate performance. The essence of developing useful KPIs with regard to supply chain performance is the identification of the gap between planning and executing while KPIs also give an indication about areas that are in need of corrective action. However, due to the fact that the Greek region has maintained narrow manufacturing activities as a result of its economic situation in the past five years, the research is focused on that part of the supply chain associated to logistics and customer service.

DOI: 10.4018/978-1-4666-3914-0.ch010

INTRODUCTION

This paper portrays the strategic significance of a metrics system formulated by appropriate data derived from an ERP system in order to measure and tackle performance in logistics' associated activities. The specific issue, the issue of performance evaluation is of great importance since there are already positive correlations researched and found by rich streams of literature concerning performance evaluation and non-financial performance measures. Thus, the importance of this study lies in the fact that performance evaluation is explored through being narrowed down to logistics activities and defined through the implementation and use of ERPs (Enterprise Resource Planning Systems). Based on research conducted in a number of SME's in Northern Greece, significant correlations have been found with respect to properly set non-financial performance measures (KPIs) and logistics activities such as procurement, purchasing, supplier evaluation, warehousing, order processing and customer satisfaction in order to determine factors that adversely affect the efficient flow of goods within the supply chains. With the evolution of technology and Information Systems (IS), customers at any level of the supply chain are able to have access to vital information concerning processes and outcomes of interest so that proper integration and visibility through the supply chain is attained.

Aims and Objectives of the Study

The interviews have provided adequate info concerning the use of ERPs—and other in house developed IS—and the extent to which ERPs support logistics activities and contribute to the formulation of suitable non-financial performance indicators. The goal of the research is to realize whether ERPs or IS systems in the Northern Greek market are utilized adequately so as to tackle and evaluate performance. The most commonly used method for attaining this without contending with

financial data—since the cost and expenses factor is not used in parallel in this chapter—is through using non-financial performance measures. Following, the methodology of approaching this research is provided for the needs of the dissertation and outcomes are interpreted while being grouped into research questions and justified in order to finalize conclusions and areas that call for further research.

LITERATURE REVIEW

In turbulent times, organizations are struggling to perform in a rather dynamic business environment which requires a flexible-although structured-strategic approach in order to be tackled. Among various activities such as manufacturing, purchasing, operations, procurement and marketing, logistics has grown to be a viable component of the supply chain within the last fifteen years since it acts as an enabler of supply chain management (Panayides, 2004; Bienstock et al., 1997; Mentzer et al., 1989). For the purpose of this paper there is a necessity to address the goal of supply chains in a global context given the interdependence and interrelation of business entities within any given industry.

Supply Chain Management and Its Relation to Strategy

Supply chain management has shifted the global business rationale from cooperation and competition between business entities to interrelation between supply chains (Van der Vorst et al., 2002). The procedure through which products flow—with the form of materials—from manufacturing until the end consumer—as finished goods—needs coordination and constant control since any failure to keep up within schedules and specifications entails excessive costs (Johnson et al., 1999) not only in money terms but in terms of performance and reputation as well (Green Jr. et al., 2008). Lee et al. (2007) in their research paper pointed out that "it has been well-known that supply chain integration creates strategic advantages" while it is also widely accepted in theory that the effective monitoring of business processes leads to a well-executed overall strategy (Prajogo et al., 2006).

Strategy could be defined as managing long-term while sustainable maximum performance, according to Kluyver and Pearce (2006). Contemporary supply chains experience an immense requirement to integrate and coordinate all activities in order to attain superior accomplishment (Jahre, et al., 2005) in terms of delivering supreme value to its customers—both internal and external—while simultaneously targeting on considerable return on investment and profit results (Johnson et al., 1999). Logistics then is that part of the supply chain that creates and preserves value to the goods through time and place variation (Mentzer et al., 2008). In this context, logistics appears to be in the focal position facilitating internal, customer and supplier linkage (Lee at al., 2007) through managing transportation, inventory, order fulfillment and purchasing at any stage of the supply chain (Mentzer et al., 1989).

Support logistics activities although designed to reinforce and sustain key logistics activities, appear to be of equal importance since they involve product purchasing, storage, handling and information collection, warehousing and management. Information management facilitates the coordination of multiple and various functional areas within the supply chain through information sharing (Mithas et al., 2011). However, random information is seldom useful and able to be interpreted (Rennolls et al., 2008) therefore the necessity of information systems is apparent in order to organize, store, process and retrieve information so that this information is meaningful to the users who perform decision-making (Adams, 2009).

Lack of proper information sharing can cause lack of coordination and integration between supply chain members (Zhang et al., 2006) within the same or related supply chains. One very common

example is the unevenness of demand pattern as we move upstream to the supply chain which can have adverse effects, one of which is fairly the bullwhip effect (Li et al, 2001). The inability to provide accurate demand forecasts is inextricably associated to the lack of visibility through the supply chain since demand variability is magnified (Ericsson, 2011).

Information sharing is of strategic importance due to the fact that it gives the organization an insight about which activities are performed efficiently (Li et al., 2001), whether processes run in order to create proper value while it can be used in order to formulate performance measures and metrics in order to answer questions and tackle drawbacks that traditional financial measures cannot (Chow et al., 2006). Measuring specific activities in order to recognize and set performance levels is a good start however this procedure should not be faced as a checklist since there are implications and interpretations involved which are more critical than the data itself (Campo et al, 2010). Most managers are unaware of what they would like to measure in order to evaluate performance in specific sectors while in most cases data can be easily retrieved (Ittner et al., 2003).

According to numerous studies made upon the subject of information sharing and performance measures, the outcome is drawn through defining the industry from a generic perspective to a process-oriented perspective with a few overlaps (Van der Vorst, 2006).

- Identification of the margins within which a specific supply chain system operates in order to identify the business partners/entities that are of a trigger importance in terms of the organizations' strategic objectives.
- Identify existent processes that are organized, measured in order to deliver specific outcomes so as to create proper value aligned to strategy.
- Ensure that processes within the supply chain are coordinated and integrated to-

wards common strategic goals exemplified by related commitment and trust.

- Human and tangible resources including IT systems are combined and utilized in order to facilitate value-driven outbound activities.

IS and SCM

Since dot com schemes made their appearance threatening established companies, the business world has been intimidated while searching for approaches to develop in an "electronic" manner (Helo eta al., 2006). This evolution has moved interest towards Information and Communication Technologies (ICT), Electronic Data Interchange (EDI) and more specifically, systems able to provide established and controlled buyer-supplier relationships such as various CRM modules, systems to monitor resources and turnover and systems to oversee warehouse activities and inventories (Hill Associates, Inc., 2006). In essence, the complexity of SCM per se has forced businesses to frame and control activities given that they are not restricted to arm-length operations.

SCM information systems are user-interfaced and they provide the ability to gather and process information within the supply chain, associated to strategy, operations, orders, inventory levels and handling (Soroor et al., 2009) while they embrace the decision making process based on information sharing. Enterprise systems belong to the most important tools of information technology within supply chains while their most famous and widely used representatives are the ERP (Enterprise Resource Planning) systems which appear to support a wide range of everyday tasks and processes (Haines, 2009). Logistics and order processing found themselves very high in the support agenda of ERPs due to the fact that they are highly correlated to performance improvement initiatives (Cotteleer et al., 2006).

ERP Systems

ERPs, when fully integrated and properly performed, provide timely information in an operational, tactical and strategic context while the manner based on which information is shared could turn them in JIT-information (Green et al., 2007). The evolution of MRP and MRP II shifted focus from production wise and planning production procedures to an interface that attempts to fit all functions through seamless integration in order to attain better information and knowledge management and as a consequence, better processes (Huang et al., 2009). Real time information can be a differentiating factor in competitive advantage formulation and core competencies' enhancement (Li et al., 2001); however, each supply chain faces different needs especially when a business entity belongs to more than one supply chains.

ERP Benefits and Risks

Working with an ERP entails a plethora of benefits as well as risks. There is no standard way of identifying a given number of both categories since enterprises and supply chains differ as much as strategy among enterprises and industries. ERPs provide companies with the opportunity to gain better insight about their customers' behaviour (Huynh and Chu, 2011) while at the same time they enable reengineering of processes through attaining strategic relationships with the company's partners (Singla, 2008) in order to tackle the desires hidden within customers' behaviour. More and more companies nowadays are seeking for ways to narrow their operating costs in order to make their profits emerge. Through the ERP, manual processes are automated and standardized in order for companies and supply chains to be able to be competitive and claim sustainability while at the same time enterprises are allowed to grow in a systematic and tactical way which is embraced by the number of users having access on the information (Sage ERP, 2011).

Despite the remarkable benefits that an ERP adoption can entail, such a tool can be transformed to a huge cost should it be implemented by unstructured strategic objectives. Major drawbacks find themselves in improper communication of strategic goals and support towards the employees, resistance to change and unclear job functions (Campo et al., 2010, Gunasekaran et al., 2004). Goals related to an ERP implementation are generally considered to be focused on information gathering, sorting, storing, retrieving and processing either financial or customer-related. Since the goal of ERP adoption lies in the field of information handling (Singla, 2008) in order to attain visibility and performance, technology vendors have specialized or modularized their products in order to adapt to a sample upright market model while they have also left room for customization (Huynh et al., 2011). Therefore, choosing an ERP randomly is far different from choosing the modules that serve an organization's strategic goals.

The implementation of an ERP system entails a combination between the manner a company desires the ERP to perform and the way the system itself allows the company to perform (El Amrani et al., 2006). ERP systems are based on absolutely precise data entry due to their unified logic, in any other case wrong data entry is transferred to the whole supply chain as a domino; therefore the prior education of the users is of crucial importance (IFS, 2007). Apart from the already mentioned subsystems, there is a plethora of complementary subsystems supported by an ERP depending on the level of complexity a company's processes bear. Such subsystems could support functions such as human resources, quality control, work planning and resource management (IFS, 2009). In this paper research is drawn upon subsystems supporting logistics activities such as purchasing, warehouse and distribution as well as marketing and sales through which relative KPIs are going to be formulated.

From a cost perspective, ERPs can be a low-cost solution if the support is totally susceptible to the vendor's authority provided that upgraded versions are installed upon launch (Haines, 2009). In case the software is customized, a private consultant needs to perform maintenance and support in order for the software to bear appropriately tailored modules for meaningful information processing (Hill Associates, Inc., 2006). Backbone costs include licensing, implementation and maintenance costs but these are not costs that a business unit could find difficult to afford (IFS, 2007). The implementation process of an ERP project is the costlier phase of all since it involves finding the right people who will be trained and be able to gain knowledge on this project (Moller, 2005). The cost factor comes in when some considerable workload burden will have to be lifted of those people's shoulders and be shared among other employees-already existent or newly hired (IFS, 2007). Bottom line, the implementation of an ERP system should be faced as a project implemented from a project team with whatever that entails.

ERPs and Performance Measures

While the benefits of IS in relation to business performance are readily analysed further above in this paper and bear a rather extensive theoretical background there is very little theoretical and empirical evidence concerning the contribution of the ERP *per se* in organizational performance. Since the ERP issue is a newly advanced issue due to the fact that it made its appearance in the 90s, it practically merges the IT with the business world which is a rather rapidly developing combination. Therefore, one of the reasons that the academia has not sufficient evidence concerning the integration of ERPs lies in the complexity of these systems and the insufficiency and inability of common IT principles to adapt to ERP as well (Amoako-Gyampah et al., 2004). The continuous evolution of the IT part and its constant extension in order to support emerging business activities and needs more efficiently, made every theoretical framing attempt outdated (Uwizeyemungu et al., 2010).

In this study, it is not aimed to investigate the responsiveness of ERPs to processes, however it is desired to use performance indicators actually used by managers in Northern Greece in order to understand whether ERPs contribute to the formulation and use of performance indicators and whether people are familiar with extracting data from an ERP in order to measure business performance in supply chain activities. However, prior to the empirical analysis there is a necessity to address KPIs in relation to performance and logistics activities.

Performance Measurement and KPIs

Performance—especially in the logistics field—in the contemporary business world is a trigger topic that has drawn global attention in terms of finding the finest tradeoff between effectiveness and efficiency in order to attain optimal customer service and thus satisfaction (Fugate et al., 2010). Logistics activities and their implications are of extreme interest for the companies and supply chains, nevertheless logistics managers have made efforts for years in order to prove the business world that logistics do contribute to overall organizational performance (Griffis et al., 2007; Fugate et al., 2010). Logistics performance is no old fashioned area based on boxes, trucks and warehouses, on the contrary it needs to be up-to-date in order to complement shorter product life cycles, changing consumer needs and hypercompetition. However, there is a need to define performance evaluation and measurement in a logistics concept in order to further outline the measuring method that is going to be utilized in this paper, namely KPIs.

With the aim of performance evaluation, a company's management should be well aware of the underlying strategic processes and procedures (Germain et al., 2006) in order for the data and

criteria of the evaluation to be meaningful and based on actual extents of achievement on actual objectives related to goals and strategy (Fawcett et al., 1997; Ramos, 2004).

KPIs and Logistics Activities

Developing KPIs in order to measure performance in each one of the areas within a supply chain is a complex task and can be easily turned into a rebound in a case an organization is engaged into the formulation of many KPIs for many operations simultaneously. In case we isolate the five stages in logistics, namely purchasing, inventory management, warehouse management, transportation management and customer service, it can be easily noticed that there are numerous common non-financial KPIs such as fill rate, stock turn over (for both materials and finished goods), order picking accuracy rate, service level – DIFOT (delivered in full on time), amount of back loading, on time deliveries etc. (Onwubolu et al, 2006). However, it can also be observed that KPIs and their implications affect all stages in supply chains from production to delivery and the outcomes of KPIs set in one stage, directly affect the performance of the next stage. Broken down to activities, KPIs are giving an indication of how well the organization is performing with compliance to its strategic goals.

KPIs Benefits and Drawbacks

Successful performance measurement and evaluation based on KPIs is assumed based on how well these KPIs are formulated and designed. KPIs should motivate desired outcomes while at the same time they should be measurable and affordable (Chow et al, 2006). Moreover, the set of objectives established and aimed to be met through KPIs should be able to be attained and the results should be meaningful to all the parties involved (Griffis et al., 2007).

More extensively, Theurer (1998) demonstrates in his paper some drawbacks and advise of performance measurement systems:

- Data by themselves have no meaning.
- There must be a strong commitment from leaders to move toward measuring performance and not just collecting data on effort.
- Employees must have the capacity to develop measures, or they will use whatever 'measures' are already available.
- If measurement focuses on negative accountability, managers and employees will seek to avoid accountability when things go wrong.
- A performance measurement system should provide information to policymakers and managers so they can make better decisions.
- For many governments, the ultimate aim of management based on performance measures is to integrate program performance and outcome information with the budget process.
- Provide reliable and valid information on performance.

METHODOLOGY

Definition of Research Problem

ERPs seem to assist the implementation and control of the overall logistics performance while they boost and have a positive correlation with performance measurement; however, it has not yet been clarified whether ERPs facilitate the formulation of non-financial performance measures through information and data sharing in the Greek market. Given the fact that Greece has an underdeveloped manufacturing sector, logistics in an operational context exist in a very restrained manner. Therefore, supply chain and logistics activities are observed in a broader context and the research framework as well as the structure of the interviews are adapted to that part of the chain beginning from the wholesaler and ending to the final customer.

This study aims to look deeper into the formulation of proper KPIs measuring logistics activities, while at the same time it seeks to reveal whether non-financial performance measures' formulation can be supported through information and data derived from ERP systems. The goal is to assist organizations conducting business in the Greek business environment in order to align their processes within a broader strategic perspective in the context of ERP usage.

By taking into account the nature of this paper, an inductive approach is going to be followed. This paper is based upon research among a number of wholesalers in Northern Greece. The industry in which the organizations conduct business in has been found to be of secondary importance since the aim of the paper focuses on the activities and processes per se rather than the nature of products or services entailed. Moreover, the research design applied is exploratory since there is no adequate theoretical framework that deals with the direct contribution of ERP and its contribution to KPI formulation while empirical evidence is going to be crucial in order to determine the implementation parameters of the topic. Finally, qualitative research is going to be conducted in order to express peoples' perception concerning ERPs, their use and their involvement in performance measurement embraced by KPIs. Moreover, since the research procedure is going to be conducted within the wider area of Northern Greece, it is important to take into account the norms based on which local organizations view performance measurement and up to what extent they find ERP integration useful.

Research Design

For the purpose of the research, interviews with IT, logistics and warehouse managers as well as managing directors took place after having drawn adequate literature review in order to gain a proper insight of what should be addressed in specific. Questionnaires have been provided to the interviewees before the interviews took place therefore they could be prepared to respond to the demands of the interview. The Questionnaire (see Appendix) included 18 questions related to whether Greek companies (SMEs) use an ERP system and up to which extent they utilize it in order to evaluate and control performance through the use of KPIs. Out of the 20 attempts made to arrange interviews, 15 of them where successful. The reason why 5 of them failed to be performed and completed was the ignorance of the supervisors concerning KPIs mostly and performance measurement in general. They claimed to be familiar only with financial metrics related to turnover and sales figures.

Sample

This study examines the ability of Greek companies in the northern Greek region to combine the management of vital information concerning logistics activities through an ERP system, with the formulation of performance indicators (KPIs) and the extent to which those KPIs are able to help them evaluate performance and take corrective action furthermore.

The sample monitored is not based on a sole industry, however there are certain criteria used for its selection. Fifteen companies conducting business in the northern Greek region were monitored and interviewed. Companies selected could be grouped upon the position they hold within the supply chain in the industry each is engaged in. In essence, out of the 15 companies interviewed, 6 are wholesalers, 4 are retailers, 3 are LSPs (Logistics Service Providers) and 2 companies are engaged in the service sector, namely education

and health services. As expected, not all companies interviewed held a separate logistics department therefore there was adequate emphasis given in order to trace and interview the employee that is in charge of monitoring the logistics activities ran in the company. Logistics and warehouse managers existed only in 7 out of the total of 15 companies visited where physical inventory is held in bulk. In the other 8 cases, interviews were taken from IT managers occupying with the ERP settlement and implementation as well as from general managers that made use of the metrics and measures derived from the ERP in order to evaluate results and performance.

Limitations and Ethical Issues

Ethics and limitations are particularly significant components throughout the research procedures and if failed to be taken into account, they can lead to misinterpretation or even invalid conclusions. Due to the fact that the business environment in Greece is under deep crisis, Greek organizations avoid publishing information concerning procedures and processes followed since they perceive them as core competencies or weaknesses that would assist competition to grow. Additionally information will not go under any form of bias or change. Therefore, this chapter will not include the original names of the companies surveyed, however it will portray the sector in which each company is engaged in and all companies will be referred to as XYZ Company.

As far as limitations are concerned, the research procedure has taken place in companies within the region of Northern Greece since there is direct access from a geographical point of view. Those companies are engaged into logistics activities and they use ERP systems. Moreover, research has been conducted within the summer period and early autumn period, therefore business activity is expected to be restricted and it may have affected the quality of responses concerning the specific period up to a limited extent.

The initial goal portrayed in the introduction section of this paper was to find answers concerning the five research questions that embrace and tackle the issue of this research paper which is the contribution of the ERP concerning the formulation of KPIs that are used for monitoring strategic logistics activities.

FINDINGS AND DISCUSSION

Do Companies use ERPs in Order to Tackle Performance in Logistics Activities?

Respective questions from the questionnaire that answer this research question are numbers 14, 16 and 17. Companies are divided into two groups concerning the use of ERPs with regard to performance initiatives, companies that use the ERP as an enabler of performance evaluation and companies that do not use an ERP since they use another information system with more restricted capabilities.

Companies that use an ERP system so that they can tackle performance in performed logistics activities confirm that real time information provided by an ERP system lead to a strong competitive advantage and contributes to strategic performance as Li et al (2001) has claimed. Furthermore, being engaged in the procedure of integrating the ERP to their logistics activities they have realized that ERPs allow people participating in this integration to gain better insight about customers' behaviour (Huynh and Chu, 2011) while they support strategic relationships with the company's partners (Singla, 2008) and find that ERP implementation and performance are in positive correlation for the supply chain overall. The companies that utilize an ERP system account for 66.6% of the total sample.

Companies that do not use an ERP system have reported drawbacks that make them postpone or even reject the future adoption and implementation of such a system. Those drawbacks are not as innocent as they seem however they appear to have rather strategic extensions related to bad strategy execution and communication to employees and resistance to change (Campo et al., 2010, Gunasekaran et al., 2004). Therefore they prefer performing arm-length activities since they believe that they can better control performance as well. Shortsighted strategy implemented by shortsighted tools.

Do Companies Keep Record of Day-to-Day Tasks Related to Logistics Activities with the Assistance of an ERP System?

This research question is associated to the efficient data entrance, retrieval and processing with extension to performance monitoring and evaluation through the ERP is linked with questions 3 and 15. Companies that use an ERP system, namely 10 out of the total 15 interviewed are entering the data based on transactions in logistics activities on a daily basis and reviewing them at the end of each week. These companies have realized that it is unfeasible to monitor and control these transactions without entering the data into the system (Rennolls et al., 2008). As mentioned earlier in theory, this data is useless unless it can be stored, analysed, combined and translated into meaningful information that will contribute to the decision making process (Adams, 2009). Through this procedure and the frequent review of information the organization attempts to discovering the underlying reasons for high or low sales, gained or lost clients or orders and lead times (Hill Associates, Inc., 2006).

Companies that are reluctant adopting therefore they do not use an ERP system are proving in fact Dery et al.(2006) correct since the drawback in essence does not lie in the use of the ERP or in the training of employees to adapt to the ERP, but it lies in the business part of the procedure which can reveal that until now, critical functions have been performed the wrong way (Dery et al, 2006).

What Kind of Information Derived from an ERP Contributes to Non-Financial Performance Measures' Formulation?

Based on the transactions that each company records related to logistics activities performed, the answers to this question vary among companies grouped into wholesalers, retailers, LSPs and service companies. Given the fact that retail companies do not use an ERP system however they use some IS applications that resemble to some ERP modules such as the ones supporting purchasing, order processing activities and accounting, it would be difficult to adapt their answers to the present research topic since the data is not sufficient and it cannot be extended to a rule.

Wholesalers and LSPs that find the use of an ERP necessary and record transactions which are mostly related to supplier evaluation, inventory handling and storage and in some cases transportation in terms of loading optimization with reference to picking, are subject to be contributing to this research because they fulfill all the prerequisites. Evidence from these companies has shown that the implementation of an ERP system in order to support and evaluate these activities affects the activities and the business processes entailed (Uwizeyemungu et al., 2010). Service companies have not contributed much in order to gain a specific insight concerning activities recorded through the ERP, although company A has given some really interesting answers regarding the handling of consumables and its support through the ERP. Nevertheless the latter cannot be generalized but could be easily a topic for future research about ERPs and logistics activities in service companies.

Do Companies Use KPIs in Order to Measure Performance in Logistics Activities?

With respect to the sample researched, companies have found to be formulating and consulting KPIs in order to measure and evaluate performance. Representatives that perform pure logistics activities such as purchasing activities, inventory handling, and transportation have reported that they use and review their KPIs weekly and sometimes daily in case they aim to maintain their customer service initiatives—after all—in high levels. Specifically, wholesalers, retailers, and LSPs confirm theory embracing customer service from a logistics perspective, which claims that there are three performance parameters that affect customer service and satisfaction: product availability, cycle time and customer responsiveness (Dadzie et al., 2005). Those parameters are the ones that companies nowadays attempt to tackle through the use of KPIs.

Performance however does not have the same meaning for all companies. Service companies, although sharing the aspects of the wholesalers, retailers and LSPs mentioned above, do not have procedures involving tangible goods in order to mathematically measure and are engaged on other resources' utilization evaluation such as technology, rooms and efficiency of information flow in general. Surprisingly, service companies that belong to this sample utilize KPIs and take them into account in the decision making process.

Which Logistics KPIs are of Strategic Importance?

Answering this question is giving an insight towards the linkage between performance evaluation and strategy. Not all companies have readily available KPIs in order to be more specific in what they evaluate, however it has been realized through discussion that not all companies have fully implemented the correct KPIs that are going to specifically tackle performance to the activities that they consider as strategic. Back to theory and KPIs' formulation, there is a difficulty on behalf of the companies to measure exactly what they are in need of, based on their strategy (Chow et al., 2006). In the case of this sample, companies that do not have specific KPIs have claimed to have identified the activities that are of strategic importance for their company, so this is a paradox. What those companies have failed to do is to formulate KPIs that are in direct link with their already identified strategic logistics activities.

Still, contrary to companies that have specific KPIs mentioned in question 18 of the questionnaire, companies that do not, seem to have failed to take into account the multidimensional nature of business entities cooperating in an environment characterized by interdependence (Hervani et al., 2005). Then again, companies that have portrayed some indicative KPIs, have reported to believe that non-financial performance measures have more direct correlations with strategic goals than pure financial quantitative measures since they give a more reliable proxy for performance (Lunnan et al., 2002).

CONCLUSION

After deploying the answers to questionnaires and research questions, it has been realized that the complexity of this topic is intense since all factors involved, no matter if they are related to technology, supply chain integration, and coordination or soft aspects are interacting with each other and provide diverse results. An attempt was made to group interviewed companies into four categories, namely wholesalers, retailers, LSPs and service companies. Unfortunately, the sample of service companies was not considerable enough in order to generalize findings, however, their answers hold important remarks in this research and give a stimulus for further research.

LSPs were more specific about their KPIs and the manner their WMS contributes to their formulation while wholesalers are coming second with less precise answers but the same levels of KPIs and ERP utilization. Retailers were more attached to financial metrics and indications of performance while they did not reject the use of an ERP, yet they do not find it necessary since they have been assigned to the drawbacks related to cost in time and money, while service companies portrayed two opposite cases of having and not having an ERP; however through utilizing a good number of performance indicators for performance evaluation.

Although all companies have reported that they measure performance through performance indicators, 5 out of 15 are considering it difficult to link performance with ERPs since they have major drawbacks regarding their adoption and implementation. Reduced turnovers have resulted in demotivation and distorted strategic goals which prevent these 5 companies from realizing the domino effect affecting the whole supply chain (IFS, 2007). Those companies are experiencing drawbacks while dealing with the complexity of the supply chains in general rather than with the complexity of the ERPs and demonstrate a rather egocentric behaviour and resistance to change (Campo et al., 2010; Gunasekaran et al., 2004). Yet, there are high hopes that the results and argumentation of this research will have positive effects towards changing their minds.

Companies that have adopted and implemented ERPs have replied that they have gained visibility within the supply chain (Ericsson, 2011) and can efficiently coordinate activities and share information with their business partners and customers (Germain et al., 2006). Those companies have also reported that they have switched from conventional IS systems to ERP systems since they have higher chances of being integrated and provide the company with higher levels of flexibility than any conventional IS (El Amrani et al., 2006). Those companies that account for 66.6% of the sample (10 out of 15) have reported that their ERP has supported their attempts to link performance with technology and has provided all necessary information for KPIs formulation and therefore performance evaluation.

Based on theory, companies being engaged in performance evaluation maintain considerable levels of supply chain logistical integration (Zhao et al., 2001) and technological readiness (Richey et al., 2007). Companies have reported that the communication and the information flow have been better off even from suppliers and other partners' perspective within the supply chain with the use of ERPs while their strategic goals have become clearer and effectively communicated. The first half of the questionnaire attempts to define the companies' position, goals, and background in order to define the supply chain in which they belong and consequently demonstrate that these companies interact with partners and customers as the new era compels.

As reported by all companies through discussion, customer service is a top priority nowadays, especially with reduced workloads and turnovers in the Greek region; however it seems that more effort is being put on good relationships with suppliers than on good relationships with customers. This conclusion has been reached since none of the companies, even the ones maintaining an ERP system, reported having an integrated CRM in order to boost demand and not supply for once. Back to what Ericsson (2011) supports that the Demand Chain Management (DCM) concept is designed to tackle this new challenge through times of crisis and limited resources by aiming on the customer and aligning inter- and intra-organizational processes accordingly which would be an excellent topic for future research.

REFERENCES

Adams, N. (2009). Perspectives on data mining. *International Journal of Market Research, 52*(1), 11–19. doi:10.2501/S147078531020103X

Amoako-Gyampah, K., & Salam, A. F. (2004). An extension of the technology acceptance model in an ERP implementation environment. *Information & Management, 41*(6), 731–745. doi:10.1016/j.im.2003.08.010

Bienstock, C., Mentzer, J., & Bird, M. (1997). Measuring physical distribution service quality. *Journal of the Academy of Marketing Science, 25*, 31–44. doi:10.1007/BF02894507

Campo, S., Rubio, N., & Jague, M. J. (2010). Information technology use and firm's perceived performance in supply chain management. *Journal of Business-To-Business Marketing, 17*(1), 336–364. doi:10.1080/10517120903574649

Chow, C., & van der Stede, W. (2006). The use and usefulness of nonfinancial performance measures. *Accounting Management Quarterly, 7*(3), 1–8.

Cotteleer, M., & Bendoly, E. (2006). Order lead-time improvement following enterprise information technology implementation: An empirical study. *Management Information Systems Quarterly, 30*(3), 643–660.

Dadzie, K., Chelariu, C., & Winston, E. (2005). Customer service in the internet-enabled logistics supply chain: Website design antecedents and loyalty effects. *Journal of Business Logistics, 26*(1), 53–78. doi:10.1002/j.2158-1592.2005.tb00194.x

Dery, C., Grant, D., Harley, B., & Wright, C. (2006). work, organisation and enterprise resource planning systems: An alternative research agenda. *New Technology, Work and Employment, 21*(3), 199–214. doi:10.1111/j.1468-005X.2006.00175.x

El Amrani, R., Rowe, F., & Geffroy-Maronnat, B. (2006). The effects of enterprise resource planning implementation strategy on cross-functionality. *Information Systems Journal*, *16*(1), 79–104. doi:10.1111/j.1365-2575.2006.00206.x

Ericsson, D. (2011). *Demand chain management – The evolution*. Retrieved from http://www.orssa.org.za

Fawcett, S., Stanley, L., & Smith, S. (1997). Developing a logistics capability to improve the performance of international operations. *Journal of Business Logistics*, *18*(2), 101–127.

Fugate, B., Mentzer, J., & Stank, T. (2010). Logistics performance: Efficiency, effectiveness and differentiation. *Journal of Business Logistics*, *31*(1), 43–62. doi:10.1002/j.2158-1592.2010.tb00127.x

Germain, R., & Iyer, K. (2006). The interaction of internal and downstream integration and its association with performance. *Journal of Business Logistics*, *27*(2), 29–52. doi:10.1002/j.2158-1592.2006.tb00216.x

Green, K., Whitten, D., & Inman, R. (2008). The impact of logistics performance on organizational performance in a supply chain context. *Supply Chain Management: An International Journal*, *13*(4), 317–327. doi:10.1108/13598540810882206

Griffis, S., Goldsby, T., Cooper, M., & Closs, D. (2007). Aligning logistics performance measures to the information needs of the firm. *Journal of Business Logistics*, *28*(2), 35–56. doi:10.1002/j.2158-1592.2007.tb00057.x

Gunasekaran, A., & Ngai, E. (2004). Information systems in supply chain integration and management. *European Journal of Operational Research*, *159*(1), 269–295. doi:10.1016/j.ejor.2003.08.016

Haines, M. (2009). Understanding enterprise system customization: An exploration of implementation realities and the key influence factors. *Information Systems Management*, *26*(1), 182–198. doi:10.1080/10580530902797581

Helo, P., Xiao, Y., & Jiao, R. (2006). A web-based logistics management system for agile supply demand network design. *Journal of Manufacturing Technology Management*, *17*(8), 1058–1077. doi:10.1108/17410380610707384

Hervani, A., Helms, M., & Sarkis, J. (2005). Performance measurement for green supply chain management. *Benchmarking: An International Journal*, *12*(4), 330–353. doi:10.1108/14635770510609015

Hill Associates, Inc. (2006). *Enterprise applications: A conceptual look at ERP, CRM, and SCM*. Colchester, VT: Copyright Coordinator.

Huang, S. Y., Huang, S. M., & Wu, T. H. (2009). Process efficiency of the enterprise resource planning adoption. *Industrial Management & Data Systems*, *109*(8), 1085–1100. doi:10.1108/02635570910991319

Huynh, M., & Chu, H. (2011). Open-source ERP: Is it ripe for use in teaching supply chain management? *Journal of Information Technology Education: Innovations in Practice*, *10*(1), 181–194.

IFS. (2007). *6 steps to ERP implementation success*. MSS Technologies Inc.

Ittner, C., & Larcker, D. (2003). The use and usefulness of nonfinancial performance measures. *Harvard Business Review*, *5*(9), 1–10.

Jahre, M., & Fabbe-Costes, N. (2005). Adaptation and adaptability in logistics networks. *International Journal of Logistics: Research and Applications*, *8*(2), 143–157. doi:10.1080/13675560500110903

Johnson, E., & Pyke, D. (1999). *Supply chain management*. (Unpublished M. Ed. Dissertation). Dartmouth College. Hanover, NH.

Lee, C. W., Kwon, I., & Severance, D. (2007). Relationship between supply chain performance and degree of linkage among supplier, internal integration, and customer. *Supply Chain Management: An International Journal, 12*(6), 444–452. doi:10.1108/13598540710826371

Li, J., Shaw, M., Sikora, R., Tan, G., & Yang, R. (2001). *The effects of information sharing strategies on supply chain performance*. (Unpublished M.Ed. Dissertation). University of Illinois. Urban-Champaign, IL.

Lunnan, R., & Haugland, S. (2007). Research notes and commentaries: Predicting and measuring alliance performance: A multidimensional analysis. *Strategic Management Journal, 29*(1), 545–556.

Mahto, R., Davis, S., Pearce, J., Robinson, I. I. Jr, & Richard, B. (2010). satisfaction with firm performance in family businesses. *Entrepreneurship. Theory into Practice, 34*(5), 985–1001.

Mentzer, J., Gomes, R., & Krapfel, R. (1989). Physical distribution service: A fundamental marketing concept? *Journal of the Academy of Marketing Science, 17*, 53–62. doi:10.1007/BF02726354

Mentzer, J., Stank, T., & Esper, T. (2008). Supply chain management and its relationship to logistics, marketing, production and operations management. *Journal of Business Logistics, 29*(1), 31–46. doi:10.1002/j.2158-1592.2008.tb00067.x

Mithas, S., Ramasubbu, N., & Sambamurthy, V. (2011). How information management capability influences firm performance. *Management Information Systems Quarterly, 35*(1), 137–150.

Möller, M., & Watanabe, M. (2010). Advance purchase discounts versus clearance sales. *The Economic Journal, 120*(547), 1125–1148. doi:10.1111/j.1468-0297.2009.02324.x

Onwubolu, G., & Dube, B. (2006). Implementing an improved inventory control system in a small company: A case study. *Production Planning and Control, 17*(1), 67–76. doi:10.1080/09537280500366001

Panayides, P. (2004). Logistics service providers: An empirical study of marketing strategies and company performance. *International Journal of Logistics: Research and Applications, 7*(1), 1–17. doi:10.1080/13675560310001619231

Prajogo, D., & Brown, A. (2006). Approaches to adopting quality in SMEs and the impact on quality management practices and performance. *Total Quality Management, 17*(5), 555–556. doi:10.1080/14783360600588042

Rennolls, K., & Al-Shawabkeh, A. (2008). Formal structures for data mining, knowledge discovery and communication in a knowledge management environment. *Intelligent Data Analysis, 12*(1), 147–163.

Richey, R. G., Daugherty, P., & Roath, A. (2007). Firm technological readiness and complementarity: Capabilities impacting logistics serving competency and performance. *Journal of Business Logistics, 28*(1), 195–228. doi:10.1002/j.2158-1592.2007.tb00237.x

Sage, E. R. P. (2011). *7 steps to building a business case for ERP*. Irvine, CA: Sage ERP.

Singla, A. (2008). Impact of ERP systems on small and mid-sized public sector enterprises. *Journal of Theoretical and Applied Information Technology, 14*(1), 119–131.

Soroor, J., Tarokh, M., & Keshtgary, M. (2009). Preventing failure in IT-enabled systems for supply chain management. *International Journal of Production Research, 47*(23), 6543–6557. doi:10.1080/00207540802314837

Theurer, J. (1998). Seven pitfalls to avoid when establishing performance measures. *Public Management, 80*(7), 21–24.

Uwizeyemungu, S., & Raymond, L. (2010). Linking the effects of ERP to organizational performance: Development and initial validation of an evaluation method. *Information Systems Management, 27*(1), 25–41. doi:10.1080/10580530903455122

Van der Vorst, J., & Beulens, A. (2002). Identifying sources of uncertainty to generate supply chain redesign strategies. *International Journal of physical Distribution and Logistics Management, 32*(6), 409-430.

Zhang, C., & Li, S. (2006). Secure information sharing in internet-based supply management systems. *Journal of Computer Information Systems, 46*(4), 18–24.

Section 3
Evolving Business

Chapter 11
The Use of RFID Technologies for E-Enabling Logistics Supply Chains

Zenon Michaelides
University of Liverpool, UK

Richard Forster
University of Liverpool, UK

ABSTRACT

This chapter reviews the potential benefits and challenges of introducing Radio Frequency Identification (RFID) technologies as a means of e-enabling logistics supply and distribution systems. It introduces RFID and associated technologies as a catalyst for e-enabling optimised supply and distribution activities. In particular, the emerging role of RFID in integrating logistics supply chains is considered key to aligning tasks and achieving operational efficiencies. Other benefits include better visibility resulting from proactive task and process management, and improved risk assessment associated with better data accuracy/quality. In addition, the optimisation of planning and control functions is enhanced through the introduction of key RFID technologies and their integration into logistics systems and operations. Finally, the use of RFID technologies is reviewed in a variety of diverse sectors and areas, from assisting humanitarian efforts through solutions aimed at recovering from the effects of natural disasters to providing accurate and effective methods of recording race times for the Los Angeles marathon.

INTRODUCTION

Logistics and supply chain management are key areas where developments in Information and Communication Technologies (ICTs) are enabling a paradigm shift in the evolution of traditional business practices. The introduction of e-logistics and e-supply chain management has brought on new challenges in the way that tasks are fundamentally assigned, executed and managed, from an operational as well as an organisational perspective. The adaptation and use of

DOI: 10.4018/978-1-4666-3914-0.ch011

e-enabled technologies such as RFID has resulted in optimisation gains across extended logistics and manufacturing supply chains. The immediate availability of information and the dynamic nature of data enables amongst others, better visibility, more agility, more awareness, better pro-activeness and better decision support, all of which translate to higher efficiency gains. In this Chapter, we aim to introduce RFID technologies and demonstrate their positive impact on e-logistics and e-supply chain, in supporting and enabling the overall optimisation of operations management practices required to maintain competitiveness.

A historic overview of the development of RFID technologies shall be presented, and examples of key RFID applications and their use will follow. Case studies shall be presented demonstrating the challenges of introducing RFID technologies and their potential benefits.

The objective of this chapter is to critically review recent developments in the field of RFID technologies, and to discuss their suitability, adaptation and use in a variety of sectors, from production to services. The aim is to familiarize readers with the challenges associated with the various types of RFID technologies available and to present examples of their use in the fast evolving e-logistics and e-supply chain sectors. The special focus of this chapter is to identify suitable methods of integrating the extended logistics supply chains through the use of RFID technologies, in order to enable visibility and competitiveness

On a critical note, the suitability of RFID technologies will be discussed in depth, demonstrating that RFID is not a "one size fits all" solution, rather an e-enabled approach for optimally aligning and integrating key logistics operations with a focus on sustainability and competitiveness. We will present a critical review of the literature, supporting key arguments and identifying areas of future research.

BACKGROUND

Radio Frequency Identification (RFID) is defined as a type of wireless information and communication technology, which has the ability to identify, record, verify, and process data associated with various tangible items, such as physical location of goods and the associated movement or variations thereof, as well as supporting intangible tasks, such as information processing and data execution operations associated with the provision of services.

Examples of data and information pertaining to tangible goods, which are typically captured by RFID systems are inventory quantities measured against time, date and location. Other types of measured data may include monitoring of ambient conditions, such as temperature, humidity and/or pressure, which make the use of RFID very appealing to specific sectors, such as perishable goods and pharmaceuticals. RFID has a wide use in many diverse sectors, from retail to banking, particularly in the areas of inventory management and control, such as tracking and security. RFID is key in supporting e-logistics and e-supply chain operations through its ability to exchange information with systems such as Enterprise Resources Planning (ERP) systems. The integration of RFID with ERP systems and more recently cloud computing, offers new opportunities for enabling visibility, particularly in supply chains, where the exact location and movement of parts enables proactive planning and control, thus enhancing efficiencies and enabling competitiveness.

The roots of RFID date back to World War II and were born out of necessity to identify friendly or enemy aircraft in the air. This system, which is still in use to this day in the form of radar, was called Identify Friend or Foe (IFF). IFF used transponders placed on-board the friendly aircraft which, when interrogated by base radar stations, would return a unique code identifying them as being friendly or, in the absence of this code, the enemy. After the war, and in particular in the 1950s,

IFF evolved further as many military spinoffs do, and is common place in both military and civil aircraft flying today (Roussos, 2008).

More applied developments of RFID took place in the 60s and 70s, primarily by the Los Alamos National Laboratory in the USA, as a means of tracking nuclear materials, and would later evolve into Electronic Article Surveillance (EAS) for controlling stock theft (Roussos, 2008). This placed an emphasis on stock control, and was the forerunner of the typical security tag operations used in many retail outlets today. During the 90s, several large-scale deployments of RFID solutions were undertaken, notably electronic toll collection in the United States and on rail cars in North America (Landt, 2005). Widespread adaptations of RFID were further driven by large retail companies, such as Wal-Mart and METRO. However, in spite of its promising potential, the successful use of RFID in e-enabling and optimising end-to-end logistics supply chains remains a challenge and has not been fully realised in recent years, suggesting that the process of RFID adaptation is more complex than previously anticipated (Ustundag, 2010).

Literature Review

There has been a significant academic interest surrounding RFID since its inception. This interest stems from the potential which RFID technologies have to redefine the way organisations traditionally identify and manage their products, and the way that they exchange information between partnering supply chain echelons. Much research attempts to identify key success factors and barriers to RFID adoption (Attaran, 2012; Charikleia 2010; Sabbaghi and Vaidyanathan, 2008). Within the literature, efficiency gains resulting from better insight and speed arising from the use of RFID technologies is discussed prolifically, with only fleeting acknowledgment of the fact that RFID might be in fact unsuitable in some instances. As a result, negative connotations to RFID are only visible in the research though the perspective of 'barriers to adaption' and not as important differentiating characteristics which could render the technology ineffective or unsuitable.

Over the years significant applied research has been conducted in the area of RFID adaptation. Such research focuses primarily on Return On Investment (ROI) through the review of several successful case studies, such as Walmart, Tesco and also the US Department of Defence (Wamaba and Boeck, 2007; Charikleia, 2010). Recently however, research has focused on the application of RFID in specific areas such as supply chain management, inventory management, logistics and transportation, assembly and manufacturing, asset tracking and object location (Sarac et al, 2009; Coltoman et al, 2008).

By comparing research conducted from an applied perspective, which details information pertaining to specific cases, to that of an academic or research perspective, which analyses theoretical benefits, there is evidence of only a limited range of positive applications which have been adapted for RFID solutions across both perspectives. These are: inventory transparency from strategic viewpoint and actual real-time inventory tracking of physical products. Specific areas of interest derived from these two points have been focused on intermittently, but rarely does RFID adaptation vary from the above areas at the fundamental level.

While these reasons are prolific and there is much consensus as to their value, they are the only factors which appear to be attracting consensus with the literature. This shows a clear disparity between the enthusiastic imaginings of the applications for RFID technology and the practical reality of its application. This suggests one of three possible concluding reasons: Firstly, that the barriers to RFID implementation are more obstructive than the widely popular opinion would suggest, despite its theoretical promise. Also, potential barriers such as cost, integration commitments and error prevention are significant enough to hamper diffusion into a diversified range of sectors. Secondly, that the benefits are not sufficiently persuasive or sufficiently well developed to influence perspective adopters to commit. Lastly, that the enthusiastic ideas of RFID proprietors have encapsulated the imagination of interested parties to the extent where this enthusiasm is causing an un-cautioned support of a technology not yet matured in its application. This idea is given further weight by Whang (2010), who suggests that early adopters of RFID have had a number of issues and that adopting a 'cautious posture' regarding this innovation may be the better ideology.

In addition to the typical barriers and success factors discussed throughout the literature, Whang (2010) discusses RFID from another important viewpoint, namely the perspective of the supplier/buyer power relationship. Large retailers, such as Wall-Mart and Tesco have set a mandate requiring their suppliers to integrate with their RFID systems. This creates a 'free-rider' situation, where the receiving company in a supply chain can reuse the RFID tags placed upon products from the sending organisation. As a result, this affects the dynamics and places additional stress on the formation of supplier buyer partnerships.

Another disparity between the theoretical possibilities of RFID and the practical reality that arises is that most of the areas analysed throughout the literature are limited to one product, one service or one part of a business that has implemented RFID. There are very few examples within the literature of any extensive company-wide RFID implementation. The reasons are that for such a wide scope implementation, the technology is still by comparison, significantly more expensive than alternative methods. In addition, while RFID offers greater utility, alternative tracking and ID solutions such as bar-coding are still fit for purpose and remain economically attractive. With there being little research penetrating to multiple operating concerns within an organisation, it is unsurprising that the literature examining supply chain wide RFID usage is also found to be somewhat lacking. Conversely, while RFID

usage is prevalent throughout 3PL companies (as well as in large organisations operating within the same supply chain) these appear to be discreet RFID implementations, joined to accommodate each other as opposed to a deliberate, coherent and homogenous set of technologies and process implemented from a strategic perspective (Sarac et al, 2009; Narsing, 2005; Ganesan, 2009).

This lack of coherence within RFID enabled systems appears to be a central theme in much of the literature. Potential reasons for this include: technological maturity, number of deployment styles, sensitivity to processes within an organisation and commitment of strategic management.

Due to the pervasive nature of RFID technologies, the adaptation and widespread use of various RFID applications has raised several concerns relating to privacy and data security. Near Field Communication (NFC) chips, essentially used in mobile phones for contactless payment and data transfer between devices, are in essence RFID tags. However so prevalent are the security concerns regarding RFID that mobile phone organisations felt that rebranding was necessary to disassociate the term RFID from their own devices (Damgard and Pedersen, 2008; Madlmayr, 2008). This negative depiction of RFID highlights the industry's concerns with standard RFID tags, in that they offer little defence against unauthorised access. However, in supporting specific types of RFID implementations, such as in the use of NFC chips which contain sensitive data e.g. e-passports, safety measures are employed, such as encryption which can be used in conjunction with mobile phones or radio proof sheath's to prevent unwanted access in the case of e-passports.

However, in terms of RFID deployments which are typically used in supply chains, the above described countermeasures are often not practical or cost-effective to implement. In addition, a consumer privacy problem may arise if an RFID tags are not removed from items at specific intervals, such as before being shipped or sold to the public. There are two typical characteristics of RFID tags used in supply chains, which if not adequately monitored, have the potential to create this problem. Firstly, RFID tags are indiscriminate as to what device is reading them: their utilisation within supply chains is feasible due to the fact that tags are easy and cheap to use, and 'universal' type reading devices may be located at many points in extended supply chains. As a result of their widespread adaptation, they are unable to support any electronic countermeasures, such as those countermeasures which are present in mobile phones or laptop computers. Secondly, passive tags cannot be instructed to stop transmitting at the point of purchase. This could result in situations where either individuals or organisations acquire RFID scanners and profile specific items based on their value (Grimaila, 2007; Juels, 2005; Wang et al, 2012). The above issue remains unresolved and is further evidence of the immaturity of this revolutionary technology.

In conclusion, it seems that while RFID holds much promise, there are still a wide variety of constraints in terms of process re-engineering, external and internal integration, understanding the scale, security implications inside and outside the organisation and in considering the future of the technology within a wider context before adoption.

RFID in Logistics Supply Chains

RFID may be viewed as an evolutionary successor of barcodes, but in reality RFID has unique functionality and its selection must be carefully considered. RFID can either be deployed as a stand-alone solution or could work well in conjunction with a typical barcode implementation. RFID should neither be seen as a technology that supersedes all existing barcode implementations regardless of their functionality nor viewed as the solution to all barcode shortcomings. Selection needs to be informed, with a clear understanding of the business objectives for which the required RFID implementation is sort, as well as a clear understanding of possible limitations for its use.

A comparison between RFID and Barcodes is presented in Table 1.

In its basic configuration an RFID tag comprises of an antenna and microchip, but can also include other components such as sensors (e.g. temperature) and a power source (battery, solar panel). The RFID tag contains a small amount of virtual memory that can be used to store information pertaining to an item to which it is attached. This information could be a unique identification code, e.g. part number and in addition may include other information, such as specific instructions, dates, limits, warnings, etc.

In the case of an active RFID tag, data and information are broadcast using the tags' own power source. Alternatively, for passive RFID tags, data and information can be sent as a response when the passive tag is activated within the proximity of an RFID reader. Once in communication, the reader can read the information from the tag, and update or add new information relating to the item to which the RFID tag is attached, to either the tag itself and/or to an ERP or similar system. This functionality offers a wide scope of use for RFID technology. An example of an RFID implementation is presented in Figure 1.

The RFID chip can be attached directly to a single item or to packages with a set quantity of the same item, e.g. one dozen. In addition, pallets can also contain their own RFID tag, which would record the number of packages on each pallet. This is useful for warehousing operations, including storage and location, and for integrating such information with Warehouse Management Systems (WMS). Once this chip is in the proximity of a reader, for example at the loading bay, the chip is activated and causes it to respond. The reader then relays the information to a stand-alone computer of a centralised database. This new information is then analysed and an appropriate response is generated. This response could simply be updating the status of that particular product, such as an inventory adjustment, or in the case of an unauthorised movement, sending a warning

Table 1. Comparison between RFID and barcodes (after: Attaran, 2012; Wamaba and Boeck, 2007; Wamaba and Chatfield, 2009)

Factor	RFID	Barcode
Line of Sight	RFID does not require direct line of sight.	A bar code required direct line of sight to be scanned.
Multiplicity	RFID can interact with a reader autonomously and therefore does not require individual attention. A huge number of RFID tags can pass by a reader and be processed without individual attention or delay.	A barcode scanner is required by the user to scan one code at a time, delay in processing time when dealing with a large volume of items.
Capacity	RFID's memory is limited but, depending on the design and cost of the chip, can contain up to around 1MB of data. This allows one tag to contain much more than a simple product code.	Barcode memory capacity is limited; in the case of one-dimensional barcode it works on a similar basis to Morse Code and can contain only a series of numbers. In most instances this is a unique identifier.
Read/Write	An RFID chip can read the information on this chip but also amend it. This gives many powerful applications in terms of monitoring expiry dates, health and safety, or even a running credit system (where a chip can be credited and debited with amounts) or simply augment a tally as in the case of bus and train passes.	A barcode only has the capacity to provide a reader with a piece of information. This leaves its function as only being an identifier. There is an argument however that if readers are sufficiently well equipped with software and/or Internet connection then there is little advantage to being able to write to a chip.
Longevity	In terms of passive RFID chips there is very little limit on how long they can last, as they do not contain any internal power source that might deplete. Active RFID chips however, like those used to ascertain proximity in a warehouse or shipping area, will spend their energy in time. There are some innovative solutions around this, such as the inclusion of a solar panel on the chip. However this is still considerably more expensive and not useful in all areas of application.	A bar code can theoretically last forever, but its functional constraints make this more of a symptom of inadequacy rather than a testament to function.
Environmental Constraints	One major problem with RFID is the constraints on its operating conditions. Proximity to reader, proximity to metal, amount of material in the way, background noise and liquid all have to be considered in an RFID enabled solution. This is very much dependant on the type of tag.	A barcode has no environmental constraints. It cannot be scanned through a liquid but no amount of surrounding metal and or electronic noise will hamper its function.

Figure 1. Components of basic RFID enabled system (after: IDTechEx, 2005; Veryfields, 2012; Gunther and Spiekermann, 2005)

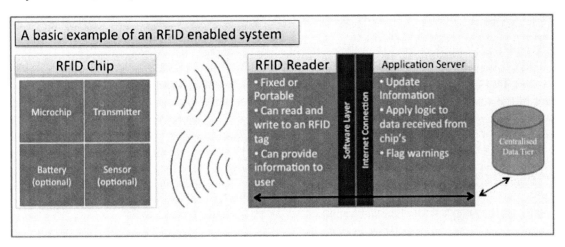

message to the reader, stating that there is no associated order for that product.

RFID Tag Types

There are many RFID tag types and various deployments that can be used depending on the particular situation on hand. The RFID tags vary significantly in terms of operating conditions, functionality and cost. Therefore, their selection must be carefully mapped to their use and the specific type of RFID tag should be considered in detail before adoption. While there are numerous types of tags, they can mostly be categorised into two broad groups: passive tags and active tags.

Passive RFID Tags

A passive RFID tag is called such because it does not actively seek to share information: it is simply activated when in proximity to a reader. It therefore does not need to contain a power source. This gives the tag far greater longevity because there is no battery integrated within it, which potentially would limit the tags' use by linking it to the battery operating life. It does however have additional constraints due to this factor, because it cannot activate itself and therefore it cannot be used to locate items. Also, the range or proximity can be challenging: depending on the frequency being used (low to ultra high frequency) the distance fluctuates substantially but never exceeds approximately 3 metres in range (Chawla 2007). That said, the most notable characteristic of passive RFID tags is that they are substantially cheaper than active tags: typically between 5% and 8% percent of the cost of an active tag.

Active RFID Tags

Active RFID tags contain batteries and because of this, they have a variety of different applications. For example, they can activate themselves which makes them useful in real time location systems

(RTLS). These are also known as 'beacon' tags, as they transmit their location intermittently. This is only made possible because the range of active tags is substantially greater. Using the onboard battery to generate Radio Frequency (RF) energy typically allows a range of 100m or more, which is significant over passive tags. Additionally, the battery can be used to power other sensors attached to the tag, which can record other associated information such as temperature, humidity, pressure, etc. In addition to the substantial increase in cost, there are a further two limitations created by the inclusion of a battery, these being; the tags longevity and diversity of environments in which they can be deployed (Chawla, 2007; Weinstein, 2005).

Semi Passive Tags

There are now a multitude of hybrid tags that combine functionalities from each of the active and passive categories. A battery assisted passive tag can be thought of as essentially a passive tag that has a battery included, in order to perform additional tasks such as the powering of a temperature sensor. Their power usage is minimised through the use of an RFID tag as a power source to transmit information. Once the battery is depleted these tags stop transmitting (Jedermann, 2007).

Battery Assisted Passive Tags (BAP) RFID Tags

These are tags that contain a battery only for the purpose of assisting with the 'wake up' problem of passive tags. While a passive tag has to retain enough energy from a reader before transmitting a battery assisted passive BAP RFID tag does not. They therefore have a significantly larger range than passive tags whilst using less power than active tags which transmit there signal without using the power from the reader. Collecting power from the reader before transmitting is called the "backscatter technique."

Passive RFID Tags with Light Panel

Passive tags can be thought of as battery assisted passive BAP RFID tags, however instead of a battery they use a small solar panel to acquire the power needed. The obvious advantage to this is that it does not having its lifespan limited by battery life, however it is also reliant on intermittent exposure to a light source or sunlight to function.

RFID Tag Frequency Types

Various frequencies can be used in order to communicate with a passive RFID tag. These frequencies have a profound effect on a number of factors, which make each one more suited to various situations. Table 2 shows the types of frequencies used for typical RFID solutions and their characteristics.

RFID Implementation Challenges

RFID technologies has been present for over 60 years, however it is only now that they are being rapidly adopted in industry and adopted on a widespread basis. There is evidence that the technology has not fully matured yet and is still developing in terms of the cost per tag and the capabilities of the system in terms of distance, interference, power acquisition. Additionally the infrastructure that support the technology is poorly developed and currently lacks a global uniform RFID standard, which gives significant challenges when attempting to integrate a number of different partners that are not committed to supply chain consistency. In firms that are largely vertically integrated, a single solution can be deployed across the entire supply chain. However, in industries where the supply chain is open there are significant issues in terms

Table 2. Types of frequencies used in typical RFID solutions and their characteristics (after: Ward and Kranenburg, 2006; Liu et al., 2010)

Characteristic	Low Frequency	High Frequency	Ultra High Frequency
Distance	The low frequency tag has the shortest operating distance of all frequencies. The proximity between reader and low frequency tags can be around 1.5ft at a maximum.	High frequency tags have a greater operating distance than low frequency tags with an maximum of around 3ft.	Ultra high frequency tags have a substantially larger range, a maximum average of around 10ft
Issues with Liquid and Metal	Low frequency tags can operate most effectively through liquid and metal.	Can operate though liquid and metal to some extent, but can suffer from the interfering effects.	Are hugely affected by liquid and water making them unsuitable for many applications.
Background Noise	Ignores the vast majority of background EM noise and can operate in most conditions	High frequency chips are a middle choice, being more sensitive than low frequency but not as sensitive as high frequency.	The most sensitive to background noise, which can lead to a lack of read ability or false reads.
Cost	High relative to the other two options	The price of these chips is the lowest out of the three options	Comparable with the cost of high frequency chips.
Read Speed	The speed at which information can be transferred between tag and reader is slowest with low frequency tags.	High frequency offers a greater read speed than low frequency, not as much as ultra high	Provides the greatest read speed of all passive tags.
Typical Applications	• Point of Sale • Vehicle immobilisers • Healthcare application • Product Authentication • Animal tracking	• Smart Cards • Smart Shelves • Library books • Healthcare Patients • Airline baggage	• Supply chain functions • Electronic Product Code • Electronic Toll Systems (Motorway) • Parking lot access

of compatibility of infrastructure as well as with the cost of the significant middleware requirements (Chan et al, 2012). This can be seen in Figure 2.

In an open supply chain set-up, where various supply chain echelons will be servicing several clients, no prescription exists that each of these clients will be using the same RFID systems. Indeed is likely that the same solutions will not be suitable to support the different functions required by the various parties involved. Therefore, as shown in Figure 3, each retailer RFID generated data will be entered into their respective ERP systems via a piece of middleware, the purpose of which is to facilitate integration. Their ERP information will then be sent to the suppliers system via the Internet. If the retailer wishes to promote total transparency, then the RFID codes and tags will be placed onto the products at the distributor level. This will require the use of different tags for each retailer, depending on their

own requirements. In addition, it shall require a different piece of middleware in order to integrate the RFID tag with distributors own ERP system. It is probable that the distributor shall need to have the ability read the incoming RFID tags from the suppliers, thus requiring yet another set of readers and middleware. This is costly and undesirable, and it is likely that firms who wish to benefit from supply chain transparency and RFID efficiency will need a consolidated effort, which in itself presents huge challenges. It is therefore clear that in each situation where RFID is being considered as a solution, a full return on investment analysis should be carried out to assess the total cost of integration with existing company data structures as well as the data structures used in by value chain partners. This is a current drawback of RFID in that it can rarely be considered an addition to current systems and often requires redesign of exiting processes (Angeles, 2005).

Figure 2. Integrating RFID in an open supply chain (after: Narsing, 2005; Wamaba & Boeck, 2007)

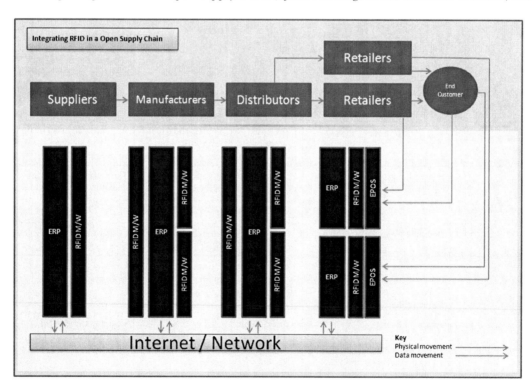

Figure 3. RFID in logistics supply chain system

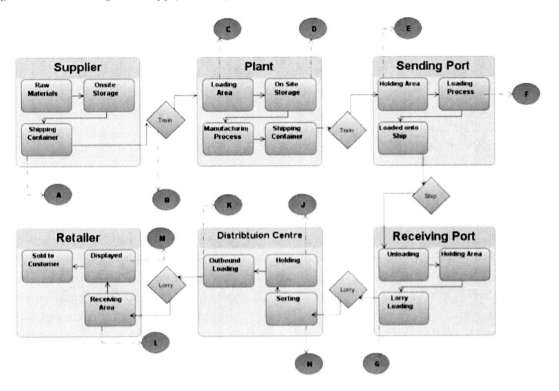

The future will require a standardised set of RFID technologies that offer interoperability between readers and tags for all stakeholders across extended supply chains.

Cost Related Challenges

While RFID technologies are steadily coming down in price they are currently still relatively expensive. The total cost is also relatively difficult to consider as it depends on the deployment design, how many passive tags are needed, how many active tags, type of active and passive tags, special sensor requirements, number of readers, amount of data required to be exchanged, operating conditions etc. Cost has long been a significant factor in deterring potential investors from investing in the technology and this seems likely to continue to be true (Michael and McCathie, 2005). The complicated pricing of the technology as well as the lack of maturity and standardisation may understandably make potential investors nervous about using RFID.

Reliability Challenges

There are numerous reliability issues surrounding RFID, which need to be considered in any RFID deployment. Passive tags for example take time to charge in order to acquire the energy to return a signal. Higher frequency tags charge faster but are very poor at signalling thought water or metal. Tags with a power source could cause potential disturbance of processes if the battery fails at a key moment. All of these issues must be considered in order to address the individual needs of RFID users whilst taking each specific deployment into consideration based on its characteristics and idiosyncrasies (Mishra et al, 2012; Derakhshan et al, 2007).

Data Challenges

It is not unusual for a reader to be able to interact with 800 or more RFID tags in a second and with the increased memory on the tags the demand on virtual storage is significant. Wal-Mart suggested that RFID generates 7.5 terabits of information per day. The volume of information places extra demands on hardware and software to be able to extract the desired information. There may also be unnecessary and misleading information generated by an RFID system e.g. when a member of staff moves an item to simply let something past or if a customer changed what shelf an items was on. This volume of data will require some element of redesign in terms of both the process mapping and software deployment used to extract business intelligence from operational data.

RFID IN LOGISTICS AND SUPPLY CHAINS

There are many examples of RFID solutions in logistics and supply chain sector. RFID is particularly suited due to its ability to track and control inventory movements and control the location of stocks.

Figure 3 is a typical supply chain process, whilst viewing the roles of RFID in logistics. These functionalities are based on actual cases used in international logistics companies such as DHL and FedEx.

Process A: The supplier, of what in this instance are raw materials, has to transport these materials from their facility to the manufacturing plant. In order to do this they are loaded into standardised shipping containers. If we assume that the materials are palletised before placing them into a container, then there are multiple opportunities for RFID use on offer. Since these are raw materials it is likely the value is reasonably low. We will therefore assume these items are potentially not worth tagging individually. Instead, the pallets and containers are tagged. Pallets with passive ID tags can be loaded and the tags programmed. These pallets can then be loaded into a shipping container in proximity to RFID reader, which will feed back information on weight, approximate value and time of loading through the Internet into a centralised database.

Process B: These shipping containers are to be loaded into a train. When the tagged pallets where placed into the container they became associated with that specific container in the ERP system. Each of the containers also has a tag and while the passive tags on the pallets cannot be scanned through the metal container their contents are known. The ERP system already lists the approximate weight of each of these containers, pallets and the associated value. This can guard against theft and aid the supplier's case for reliability by having each container weighed when it gets to its destination.

Process C: Once at the manufacturing plant the containers can be off-loaded from the train and scanned. It is possible that the container scanners can be fitted with a movement sensor to detect the likelihood of damage to the materials due to shifting, in order to aid in quality control. In the event that there has been significant movement to the products, they can undergo an inspection and be send back without wasting time unloading.

Process D: Once the pallets have been removed from the train they can be placed in site storage though an RFID reader, which can detect the nature of the contents of each pallet. This information can instantly be fed back to the handler to instruct them where in the storage area the pallets should go. For example, if they are in short supply they may be required immediately; if they are hazardous special precautions can be adhered to.

Process E: After the manufacturer has produced, palletised and added to a shipping container, the new products can be sent to a shipping port for distribution. Each major shipping port has used RFID technology for a number of years in increasingly diverse ways. Shipping ports do not belong to one supply chain alone, and have a huge volume of containers present in any given time. In order to effectively locate each of these containers, each of the containers or indeed pallets can contain active RFID beacon tags that intermittently broadcast there location. Therefore also helping to efficiently manage and control all the items on the site.

Process F: When loading the shipping containers it is appropriate to consider weight distribution, weight sensors attached to an active RFID tag on each of the container will allow appropriate allocation of weight on the ship itself. Once again, all containers are read by readers as they are loaded. This information can be fed back to the expecting customer, allowing them to plan resources such as lifting equipment or manpower and expertise, thus enabling pro-activeness and maintaining supply chain visibility.

Process G: After processing at the receiving port, the containers will be loaded onto transportation vehicles. The arrival time of each product can be automatically updated. The distribution centres most in need of the products can be identified by the ERP system, in order to determine the order of delivery and to track any change in delivery method or process. DHL have labelled this kind of automated RFID-enabled recalculation of product logistics as 'The Internet of Things' since the products are effectively informing their destination depending on time, market demand, potential damage, etc.

Process H: Logistics has a long-standing issue with the time delay in sending goods the 'last mile', which is a term used to identify the final stages of delivery of a product to a customer. Using on-line shopping as an example, it can be seen that the international shipping process is arguably more efficient than the regional Distribution Centres (DCs) complex system deliveries. RFID can offer a solution for the above by having the items scanned into the DCs in bulk without the need to laboriously scan each of the bar codes. The functionality offered by movement sensors in quality control can also have a profound impact here.

Process J: When products have been entered in a DC, there can be multiple RFID readers in order to track movement and order progress. These status updates give greater transparency both internally and supply chain wide, such as low stock levels, in order to tackle the problem of stock-outs. This also does not slow down the processes within the DC because RFID requires no manual involvement beyond initial installation, or line of sight between product and scanner.

Process K: Outbound loading in a DC is made easier with RFID. Having the RFID readers either at the outbound loading station or actually in the vehicles themselves allows an efficient and non-laborious loading process. In addition, having portable RFID scanners in the vehicle offers added opportunities to monitor goods in transit, particularly if they are perishable, subject to heat damage or if there is potential for damage caused by driving. The goods can return to the DC, without undergoing the process of delivery, rejection, and return.

Process L and Process M: There is a drive by proprietors of RFID technologies and some prominent retail industry players to have RFID tags moved from the logistics equipment and onto the products themselves, totally replacing barcodes. This would allow dramatic application for both the supply chain and the customer. A customer could pick up a product with an RFID tag from a 'smart shelf' and the shelf could then display the price, expiry date, offers involving the product etc. If the product is not replaced the system can deduct this item from the in-store inventory and inform the stock area thought the ERP system regarding re-supply. Finally, all items could be simultaneously scanned at the checkout by RFID readers.

Eventual integration with NFC (near field communication) chips in phones, which is being perused by Nokia, could simply allow customers to enter a store, pick up items and leave the store. All payment could be automated through RFID and the mobile phone. Biometrics could be incorporated into the phone for a more secure system. The potential for the technology is clearly extensive, with the RFID cost dropping and contactless infrastructure growing, the possibly of these seemingly science fiction style applications are coming a more viable option.

Case Studies: RFID in Logistics

The following section discusses several case studies presented by the Association for Automatic Identification and Mobility (AIM) (2012), which implemented a number of RFID solutions in various sectors. Each case study is described and summarised in Table 3 by presenting suitable scenarios detailing the specific challenges faced by each company and the RFID solutions implemented.

Case Study 1 (Griva Textiles): Italian Textile Firm. (Access to full case study at http:// www.aimglobal.org/members/news/ articlefiles/3361-CS_Alien-Griva.pdf). Griva Textiles is a high-volume textile manufacturer. Their biggest challenge was managing inventory through each production stage and introducing an RFID solution to manage the manufacturing and distribution

process, from raw materials to finished product.

Case Study 2 (The State of Texas, US): (Access to full case study at http://www.aimglobal. org/members/news/articlefiles/3454-CS_ motorola-StateofTexas.pdf). This case addresses the challenges faced by the State of Texas when addressing the effects of natural disasters and describes how RFID played a key role in assisting the humanitarian efforts that arose as one million people evacuated from Hurricane Katrina in August 2005 and more than 2.7 million people fled from Hurricane Rita the following month. The solution includes an RFID automated evacuee tracking system using wrist bands.

Case Study 3 (McCarran International Airport): (Access to full case study at http://www.aimglobal.org/members/news/ articlefiles/3456-CS_motorola-McCarran_ Intl.pdf). McCarran International Airport is the 7th busiest airport in the USA, and handles nearly 70,000 passengers and over 460 flights daily. The airport has experiences a large growth in passenger numbers primarily due to its proximity to the popular city of Las Vegas and its resorts. To meet such high demand, the airport introduced an RFID solution to manage passenger's baggage.

Case Study 4 (American Apparel Clothing): (Access to full case study at http://www.aim-global.org/members/news/articlefiles/3457-CS_motorola-American_Apparel.pdf). American Apparel is a leading retailer with a unique selling point: they stock only one item of each style, colour and size on the shop-floor at any time. This makes inventory management challenging for its manufacturing, distribution and retail operations, and relies on RFID to provide accuracy in ensuring minimising out-of-stock situations.

Case Study 5 (Southeastern Container Company): (Access to full case study at http://www.aimglobal.org/members/news/

Table 3. Analysis of RFID case studies

Case	Scenario	Benefit
Griva Textile Company *(AimGlobal, 2012)*	Griva an Italian textile company had previously been identifying their rolls of material with barcodes at the base. The fabric is exposed to chemicals and harsh temperatures as a method of quality control. This often destroyed the barcode and made a chaotic environment to attempt the kind of highly controlled inventory management that the industry demands.	Griva contacted a RFID enabling company called Simet. With the use of highly durable passive tags from Alien Technologies, Simet succeeded in replacing the existing barcode system, solving the problem of harsh environment and integrated the information in real time with their current ERP thought a bespoke development of middleware.
The State of Texas *(AimGlobal, 2012)*	The state of Texas was flooded with over 450,000 refugees after Hurricane Katrina hit the southern coast of America, 145,000 of these had no identification whatsoever. It became clear that current methods of dealing with the refuges where ineffective as families where separated and the logistical and housing confusions that arose cost the state a large amount of money.	The head of state contacted Motorola and a number of partner companies to help solve this by using RFID. The state now has RFID wristbands that will be given to refugees and associated family members stored in the database. All emergency vehicles and public transport such as busses have been fitted with GPS tracking and an RFID reader. Readers can also be found at all designated Refugee centre. This allows the state authorities to track individuals and traffic, and resource requirements across state
McCarran International Airport *(AimGlobal, 2012)*	This airport located in Las Vegas is the 7th largest airport in the world with 70,000 passengers and 460 flights each day. McCarran International Airport has experienced growth into double digits for the past few years due to the increased popularity of Las Vegas to tourists' hot spot. This had lead to the processes in place being overwhelmed and unable to scale to meet the increased demand. A particular issue was the airports poor effeminacy record with baggage.	Motorola was contacted to solve the issue. Low cost passive disposable RFID tags are fitted to the baggage upon check-in and a series of RFID reader along the conveyer system directs the luggage to either a scanner, detailed inspection department or the relevant plane depending on the information contained on the RFID tag. The airport has reported near 100% accuracy rating with reference to their baggage handling since the implementation.
American Apparel Clothing *(AimGlobal, 2012)*	American Apparel are a large clothing manufacturer in the US. They were suffering losses from excessive internal shrinkage due to internal theft and processing errors (60% of total shrinkage). They are heavily vertically integrated and system wide transparency had significant potential to affect profits in the origination and theirself-controlled supply chain.	American Apparel introduced a supply chain wide RFID system to control all assets with the chain. This involved scanners and tags in the textiles plant thought to the distribution centre. The result of this was a 55% reduction in total shrinkage.
Southeastern Container Company *(AimGlobal, 2012)*	The Southeastern Container Company produces more than 70% of the bottles for Coca-Cola in the US. In 2012 they changed the container used to transport there product from a of the shelf disposable plastic container in favour of a bespoke hard plastic bin that was designed to carry more of their product in a safer way. The problem however was that they already suffered significantly from damage and loss of other non-disposable containers used and given that the bins where ten times more expensive than any of the containers currently used.	In order to prevent this each of the containers was fitted with an active RFID chip to intermittently broadcast its location on site. They reduced their shrink rates hugely and expect a return on investment by 2014.
Log Angeles Marathon *(AimGlobal, 2012)*	The Los Angeles Marathon attracts over 12,000 runners at each event. Large numbers of participants crossing the finishing line at the same time posed issues in associating timings to all of the participants.	By simply placing an RFID scanner inside the finishing line itself and attacking inexpensive RFID tags to each of the runners' armbands the organisers managed to achieve a 98% success rate and save considerable amount of money when pared to any other system that could deliver that level of accuracy. This is a good example of how RFID can be used for a diverse range of industries

articlefiles/3500-CS_motorola-Southeast-ernContainer.pdf). Southeastern Container handles nearly 70% of the bottle production for Coca-Cola in the U.S., and introduced an RFID system to provide an end-to-end solution designed to address inventory control and traceability for specialized product containers. This solution, which was designed to work in association with existing barcode systems, involves approximately 30,000 bins, which will be permanently identified with an RFID tag and their locations tracked to minimise losses.

Case Study 6 (Los Angeles Marathon): (Access to full case study at http://www.impinj.com/Documents/Applications/Case_Studies/LA_Marathon_Event_Timing_Case_Study/). The innovative solution was aimed at supporting the popular Los Angeles Marathon, which is the USs fourth-largest, with 20,000 participants and 12,000 race day volunteers. The solution provided an accurate and effective way of recording race timings, which is challenging particularly when large numbers of participants cross the finishing line simultaneously. The solution provided RFID tags integrated into runner's bibs, which is a piece of material used to display a runner's number and association or attached to their running shoes.

CONCLUSION

This chapter has introduced RFID as a viable tool and contemporary solution in the areas of e-logistics and e-supply chain management. The historic evolution of RFID has been presented, detailing how early advances in radar technologies helped to develop the key functionality behind RFID. The ongoing evolution of RFID, from the research environment to an applied solution in the real world, has further focused its requirements and offered new directions for its potential use.

The recent widespread adaptation of RFID across various sectors has raised awareness of this technology, as well as questions relating its ability to meet contemporary challenges. The effectiveness of RFID in certain types of applications and under certain scenarios is undisputed. This can be seen from the case studies, where the benefits of adapting RFID solutions are clearly demonstrated. However, evidence also suggests that RFID should not be seen as the 'panacea' for all problems, and selection of this technology should be made on an informed basis, with a clear understanding of both its abilities as well as its limitations. This can be done by reviewing the objectives and business benefits for each prospective deployment against the technical, operational and cost implications. For example, under some conditions the use of RFID may be possible as a long-term solution, but not viable on the grounds of cost-effectiveness. In this case barcodes may be a more suitable solution, due to their lower cost of implementation.

RFID has proved to be a valuable tool supporting operations across extended e-logistics supply chains, through its ability to track, monitor, control and manage the movement of goods and associated processed and services. RFID has enabled efficiency gains, optimised and indeed changed the way that certain practices are traditionally carried out, such as inventory management. Due to their versatility and ability to integrate with other systems, such as Enterprise Resources Planning (ERP) systems and Global Positioning Systems (GPS), they have enabled goods tracking on a global scale. In the process RFID has demonstrated tangible cost benefits, such as reducing losses due to pilferage, theft, etc. and optimised e-supply chains by enabling better visibility.

RFID is at the forefront of technologies supporting many different types of logistics operations, such as humanitarian logistics, e.g. disaster relief. In addition, RFID increasingly plays a key role in conservation projects, from wildlife tagging e.g. studying migratory habits of animals, to the preservation of antiquities, e.g. recording of artefacts. As RFID matures further, it finds additional uses in many diverse areas, from controlling the movement of perishable items to monitoring of donor organs. RFID continues to offer a way forward in effectively recording and monitoring an increasing array of parameters, and is being integrated into a number of products aimed at, amongst others, offsetting counterfeiting such as e-Passports, and supporting effective decision making processes. The adaptation of RFID will undoubtedly increase as its costs of acquisition decrease and its use and application of its technologies find new ground.

Further Research

Future research in this area revolves around exploring the potential of Low Field magnetic auto-Identification technology, known as 'RuBee,' as a potential alternative, replacement or accessory to RFID. In many respects the technology would appear to mimic the functionality of RFID; however it has a number of differing characteristic that alter its potential application. RuBee, like Active RFID systems, consists of a tag that contains an antenna, battery and a small amount of data storage that can be read and written to by a reader. (Mishra et al, 2012).

The similarities however end there. Instead of high frequency radio waves, RuBee uses long wavelength microwaves and requires a cheaper yet potentially more physically intrusive reader. Unlike RFID, the RuBee reader utilises a long loop antenna and all tags must be contained within or close to the limits of this loop. These antennas add the undesirable requirement of having to precisely plan the area to be scanned; however, they can often be concealed in ceiling floors and are less expensive than the readers associated with their RFID counterparts (Chiu, 2010).

In addition to the infrastructure, the usage characteristics also differ: the long wavelength of RuBee means that the technology can operate irrelevant of surrounding water, metal or electromagnetic interference—indeed steel is shown to actually boost the signal. This makes that the technology is far superior to Radio based auto-identification systems, such as RFID, in many applications, circumstances and environments. A few examples include: the mining industry which has an existing requirement for auto identification of explosives in an underground setting (Mishra et al, 2012), in hospitals where current equipment typically produce a significant amount of electromagnetic interference (Kapa et al, 2012) or within logistics and distribution, to locate items amongst the large volume of metal found in the shipping containers or shelving units.

RuBee technologies also differ from RFID in that they are predominately active tags that contain a power source. Whilst this does give the tags an eventual expiry date, the low wavelength used results in a lower power usage rate, with a battery being able to last 10-15 years, essentially mitigating this draw back in many potential instances of RuBee utilisation (Jolluck and Weich, 2010). The nature of the technology and its low power usage allows RuBee to operate peer-to-peer, i.e. tags can communicate information and logic between them. This characteristic facilitates a significant number of innovative auto ID applications, such as the RuBee tag on a car being able to tell if the RuBee tag on the engine or wheels have changed. Another example is in aircraft, where a Rubee tag attached to a particular part could hold information pertaining to the last maintenance of that specific part. This tag could communicate with one in the cockpit that disallows take off until a certified mechanic with a certified reader has cleared the part.

RuBee technologies do however have significant drawbacks compared with RFID. Typically RuBee tags are more expensive and the long wavelength leads to a slow data transfer rate which would make it incapable of processing a large number of tags at speed. This would invalidate the technologies usefulness in scenarios that require high speed data transfer, such as a cross docking depot or a supermarket receiving a large number of concurrent deliveries (Stevens et al, 2010).

That fact that RuBee tags can utilise larger volumes of data on the tag and interact peer-to-peer has led to RuBee being dubbed a 'visibility tool' rather than a 'tracking tool', for use when exact location and absolute visibility is required. The two auto-identification technologies seem to significantly overlap but fundamentally fulfil different functions. It therefore seems highly unlikely RuBee will replace RFID. Neither one completely replicates the utility of the other, which suggests that the future will possibly see hybrid deployments of the two technologies mediated by a centralised computer system. What is subject to future research is the manner in which these technologies will evolve and how they will precisely manifest.

REFERENCES

AIM. (2012). *RFID cases*. Retrieved July 02, from http://www.aimglobal.org/casestudies/RFID.asp

Angeles, R. (2005). RFID technologies: Supply chain applications and implementation issues. *Information Systems Management, 22*(1), 51–65. doi:10.1201/1078/44912.22.1.20051201/85739.7

Attaran, M. (2012). Critical success factors and challenges of implementing RFID in supply chain management. *Journal of Supply Chain and Operations Management, 10*(1), 144–167.

Chan, C.-K., Chow, H. K. H., Ng, A. K. S., Chan, H. C. B., & Ng, V. T. Y. (2012, March). *An RFID case study for air cargo supply chain management*. Paper presented at the International Multi-Conference of Engineers and Computer Scientists. Hong Kong, China. Retrieved from http://www.iaeng.org/publication/IMECS2012/IMECS2012_pp278-283.pdf

Charikleia, L. (2010). *RFID in the retailing supply chain: A case study on fashion retailing industry*. (Masters Dissertation). Retrieved June 20, from https://gupea.ub.gu.se/bitstream/2077/22606/1/gupea_2077_22606_1.pdf

Chawla, V. (2007). An overview of passive RFID. *IEEE Communications Magazine, 45*(9). Retrieved from http://ieeexplore.ieee.org/xpls/abs_all.jsp?arnumber=4342873 doi:10.1109/MCOM.2007.4342873

Chiu, B. (2010). *Leveraging visibility technology for business applications*. Oracle White Paper. Redwood Shores, CA: Oracle Corporation.

Coltoman, T., Hadh, R., & Michael, K. (2008). RFID and supply chain management: Introduction to the special issue. *Journal of Theoretical and Applied Electronic Commerce Research, 3*(1).

Damgard, I., & Pedersen, M. (2008). RFID security: Trade-offs between security and efficiency. *Computer Science, 4964*, 318-334. Retrieved from http://www.bytopia.dk/blog/wp-content/uploads/2008/08/rfid.pdf

Derakhshan, R., Orlowska, M., & Li, X. (2007). RFID data management: Challenges and opportunities. In *Proceedings of the IEEE International Conference on RFID*, (pp. 26-28). IEEE Press. Retrieved from http://130.102.79.1/~xueli/IEEE-RFID-Conf-04143527.pdf

Ganesan, S., George, M., Jap, S., Palmatier, R., & Weitz, B. (2009). Supply chain management and retailer performance: Emerging trends, issues and implications for research and practice. *Journal of Retailing, 85*(1), 84–94. doi:10.1016/j.jretai.2008.12.001

Grimaila, M. (2007). RFID security concerns. *ISSA Journal*. Retrieved from https://dev.issa.org/Library/Journals/2007/February/Grimaila%20-%20RFID%20Security%20Concerns.pdf

Gunther, O., & Spiekermann, S. (2005). RFID and the perception of control: The customers view. *Communications of the ACM, 48*(9), 9. doi:10.1145/1081992.1082023

IDTechEx. (2005). *An introduction to RFID and tagging technologies.* Retrieved June 30, from http://www.idspackaging.com/Common/Paper/Paper_486/Y9268U8423.pdf

Jedermann, R. (2007). Semi-passive RFID and beyond: Steps toward automated quality tracing in the food chain. *International Journal of Radio Frequency Identification Technology and Applications, 1*(3). Retrieved from http://www.sfb637.uni-bremen.de/pubdb/repository/SFB637-B6-07-026-IJ.pdf doi:10.1504/IJRFITA.2007.015849

Jolluck, D. & Weich, C. (2010). *An oracle white paper: An introduction to rubee technology.* Oracle White Paper. Redwood Shores, CA: Oracle Corporation.

Landt, J. (2005). The history of RFID. *IEEE Potentials, 24*(4), 8–11. doi:10.1109/MP.2005.1549751

Liu, L., Chen, Z., Yan, D., Lu, Y., & Wang, H. (2010, May). E-business and e-government. In *Proceedings of the ICEE 2010 International Conference,* (pp. 2379-2382). IEEE.

Madlmayr, G. (2008). *NFC devices: Security and privacy.* Retrieved from http://ieeexplore.ieee.org/xpl/login.jsp?tp=&arnumber=4529403&url=http%3A%2F%2Fieeexplore.ieee.org%2Fxpls%2Fabs_all.jsp%3Farnumber%3D4529403

Michael, K., & McCathie, L. (2005). The pros and cons of RFID in supply chain management. In *Proceedings of the International Conference on Mobile Business,* (pp. 623-629). Retrieved form http://ro.uow.edu.au/cgi/viewcontent.cgi?article=1104&context=infopapers&sei-redir=1&referer=http%3A%2F%2Fscholar.google.co.uk%2Fscholar%3Fq%3DRFID%2Bcost%2Bmanagement%26btnG%3D%26hl%3Den%26as_sdt%3D0%252C5#search=%22RFID%20cost%20management%22

Mishra, P., Bolic, M., Mustapha, Y., & Stewart, R. (2012). RFID technology for tracking and tracing explosives and detonators in minding services applications. *Journal of Applied Geophysics, 76,* 33–43. doi:10.1016/j.jappgeo.2011.10.004

Narsing, A. (2005). RFID and supply chain management: An assessment of its economic, technical, and productive viability in global supply chains. *The Journal of Applied Business Research, 21*(2), 75–80.

Roussos, G. A. (2008). *Networked RFID, systems, software and services.* London, UK: Springer-Verlag. doi:10.1007/978-1-84800-153-4

Sabbaghi, A., & Vaidyanathan, G. (2008). Effectiveness and efficiency of RFID technology in supply chain management: Strategic value and challenges. *Journal of Theoretical and Applied Electronic Commerce Research, 3*(2), 71–81. doi:10.4067/S0718-18762008000100007

Sarac, A., Absi, N., & Dauzere-Peres, S. (2009). A literature review on the impact of RFID technologies on supply chain management. *Integrating the Global Supply Chain, 128*(1), 77-95. Retrieved June 30, from http://citeseerx.ist.psu.edu/viewdoc/download?doi=10.1.1.169.7017&rep=rep1&type=pdf

Stevens, J., Weich, C., & GilChrist, R. (2010). RuBee (IEEE 1902.1) – The physics behind, real-time, high security wireless asset visibility networks in harsh environments. *Viable Assets, Inc.* Retrieved from http://www.rubee.com/White-SEC/RuBee-Security-080610.pdf

Ustundag, A. (2010). Evaluating RFID investment on a supply chain using tagging cost sharing factor. *International Journal of Production Research, 48*(9), 2549–2562. doi:10.1080/00207540903564926

Veryfields.com. (2012). *How do RFID tags work?* Retrieved June 30 from http://www.veryfields.net/how-do-rfid-tags-work

Wamaba, S., & Boeck, H. (2007). Enhancing information flow in a retail supply chain using RFID and the EPC network: A proof-of-concept approach. *Journal of Theoretical and Applied Electronic Commerce Research, 3*(1), 92–105.

Wamaba, S., & Chatfield, A. (2009). A contingency model for creating value from RFID in supply chain network projects in logistics and manufacturing environments. *European Journal of Information Systems, 18*(6), 615–636. doi:10.1057/ejis.2009.44

Wang, M., Liu, J., Shen, J., Tang, Y., & Zhou, N. (2012). Security issues of RFID technology in supply chain management. *Advanced Materials Research, 2*. Retrieved from http://www.scientific. net/AMR.490-495.2470

Ward, M., & Kranenburg, R. (2006). RFID: Frequency, standards, adoption and innovation. *JISC Technology and Standards Watch*. Retrieved from http://www.jisc.ac.uk/uploaded_documents/ TSW0602.doc

Weinstein, R. (2005). IRFID: A technical overview and its application to enterprise. *IT Professional, 7*(3), 27–33. Retrieved from http://ieeexplore.ieee. org/xpls/abs_all.jsp?arnumber=1490473&tag=1 doi:10.1109/MITP.2005.69

Whang, S. (2010). Timing of RFID adoption in a supply chain. *Management Science, 56*(2), 343–355. doi:10.1287/mnsc.1090.1121

ADDITIONAL READING

Abad, E., Palacio, F., Nuin, M., González de Zárate, A., Juarros, A., Gómez, J. M., & Marco, S. (2009). RFID smart tag for traceability and cold chain monitoring of foods: Demonstration in an intercontinental fresh fish logistic chain. *Journal of Food Engineering, 93*(4), 394–399. doi:10.1016/j.jfoodeng.2009.02.004

Azevedo, S. G., & Carvalho, H. (2012). Contribution of RFID technology to better management of fashion supply chains. *International Journal of Retail & Distribution Management, 40*(2), 128–156. doi:10.1108/09590551211201874

Butz, C., & Bogatu, C. (2008). Empirical study regarding the successful implementation of innovative information and communication technologies such as RFID into logistics processes. In *Proceedings of the CIRP 15th International Conference on Life Cycle Engineering,* (pp. 406-411). Sydney, Australia: CIRP.

Günther, O. P., Kletti, W., & Kubach, U. (2008). *RFID in manufacturing*. Berlin, Germany: Springer-Verlag.

Kim, H. S., & Sohn, S. Y. (2007). Production, manufacturing and logistics: Cost of ownership model for the RFID logistics system applicable to u-city. *European Journal of Operational Research, 194*(2), 406–417. doi:10.1016/j.ejor.2007.12.015

Kirankumar, G., Samsuresh, J., & Balaji, G. (2012). Vehicle speed monitoring system (using rubee protocol). *IACSIT International Journal of Engineering and Technology, 4*(1).

Kyosuke, O., Tsuyoshi, T., Kenichi, Y., & Osamu, T. (2009). An efficient and secure RFID security method with ownership transfer. In *RFID Security,* (pp. 147-176). Springer. Retrieved from http://www.springerlink.com/content/ pr16198625270834/

Lee, C. K. M., Ho, W., Ho, G. T. S., & Lau, H. C. W. (2010). Design and development of logistics workflow systems for demand management with RFID. *Expert Systems with Applications, 38*(5), 5428–5437. doi:10.1016/j.eswa.2010.10.012

Meyer-Larsen, N., Lyridis, D., Müller, R., & Zacharioudakis, P. (2012). Improving intermodal container logistics and security by RFID. *International Journal of RF Technologies: Research & Applications, 3*(1), 15–38.

Nativi, J. J., & Lee, S. (2012). Impact of RFID information-sharing strategies on a decentralized supply chain with reverse logistics operations. *International Journal of Production Economics, 136*(2), 366–377. doi:10.1016/j.ijpe.2011.12.024

Tsai, W.-C., & Tang, L.-L. (2011). A model of the adoption of radio frequency identification technology: The case of logistics service firms: Creating competitive edge in operations and service management through technology and innovation. *Journal of Engineering and Technology Management, 29*(1), 131–151. doi:10.1016/j.jengtecman.2011.09.010

Will, T., & Blecker, T. (2012). RFID-driven process modifications in container logistics: SOA as a solution approach. *International Journal of Logistics: Research & Applications, 15*(2), 71–86. doi:10.1080/13675567.2012.674106

Wu, Y., Lirn, C. J., & Cherng, T. (2011). RFID technology in emergency logistics: An exploratory study. *International Journal of Management & Enterprise Development, 11*(2/3/4), 163-181.

Zacharewicz, G., Deschamps, J.-C., & Francois, J. (2011). Distributed simulation platform to design advanced RFID based freight transportation systems. *Computers in Industry, 62*(6), 597–612. doi:10.1016/j.compind.2011.04.009

Zheng, M., Fu, C., & Yang, M. (2012). The application used RFID in third party logistics. In *Proceedings of the International Conference on Solid State Devices and Materials Science*, (pp. 2045-2049). Physics Procedia.

KEY TERMS AND DEFINITIONS

Active RFID Tag: Tags which have an internal power source, which is able to transmit as well as receive information when in the vicinity of a reader.

E-Enablement: The ability to use Information and Communication Technologies (ICTs) to integrate various systems and processes, for the purposes of dynamically sharing and distributing information relating to specific tasks and operations.

Passive RFID Tag: Tags which do not have an internal power source, and as a result rely on a reader to power it up in order to enable the transmittal of date and information stored within it. The advantages of passive tags over active tags include lower cost and smaller size.

Radio Frequency Identification (RFID): A type of information and communication technology which has the ability to identify, record, verify, and/or process tangible items, intangible processes, people and operations. It has a wider use in inventory management and control, such as tracking and security, and is particularly suited to logistics and supply chain related operations.

Chapter 12
Cloud Computing in Supply Chain Management:
An Overview

Agorasti Toka
Aristotle University of Thessaloniki, Greece

Eirini Aivazidou
Aristotle University of Thessaloniki, Greece

Antonios Antoniou
Aristotle University of Thessaloniki, Greece

Konstantinos Arvanitopoulos-Darginis
Aristotle University of Thessaloniki, Greece

ABSTRACT

In the modern world, companies are investigating state-of-the-art practices to optimize both the cost and operational efficiency of their supply chain. Cloud computing emerges as a meaningful technology that could contribute to this optimization by providing infrastructure, platform, and software solutions for the whole supply chain network via Internet. The utilization of cloud-based services in supply chain management leads to financial and operational benefits, while at the same time potential risks and limitations should be taken into account by all supply chain stakeholders. In this chapter, an overview of cloud-based supply chain management is addressed. At first, a brief introduction to cloud technology is provided. Then, the application of cloud computing on supply chain activities is presented, while positive and negative aspects of adapting this technology in modern supply chains are discussed. The case for Third-Party Logistics (3PL) service providers is specially addressed. Finally, conclusions and future research steps are presented.

DOI: 10.4018/978-1-4666-3914-0.ch012

INTRODUCTION

According to the best known IT (Information Technology) consulting corporations, cloud computing emerges as a rapidly evolving technology that more and more companies are willing to adopt in order to improve their efficiency. More specifically, as stated by IDC (International Data Corporation), investments on new technologies such as cloud computing are increasing at a rate of approximately 18% per year, while it is estimated to reach at least 80% of IT expenditure until 2020 (Gens, 2011). Similarly, according to a recent study of IBM Corporation, the use of cloud computing is expected to more than double until 2014 (Berman et al., 2012). The survey revealed that 72% of the participating companies had already piloted, adopted or substantially implemented cloud technologies, while 90% of the respondents expected to follow the same direction in three years time. Meanwhile, although numerical estimations about the application of cloud computing in supply chain management have not been performed yet, the consulting company Accenture points out that cloud technology can induce a large-scale transformation in traditional supply chains driving companies that use cloud computing to innovative, more dynamic supply chains (Schramm et al., 2010).

Motivated by the aforementioned trends, the aim of this chapter it to provide an overview of implementing cloud computing in supply chain management, with a special focus on the case of 3PL (Third-Party Logistics) providers. Activities like planning and forecasting, sourcing and procurement, logistics, and service and spare parts management are considered to be the first to move to the cloud (Schramm et al., 2011). Employing cloud-based technology in supply chains could generate numerous advantages such as capital investment savings, simplified operations, scalability, real-time visibility, as well as sustainability.

However, risks and limitations such as security of private information, as well as lack of companies' awareness on state-of-the-art information sharing technologies, should be taken into consideration before applying cloud computing in modern supply chain networks. After all, well-known 3PL companies nowadays utilize cloud computing firstly in private and then in public level, in order to benefit from the competitive advantages of adopting cloud networking.

In order to address all the above issues, this chapter is structured as follows. At first, an introduction to cloud computing is provided. More specifically, cloud computing technology is defined and key cloud service models are presented, according to the existing state-of-the-art literature. In the next section, cloud-based supply chain management is addressed. Firstly, supply chain activities that have the potential to move to the cloud are described. Then, the positive impact of adapting cloud computing solutions in advanced supply chain management is discussed thoroughly, as well as the potential risks, challenges and limitations that all supply chain stakeholders have to confront when employing cloud-based systems. Following, the effect of cloud computing utilization specifically for the case of Third-Party Logistics (3PL) providers is presented, along with real-world cases from the global market. Finally, conclusions are presented and future research steps are proposed in the last section.

CLOUD COMPUTING

Prior to introducing the concept of cloud computing in supply chain management, a general description of cloud computing technology is provided following, including the definition of cloud computing and its classification in literature, as well as the presentation of three basic cloud service models.

Definition

When referring to cloud computing, significance must be given to both the applications provided as online services as well as to the hardware and software that cloud providers offer to their customers (Armbrust, 2010).

Cloud computing is an IT service model where computing services (both hardware and software) are delivered on-demand to customers over a self-service fashion, independent of device and location (Marston et al., 2011, p. 177).

Customers access cloud-based applications through a web browser while the software and data are stored either on in-house servers or on servers at a remote location. Cloud computing can be classified in general into four types: public, private, hybrid and community cloud.

Public cloud infrastructure is designed for open use by general public. It may be managed and operated by a company and its multiple partners and it exists externally on the premises of the cloud provider (Mell & Grance, 2011). The comparative advantage of public cloud against in-house systems is that companies do not have to concern about the systems' construction or maintenance (Pires & Carmago, 2010). Using public cloud, the end-user can achieve an inexpensive set-up, as the application costs are covered by the third-party provider. Moreover, the cost of using such a service is being kept at the lowest as the users pay for what they use (Zhou et al., 2012).

In contrast, private cloud is an on-premises cloud infrastructure accessed by users of different business units within a company (Pires & Camargo, 2010). Since the main motivation for employing cloud services is independence from having to operate internal computing resources, the term of private cloud is an oxymoron (Kim et al., 2009). However, the need for lower risk and high security levels makes private cloud an intriguing concept. As shown in Table 1, the choice between private and public cloud depicts a trade-off between security and flexibility respectively (Schramm et al., 2010).

Another type of cloud computing is the hybrid cloud, which is a combination of private and public cloud. In this type, "two or more distinct cloud infrastructures, while remaining unique entities, are bound together by standardized or proprietary technology that enables data and application portability" (Mell & Grance, 2011, p. 3). In a hybrid cloud, a company can maintain its private cloud and then scale out to a public when local capacity is exhausted (Sujay, 2011). In other words, when in-house systems are not able

Table 1. Trade-off between private and public cloud (adapted from Schramm et al., 2010)

Private Cloud	Data Security and Business Continuity	Full data protection
Security		Service level agreement
↑	Process and Competitive Advantage	Unique processes
⏐		Internal processes
⏐		High customization abilities
⏐	Infrastructure Flexibility and Scalability	Resources
⏐		Network
⏐		Processing
↓	Availability of New Business Capabilities	Fast & cheap access to new capabilities
Flexibility and cost	Build and Maintenance Costs	Relatively low costs per user
Public Cloud		Pay per use instead of fixed costs

to support workload peaks, the external system becomes available for the users (Pires & Camargo, 2010). Hybrid clouds balance the benefits and risks between private and public clouds, as well as the operating cost of the in-house infrastructure and the usage-based cost of the cloud provider services.

Finally, community cloud is the fourth type of cloud computing. Community cloud is designed for organizations that share common concerns, such as regulatory compliance or security requirements. This type of cloud can be managed by one or more parties of the community, a third-party or by a combination of them (Mell & Grance, 2011). Moreover, it can be hosted internally or externally.

Service Models

Cloud computing consists of three different service models namely Infrastructure-as-a-Service, Platform-as-a-Service and Software-as-a-Service, each one of them serving different requirements of cloud users.

Infrastructure-as-a-Service (IaaS). IaaS model is a platform through which businesses can avail equipment in the form of hardware, servers, storage space and others, at pay-per-use service. In this service model, cloud providers offer from physical or virtual machines to raw storage, firewalls, load balancers and networks (Mell & Grance, 2011). More specifically, the user buys these resources as a fully outsourced service instead of buying servers, software and network equipment (Conway, 2011). A remarkable example of IaaS is Amazon Cloud Services, a web-based platform that offers online services via its webpage, amazon.com. Two popular services are Amazon EC2 and Amazon S3, each of them covering specific areas of interest.

Platform-as-a-Service (PaaS). PaaS model offers a higher level of abstraction compared with IaaS model that focuses on providing raw access on virtual or physical infrastructure (Garg & Buyya, 2012). In PaaS, cloud providers host a computing environment typically including operating system, data base and programming language execution environment, where users develop and deploy applications (Sujay, 2011). Users can rent virtualized servers for running existing applications or developing new ones without the cost and complexity of buying and managing the related hardware and software (Conway, 2011). In some cases, the underlying compute and storage resources scale automatically to catch application demand so that cloud user does not have to allocate resources manually. Some examples of PaaS are Google Apps and Windows Azure. Windows Azure is a service provided by Microsoft, where someone can build, deploy and manage all the applications across a network of data centers based on a Microsoft environment.

Software-as-a-Service (SaaS). SaaS model is a software delivery model providing on-demand access to applications (Garg & Buyya, 2012). More specifically, cloud providers install and operate application software in the cloud and users access the software various client devices through either a thin client interface, such as a web browser or a program interface. The cloud users do not manage the cloud infrastructure and platform on which the application is running but have control over the deployed applications and possibly configuration settings for the application-hosting environment (Mell & Grance, 2011). This can be an attractive and low-cost solution to acquire demanding software capabilities without the need of applying and maintaining traditional software and hardware (McPherson, 2010). An example of SaaS is Salesforce CRM, which is also divided into several categories. Those are Sales Cloud, Service Cloud, Data Cloud, Collaboration Cloud and Custom Cloud.

As a rapidly evolving technology, cloud computing is constantly providing new, more specialized services, which are mainly subservices of the three existing ones as described above. More specifically, some of them are Storage as a Service (STaaS), Security as a Service (SECaaS), Data as a Service (DaaS) and Desktop as a Service (DaaS).

The different pathways through which computing resources can be accessed from a variety of customers (using different devices and from places) using one of the three different service models of cloud architecture are illustrated at Figure 1 (Marston et al., 2011).

CLOUD-BASED SUPPLY CHAIN MANAGEMENT

The application of cloud computing concept in the context of supply chain management is an innovative practice that generates a new field of study.

A cloud supply chain is two or more parties linked by the provision of cloud services, related information and funds (Lindner et al., 2010, p. 3).

However, before shifting from a traditional supply chain to a cloud supply chain, companies should first identify the technical requirements for migrating supply chain activities to the cloud. This transformation process can be executed by using the cloud lifecycle, which is an improvement lifecycle with multiple steps that allows the process of transformation to be evaluated and improved

recurrently (Lindner, 2011). However, prior to that, companies should weigh all the factors to assess the implementation of cloud technology in their supply chain. Questions about the changes, the benefits as well as the challenges that supply chain stakeholders have to face when using cloud computing should be answered well before taking the critical decision of moving to the cloud (Schramm et al., 2010).

Cloud Computing in Supply Chain Activities

In this section, the application of cloud technology on the several supply chain activities is presented. More specifically, forecasting and planning, sourcing and procurement, logistics, as well as service and spare parts management appear as the most common activities in which cloud computing can be effectively implemented.

Forecasting and Planning. Cloud-based platforms are designed to assist companies to improve their service levels by coordinating the supply chain network's partners (retailers, suppliers and distributors) that play pivotal role in demand forecasting. These platforms can gather sales data via internet, perform basic analytics and consequently

Figure 1. Cloud computing architecture (adapted from Marston, et al., 2011)

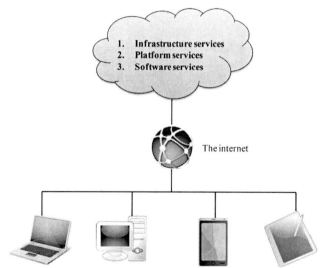

execute more accurate statistical demand forecasts for all the supply chain participants (Schramm et al., 2011). Such a process can lead to a significant decrease of the Bullwhip effect—the information distortion among different stages of the supply chain, (Lee et al., 1997)—allowing all stakeholders to be aware of the real demand volatility they have to cope with. Cloud solutions for demand and order planning combine EDI (Electronic Data Interchange) and forecast execution applications into a single multi-party platform. As shown in Figure 2, when customers generate demand, distributors send the data to the public cloud, making at the same time the information available to the entire supply chain (Pires & Camargo, 2010).

Sourcing and Procurement. Sourcing incorporates acquisition, receipt and inspection of incoming materials with procurement processes and selection of the appropriate suppliers (Schrödl & Turowski, 2011). In this case, cloud-based platforms can operate as a database, which contains multiple data about different suppliers, creating significant benefits for companies that transact with numerous suppliers. Consequently, companies are able to select their suppliers depending on their ability to provide the appropriate raw materials or semi-products according to the end product's specifications and the fulfillment of time limits. Moreover, cloud-based tools enable companies and suppliers to develop contracts, drastically developing contract management (Schramm et al., 2011).

Logistics. Cloud computing is also useful for inventory, warehouse and transportation management, as it offers logistics tracking operations to multiple supply chain partners. Processes such as replenishment planning, order processing, fleet management, transportation route planning as well as global trade compliance can migrate to the cloud (Schramm et al., 2011). More specifically, a sole integrated cloud platform provides the advantage of streamlined transportation, as well as reduced on-hand and pipeline inventory that can lead to annual freight cost savings for companies. Especially in the logistics sector, cloud services appear to be essential for 3PL companies' necessity for itinerary and warehousing management for many different customers in one single system.

Figure 2. Integration of supply chain processes (adapted from Pires & Camargo, 2010)

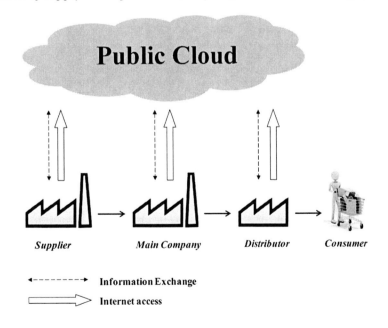

Service and Spare Parts Management. Cloud computing gives the opportunity to companies to integrate forward logistics with reverse logistics in the same closed-loop supply chain model (Guide et al., 2003). Indicatively, RFID (Radio-Frequency Identification) technology allows for tracking inventory's location and then transmitting this information to a cloud application. As a result, inventory's route can be visible to all supply chain partners, from the manufacturer to the customer and vice versa. At the same time, warranty validation, returns processing, spare parts inventory and distribution or technician dispatch are processes that can be hosted efficiently in a single cloud-based platform (Schramm et al., 2011).

Benefits

Following, the main positive implications of cloud-based supply chain management, namely cost efficiency, simplification, flexibility, visibility, scalability and sustainability are discussed.

Cost Efficiency. Cloud computing systems can be used effectively in supply chain management as involved companies can highly benefit from the derived financial advantages. Cloud services do not require any investment for software or computer power ownership, unlike common in-house ERP (Enterprise Resource Planning) systems, as they are offered by external providers (public clouds). Consequently, capital costs for supply chain management software can be converted to operational costs, further enhancing one company's cash flow (Schramm, 2010). Indicatively, the only fees that companies have to pay in order to acquire cloud-based systems are first the activation fee and then the usage fee which varies according to the level of cloud service utilization. Moreover, companies are able to save more money by reducing maintenance costs and keeping upgrade costs to minimum (Zhou et al., 2012).

Simplification. Another main advantage of cloud-based systems is the simplification they provide. Every part of the supply chain is ac- cessible through the same platform, eliminating compatibility problems as well as providing easy connection and enabling supply chain information sharing among partners in one single supply chain system (Chen & Ma Yan, 2011). In this collaborative community, members can be added any time and then enter in the cloud only with a set of password and surname (Pires & Camargo, 2010). After that, all users have the opportunity to operate simple processes and applications in the same platform, reducing the response time of one partner to another's decisions. Essentially, cloud-based services offer information control through a single centralized storage system, so that information flow is smooth among supply chain's partners.

Flexibility. From demand forecasting to warehouse or transportation management, there is a variety of applications for the entire supply chain that can be hosted in one single cloud-based platform. Moreover, supply chain partners could have access to such a platform from their own environment or company regardless their location by using common devices. In other words, running the cloud applications is location-independent (Zhou et al., 2012). This broad network access offers more agility to the whole supply chain, which leads companies to enter quickly in new markets with new products and services (Schramm et al., 2010).

Visibility. Visibility provides timely connectivity along multiple supply chain participants. In that way, companies have the opportunity to observe supply chain events at the time they occur and as a result deal with possible problems or deviations in plans (GT Nexus, 2009). Therefore, visibility is a key issue for 3PL service providers as not only does it help such companies to coordinate their operations and manage many different customers but also allows the customer network to have a transparent view of the entire system (Gillis, 2011). Cloud-based systems are able to provide real-time visibility of inventory and shipments and improve logistics tracking.

These systems, acting as a virtual warehouse for products in pipeline, offer companies the ability to make strategic order fulfillment decisions and, if needed, reroute dynamically the inventory, based on the information about the actual product location (GT Nexus, 2009).

Scalability. By employing cloud computing, supply chain stakeholders can control their system capacity more accurately. In periods of high demand, companies need enough capacity in order to be able to fulfill their customers' orders. Consequently, using common on-premises systems, they should own the necessary database for the whole year in order to respond to the excessive demand just for a short time period. However, with the advent of cloud technology, companies are given the opportunity to adjust their capacity automatically according to their needs and scale their computing power depending on demand fluctuations (Zhou et al., 2012). For example, as depicted in Figure 3, by using hybrid cloud companies are able to deescalate their in-house capacity up to the limits of the forecasted low demand and employ cloud-based capacity for sudden demand spikes (M&E Team, 2009).

Sustainability. Cloud computing can be considered as an emerging 'green' IT that can assist companies in improving their operations' efficiency, lessen their energy costs, as well as their environmental impact (Scott & Watson, 2012).

However, many experts doubt if benefits of moving to the cloud do really exist or if it is about outsourcing of environmental impact to the service provider (Abood et al., 2010). What could resolve such a controversy is the virtualization offered by cloud technology, which leads to a considerable improvement of energy efficiency by leveraging the economies of scale connected with the large number of organizations that share the same cloud infrastructure (Garg & Buyya, 2012). According to Abood et al. (2010), CO_2 emissions per user are notably decreased when using cloud platforms versus in-house systems, as by using cloud technology multiple companies can share the same infrastructure. Furthermore, the application of cloud computing in supply chain management can contribute to the conversion of the traditional supply chain to a 'greener' one in an indirect way. The aforementioned advantage of visibility can assist companies to reduce their carbon footprint. More specifically, through visibility, companies could optimize their inventory routes based on real-time events and thus reduce emissions that are harmful for the environment.

Risks and Limitations

The most common challenges and limitations that companies face when using cloud-based technologies are data security and privacy, the

Figure 3. Traditional in-house model vs. hybrid cloud model (adapted from M&E Team, 2009)

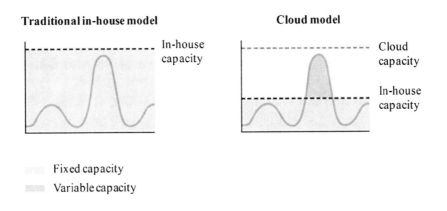

outdated business thinking, system availability, as well as lack of customization, as discussed in the following paragraphs.

Data Security and Privacy. Data in the cloud should be accessed only by authorized members, namely trustworthy supply chain's partners. However, cloud computing systems as software products cannot always ensure confidentiality and as a result run increasing risk of being infiltrated by hacking systems (Zhou et al., 2012). Additionally, possible data acquisition by competing companies would pose an imminent threat to the whole supply chain.

Outdated Mindset. The sharing of data and information with public implies a radical change on the traditional way of working and thinking, which can be a significant cultural business issue (Zhou et al., 2012). Up until now, the majority of companies have been keeping secret piece of information regarding production processes or supply chain networks. Those companies are concerned that wide sharing and disclosure of such data could lead to loss of their competitive advantage. Meanwhile, adopting cloud technology implies a radical change in the business model of the whole supply chain network (Schramm et al., 2010). In other words, all the supply chain partners, who have been managing their operations till now with common on-premises infrastructure, should learn how to use the new cloud systems effectively. Such adaptations cannot be completed in a short period of time, since the transition to a more open way of business strategy needs slow pace to carry out.

Availability. Users of cloud computing often have concerns on the consequences of a potential crash down caused by the provider's system workload and thus disruption of the delivered services. Supply chain operations are crucial for a company's financial welfare and as a result any delays due to the cloud system's malfunction can be proved fatal. At the same time, users worry about their access to the cloud, for example due to poor internet connection in different geographic regions (Zhou et al., 2012).

Lack of Customization. Most of the times cloud computing systems offer standardized services that do not fit exactly to their specific supply chain operations. For example, due to the fact that manufacturing is a complex core procedure that consists of individualized processes depending on each company's products, it requires a high degree of customization that cloud-based services cannot offer yet (Schrödl & Turowski, 2011). More specifically, lack of customization would lead to slow market response or even worse loss of the company's competitive advantage (Schramm et al., 2010).

CLOUD COMPUTING IN 3PL SERVICES: REAL-WORLD CASES

In the context of cloud-based supply chain management, the impact of cloud computing utilization by 3PL service providers emerges as an interesting issue. Real-time visibility of shipments and inventory, either within the company's borders or throughout the whole supply chain network, is of utmost importance to every 3PL company. Cloud computing as private, public or hybrid cloud structure is able to enhance internal or external visibility with consequent operational, as well as financial benefits. In the following subsections, cases of real-world successful 3PL providers are presented in order to demonstrate the effect of adapting cloud technology in their supply chain operations.

The Case of Private Cloud

The introduction of cloud computing as a new technology could not have been so abrupt. Being utilized at first by companies internally, it enhanced their infrastructure and processes. Private clouds enabled sharing of computing resources among different business units, all powered by one single infrastructure.

In the context of 3PL companies, FedEx is considered to be a pioneer in cloud computing. FedEx introduced this technology in 2011 at a private level in collaboration with CloudX (Watkins, 2011). CloudX enabled the company to focus on its customer relationship management and obtain a single interface for many of its sales processes. Before using private cloud, the company faced several problems concerning large sets of data, which needed a lot of computing power to be analyzed. Furthermore, response time had been deteriorated due to large integrated batch processes (Cearley & Phifer, 2009). After turning to cloud computing, FedEx achieved to reduce its response time by 60%, further allowing the parallel execution of batch processes. The company also managed to develop a new analytical application for processing data, something that was not affordable using previous infrastructure models. Apart from the collaboration with CloudX, the company used other three cloud services, namely FedEx® CLI (Critical Inventory Logistics), ROADS (Route Planning and Optimization System) and Salesforce Automation (Dack, 2011).

FedEx enabled a thorough control of its activities throughout the world by providing global order-to-delivery status and global inventory visibility. The company manages FedEx® CLI for over 60 regional and multi-regional customers in over 200 order fulfillment locations around the world. That indicates an average of 160,000 orders per month consisting of 200,000 packages which means 4,500,000 pieces. Furthermore, FedEx is able to optimize courier delivery routes and measure route efficiency through ROADS. This system runs in 500 locations and manages 20,000 daily service plans. It also assists the company to reroute deliveries and better predict delivery times.

FedEx has used its internal cloud structure at its best utilization. However, it became clear that cloud computing had to run public, in order for the company to take advantage of its full spec-trum. For this reason, FedEx turned to the hybrid cloud (Salesforce.com), which utilizes features of both private and public cloud. This hybrid cloud system provided company's sales teams with a full featured mobile solution increasing their effectiveness and improving service level for the customers.

The Case of Public Cloud

As a consequence, private cloud cannot be enough for large 3PL providers with numerous partners and customers. What should actually lead these companies to public cloud is the absolute need of real-time visibility of their shipments, carried out by information collaboration between all the supply chain partners.

Regarding supply chain tracking, most of the traditional 3PL companies have been using emails or phone calls in order to collect the necessary data. However, these ways cannot offer timely shipment visibility nor do they offer network connection between all the stakeholders. As a consequence, the inability of monitoring vast supply chain flows, which large 3PL companies have to deal with, is a significant bottleneck for their supply chain network's efficiency. Moreover, common ERP systems used for organizing collected data or perhaps private cloud infrastructures, which both are deployed within the company, are unable to suggest the dimension of connectivity between the 3PL and its collaborators (Gillis, 2011).

On the contrary, by using a cloud-based public platform which offers an EDI system, 3PL providers are capable of connecting all their carriers and customers in the same network and getting in-time information of their cargo in transit. It is generally known that the variability of lead time is an 'enemy' for 3PL companies. For example, shipments lingering in ports because of mismatches on ship sailing timetables, or due to port strikes, could dramatically prolong lead times (Gillis, 2011). In addition, possible natural disasters can set back many company's transportation schedules. However, cloud technology can assist 3PL providers to avoid such obstacles as their carriers will be able to alert them about the location of their shipments. Consequently, having the right information in the right time will facilitate 3PLs to rearrange their routes and deliver the orders to their customers while satisfying lead times.

Apparently, moving to the public cloud also implies essential financial benefits for 3PL providers. The direct cost reduction is derived from the absence of ownership cost of an EDI system, as well as of other consequent maintenance and upgrade costs. Nevertheless, the most significant profit is gained from the timely fulfillment of customer's orders and as a result the lack of cost of delays and unsatisfied demand.

A noteworthy example of a 3PL provider that has recently moved to public cloud is COSCO Logistics, the largest 3PL company of China and the world's second largest ocean shipping company. In 2009, the company started to reestablish its supply chain management system upon a cloud computing architecture. Their goal was to provide a SaaS service to their customers, subsidiaries and distributors, in order all of them to use the same logistics management software (Harris & Alter, 2010). COSCO contracts contained confidentiality agreements so as to secure information that was shared among all supply chain partners. Although this cloud network collaboration was still in trial stage, the company managed to offer real-time visibility across shipments worldwide.

CONCLUSION

As thoroughly discussed in this chapter, the concept of cloud computing can be effectively used in the field of supply chain management facilitating mainly the collaboration among the supply chain stakeholders through the integration of supply chain activities. More specifically, forecasting on the cloud can reduce the distortion of demand when moving away from the real customer's demand.

Furthermore, cloud-based procurement enables companies to manage different suppliers in one integrated database. Last but not least, cloud systems can provide tracking in forward and reverse logistics in one closed-loop supply chain model. Therefore, companies that are willing to improve their supply chain activities are recommended to adopt cloud technology with consequent positive aspects. Cost efficiency, simplicity, flexibility, system scalability as well as timely visibility are the main benefits for businesses that choose to apply cloud computing on their operations.

At the same time, implementing cloud computing in supply chain management also implies some challenges. Uncertain data security, unfair data acquisition from competitors, system's crash down or poor internet connection appear to be the most common. Especially in core processes such as manufacturing, the lack of customization that characterizes cloud systems, which are designed to be used by several customers, could lead to loss of competitive advantage. For this reason, cloud providers should strive to mitigate cloud disadvantages either by strengthening the system's protection or by offering customization options for their customers in order to persuade them to buy and apply the cloud services. Nevertheless, one of the major obstacles that companies need to overcome when applying cloud technology is the transition from the traditional non-functional working concepts and methods to new innovative modern practices. Thus, companies that intend to apply cloud technology should radically change this myopic attitude by adopting a new one which entails real-time sharing of information as well as collaboration with all the supply chain stakeholders.

In practice, cloud-based models have already been implemented by leading international 3PL companies with great success so far, firstly at private and later on at public cloud structure. These real-world cases, as presented in this chapter, indicate that these companies have succeeded in adopting the new collaborative thinking in supply chain management and enjoy the benefits of cloud computing, especially real-time visibility throughout their customer network.

The field of cloud computing appears to be vast yet relatively new. For this reason, literature about cloud computing in supply chain management is quite limited but rapidly increasing over time. As a consequence, many aspects of cloud implementation in supply chain management have not been thoroughly studied and its full potentials has not been yet adequately discovered. Quantitative models as well as cost analyses of companies, which have already implemented cloud technology, could document more accurately the cost benefits of cloud in comparison with traditional ERP systems or other on-premises infrastructure. Finally, subsequent academic research could possibly develop new advanced integrated cloud models for supply chain management, which will encourage the majority of companies, including 3PLs, to innovate and drive forward their enterprises by moving to the cloud.

REFERENCES

Abood, D., Murdoch, R., N'Diaye, S., Albano, D., Kofmehl, A., & Tung, T. … Whitney, J. (2010). Cloud computing and sustainability: The environmental benefits of moving to the cloud. *Accenture*. Retrieved September 14, 2012, from http://www.accenture.com/us-en/pages/index.aspx

Armbrust, M., Fox, A., Griffith, R., Joseph, A., Katz, R., & Konwinski, A. (2010). A view of cloud computing. *Communications of the ACM, 53*(4), 50–58. doi:10.1145/1721654.1721672

Berman, S., Kesterson, L., Marshall, A., & Srivathsa, R. (2012). The power of cloud - Driving business model innovation. *IBM Institute for Business Value*. Retrieved September 14, 2012, from http://www.ibm.com/us/en/

Cearley, D., & Phifer, G. (2009). Case studies in cloud computing. *Gartner*. Retrieved September 14, 2012, from http://www.gartner.com/technology/home.jsp

Chen, J., & Ma Yan, W. (2011). The research of supply chain information collaboration based on cloud computing. *Procedia Environmental Sciences, 10*(A), 875-880.

Conway, G. (2011). Introduction to cloud computing. *Innovation Value Institute*. Retrieved September 14, 2012, from http://ivi.nuim.ie/

Dack, A. (2011). Cloud computing in FedEx. *FedEx*. Retrieved from http://www.apecscmc.org/

Garg, S., & Buyya, R. (2012). Green cloud computing and environmental sustainability. In Murugesan, S., & Gangadharan, G. (Eds.), *Harnessing Green IT: Principles and Practices* (pp. 315–340). London, UK: Wiley Press.

Gens, F. (2011). IDC predicts 2012 will be the year of mobile and cloud platform wars as IT vendors vie for leadership while the industry redefines itself. *IDC*. Retrieved September 14, 2012, from http://www.idc.com/

Gillis, C. (2011). Visibility through CAT's eyes. *American Shipper Journal, 53*(12), 8–15.

Guide, V., Harrison, T., & Van Wassenhove, L. (2003). The challenge of closed-loop supply chains. *Interfaces: The INFORMS Journal of Operations Research, 33*(6), 3–6.

Harris, J., & Alter, A. (2010). Cloudrise: Rewards and risks at the dawn of cloud computing. *Accenture*. Retrieved September 14, 2012, from http://www.accenture.com/us-en/pages/index.aspx

Kim, W., Kim, S., Lee, E., & Lee, S. (2009). Adoption issues for cloud computing. In *Proceedings of MoMM2009*. Kuala Lumpur, Malaysia: MoMM.

Lee, H., Padmanabhan, V., & Whang, S. (1997). Information distortion in a supply chain: The bullwhip effect. *Management Science, 43*(4), 546–558. doi:10.1287/mnsc.43.4.546

Lindner, M., Galan, F., Chapman, C., Clayman, S., Henriksson, D., & Elmroth, E. (2010). The cloud supply chain: A framework for information, monitoring and billing. In *Proceedings of the 2nd International ICST Conference on Cloud Computing (CloudComp 2010)*. Barcelona, Spain: ICST.

Lindner, M., McDonald, F., Conway, G., & Curry, E. (2011). Understanding cloud requirements – A supply chain lifecycle approach. In *Proceedings of the 2nd International Conference on Cloud Computing, GRIDs and Virtualization*. Rome, Italy: IEEE.

Marston, S., Li, Z., Bandyopadhyay, S., Zhang, J., & Ghalsasi, A. (2011). Cloud computing - The business perspective. *Decision Support Systems Journal, 51*(1), 176–189. doi:10.1016/j.dss.2010.12.006

McPherson, A. (2010). How private equity firms can use software as a service to improve portfolio company management. *IDC Financial Insights*. Retrieved September 14, 2012, from http://www.idc-fi.com/

Media & Entertainment (M&E) Team. (2009). Not just the blue-sky thinking: Cloud computing and the digital supply chain. *Accenture*. Retrieved September 14, 2012, from http://www.accenture.com/us-en/pages/index.aspx

Mell, P., & Grance, T. (2011). The NIST definition of cloud computing. *National Institution of Standards and Technology (NIST)*. Retrieved September 14, 2012, from http://csrc.nist.gov/

Nexus, G. T. (2009). Visibility in the import supply chain. *GT Nexus Inc*. Retrieved September 14, 2012, from http://www.gtnexus.com/

Pires, S., & Camargo, J. B. (2010). Using cloud computing to integrate processes in the supply chain. In *Proceedings of the POMS 21st Annual Conference*. Vancouver, Canada: POMS.

Schramm, T., Nogueira, S., & Jones, D. (2011). Cloud computing and supply chain: A natural fit for the future. *Logistics Management*. Retrieved September 14, 2012, from http://www.logistic-smgmt.com/

Schramm, T., Wright, J., Seng, D., & Jones, D. (2010). Six questions every supply chain executive should ask about cloud computing. *Accenture*. Retrieved September 14, 2012, from http://www.accenture.com/us-en/pages/index.aspx

Schrödl, H., & Turowski, K. (2011). SCOR in the cloud – Potential of cloud computing for the optimization of supply chain management systems. In *Proceedings of the European, Mediterranean & Middle Eastern Conference on Information Systems*. Athens, Greece: IEEE.

Scott, W., & Watson, R. (2012). The value of green IT: A theoretical framework and exploratory assessment of cloud computing. In *Proceedings of the 25th Bled eConference - eDependability: Reliable and Trustworthy eStructures, eProcesses, eOperations and eServices for the Future*. Bled, Slovenia: IEEE.

Sujay, R. (2011). Hybrid cloud: A new era. *International Journal of Computer Science and Technology, 2*(2), 323–326.

Watkins, B. (2010). Cloud computing: Theirs, mine, ours. *FedEx*. Retrieved September 14, 2012, from http://itri.uark.edu/

Zhou, L., Zhu, Y., Lin, Y., & Bentley, Y. (2012). Cloud supply chain: A conceptual model. In *Proceedings of International Working Seminar on Production Economics*. Innsbruck, Austria: IEEE.

ADDITIONAL READING

Buyya, R., Yeo, C. S., Venugopal, S., Broberg, J., & Brandic, I. (2009). Cloud computing and emerging IT platforms: Vision, hype, and reality for delivering computing as the 5th utility. *Future Generation Computer Systems*, 25(6), 599–616. doi:10.1016/j.future.2008.12.001

Cegielski, C. G., Jones-Farmer, A. L., Wu, Y., & Hazen, B. T. (2012). Adoption of cloud computing technologies in supply chains: An organizational information processing theory approach. *International Journal of Logistics Management*, 23(2), 184–211. doi:10.1108/09574091211265350

Demirkan, H., Cheng, H., & Bandyopadhyay, S. (2010). Coordination strategies in an SaaS supply chain. *Journal of Management Information Systems*, 26(4), 119–143. doi:10.2753/MIS0742-1222260405

Fiala, P. (2005). Information sharing in supply chains. *Omega*, 33, 419–423. doi:10.1016/j.omega.2004.07.006

Haq, I. U., Huqqani, A. A., & Schikuta, E. (2011). Hierarchical aggregation of service level agreements. *Data & Knowledge Engineering*, 70, 435–447. doi:10.1016/j.datak.2011.01.006

Huang, Z., & Gangopadhyay, A. (2004). A simulation study of supply chain management to measure the impact of information sharing. *Information Resources Management Journal*, 17(3), 20–31. doi:10.4018/irmj.2004070102

Jun, C., & Wei, M. Y. (2011). The research of supply chain information collaboration based on cloud computing. *Procedia Environmental Sciences*, 10, 875–880. doi:10.1016/j.proenv.2011.09.140

Kim, W., Kim, S. D., Lee, E., & Lee, S. (2009). Adoption issues for cloud computing. In *Proceedings of the 7th International Conference on Advances in Mobile Computing and Multimedia (MoMM 2009)*. ACM Press.

Leukel, J. (2011). Supply chain as a service: A cloud perspective on supply chain systems. *IEEE Systems Journal*, 5(1), 16–27. doi:10.1109/JSYST.2010.2100197

Schrödl, H. (2012). Adoption of cloud computing in supply chain management solutions: A SCOR-aligned assessment. In *Web Technologies and Applications* (pp. 233–244). Berlin, Germany: Springer. doi:10.1007/978-3-642-29426-6_27

Sundarakani, B., de Souza, R., Goh, M., Wagner, S. M., & Manikandan, S. (2010). Modeling carbon footprints across the supply chain. *International Journal of Production Economics*, 128(1), 43–50. doi:10.1016/j.ijpe.2010.01.018

Vouk, M. A. (2008). Cloud computing - Issues, research and implementations. *Journal of Computing and Information Technology*, 4, 235–246.

KEY TERMS AND DEFINITIONS

3PL Service Provider: A firm that provides service to its customers of outsourced (or "third party") logistics services for part, or all of their supply chain management functions (e.g. warehousing and transportation services).

Cloud-Based Supply Chain Management: The planning and management of all activities involved in sourcing and procurement, conversion, and all logistics management activities that prerequisites coordination and collaboration within supply chain stakeholders with information sharing using cloud computing technology.

Cloud Computing: An IT service model that relies on sharing computing services (both hardware and software) rather than having local servers or personal devices to handle applications.

Chapter 13
A University of Greenwich Case Study of Cloud Computing:
Education as a Service

Victor Chang
University of Greenwich, UK, University of Southampton, UK
& School of Computing and Creative Technologies, UK

Gary Wills
University of Southampton, UK

ABSTRACT

This chapter proposes a new Supply Chain Business Model in the Education domain and demonstrates how Education as a Service (EaaS) can be delivered. The implementation at the University of Greenwich (UoG) is used as a case study. Cloud computing business models are classified into eight Business Models; this classification is essential to the development of EaaS. A pair of the Hexagon Models are used to review Cloud projects against success criteria; one Hexagon Model focuses on Business Model and the other on IT Services. The UoG case study demonstrates the added value offered by Supply Chain software deployed by private Cloud, where an Oracle suite and SAP supply chain can demonstrate supply chain distribution and is useful for teaching. The evaluation shows that students feel more motivated and can understand their coursework better.

INTRODUCTION

The Joint Information Systems Committee (JISC) has announced Cloud Computing is increasingly attractive for research and education, and they believe there are the following five reasons for University Cloud adoption (JISC, 2011):

DOI: 10.4018/978-1-4666-3914-0.ch013

- Reduce environmental and financial costs where functions are only needed for short periods.
- Share the load when a university is working with a partner organisation so that neither organisation need develop or maintain a physical infrastructure.
- Be flexible and pay as you go. Researchers may need to use specialised web-based

software that cannot be supported by in-house facilities or policies

- Access data centres, web applications, and services from any location.
- Make experiments more repeatable. Write-ups of science experiments performed in the cloud can contain reference to cloud applications like a virtual machine, making the experiment easier to replicate.

The UK Universities are adopting Cloud computing, either private cloud or hybrid cloud, to save operational costs, enhance quality of service and improve efficiency (Chang et al., 2011e; JISC, 2011). Indeed, Cloud Computing offers a variety of benefits including cost-saving, agility, efficiency, resource consolidation, business opportunities and green IT (Chang et al., 2010a, 2010b, 2011b, 2011d, 2011e, 2012; Foster et al, 2008; Kagermann et al., 2011; Schubert, Jeffery and Neidecker-Lutz, 2010). As more organisations adopt Cloud, there are challenges such as security, interoperability, migration measurement of Cloud business performance (Chang et al., 2011b, 2011c, 2011d). To address these increasing requirements, a structured framework is necessary to support business needs and recommend best practice which can be adapted to different domains and platforms. Cloud Computing Business Framework (CCBF) is the proposed solution (Chang et al., 2011a, 2011b, 2011c, 2011d, 2011f). The goal is to help organisations achieve good Cloud design, deployment, and services, and deliver solutions, recommendations and case studies to businesses.

Clouds are commonly classified into Public Clouds, Private Clouds and Hybrid Clouds (Ahronovitz et al., 2010; Boss et al., 2007; Sun Microsystems, 2009). Their definitions are summarised as below:

- **Public Cloud:** Cloud services offered in public domains such as Amazon EC2 and S3. This approach is for organisations wishing to save costs and time without obliga-

tions on deployment and maintenance. For organisations without Cloud Computing deployment, this is the quickest way to make use of Cloud Computing. The down side is there are concerns for data security in public domains including data loss and conflicts, legal and ethical issues (Krutz and Dean Vines, 2010).

- **Private Cloud:** Bespoke cloud services are deployed within the organisation, thus data and accessibility are only for internal users. This approach is suitable for organisations focusing on privacy and data security, or to change or simplify the way people work. The downside is that some implementations are complicated, time consuming or costly to complete.

- **Hybrid Cloud:** An integrated approach is to use part public and part private cloud to deliver a solution. This approach is suitable for universities wishing reducing costs, whilst maintaining privacy and data security. Downside is that integrating the different architectures is not easy and it is likely this model ends up either public cloud or just private cloud due to complexity and time involved.

- **Community Cloud:** Ahronovitz et al. (2009) from National Institute of Standard and Technology (NIST) proposes four types of Clouds, the fourth is Community Cloud, which they define as "A community cloud is controlled and used by a group of organisations that have shared interests, such as specific security requirements or a common mission." The downside is that it takes years to establish a working community for sharing and mutual learning. However, the added values and benefits for Academic Community could be worth far more than the time and effort spent. Briscoe and Marinos (2009) propose that the concept of the Community Cloud draws from Cloud Computing, Digital Ecosystems and

Green Computing, with these five major characteristics: Openness; Community; Graceful Failures; Convenience and Control; and Environmental Sustainability.

This paper is not about the literature of Cloud Computing but how it can be adopted in the education domain. It proposes Education as a Service (EaaS) and explains its business model, content, technology, impacts to education and benefits involved.

Education as a Service Definition

Educause and Nacubo (2010) jointly propose shaping the Higher Education by using Cloud Computing services to improve delivery and content of Education. They explain the term Education as a Service (EaaS), which includes Cloud architecture, applications and services delivered by Cloud to education in the form of lectures, quizzes, assignments, marking, tutorial, discussions, debates and student support. They focus more on the benefits of doing so, rather than the details of how to achieve EaaS. They explain this is a sustainable business model and may shake up the way education goes forward. Fogel (2010) explains the benefits of adopting EaaS and presents EaaS some information of how to do it by emphasising the architecture of services, connectivity, and service integration. He argues that education can get more benefits by service integrations of EaaS. Both papers strongly support that EaaS is not only a new way of delivery of education but also an economical and sustainable business model.

University of Greenwich (UoG) Case Study Overview

In the University of Greenwich (UoG) case study, the aim is to present how Cloud Computing can offer a unique business model for higher education and transforms the way modern higher education

is delivered. This includes demonstrations of the followings:

- The use of Cloud Computing Business Framework (CCBF) recommends suitable business models for Education such as Education as a Service (EaaS). The use of the pair of Hexagon Models assessing Cloud projects against elements of success criteria.
- Demonstration of Oracle supply chain private cloud that has been used in teaching to improve learning efficiency.
- Strategic plan of adopting enterprise software for quality teaching and learning.

The structure of this chapter is as follows. Section 2 present a classification of Business Models and their application in an EaaS. Section 3 introduces the use of a pair of Hexagon Models. Section 4 presents the use Oracle to help Supply Chain Business Model, the results of the evaluation. Section 5 describes a strategic plan for adopting SAP using a supply chain business model in higher education. Section 6 presents topics for discussions and Section 7 sums up with the Conclusions and Future Work.

BUSINESS MODEL CLASSIFICATIONS AND THEIR USES

The Cloud Cube Model (CCM) proposed by the Jericho Forum (JF) is used to enable secure collaboration in the appropriate cloud formations best suited to the business needs (Jericho Forum, 2009). However, CCM does not classify Cloud operations into different business models and additional work is required, where Chang et al. (2010a, 2010b, 2011a) demonstrate key area of Cloud Computing Business Framework (CCBF) by categorising eight business models and explain how CCM fits into each business model with strength and weakness presented. These eight models proposed by CCBF are categorised as follows:

- Service Provider and Service Orientation
- Support and Services Contracts
- In-House Private Clouds
- All-In-One Enterprise Cloud
- One-Stop Resources and Services
- Government funding
- Venture capitals
- Entertainment and Social Networking

The education sector is increasingly regarded as a service industry for providing training, knowledge and skills for students and general public. Cloud Computing for higher education is identified a key strategic area in the UK (JISC 2011) and this provides a unique business model to meet demands from continuously-improved education and services. UoG adopts multiple business models including Support and Services Contracts; In-House Private Clouds and One-Stop Resources and Services to deliver educational services. There will be detailed descriptions about Business Models and their examples and business cases.

How These Business Models Help Organisations for Cloud Adoption

Having the winning strategies also greatly influences decision-makers from traditionally non-cloud organisations. Wolfram is a computational firm providing software and services for education and publishing, and it has considered adopting "Support and Services Contracts", the second business model (HPC in the Cloud, 2010). Upon seeing revenues in iPhone and iPad, they added a new model, the eighth model, by porting their applications onto iPhone and iPad. Similarly, MATLAB, adopted the first and second model,

and began the eighth model by porting their application to iPhone and iPad in order to acquire more income and customers. There were start-ups such as Parascale using the seventh model to secure their funding, and they adopted the first model by being an IaaS provider. They moved onto the second model to generate more revenues. The National Grid Service (NGS) has used the sixth model to secure funding, and their strategy is to adopt the fifth model by becoming the central point to provide IaaS cloud services for the UK academic community. Facebook has used multiple business models, the first, seventh and eighth model to assist their rapid user growth and business expansion.

Guy's and St Thomas' NHS Trust (GSTT) and Kings College London (KCL) spent their funding on infrastructure and resources to deliver a PaaS project. Knowing that outsourcing would cost more than they could afford financially with possibility in project time delays, they decided to use the third business model, "In-House Private Clouds", which matched to cost-saving, a characteristic of Cloud. They divided this project into several stages and tried to meet each target on time. In contrast, there was another NHS project with more resources and funding, and they opted for vendors providing the second and forth business models, "Support and Service Contract" and "All-in-One Enterprise Cloud."

Multiple uses of business models are useful for Cloud-adopting organisations. An example is Facebook, which adopts the first, seventh and eighth model, and have seen growth rate of active users begun in 100 million to more than 500 million between Year 2008 and 2010 (Sullivan, 2010). Another example is Microsoft, which adopts the first and fourth business model, and they plan providing other service models such as the fifth and eighth to maximise their sources of revenue and maintain the competitive status.

Education as a Service: Multiple Uses of Business Model

The year 2012 is a challenging year for UK academic institutions due to the rise of annual tuition fees from £3,350 to approximately £9,000 for each UK and EU student. The level of funding and support have been shifted from the government support model to the university independence model where each university should find additional funding itself to support academic programmes and research projects (Guardians, 2011, 2012). This makes universities look for additional funding and to transform the way higher education content and activities are delivered, so that students can perceive as values for such a fee rise. Transformation includes the way the higher education content and activities are delivered as a value-added service which can highlight the strengths in each university, improve learning efficiency and integrate different learning activities and outcomes. The new term is called Education as a Service (EaaS), which can offer the followings:

- A blended learning (Ginns and Ellis, 2007; Samarawickrema and Stacey, 2007) environment to allow students learning from face-to-face lectures and tutorials, and online resources such as videos, games and simulations.
- A platform to integrate different learning resources and to encourage students with peer learning and interactions with tutors.

EaaS requires a unique strategy and the multiple uses of business models can help to achieve this goal. This includes the use of suitable business models such as:

- **Support and Services Contracts (second model):** A small number of projects can be outsourced to selected vendors.
- **In-House Private Clouds (third model):** A few projects can be done in-house.

- **One-Stop Resources and Services (fifth model):** Working with central IT services and joint project with another department, Cloud-based services and initiatives can start from a central place which offers resources, advice and training.
- **Government Funding (sixth model):** European and UK government funding offers several Cloud projects.
- **Venture Capitals (seventh model):** Additional funding from industry and external collaborators are in place.
- **Entertainment and Social Networking (eighth model):** Cloud services should have online forum and functionalities similar to social networking to encourage peer learning and ensures students are on learning activities when they are online.

EaaS includes these business models to ensure the maximum Return on Investment (ROI) can be achieved, which Chang et al (2011e) demonstrate the benefits of Cloud adoption for the University of Southampton, and ROI include cost-saving and improvement in services and user satisfaction. This helps universities to sustain their business model and also enhance the quality of education in the use of Cloud Computing. In this paper, all Cloud projects are designed, deployed, and serviced based on EaaS and demonstrations include technologies and activities for e-Procurement and supply chain.

THE PAIR OF THE HEXAGON MODELS

The origins of the Hexagon Model are from Sun Tzu's Arts of War which Chang et al. (2010b, 2011b) demonstrate the use of the Hexagon Model (Business Model, strategic focus) to review Cloud business performance against six success criteria. Another Hexagon Model (IT Services, operational focus) can be used to review service performance

(Hosono et al. 2009; Chang, 2010b). This pair of the Hexagon Model can be used for any Cloud projects, providing managers and stake holders a quick review of the project performance. In addition, the pair of the Hexagon Model is related to the CCBF by providing the bridge between qualitative and quantitative Cloud research methods. For example, if a project is difficult to measure its ROI, the pair of the Hexagon Model can be used to measure the performance of each success criteria and the area occupied within the Hexagon Models can indicate a business or a project's strengths and weaknesses visually for decision-makers.

Success criteria include the followings:

- Popularity, investors, valuation, innovation, consumers and Get-The-Job-Done (GTJD) for the Hexagon Model with Business Model focus. These six elements are supported by Anderton (2008), Waters (2008), Hull (2009).
- Usability, performance, portability, security reliability and scalability for the Hexagon Model with IT Services focus. These six elements are supported by Hosono et al. (2009, 2010).

The Overview for Cloud Adoption at University of Greenwich (UoG)

University of Greenwich (UoG) started Cloud adoption since 2010 in the following IT initiatives:

- **The e-procurement project:** It allows procurement activities from different departments to take place on a central platform where different products, services and suppliers can be selected. Users include Procurement Manager, Director of Resources and Finance officers from each School.
- **Oracle development for supply chain and business process:** Enterprise Oracle

software was installed and used to demonstrate the concept of supply chain, operation management, and business process. It was used in lectures and tutorials to demonstrate how they can work.

- **Sharepoint 2007 and 2010 projects:** Sharepoint 2007 has been developed to serve as a digital repository, and is offering automated administrative process to improve efficiency and reduce the level of printing. Migration to Sharepoint 2010 can improve the existing functionality, but can integrate different and more services than Sharepoint 2007. Additional features for Sharepoint 2010 can cope with increasing demands. Active users are all members of staff who have different levels of administrative duties.
- **Media server project:** It allows improves learning services for members of staff and students, and offers a platform to upload, share and review video clips related to teaching, learning, and research. Active users are some academic staff and their students.

The Hexagon Model (Business Model) Review for Cloud Adoption (University of Greenwich)

Figure 1 shows the Hexagon Model (Business Model) for University of Greenwich. Each of six elements is assessed and marked (Chang et al., 2010b, 2011a). The area occupied by the shaded region shows the overall performance of the project. Brief explanations are as follows. Innovation and GTJD score very highly because these initiatives have unique designs to ensure requirements are met. Projects are served for its purpose, which integrates different resources and provides a platform for students to learn and share. Simulations or workflows are provided to simplify complex processes which can be presented in a way that students can understand with ease. This

Figure 1. The hexagon model (business model) for University of Greenwich

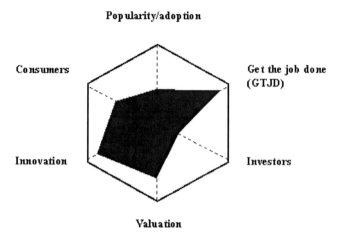

also ensures valuation of these Cloud projects is high. In addition, the student feedback on simulation and workflow demonstrations is rated highly, and thus consumers are marked in a good score. There are two issues. Firstly, some features in the Cloud projects are not as easy to use, since it requires specific knowledge and training prior using these initiatives. Secondly, some of these projects are not getting stakeholders and investors financial support. These two issues make the score for popularity and investors lower. Communication and funding availability are important factors to make overall scores better.

The Hexagon Model (IT Services) Review for University of Greenwich (Redraw)

Figure 2 shows the Hexagon Model (IT Services) for University of Greenwich. These six elements are assessed and the area occupied by the shaded region shows the overall performance. Performance, Portability, Reliability and Scalability are high to reflect the strengths of these services. Security is good as there are security technologies and measure in place. Usability is lower because some systems are not entirely open.

Supply Chain Business Models in the Education Domain

Section 2 and Section 3 explain the significance of Business Models and present how EaaS can be delivered as multiple uses of Business Models. There is an increasing demand in higher education to adopt the emerging technologies and concept for various benefits such as motivating more students, improving quality of higher education, making teaching more interesting and enhancing the opportunities for funding and collaboration (Chang, 2003, 2006; Zhou et al., 2008; Chang

Figure 2. The hexagon model (IT services) for University of Greenwich

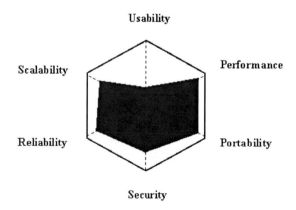

et al., 2011e). Therefore, it becomes apparently important to demonstrate new business model for higher education. Supply Chain Business Model is proposed to meet this demand, and it consists of using private cloud to demonstrate supply chain teaching and delivery, where Section 4 and 5 have more to discuss.

THE USE OF OPEN SOURCE ORACLE FOR TEACHING

Introduction to Business process at UoG is a subject with emphasis in operation management, supply chain management, and marketing. Management of Information Systems (MIS) at UoG is a subject introducing different aspects of IS to explain how it can be useful and adopted by organisations, which include technological, economical, social, political, and cultural factors. Teaching has become more challenging since different concepts and different subject areas have to be taught to different levels of students who are from different backgrounds and expectations. There is an IT initiative to adopt IT systems to enhance teaching, where the major benefits include "Simulations of business processes and supply chain management can be used for effective teaching" (Zhou et al., 2008). Details are discussed in Section 4.1 to demonstrate how Oracle can be used for supply chain in the private cloud.

Demonstration of Supply Chain

Candido et al. (2009) propose SOA approach for Supply Chain, and review a number of research papers and analysis. They explain two models, Orchestration and Choreography, and compare their strengths and weaknesses. Drawbacks for these two models are summed up in terms of orchestration and choreography:

- **Orchestration:** Use a centrally control set of workflow logic to facilitate inte-

gration or interoperability of two or more applications.
  ◦ No horizontal interaction by definition.
  ◦ Use middleware and a device is always a "slave" in a master-slave model.
  ◦ No particular research challenge.
- **Choreography:** A schema or process to set up an organized collaboration between different distributed services, without any other entity controlling the collaboration logic.
  ◦ Need to distribute the workflow logic to all involved devices, although less complex.
  ◦ No consensus about possible solution, such as within industrial automation scope.
  ◦ Possible network traffic boost when a large number of services are connected and active.
  ◦ Difficult to scale to large and complex applications.

The use of Cloud can minimise these two drawbacks and offer more opportunities to offer better delivery of supply chain education and supply chain business model (Chang et al., 2011e, 2011f, 2012; Leukel, Kirn, and Schlegel, 2011). This explains the importance of adopting the right technologies. The use of Supply Chain in SOA-based Private Cloud enabled by Oracle technologies offer improvements, which are described as follows. It offers any processes the ability to link to the next related phase, and also report to the correct application or department. The use of middleware or Web Services is optional, and even where they are in use, it is an open and free linkage-oriented model which has horizontal and vertical connections. Supply Chain can be demonstrated by simulations done by Oracle software to show the relationship between goods, services, suppliers, distributors and consumers. See Figure

3 for the example to demonstrate coffee supply chain network between South America and different states in the America.

Oracle provides a platform to demonstrate visually how supply chain distribution can work, and explains relationships between different sites, where cash flow, goods, demands, and supplies can be checked and monitored in a private cloud environment. Supply chain distribution in Figure 4 can calculate accounting and cash flow between different suppliers, distributors, and customers. It offers reporting functionality to display all the cash flow in each entity and between two entities by clicking the object (entity) on the screen. Figure 5 shows an example of the cash flow in the distribution network between customers and suppliers between January and May 2007.

Supply Chain distribution can show the Demand functionality in each supplier. Upon clicking each object (entity), it shows the report for Demand. This is useful for customers and suppliers to keep track of supply-demand relationship and understand any changes in the order and consumer behaviour. Figure 5 is the screenshot with details about different product demands between January and May 2007.

The use of Cloud technologies for Supply Chain helps to motivate students and improve their learning satisfaction, and details are in another Section.

Students' Learning Satisfaction

Students feel more motivated and interested in learning and undertaking coursework. This may help to improve efficiency and enhancing the student's learning experience (Klassen and Willoughby, 2003; Nix, 2004; Zhou et al., 2008). The use of open source Oracle e-Business applications is an IT initiative to meet both criteria. Virtual servers have been allocated where the virtual machines can be used to install different versions and application suite. There is a virtual

Figure 3. Coffee supply chain network between South America and different states in the US

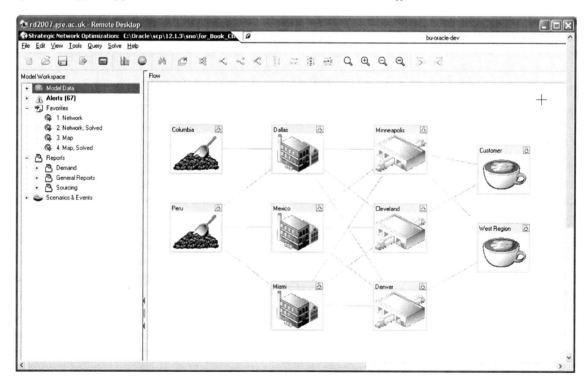

Figure 4. Reporting functionality to show cash flow in the distribution network between customers and suppliers between January and May 2007

			01-Jan-2007	01-Feb-2007	01-Mar-2007	01-Apr-2007	01-May-2007
Custo.	Mello...	Dem...	1,200.00	1,200.00	1,200.00	1,200.00	1,200.00
		Satis..	1,200.00	1,200.00	1,200.00	1,200.00	1,200.00
		Price	30.50	30.50	30.50	30.50	30.50
	Perk...	Dem...	1,200.00	1,200.00	1,200.00	1,200.00	1,200.00
		Satis..	1,200.00	1,200.00	1,200.00	1,200.00	1,200.00
		Price	30.50	30.50	30.50	30.50	30.50
	Susta..	Dem...	1,875.00	1,950.00	1,200.00	2,062.50	2,156.25
		Satis..	1,875.00	1,950.00	1,200.00	2,062.50	2,156.25
		Price	30.50	30.50	30.50	30.50	30.50
	Turb...	Dem...	1,875.00	1,950.00	1,200.00	2,062.50	2,156.25
		Satis..	1,875.00	1,950.00	1,200.00	2,062.50	2,156.25
		Price	30.50	30.50	30.50	30.50	30.50
West...	Mello...	Dem...	1,950.00	2,025.00	1,950.00	2,145.00	2,242.50
		Satis..	1,950.00	2,025.00	1,950.00	2,145.00	2,242.50
		Price	30.50	30.50	30.50	30.50	30.50
	Perk...	Dem...	1,875.00	1,950.00	1,875.00	2,062.50	2,156.25
		Satis..	1,875.00	1,950.00	1,875.00	2,062.50	2,156.25
		Price	30.50	30.50	30.50	30.50	30.50
	Susta..	Dem...	1,875.00	1,950.00	1,875.00	2,062.50	2,156.25
		Satis..	1,875.00	1,950.00	1,875.00	2,062.50	2,156.25
		Price	30.50	30.50	30.50	30.50	30.50
	Turb...	Dem...	1,875.00	1,950.00	1,875.00	2,062.50	2,156.25
		Satis..	1,875.00	1,950.00	1,875.00	2,062.50	2,156.25

server specifically used for that purpose and is installed with Oracle e-Business suite that shows some examples of supply chain management. Workflows and business process technologies are used to demonstrate supply chain and operation management. Students feel they can understand much better. To demonstrated the effectiveness of using simulation in a lecture, two cohorts at the UoG where both given the same lecture on supply chain management. Each cohort received two lessons, where one was focused on supply chain and operation management theories and case studies without software demonstration. The other lesson contained class-based teaching and software simulations. Each time their feedback was collected and learning satisfaction was rated by students in terms of percentages. The learning satisfaction with and without Oracle simulations was recorded and compared. Results are presented in Figure 6.

Learning satisfaction for Group 1 was 76% on average without software simulations and was raised to 91% with software simulations. Similarly, learning satisfaction for Group 2 improved from 78% to 93% when software simulations were included. Some feedback suggested that students can pay more attention and can understand some complex theories much better with the aid of software simulations. Two groups of cohort studies conform there is 15% improvement in learning satisfaction. Details are presented in Section 4.2.1. Students could understand better the management of a supply chain and they could articulate what they learned well. This is particularly helpful for

Figure 5. Different product demands between January and May 2007

Plant	Blend	Bean	Jan-07	Feb-07	Mar-07	Apr-07	May-07
Dallas	MellowMix	Light	65.00	65.00	65.00	65.00	65.00
		Medium	35.00	35.00	35.00	35.00	35.00
		Blend Total	100.00	100.00	100.00	100.00	100.00
	PerkMix	Dark	80.00	80.00	80.00	80.00	80.00
		Light	5.00	5.00	5.00	5.00	5.00
		Medium	15.00	15.00	15.00	15.00	15.00
		Blend Total	100.00	100.00	100.00	100.00	100.00
	SustainMix	Light	50.00	50.00	50.00	50.00	50.00
		Medium	50.00	50.00	50.00	50.00	50.00
		Blend Total	100.00	100.00	100.00	100.00	100.00
	TurboMix	Dark	80.00	80.00	80.00	80.00	80.00
		Medium	20.00	20.00	20.00	20.00	20.00
		Blend Total	100.00	100.00	100.00	100.00	100.00
Mexico	MellowMix	Light	65.00	65.00	0.00	0.00	65.00
		Medium	35.00	35.00	0.00	0.00	35.00
		Blend Total	100.00	100.00	0.00	0.00	100.00
	PerkMix	Dark	0.00	0.00	80.00	80.00	0.00
		Light	0.00	0.00	5.00	5.00	0.00
		Medium	0.00	0.00	15.00	15.00	0.00
		Blend Total	0.00	0.00	100.00	100.00	0.00
	SustainMix	Light	0.00	50.00	0.00	50.00	50.00
		Medium	0.00	50.00	0.00	50.00	50.00
		Blend Total	0.00	100.00	0.00	100.00	100.00
	TurboMix	Dark	80.00	80.00	80.00	80.00	80.00
		Medium	20.00	20.00	20.00	20.00	20.00
		Blend Total	100.00	100.00	100.00	100.00	100.00
Miami	MellowMix	Light	65.00	65.00	65.00	65.00	65.00
		Medium	35.00	35.00	35.00	35.00	35.00
		Blend Total	100.00	100.00	100.00	100.00	100.00
	PerkMix	Dark	80.00	80.00	80.00	80.00	80.00
		Light	5.00	5.00	5.00	5.00	5.00
		Medium	15.00	15.00	15.00	15.00	15.00
		Blend Total	100.00	100.00	100.00	100.00	100.00

lecturers' perspective to enhance students' learning experience and students felt they had a greater sense of learning satisfaction when they could understand the topics of discussions in lectures and tutorials. Another round of surveys will take place to see the knowledge they have learnt and experience they had retained. The next few sub-sections describe the effective use of blended learning, which is the combination of class-based teaching and online/IT learning.

Figure 6. Learning satisfaction without/with software simulations

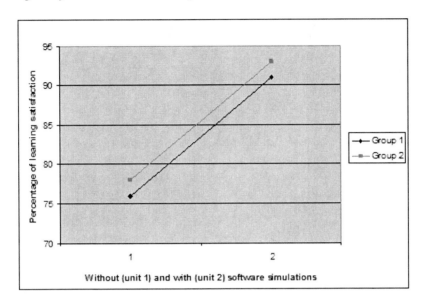

Statistical Analysis for Two Cohorts

There are two cohorts taking part in this case study. The first group has sixteen students where an hour lesson was taught without simulations and another similar lesson was taught with the aid of simulations to help explaining complex theories. Rating for learning satisfaction for each student was recorded and results are computed by STATA 11 and are recorded in Figure 7. The first variable is "group1_without_simu" which refers to learning satisfaction without simulation and the second variable is "group1_with_simu" which means learning satisfaction with simulation. Their detailed statistics are broken down, where "group1_without_simu" has a mean of

Figure 7. Statistical summary of first cohort computed by STATA 11

Variable	Observations	Mean	Std. Dev.	Min	Max
group1_without_simu	16	76	3.596294	70	83
group1_with_simu	16	91	3.405877	83	95

	Variable: group1_without_simu					Variable: group1_with_simu			
	Percentiles		Smallest			Percentiles		Smallest	
1%	70	70			1%	83	83		
5%	70	70			5%	83	87		
10%	70	73	Obs	16	10%	87	88	Obs	16
25%	74	74	Sum of Wgt.	16	25%	88	88	Sum of Wgt.	16
50%	76		Mean	76	50%	92		Mean	91
		Largest	Std. Dev. 3.596294				Largest	Std. Dev. 3.405877	
75%	78	78			75%	93	93		
90%	81	80	Variance 12.93333		90%	95	95	Variance 11.6	
95%	83	81	Skewness .0977015		95%	95	95	Skewness -.7528698	
99%	83	83	Kurtosis 2.566904		99%	95	95	Kurtosis 2.8696	

76, standard deviation of 3.596294, variance of 12.93333, Skewness 0.0977015 and Kurtosis of 2.566904. Second variable, "group1_with_simu", has a mean of 91, standard deviation of 3.405877, Variance of 11.6, Skewnes -0.7528698 and Kurtosis of 2.8696.

The second group has thirty-three students where an hour lesson was taught without simulations and another similar lesson was taught with the aid of simulations to help explaining complex theories. Rating for learning satisfaction for each student was recorded and results are computed by STATA 11 and are recorded in Figure 8. The first variable is "group2_without_simu" which refers to learning satisfaction without simulation and the second variable is "group2_with_simu" which means learning satisfaction with simulation. Their detailed statistics are broken down, where "group2_without_simu" has a mean of 78, standard deviation of 3.942772, variance of 15.54545, Skewness 0.4322148 and Kurtosis of 2.745675. Second variable, "group2_with_simu", has a mean of 93, standard deviation of 2.153222, variance of 4.636364, Skewnes –0.642455 Kurtosis of 2.745675.

Analysis of Variance (ANOVA)

Analysis of variance (ANOVA) provides statistical test of whether means of several groups are equal and can generalise t-test to two or more groups (Stevens, 2002). ANOVA can be used when these two cohorts have close means and each group has two sets of data. Figure 9 shows the ANOVA with t-test for Cohort one and two. Cohort one has t-value=1.56 and Prob>t-value is 0.2732. Cohort two has t-value=3.94 and Prob> t-value is 0.0123.

The Use of Blended Learning

Blended learning uses video, web-based materials and class-based teaching makes learning more interesting and effective, where there are reports of added values offered by blended learning (Ginns and Ellis, 2007; Samarawickrema and Stacey, 2007). In my other course, blended learning has been used and students find it interactive to learn and share. They can keep their learning progress up-to-date and can develop learning culture and peer learning with the assistance of Web 2.0 technologies. In addition, the benefits of e-Learning

Figure 8. Statistical summary of second cohort computed by STATA 11

```
Variable   |   Obs   Mean  Std. Dev.  Min   Max
-------------+-----------------------------------------------
group2_without_simu |   23    78   3.942772    72    86
group2_with_simu    |   23    93   2.153222    88    96


  group2_without_simu                          group2_with_simu
-----------------------------------------    -----------------------------------------
   Percentiles  Smallest                        Percentiles  Smallest
 1%    72      72                              1%    88      88
 5%    73      73                              5%    89      89
10%    74      74    Obs        23            10%    90      90    Obs        23
25%    74      74    Sum of Wgt. 23           25%    92      91    Sum of Wgt. 23

50%    77          Mean       78             50%    93          Mean       93
       Largest   Std. Dev.  3.942772                 Largest   Std. Dev.  2.153222
75%    81      83                             75%    95      95
90%    83      83    Variance   15.54545      90%    95      95    Variance    4.636364
95%    85      85    Skewness    .4322148     95%    96      96    Skewness   -.642455
99%    86      86    Kurtosis   2.198061      99%    96      96    Kurtosis   2.745675
```

Figure 9. ANOVA test for cohort one and two

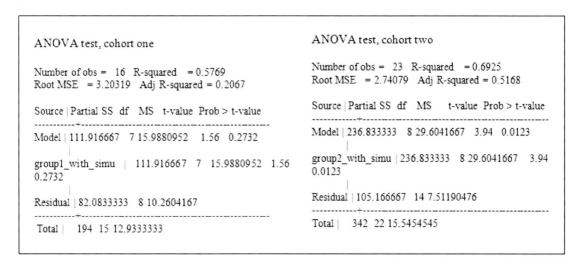

and blended learning are observed when the students' motivation and their learning interests have increased (Freeman and Capper, 1999). Strengths of blended learning are summed up in Table 1.

Extent of Interactions in Learning and Assessment

I have another class which adopts blended learning as part of curriculum where feedback has been collected. Figure 10 shows results, where 45% of them strongly agree blended learning is useful for their learning and assessment, 30% agree, 25%

Table 1. Strengths of blended learning (Horton, 2000; Chang 2003)

Advantages	Descriptions
1. Blended learning saves costs	Saves 40-60% of the expense of training by traditional means. Savings include (1) travel expenses; (2) facilities and supplies costs; (3) administrative costs; (4) salaries and (5) lost opportunity costs.
2. Blended learning improves learning	• Blended learning uses learning technologies that assist students and trainees towards learning. • The interactions between peers and instructors can 'activate learners.' • Blended learning exposes learners to real-world data, which saves learners time in searching information and also assists learners analysing large collections of data. • Blended learning provides a more in-depth learning experience.
3. Extra advantages for learners	• Learners can get the best instruction available. • Training occurs "just in time." • Learners set the pace and schedule. • Learners can have better access to instructors. • Training adapts to the learning styles. • Blended learning produces positive effects.
4. Extra advantages for instructors	• Instructors can teach from different locations. • Instructors travel less. • Course content can be dynamic.
5. Extra advantages for organisations	• Blended learning delivers high-quality training, including training around the globe without travel or minimum travel. • Blended learning creates valuable learning resources.

Figure 10. Students' feedback: whether blended learning is useful for their learning and assessment

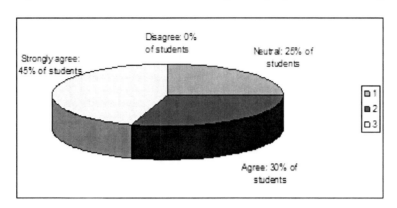

stay neutral and 0% disagree. Some of those 25% of students are the ones who seldom attend class and online participation.

Based on students' feedback, the degree of interactivity is another highlight of the present effective blended adoption. The purpose of getting a high degree of interactivity in blended learning is to strengthen the ease of communications and knowledge sharing among learners and instructors, eventually leading to improvement in learning efficiency. When students have questions, they get feedback from tutors. Peer blended learning allow them to improve on the quality of work based on genuine feedback they receive (Chang, 2003; Ginns and Ellis, 2007; Samarawickrema and Stacey, 2007). Peer blended learning ensures they feel motivated and rewarding to learn and share.

STRATEGIC PLAN OF ADOPTING ENTERPRISE SOFTWARE SUCH AS SAP

The motivation is similar to Section 4 except most of Business School members of staff at UOG do not come from technical IT backgrounds and the use of open source software is time consuming to fix issues and errors. The use of enterprise solution is acknowledged and supported by recent review programme since it helps improving quality of

teaching and learning efficiency. Another reason is when students are equipped with skills in the enterprise software, it improves their employ-ability since they are relevant skills for industry. This is another IT initiative (strategy focus for Business School) to acquire the right software for teaching, where a number of them such as SAP and commercial options will be proposed. The management decides the use of SAP can meet their strategic goals briefly as follows.

- Curriculum
  - ERP software skills expected from graduates today.
  - Students demand teaching of ERP software.
  - Using SAP software leads to compet-itive advantages for study programs.
- Cost
  - Hosting of SAP software more cost-effective than self-hosting.
  - High-quality SAP system operations and support.
  - Maintenance
- Quality
  - Competence Center approach.
  - Development of curriculum material.
  - Fast problem solving through prob-lem solution database.
  - High service level quality.

The New Supply Chain Business Model in the Higher Education Domain

The SAP enterprise architecture can enhance the quality of higher education and offer the proposed "Supply Chain Business Model" where Education as a Service (EaaS) can be delivered by UoG Business School. Joint collaboration between Business School and School of Engineering of UoG is in place to ensure courses offered by SAP can be fully utilised for undergraduate and postgraduate training, which also promote transferrable skills in the higher education. The logistics programme suite in Business School is focused on the specialisation of supply chain management. There are the SAP Distributed Requirement Planning (DRP) and SAP Fulfilment packages which focus on SCM and the decision is to take on two SAP modules, which are Fulfilment and DRP. More courses can be added on later on. Collaboration with SAP based in Munich can ensure instructor training is provided so that academic staff can be well equipped with up-to-date skills and knowledge.

Although the first two courses offered are related to e-Logistics, new courses are likely to be developed jointly with SAP. There are different services under its enterprise architecture which include:

- **Customer Relationship Management (CRM):** A service and tool to manage relationship and interactions between clients, stakeholders, and sales. It can be used for marketing, business development, customer service, and support.
- **Supplier Relationship Management (SRM):** A service and tool to work collaboratively with suppliers and to get the knowledge about their stock, pricing, and update.
- **Supply Chain Management (SCM):** A service and tool to manage a network of interconnected businesses involved in the provision of products and services required by customers.
- **Product Lifecycle Management (PLM):** A service and tool to manage the process of the entire lifecycle of a product from its conception, through design and manufacture, to service and disposal.
- **Enterprise Resource Planning (ERP):** A service and system to integrate internal and external information management systems across the entire organisation. This may include integration of some functionality described above.

All these services can be jointly integrated and used in a central platform, the SAP Business Suite, and enterprise architecture (Krcmar, 2011). EaaS should contain all these services. Using SAP rather than Oracle can achieve the following two benefits:

- Learning satisfaction can offer an additional of 15% as described in a previous section.
- More time and effort can be focused on curriculum development rather than troubleshooting in the case of using Oracle.

Staff Development and Service Development of SAPious Section

A workshop was organised in April 2012 to help staff members to get familiar with SAP which had around 95% of participant satisfaction rate. Advanced user such as the lead author was involved in architecture development. SAP is useful for staff development since academic staff can learn new skills and update their existing skills. It ensures staff can understand how EaaS service such as SAP can allow them to use CRM, SRM, SCM, PLM, and ERP efficiently. When the staff members become competent in the use of SAP, they can teach their students to understand how to use software to get their jobs in CRM, SRM,

SCM, PLM and ERP done. Acquiring skills relevant to industry, it helps students having a better employability perspective (Krcmar, 2011). When some of staff members have the competent skills and plan to upgrade their skills as a developer/architect, they can learn the back-end technologies and relevant computer languages to modify functionality in SAP. This includes performance optimisation and tuning, which allows SAP to take on more jobs/services, or complete the jobs/services much faster, or both of these.

DISCUSSIONS

UoG case study has demonstrated how Cloud Computing can be used as a Business Model and an innovation for modern Higher Education. This includes the use of technologies to improve education and the way education content and activities are delivered, including Moodle, GradeMark, media streaming, video-conferencing and mobile learning. Success elements include technological, social, economic, political, cultural and environmental factors centred on Cloud Computing Education. This leads us into the proposal in EaaS, where education content and activities can be delivered and accessible to learners and students, who can demonstrate they meet their learning criteria and tutors can monitor their progress. There are four issues for discussions.

The Role of CCBF for Supply Chain, E-Procurement, and Other IT Projects

The role of CCBF is strategic in directing the right direction that EaaS is heading into and providing support and assistance to offer a good Cloud Education design, deployment, and services, including the following:

- Consolidate existing resources and services. Ensure Business Model integrate with EaaS.
- Design of new curriculum and development of existing curriculum including the use of simulations for teaching.
- Continuously improvement in the way learning and teaching is delivered. Investigate new ways to get students motivated in learning and to improve their academic performance.

Oracle and SAP: SAP is More Suitable for Business School of UoG

Section 4 presents a case study for Oracle development used for teaching and the effectiveness in demonstrating supply chain distribution, cash flow, and demands between different entities. Section 5 presents strategic plans of adopting SAP for undergraduate and postgraduate training and benefits of such adoptions. Both are usable for Supply chain management and course delivery. However, their differences can determine suitability for Business School. The summary is presented in Table 2.

Comparisons in Table 2 demonstrate that SAP is more suitable for Business School to adopt since more focus can be spent on content development and delivery of the course rather than development of software-related work. The content can be customised for students who desire to work as business analysts upon graduations.

How to Model Supply Chain in the Cloud

Figure 11 shows the architectural view of how to model supply chain in Cloud from service provider and infrastructure provider perspective. Service provider (Greenwich) accepts Service Level Agreement (SLA) and gets to infrastructure provider (SAP), where they have service management

Table 2. Oracle and SAP supply chain software comparisons

Oracle	SAP
Software is provided without support. Support and training comes to an additional cost.	The entire package such as software, support and training is provided at an agreed price.
Supply chain software – the orientation and content is more suitable for those with technical backgrounds.	Supply chain software – the orientation and content is more suitable for business analysts.
More time is spent on development and making software to work.	More time can be focused on content development and delivery of course. Support team can take care of technical issues.

Figure 11. How to model supply chain in the cloud

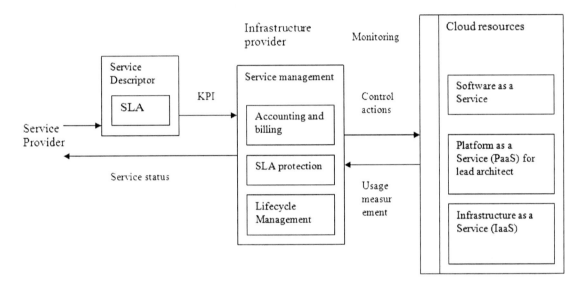

to monitor accounting and billing, SLA protection and service lifecycle management. Once they pass on this, control actions are required to access to monitoring channel, and users can access all Cloud resources. Applications are available in the Cloud resources but the lead architect is required to be involved in programming on Platform as a Service (PaaS) to ensure SAP on Software as a Service (SaaS) are running. Another alternative is to use outsourcing model and contract work to SAP in UK or Germany to achieve the same level, but it is not the model discussed in this paper.

Education as a Service (EaaS) in Summary

Section 2 proposes that EaaS has multiple Business Models and Section 3 proposes Supply Chain Business Model that uses private cloud tom demonstrate supply chain teaching and delivery. Section 4 demonstrates EaaS in the form of Oracle software to simulate supply chain distribution and the relationship between different entities, suppliers, distributors, and customers. Statistical analysis confirm that the use of simulation for teaching can improve student learning satisfaction by an additional 15% and results show two cohorts agree with this outcome. Section 5 explains the strategic plan of using SAP to meet Business School of UoG education and delivery. SAP enterprise

Figure 12. The hexagon model (business model) to forecast the likely performance for our EaaS

Popularity/adoption

Consumers

Get the job done (GTJD)

Innovation

Investors

Valuation

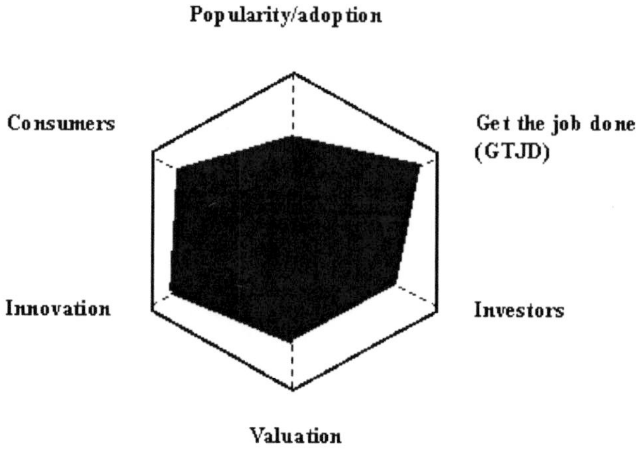

architecture also includes different services such as CRM, SRM, SCM, PLM, and ERP. All these examples fully support EaaS can be implemented in the educational environment to provide good quality of services, improve curriculum, reduce costs and improve students' learning satisfaction.

The Use of Hexagon Models for EaaS

Previous sections present the pair of the Hexagon Models with Business Model and IT services focuses to evaluate Cloud project performance. Key criteria are presented in the visual form in the Hexagon which can indicate strengths and weaknesses of overall services. However, they are not just for Oracle and SAP adoption, which are essential part of EaaS at UoG. The strategic plan of using SAP for undergraduate and postgraduate education can improve performance in various key criteria. Based on review meeting and stakeholders' feedback, both Hexagon Models can be used to forecast the likely performance for our EaaS, which curriculum delivery offered by SAP plays a central role.

Figure 12 shows the Hexagon Model (Business Model) to forecast the likely performance for our EaaS, where there are significant improvements comparing to Figure 2. Main reasons include the

full support from management and the University as the whole, which makes investors and popularity higher. SAP or business analyst software for supply chain is one of the most favourite lists amongst academic staff and students. There will be a slight increase in customers due to improvement in user confidence. Figure 13 shows the Hexagon Model (IT Services) to forecast the likely performance for our EaaS, where the significant improvement is seen on Usability because troubleshooting will be fully supported and staff can focus on teaching and delivery. Chang et al. (2011b, 2011c, 2011d) use quantitative techniques to compute performance

Figure 13. The hexagon model (business model) to forecast the likely performance for our EaaS

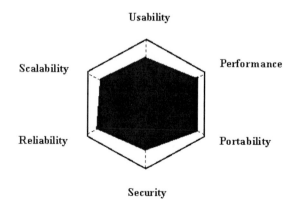

Usability

Scalability

Performance

Reliability

Portability

Security

forecasting. One major benefit of using both Hexagon Models can make sensible performance forecasts without the need of detailed quantitative analysis. This ensures any project managers to assess project performance against key criteria.

CONCLUSION AND FUTURE WORK

In UoG case study, we present that Cloud Computing offers a new business model and transforms the way Education is delivered. We use of four-step sequence to demonstrate Education as a Service (EaaS), which offers the following benefits:

- Cloud Business Model can integrate with EaaS and consolidate existing resources and services.
- Improves an additional 15% of learning satisfaction in the use of Oracle simulations for teaching supported by statistical analysis. Simulations of business processes and supply chain management can be used as an effective tool for teaching.
- Students feel more motivated and interested in learning and undertaking coursework, enhancing the student's learning experience (Klasen and Willoughby, 2003; Nix 2004). Adoption of blended learning is particularly useful.
- SAP application (part of EaaS) meets strategic plans for Business School and can improve our quality of teaching and suitability of our curriculum to match requirements of job market.

EaaS is a new Supply Chain business model useful for academic institutions such as UoG. Oracle suite has been used to demonstrate supply chain distribution to explain relationship between suppliers, distributors, and customers and to help to calculate cash flow and demand/supply. SAP is strategic in EaaS adoption since it can integrate CRM, SRM, SCM, PLM, and ERP. SAP is more suitable for Business School since they offer the whole package of software, training and support and staff can focus more on content and delivery rather than troubleshooting. Courses are relevant to train those who pursuit careers as business analysts. The use of Hexagon Models can evaluate all these projects and also Oracle/SAP initiatives in particular, so that performance against key criteria can be assessed in regular periods. Both Hexagon Models are effective to make sensible performance forecast for EaaS, which SAP plays a central role.

The UoG case study can fully support that Education can be further improved for learning and this is particularly important for Universities to adopt Cloud strategies and migration. The CCBF is strategic in directing the right direction that EaaS is heading into and has helped the Universities to achieve good private cloud design, deployment, and services while meeting their requirements and challenges. This paper also strongly supports JISC vision of University Cloud adoption, which offers key benefits to education and research. Future work will include EaaS case studies and demonstrations, and development of new academic programs and its impacts at UoG.

REFERENCES

Ahronovitz, M., et al. (2010). *Cloud computing use cases white paper, version 4.0.* Washington, DC: National Institute of Standards and Technology.

Anderton, A. (2008). *Economics AQA* (5th ed.). Causeway Press.

Boss, G., Malladi, P., Quan, D., Legregni, L., & Hall, H. (2007). *Cloud computing.* IBM White Paper. New York, NY: IBM.

Candido, G., Barata, J., Colombo, A. W., & Jammes, F. (2009). SOA in reconfigurable supply chains: A research roadmap. *Engineering Applications of Artificial Intelligence, 22,* 939–949. doi:10.1016/j.engappai.2008.10.020

Chang, V. (2003). The role and effectiveness of e-learning: Key issues in an industrial context. In *Proceedings of the First International Conference in the United Nations Information Society*. Geneva, Switzerland: United Nations.

Chang, V. (2006). Web service testing and usability for mobile learning. In *Proceedings of IEEE Computer Society: The First International Conference on Mobile Communications and Learning MCL*. IEEE Press.

Chang, V. (2011a). *A proposed cloud computing business framework*. Eighteen-Month Thesis Technical Report. Southampton, UK: University of Southampton.

Chang, V., David, B., Wills, G., & De Roure, D. (2010a). A categorisation of cloud business models. In *Proceedings of the 10ᵗʰ International Symposium on Cluster, Cloud and Grid Computing*. Melbourne, Australia: IEEE.

Chang, V., De Roure, D., Wills, G., & Walters, R. (2011d). Case studies and organisational sustainability modelling presented by cloud computing business framework. *International Journal of Web Services Research*, 8(3), 26–53.

Chang, V., De Roure, D., Wills, G., Walters, R., & Barry, T. (2011c). Organisational sustainability modelling for return on investment: Case studies presented by a national health service (NHS) trust UK. *Journal of Computing and Information Technology*, 19(3), 1846–3908. doi:10.2498/cit.1001951

Chang, V., Li, C. S., De Roure, D., Wills, G., Walters, R., & Chee, C. (2011b). The financial clouds review. *International Journal of Cloud Applications and Computing*, 1(2), 41–63. doi:10.4018/ijcac.2011040104

Chang, V., Walters, R., & Wills, G. (2012). Business integration as a service. *International Journal of Cloud Applications and Computing*, 2(1). doi:10.4018/ijcac.2012010102

Chang, V., Wills, G., & De Roure, D. (2010b). A review of cloud business models and sustainability. In *Proceedings of IEEE Cloud 2010, the 3rd International Conference on Cloud Computing*. Miami, FL: IEEE Press.

Chang, V., Wills, G., De Roure, D., & Chee, C. (2010c). Investigating the cloud computing business framework - Modelling and benchmarking of financial assets and job submissions in clouds. In *Proceedings of UK e-Science All Hands Meeting 2010, Research Clouds: Hype or Reality Workshop*. Cardiff, UK: IEEE.

Chang, V., Wills, G., & Walters, R. (2011f). Towards business integration as a service 2.0 (BIaaS 2.0). In *Proceedings of the IEEE International Conference on e-Business Engineering, The 3rd International Workshop on Cloud Services - Platform Accelerating e-Business*. Beijing, China: IEEE Press.

Chang, V., Wills, G., Walters, R., & Currie, W. (2011e). Towards a structured cloud ROI: The University of Southampton cost-saving and user satisfaction case studies. In *Sustainable Green Computing: Practices, Methodologies and Technologies*. Hershey, PA: IGI Global.

Educause & Nacubo. (2010). *Shaping the higher education cloud*. Educause and Nacubo White Paper. Educause and Nacubo.

Fogel, R. (2010). *The education cloud: Delivering education as a service*. Intel White Paper. Intel.

Foster, I., Zhao, Y., Raicu, I., & Lu, S. Y. (2008). Cloud computing and grid computing 360-degree compared. In *Proceedings of IEEE Grid Computing Environments (GCE08)*. Austin, TX: IEEE.

Freeman, M. A., & Capper, J. M. (1999). Exploiting the web for education: An anonymous asynchronous role simulation. *Australia Journal of Educational Technology*, 15(1), 95–116.

Ginns, P., & Ellis, R. (2007). Quality in blended learning: Exploring the relationships between on-line and face-to-face teaching and learning. *The Internet and Higher Education, 10*, 53–64. doi:10.1016/j.iheduc.2006.10.003

Horton, W. (2000). *Designing web-based training.* New York, NY: John Wiley & Sons Publisher.

Hosono, S., Hara, T., Shimomura, Y., & Arai, T. (2010). Prioritizing service functions with non-functional requirements. In *Proceedings of the CIRP Industrial Product-Service Systems Conference*, (pp. 133-140). Linkoping, Sweden: CIRP.

Hosono, S., Kuno, A., Hasegawa, M., Hara, T., Shimomura, Y., & Arai, T. (2009). A framework of co-creating business values for IT services. In *Proceedings of the 2009 IEEE International Conference on Cloud Computing*. Bangalore, India: IEEE.

Hull, J. C. (2009). *Options, futures, and other derivatives* (7th ed.). Upper Saddle River, NJ: Prentice Hall.

Jericho Forum. (2009). *Cloud cube model: Selecting cloud formations for secure collaboration version 1.0*. Jericho Forum Specification.

Kagermann, H., Österle, H., & Jordan, J. M. (2011). *IT-driven business models: Global case studies in transformation*. New York, NY: John Wiley & Sons.

Klassen, K. J., & Willoughby, K. A. (2003). In-class simulation games: Accessing student learning. *Journal of Information Technology Education, 2*.

Krcmar, H. (2011). *SAP UCC products / services and their use within university curricula*. Paper presented at the SAP UCC Munich Workshop. Poznan, Germany.

Krutz, R. L., & Dean Vines, R. (2010). *Cloud security: A comprehensive guide to secure cloud computing*. New York, NY: Wiley Publishing.

Leukel, J., Kirn, S., & Schlegel, T. (2011). Supply chain as a service: A cloud perspective on supply chain systems. *IEEE Systems Journal, 5*(1).

Nix, N. (2004). *Adapting and enhancing links for multiple audiences*. Fort Worth, TX: Texas Christian University.

Samarawickrema, G., & Stacey, E. (2007). Adopting web-based learning and teaching: A case study in higher education. *Distance Education, 28*(3), 313–333. doi:10.1080/01587910701611344

Schubert, H., Jeffery, K., & Neidecker-Lutz, B. (2010). *The future for cloud computing: Opportunities for European cloud computing beyond 2010*. Expert Group.

Stevens, J. (2002). *Applied multivariate statistics for social sciences* (4th ed.). Hoboken, NJ: Lawrence Erlbaum Associates Publisher.

Sullivan, D. (2010). *Has Facebook's active user growth dropped 25% to 50*. Search Engine Land.

Waters, D. (2008). *Quantitative methods for business* (4th ed.). Upper Saddle River, NJ: Prentice Hall.

Zhou, L., Xie, Y., Wild, N., & Hunt, C. (2008). Learning and practising supply chain management strategies from a business simulation game: A comprehensive supply chain simulation. In *Proceedings of the Winter Simulation Conference 2008*. IEEE.

Chapter 14

Investigating the Effect of E-Learning Technologies on Supply Chain Activities:
The Evidence of ELT Book Market

Dimitrios Terzidis
ELT Sales Consultant, Greece

Fotios Misopoulos
University of Sheffield, Greece

ABSTRACT

This chapter's concern is the impact of new technologies in the supply chain of the English Language Teaching (ELT) book market. The chapter's research starts with a literature review that presents the modern technological solutions for an educational system that can alter the book market's supply chain. The electronic teaching and reading facilities can reduce costs of production and distribution, but they can also become an ecologically friendly solution to the environmental problems that the world faces today. The statistical analysis of questionnaires has resulted in the Greek ELT market not being willing to change the existing supply chain operations of the ELT sector. Even though the market does not believe that the use of new technologies can result in the replacement of printed books, there is a trend of using them because they provide marketing benefits to their users. This trend can become the reason of a new era within the ELT book market's supply chain operations.

INTRODUCTION

According to Greek tradition, education is reflected to their sociopolitical and cultural profile. Education is regarded as the means of achieving social and personal progress and sustaining na-

tional cultural identity. According to the Greek constitution, every citizen has a right to equal educational opportunities. The first foreign language of Greece is English and is considered as the key to communication with the European Union and the world. Good English skills are considered by

DOI: 10.4018/978-1-4666-3914-0.ch014

parents and employers to be an essential ability so the demand for it is very high and many thousands of Greeks take English language examinations every year.

The aggregate sector of English Language Teaching education industry in Greece has been very profitable since its existence making the ELT book market one of the most profitable publishing sectors in Greece. The market has been in operation since the Second World War and in a more advanced form since the 1950's. Initially there were few book publishing companies and Greek customers imported their books straight from England. In the following years and especially during the decade of the seventies, the need for learning English had increased and that resulted in an expansion of teaching resources. From then on the ELT book market boomed until the millennium. Student numbers were increasing and book publishing companies likewise. Books were published in Greece for the needs of the Greek market and Greek publishing companies became a major player of the Greek market. Companies from the USA, UK, Cyprus, and Greece were actively profiting from the Greek ELT market.

The decrease in the numbers of population as also the Greek phenomenon of private lessons and photocopies is responsible according to Esplen (2002) and (2008) for the decline of revenue and operational mode of the Greek ELT book market. The status of the ELT market has changed during the last decade because of technological innovations and new teaching methods. According to Weissberg (2008) and Buzzetto et al. (2007), the digital direction of teaching is the primary aim of the Greek and foreign publishers but the book continues to be the basic teaching material. The replacement of printed books by other electronic sources of teaching such as electronic books, interactive white boards, and internet is upon the progress of the book market internationally. Electronic learning holds only a very small percentage of the aggregate global publishing market but is a worldwide rising market.

This paper focuses its interest on the effect of the new teaching and reading technologies to the supply chain of the Greek ELT publishing sector. Subsequently the paper presents how these technological changes can possibly cope to improve the financial condition of publishing companies and reduce the environmental harmful production and distribution activities of the aggregate supply chain. Moreover, it provides a picture of the ELT's book market future and a path for other publishing markets to possibly grow in Greece. The adoption of new technologies into the existing educational system is expected to provide costless but very profitable solutions to book publishers by reducing the supply chain activities and the overall cost of production. Those changes are expected to reduce the harmful environmental distribution and production activities by introducing the concept of green logistics.

THE COST OF THE ELT PUBLISHING SUPPLY CHAIN IN GREECE

The Developments in the Publishing Sector

The issues of the Greek publishing sector is according to Banou (2006), Banou and Kostagiolas (2007) as also Banou et al (2008), a major subject of analysis and research for the last decade. According to Esplen's (2002) and (2008), the Greek ELT publishing sector is presented as mature. The sales unit decline of the Greek ELT publishing market during the last decade which was upon demographic reasons, guided publishers to increase their products' prices in order to maintain shareholders' profitability.

Laband and Hudson (2003) stated that book prices are highly correlated to the cost of operations such as writing, editing, printing, transporting, warehousing, distributing and final purchasing in book stores. The amazing finding though is that according to the aforementioned researchers, the greatest percentage of each books' price returns to distributors and book sellers. On a benchmarking operation of those findings with another developed book publishing market it has been found that the same operating conditions also occur in the Australian publishing market (Gallagher, 2007). The researches of Cigolini et al (2004) as also Tyan et al (2003), specified that the expenses for storage and distribution provide to publishers a safety cushion, 1) by reducing the risk of collecting their returns from many different books selling points in a large operating area, as also 2) by keeping their customers satisfied because distributors keep an optimum time and schedule management of distribution and warehousing operations. In the research of Mikko et al (2001), it is clarified that there are various advantages of a well focused and concentrated distribution operation. That explains why publishers' accept the condition of providing a large amount of their returns for fulfilling third party logistic operations.

E-Commerce and E-Publishing

Golicic et al (2002) study of about developments in the trade sector referred to the issue of electronic commerce and how it affected the supply chain relationship. The ELT book market could not stay out of such developments and so the aforementioned analysis fits to ELT book publishing operational environment. The first step of that research has based on the references of Banou and Kostagiolas (2007) and leaded to further research on this part of the paper. The concept is based on the analysis of the aggregate publishing industry in Greece and the perceptions about future developments in the general Greek book market which has been an excellent guidance to study the particular ELT book sector. The importance of the overall analysis concludes that the Greek market is not resistant to new ideas and different operating ways. In addition, the main consideration of the market is the creation of a secure system that can confirm safety.

The use of e-commerce and e-teaching technological sources are leading the global publishing market to a new era. During the last decades, the main discussion issue in the publishing sector is the progress of the e-publishing market. Peters (2001), Gold (1994), as also Fischer and Lugg (2001), reported that the evolution for reading and teaching is e-publishing. A resent research of Buzzetto et al (2007) about the educational role of electronic books and other electronic devices shows that younger students feel more motivated and confident about using these electronic tools for their studies.

The Greek ELT book market has a common supply chain process that does not differentiate from the general book market supply chain logic. The ELT Greek market though faces a more complex difficulty in this market which is the optimization of the forecasting for the print quantities of every different book. The annual report of Esplen (2008) as also Laband and Hudson (2003), identified that books' cost depend on the volume of copies. According to economies of scales, the more the print outs the less the unit cost per book. On the contrary there is an increase in the cost of distribution and storage in an ultimate symphony to the unit cost value for greater volumes of printed books.

New printing technologies increased the range of profitability of the Greek ELT publishers during the recent years but that opportunity is usually available only for those publishers that operate internationally. People's perception of reading has changed radically because of the new technologies. Electronic networks are like the motorway system that connects people's needs. E-publishing liberates customers and producers of all previous environmental harmful operations such as cutting trees, creating paper, printing, binding, transporting and storing books for distribution and sales to the book stores. The technological innovations in the publishing sector have generated quicker and cheaper ways to publish and read a book that would be more beneficial for customers, the environment and the scientific society in total. According to Lloyd (2008), the future of the publishing industry is the digitalization of publications. Those developments in the ELT publishing sector reduce the tangibility of books. Printed books' option is expected to expire and that means a great reduction of the aforementioned costly operations such as printing, transporting, warehousing and distribution of books. The use of electronic ink and electronic books is gradually growing. Moreover, the advantages of their use created a new perspective about the ELT publishing market.

The Scientific Technical and Medical (STM) publishing sector has recently faced the results of the internet usage. According to Seeley (2006), the digitalization of the scientific articles made easier the movement of information, improved the quality of publications and increased the accessibility by peer viewers. The day that publishers or even authors will become sellers is probably not too far away according to Rawlins (1993). That development is expected to change the profile of the publishing sector to higher qualitative standards. The financial benefits that will yield from changing the production and distribution operations can be invested to marketing and research activities. According to Weissberg (2008), the full digitalization of the book market will not change the existence of International Standard Book Number (ISBN). By the use of ISBN the market can keep the books' content tracks and make the supply chain of e-books to be efficient. E-book consumers can always benefit from high quality content by either perpetual purchase of it, time based rent or even on a subscription for pay per view model.

E-Publishing and Green Logistics

According to Vasileiou and Rowley (2008), the confusion about the definition of e-books is caused by the expansion of network technology used for retrieving information in a fast and accurate way. In addition to that, it has been stated that there is no commonly accepted universal definition of e-books even though there is an extended use of e-books to support learning activities (Cox, 2004). According to Armstrong et al (2002), e-books are the online type of printed books such as electronic types of text that can be accessed via the internet. In that definition journals are excluded publications. It is also specified that there is no restriction on how these digitalised versions of books will be viewed as long the devise that is used has a screen.

According to the aforementioned definition of e-books it is commonly identifiable that this development can benefit both publishing companies and the environment in total. Electronic publishing reduces all cost from paper creation, printing, binding, packaging, transporting, warehousing, distributing, and selling operations. According to Vasilleiou et al (2009), it is not obliging for the system to eliminate all the aforementioned processes. There must always be restrictions to secure publishers copyrights so that it is still a mode for distribution and selling between the authors, the publishers, and the consumers. The cost though of making and selling a book in electronic form will be much lower than printing it.

The progression of the e-book idea is even more beneficial according to the environmental side of view. Green logistics is a new definition for ecological thinking of moving and storing products. According to Sbihi and Eglese (2007) as also Murphy et al (1996), green logistics are part of forward and reverse logistic activities. Especially for the case of the publishing sector, Sarkis (2001) presented all the activities of forward and reverse logistics that have also a specific environmental cost. For any of the above routes of the forward and reverse logistics there are specific measures about the pollution emitted and the energy loss. If the decision for producing a product is taken according to the green logistics logic then the environmental cost is always included. According to Sarkis et al (2004), e-logistics is the form that can help logistician to take under consideration the natural environment in a more accurate way than it occurs until nowadays.

Benefits from Green Supply Chain Management

According to the research of Zhu et al. (2007), there is evidence that the implementation of green SCM models resulted in the improvement of the companies' performance. There are various approaches for implementing a green supply chain management such as: the constant communication with each supplier, the implementation of Green Designing, Reverse Logistics, Green Purchasing, Green Packaging, and generally the auditing of the various resources needed for the supply chain activities by requesting the Bill of Material. There is always a need for the training of manpower in each company as also the support of top level management. Murphy (1996) defines barriers to be the high cost of implementing such policies and the expected resistance from the top management's side. The benefits though are in contradiction to that perception because the efficient implementation of a green supply chain management is expected according to Sarkis (2003) to result in a cost reduction in the long run. Moreover, products that have been processed through a green supply chain model usually have a greater public acceptance than those which are not. In addition, customers are more satisfied when companies use less material, reduce their wastes, and reduce the usage of resources and energy. Finally, the increase of customers' satisfaction reduces the risk to companies because they have achieved good publicity and also a competitive advantage.

Companies can benefit in various ways from the implementation of green supply chain management. The important constraint though is the support of the top management team and the creation of the foundations from the government to encourage these actions. According to the

literature (Green et al., 1996; Eagan and Kaizer, 2002; Lin, 2007), governmental regulations can be the major motivation to businesses for implementing an environmental policy on their supply chain operations. This is especially the case when the new policy may involve initial start up costs. Companies are known to be a little reluctant to voluntarily change their processes unless it results in cost cutting. However government legislation and usually government financial assistance helps companies adopt greener policies more easily. In addition, Zhu et al. (2005) stated that governments should set the good example and act as a model to be followed by companies. As a result of the overall idea of environmental protection during the supply chain of each product life cycle, is also the green sourcing idea. The term "green sourcing" includes the aggregate set of business activities that is needed for purchasing goods and services based on environmental friendly operations. Min and Galle (2001), defined that green purchasing is the ecological aware purchasing activity that reduces waste sources and encourages recycling and reverse logistics. This is all done without affecting the products or services quality.

The use of biological fuels, solar energy, wind energy, gas and other innovative sources of energy, can help businesses to improve their supply chain operations and their product quality by reducing their fixed costs in the long run. According to Doonan et al. (2005), consumers' perception about; "green products" and companies' environmental production performance, defines today's market's position and the aggregate demand. In addition, Lamming and Hampson (1996) stated that consumers in the US are keen to purchase ecological friendly products even when their prices are higher than common products. In addition it has been mentioned a preference in products that their companies use the method of reverse logistic. According to Dowlatshahi (2005) businesses which are preferable to the public, have created their distribution channel in order to repossess used products or parts of them to recycle, dispose or remanufacture them. According to this activity, businesses create an environmental friendly profile, gain consumers' preference and reduce their aggregate cost of production because of the raw material reuse. According to Paramasevam et al. (2001), the implementation of an Environmental Management System (EMS) provides a competitive and cost advantage to businesses. In addition to that, Watson et al. (2004) found that EMS strategies do not harm businesses financial performance. This is the main reason that according to Walker et al. (2007), there has been a role transformation of EMS strategies from legal obligation to competitive trade advantage. In the case of India, Khanna (2008) stated that the majority of companies operating in the country believe that the implementation of EMS improved their performance.

Reverse Logistics

According to Meyer (1999), reverse logistics is about taking care of product returns, their disposals, and their remanufacturing for possible reuses in their future production activity. Guide (2006) stated that the increased volume of products' returns has set, as critical, the aggregate processing of products' return. According to his estimates the products returns were calculated to be about six percent of sales. In addition to that, Gentry (1999) estimated that product returns for mass merchandisers and electronic commerce would range from fifteen percent to thirty five percent. According to Stock (2001), the product returns is a part of reverse logistics that combines activities such as recycling, renovation, restoration and the disposition of wastes. The general process of reverse logistics though is a matter of a possible win-win situation for customers and firms which have to be considered in an effective way so that firms can manage to pick up its value. Mukhopadhyay and Setoputro (2005) as also Rogers et al. (2002) stated that this process becomes more beneficial for each firm because it helps customers returns,

improves their loyalty and increases products sales. Areas of marketing and production can be affected positively if companies manage to have a good understanding of issues related to products returns. Moreover, legislative constraints about environmental issues are forcing in nowadays companies to move toward the ideas of reverse logistic theories. According to Stock (2001), companies should envision reverse logistics as a part of the traditional forward logistics because these activities can be included in the aggregate marketing mix strategy of each company.

In the case of an ELT publishing company, the reuse of their products by different consumers is both difficult to occur and unprofitable. The reason is that students have already written on their books and the use of the same book by a different student pedagogically is wrong. Publishing companies can use the method of recycling though in order to create cheaper raw material without cutting down new trees. The distribution channel should be organized well and according to the legislation of each country (Srivastava and Srivastava, 2006). Tan and Kumar (2008) stated that the profitability of the entire operation depends on the volume of returns that will occur and also on the use of the returns. If for example, the returns are not related to reuse and/or repair for further processing and remanufacturing then there will not be a direct financial beneficial opportunity for the company. Finally, there is a need for a well structured distribution channel for the products return to the company.

The Use of New Technologies in the Publishing Sector

In the ELT publishing sector there has been a shift in the direction of technological support such as the use of computers, the interactive white board, electronic - distance learning and the use of electronic books. According to the literature (Lloyd, 2008; Seeley, 2006; Gold, 1994; Fischer and Lugg, 2001; as also Peters, 2001) these unorthodox sources of teaching activities provides companies with a great motive to use them as they are popular with customers and they help to reduce the company's aggregate cost. This reduction in cost goes hand in hand with the improvement of the quality and diversity of their products and services. This can add to the ELT publishing companies' customer satisfaction and offer a competitive strategic advantage to use for obtaining a greater market share. Weissberg (2008) identified that there are financial, environmental, and operational benefits from the use of alternative to traditional educational sources of teaching such as paper printed books.

The usage of electronic and digital sources like; the internet, personal computers and e-books can change completely the supply chain structure of an ELT publishing company. ELT Books do not have to be printed when students can read, write, listen, watch, and save their notes in electronic forms. It is also not essential that all students leave the comfort of their homes purchase their books, and books don't need to be stored in great warehouses. The printing cost is minimized, if not eliminated, and the risk of production cost is extinguished because the digital form of a book has minimal purchasing and "reprint" cost. Companies can also control the fraud activity between students. In the case of the ELT book sector photocopies are the major enemy of publishing companies. The ethical issue that takes place here is about the job cutting operation that businesses of various satellite sectors may need to proceed. Sectors like paper printing, logistic activities and book shops seem to be threatened by the implementation of the technological changes. In contradiction, the benefits are in such a volume that they overcome the employment status of specific sectors. Moreover, the use of a new technology is expected to create job vacancies about the service of that technology and the protection of purchasing digital ELT book products.

In the case of e-publishing though there is no need for warehousing. The first benefit from the elimination of warehousing facilities will be the reduction of new buildings in a piece of land that could be full of trees and grass. The ecological advantage comes from the fact that there will be no need for energy to be spent during the storage operation and also the resources that have to be used for building, maintenance, and the human operational resource. E-book devices can upload according to Vasileiou and Rowley (2008) more than one thousand books and that reduces also the space needed in individual houses for storing books. It can also be seen as a revolution of expanding education's borders and also distributing them faster than ever.

METHODOLOGY

The Research Method

The structure of the paper follows a mixture of quantitative and qualitative research method. The research is separated into four main parts. On the first, there has been the exploration of what is the general belief of school owners regarding the use of new technologies into their lessons. The case in this part is that there are not significant researches that can provide an efficient statistical result. For that reason there have been created one hundred and seventy questionnaires that have been answered by English school owners from the areas of Peloponnesus, Athens, Epirus, Thessaly, Macedonia and Thrace. The sample of these areas is estimated to be about one thousand nine hundred schools out of seven thousand private English schools population number in Greece (Esplen, 2008). The collected questionnaires represent about the nine percent of the aggregate sample and are enough to secure the efficiency of significant results.

The next parts of the research are through interviews to publishers, distributors, and booksellers accordingly. The method that is selected in these three parts is qualitative but the process for each interview is based on the statistical results of the first part as also to the relevant literature review. The mixture of both methods provides to the paper the ability to interpret the results and provide the best possible explanation. Moreover, the combination of research through the empirical evidence with the statistical results is the method that includes the comparative analysis that provides to the paper the evidence for answering every research question. According to Hoepfl (1997), the combination of both methods is expected to help the research of predicting and generalizing of the findings through the quantitative method and also make a comparative analysis to improve understanding by the use of qualitative methods.

The purpose of this research is to identify the ELT market's readiness to react to the forthcoming changes as also their perceptions and believes about the future of the ELT publishing sector and their reactions to the new implemented technologies. All this research can help this study to conclude with comparative results about the future of the ELT book sector and how that will impact its supply chain.

Questionnaires

In the first part of the research, a quantitative method through questionnaires has been used. Two hundred questionnaires, addressed at school owners, have been collected and analysed. The population of ELT private schools according to Esplen (2008) is about seven thousands in Greece but only one thousand and eight hundred in the areas that the questionnaires were promoted. According to Golafshani (2003), the greater the sample of the statistical research the higher the significance of the results can be. The reason that questionnaires were selected for extracting this research is for predicting whether the Greek ELT sector is ready to adopt the forthcoming technological changes or not, and also to forecast when will it be possible for these changes to become notable in the Greek

market. Data is collected through personal visiting of each school or through e-mail and telephone conversations. The visiting method is the most effective way of collecting data because it has fewer errors and missed values. The participants kept their anonymity in order to be able to express unbiased opinions. The statistical program that is used for the analysis of those data is SPSS and various tests for the analysis. The data from that collection were treated as the base for the following qualitative research.

Interviews

For the rest of the research the paper uses the method of interviews for the collection of data that provides important information about publishers', distributors', and book sellers' opinion about how the new technologies can manage to affect the ELT book market in Greece. The interview questions took place either by e-mail or during a personal visit. The greatest difficulty of that process was to convince publishers to participate. There are eleven publishing companies that have been approached but only two of those responded positively to the request for participating to the research through an interview. The reason for the high percentage of resistance in participating to that research was because information about technological issues of the ELT book sector are considered as very important by publishers and they prefer to keep this strategic information secret.

The logic for interviewing the groups of publishers, distributors and book sellers was upon the fact that they affect with their actions the supply chain process. Their decisions and strategic thoughts for future actions give an idea to the public about the path that the ELT publishing sector will follow. Their response to the call for an interview became difficult because the issues of new technologies in the education and publishing sector are part of each company's strategy. Their resistance to answer the research questions presents the importance of information for the future movements in the book publishing sector. That resistance though is a very strong research element for any researcher because it presents the trend of the sector and their common interest.

THE RESULTS OF THE STATISTICAL ANALYSIS

Introduction

The expected outcome of this study is to forecast the time range and the possibility that the Greek ELT publishing market will proceed to changes in their teaching methodologies according to the technological developments in the publishing sector. The outcome of this study can present the impacts in the supply chain of the Greek ELT book market and the results on the economic and also the environmental sector.

The implications of this study are expected to be a further research in the aggregate Greek book sector. This research can help forecast the results of a possible implementation of these technologies to other publishing sectors of the Greek market. This would assist to maximize the benefits of e-publishing and e-searching and e-reading according to the economics and the environment.

The objective of the paper's research is to define the current condition of the Greek ELT market's supply chain and forecast possible changes that may occur in the future. The research is carried out in two parts. The quantitative part is geared towards questionnaires to the school owners and the qualitative part is interview driven with the publishers, authors, distributors and book sellers. The correlation between the responses of those groups is very important in order to identify possible trends and movements. The issue of new technologies in the ELT sector is a serious strategic part of each group.

Quantitative Analysis

The purpose of this research is to identify the ELT market's readiness to react to the forthcoming changes as also their perceptions and believes about the future of the ELT publishing sector and their reactions to the new implemented technologies. The sample that is collected for this research is one hundred and seventy questionnaires (n=170) and the greater percentage of the school owners in the areas selected are between thirty one to fifty years old (68.8%) (see Figure 1).

The schools' location is divided into five categories while the greatest percentage of the sample is from category five as the geographical sections covered are from mainland Greece not including the Aegean islands. In order to identify the relationship between two different variables it has been plotted a bivariate multi-correlation test between variables of the same identity.

According to the test results there is a significant positive correlation (r) of participants' age to the years they use computer (r=0.203, 2-tailed significance value p=0.008) which is normal because the younger the teachers the less years they possibly use computers. The opposite occurs though about how familiar teachers are feeling with the use of computers (r=-0.295, p=0.000). The same relationship of age group stands also about the frequency of PC (r=-0.281, p=0.000) and internet use (r=-0.333, p=0.000). The younger the school owners the more they use PCs and the internet. Subsequently young owners are affected more than older owners by the books' prices when they came to an adoption decision (r=-0.154, p=0.044). The older ages though do not seem to care more about the prices of new technologies (r=0.277, p=0,000) since there is a positive correlation between the age group and possible reasons that may stop a participant to install an interactive white board technology. Therefore there are other reasons that affect those groups decisions which is easy to be explained since the older people are less informed about technologies

Figure 1. Sample's age distribution

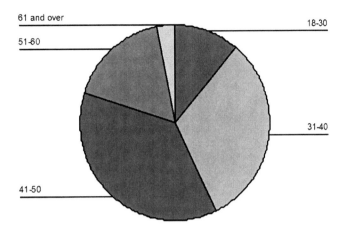

and the younger owners are more affected by the financial constrains of installing new technologies. Additionally, the use of new technologies in the classroom is less frequent by the last age group category than the first age group category. Even though the cross tabulation test presents a insignificant chi square result (p=0.087), it is clearly observable that the younger ages are more active with the new technologies when they own a new technology (see Tables 1 and 2).

Finally, older school owners recognize that ELT book prices should be lower priced (r=0.307, p=0.000) but they are affected less than their younger opponents since the correlation outcome as is shown before is negative (r=-0.154, p=0.044). According to the Greek legislation, it is possible for individuals to sell books only if they acquire a license from the Greek state. Therefore, ELT private institutions provide mainly only teaching

services so they do not have any direct benefit from the price differences between books. Younger school owners care more about the books' prices in order to gain a competitive advantage over their competitors. Assuming that older school owners may own more crowded ELT private schools than their younger competitors then it seems that they care less about the books' prices.

According to the location variable, the correlation analysis presents that in larger populated cities school owners use PCs (r=0.184, p=0.016) as also the internet more years (r=0.216, p=0.005), in higher frequency (r=0.266, p=0.000) and therefore they are more familiar (r=0.208, p=0.008) with it. People located in greater cities are using more often Interactive White Board technologies (r=0.188, p=0.014) and the book prices affect more their decision-making according to the positive sign in the correlation result (r=0.168, p=0.029).

Table 1. Correlation tests of using participants' age group as the basic factor

		How many years have you been using computers?	How familiar are you with the use of a PC?	How often do you use a PC?	How many times per week do you make use of the Internet?	Book prices affect your adoption decision.	What would possible stop you from installing an IWB?	ELT book prices are overvalued
Which is your age group?	Pearson Correlation	0.203	-0.295	-0.281	-0.333	-0.154	0.277	0.307
	Sig. (2-tailed)	0.008	0.000	0.000	0.000	0.044	0.000	0.000

Table 2. Cross tabulation test of age group category to the frequency of technology use

Chi-Square Tests	Value	df	Asymp. Sig. (2-sided)
Pearson Chi-Square	17,982(a)	16	0.325
Likelihood Ratio	21,534	16	0.159
Linear-by-Linear Association	2,932	1	0.087
N of Valid Cases	170		

The aforementioned result can make sense if one considers that the large cities' school owners have easier access to information, education and technological products than the less crowded cities. People in large urban areas have the ability to focus on the use of technologies more than the ELT school owners of smaller cities (see Table 3).

The private ELT schools in large cities are more than in smaller populated areas but the basic characteristic of large cities is also the ELT school chains. Franchised ELT schools usually have different criteria than the books' prices when

they come to an ELT book adoption decisions because they make deals for the aggregate of their business group. Although the existence of that status of ELT school chains, does not affect the open market competition system in the ELT book sector (r=0.168, p=0.029). According to this correlation result, the pure open market competition principals exist in large cities at a greater percentage than in smaller populated places. Opposing to that, book prices does not affect the school owners' majority decision making for the adoption of a book title even though the bigger percentage of them agree or even strongly agree that the ELT book prices are very expensive.

A school owner located in larger urban areas does not significantly use the internet more in their classrooms, than owners of smaller cities (p=0,063). Internet use has greater frequency in ELT schools of smaller cities than large urban areas (r=0.216, p=0.005). On the other hand, the more familiar a pc user is the more often uses internet in the classroom (r=0.239, p=0.002) and interactive white board technology (r=0.234, p=0.002). The

Table 3. Correlation test of schools' location as the basic factor

		How many years have you been using computers?	How many times per week do you make use of the Internet?	How often do you use it?	How familiar are you with the use of a PC?	How regularly do you make use of the Interactive White Board in your class room?	Book prices affect your adoption decision.	How regularly do you make use of the Internet in you class room?
Where is your school located?	Pearson Correlation	0.184	0.216	0.266	0.208	0.188	0.168	0.144
	Sig. (2-tailed)	0.016	0.005	0.000	0.008	0.014	0.029	0.063

Table 4. Correlation test of participants' computer literacy to other factors

		How many times per week do you make use of the Internet?	How regularly do you make use of the Interactive White Board in your class room?	How many different ELT book publishers do you use every year?
How familiar are you with the use of a PC?	Pearson Correlation	0.239	0.234	-0.220
	Sig. (2-tailed)	0.002	0.002	0.004

more familiar to pc use a school owner is the fewer ELT book publishers uses every year (r=-0.220, p=0.004) (see Table 4).

That last finding gives an indication that the more familiar pc users have a tendency to replace the book usage in the classrooms with technological means. In order to identify the possibility that this trend may be significant, it has been stretched out a cross-tabulation and a chi-square test between the two variables. The result of the test shows that there is a significant relationship between the two variables while the asymptotic significance 2-sided (p) equals 0,000 and therefore it verifies that there is a significant relationship between pc users abilities and the possible replacement of ELT books in the classroom by other educational methods like e-books, e-learning, distance learning, internet sites and personal pc databases. It is important to mention at this point that the use of the pc as also the internet and other technologies does not affect school owner's belief about what percentage of their students use a pc at their home. Opposing this and according to a t-test, a significant relationship has been defined between the students that study their lessons by pc and the variables "ELT schools that have a computer room (p=0.000)" as also to "ELT schools that have internet connection in their classroom (p=0.000)". These school owners are shown to be using more regularly the internet (r=0.370, p=0.000) as also modern technologies like interactive white boards in the classroom for their lessons (r=0.278, p=0.000). According to the aforementioned results, the technological progress of the school and the technological skills of the school owners have a significant effect to the percentage of their students that use their PCs to study their lessons at home. Finally, the more often a school owner uses interactive white board in the classroom the less ELT book publishers are used for its book list every year. This effect can also be explained by the recent trend in the market that the school owners are making deals with the publishing companies in order to adopt their

books and get sponsored the technological equipment required for operating an interactive white board into their classrooms. According to our research, 80% of the school owners that uses only one book publisher in their book list also use an interactive whiteboard in their classrooms.' In order to identify if the trend between those two variables is significant it has been set up an independent sample t-test. The result presents the existence of a correlation with an acceptable 2-tailed significant value (p) equal to 0.006.

The positive significant relationship between the technologies related variables (pc and internet use frequency of school owners and students) with the owners' belief that their customers may purchase a book through an e-shop for a cheaper price, presents that there is a possible trend in the Greek ELT market that can guide the market to operate within a different purchasing approach other than through the direct book shop physical presence. The school owners believe that customers which haven't yet purchased a book from an e-shop would not purchase a book even if the price would be cheaper since there is a negative correlation (r=-0.161) and the significance p value of independent t-test is equal to 0.002. The opposite correlation relationship stands for the owners that believe ELT books are more expensive than they should be so their customers will eventually purchase an ELT book if he could get it from an e-shop (r=0.232, p=0.002). The main reason for not using an e-shop, is shown to be that they're afraid to do transactions through the internet (44.7%) and secondly that they don't know how to make a purchase through an e-shop (34.7%). According though to Eurostat (2008), 12% in the EU27 avoids e-shopping because of security concerns while the higher rate is for Spain (27%), Finland (26%) and for Cyprus (20%). The same rate for Greece was 14% which shows that there is a great difference between the real reasons and the school owners' expectation (see Table 5).

Only 9.4% of the participants have chosen that the main reason for not using the e-shop option

Table 5. Correlation test according to e-shop use and ELT book price factors

		Do you believe that your students or their parents ever tried to buy an ELT book from an e-shop?
Your customers will eventually prefer buying books from e-shop if book prices will be cheaper than in a physical book shop.	Pearson Correlation	-0.161
	Sig. (2-tailed)	0.002
		Your customers will eventually prefer buying books from e-shop if book prices will be cheaper than in a physical book shop.
ELT book prices are overvalued	Pearson Correlation	0.232
	Sig. (2-tailed)	0.002

is that they are willing to keep their good relations with the booksellers. The higher percentage of school owners that have chosen this answer in the aforementioned question is mainly from middle and small populated areas. This result strengthens the belief that in smaller cities human relations have a stronger impact to the purchasing behavior of people than in large cities.

The mean value of the students that own a pc according to the expectations of the school owners is 68.02%. That percentage is an expected outcome of the school owners for their students without having the real exact numbers. Although this variable presents to us the owners' belief about what percentage of their students have a relation with modern technologies that can be also used for educational purposes. According to that belief one can foresee that younger school owners believe that technology can play an important role for the educational operations.

In conclusion, the market does not seem to be unaware about the technological developments that occur in the sector of publishing and education. The majority of the school owners have at least the basic knowledge of using a personal computer and the internet so they are familiar enough to operate other relative technologies also. They also believe that their customers from the student perspective are familiar with the use of PCs but their parents are not trained to do the same. Because of that result, school owners believe that their customers are not ready to use an e-shopping operation

therefore do not purchase ELT books even if the books' prices are much cheaper than from a book store. Teachers and owners response about the use of new technologies is in accordance to their ages and their location. School owners are more familiar with the use of new technologies in teaching when they are located in large cities and they have small age. The problem that younger owners face for using those technologies is that they usually do not have the financial resources to acquire them. So according to the statistical analysis they use technology more than older school owners when they have the opportunity to own them.

Qualitative Analysis

The next stage of the analysis is based on the interviews of authors, publishers, distributors and book sellers. These interviews have been studied and analyzed in a critical manner in order to allow any individual reader to come on a critical result even if that result may be different from the writer's results. According to authors, the Greek market is ready to accept new technologies in their daily lesson operations mainly because they already use a few of them such as various forms of e-learning, eBooks, and interactive whiteboard technologies. The basis of those technologies and the "know-how" already exist in the ELT market but there is a strong belief that printed books are fundamental for the educational operation of schools and the learning activities of students. On behalf of that statement, publishers have questioned the possibility to have changes in the operational status of the ELT book market. Moreover, publishers as also distributors and booksellers strongly believe that the education system is highly interconnected with the existence of printed books. Among the respondents, it is observable that publishers and authors have been better informed about technological developments than booksellers and distributors.

Regarding the issue of how the Greek ELT publishing market is going to react in the technological changes authors answered had a common response. They all believe that books will never extinguish even if other digital methods of teaching will take off the Greek market. They still say that the non-printed era does not exclude the use of printed books from the market. The e-learning and digital teaching methods already exist but their use is supplementary. Publishers have been more inflexible than authors according to their sayings about the same issue. The main issues for them are; the quality of books and services; as also the reduction of the aggregate cost for the best benefit of their customers. At the same time, distributors and book sellers have mentioned similar cases of technological mediations in the ELT market at the past. They parallelize that era of pc use in the ELT schools that took place a few decades ago with the modern technologies such as the interactive whiteboards. Distributor's main concern is how to modernize their operations in order to reduce their main costs. These costs are not coming only from transferring the products, from the human resource's expenses and from storing. The cost that cannot easily be controlled by distributors is bad debts which accrue from the collection of finances from book sellers. Distributors agree that they are also responsible for books' prices because they get high percentages out of books' sales but they also have the risk to administrate every stage of the supply chain as also all payments from booksellers to them and pay back the publishers. Therefore, distributors do not believe that the supply chain in the book

market is likely to change because risk and high costs of administrating the aforementioned operations discourages publishers.

Publishers have contradicting opinions about the cost that the technological innovations may create to publishing companies as also to school owners. Some of them state that cost will play a primary role in the progress of those changes without affecting books' role in the educational system. On the other hand, the more traditionally thinking publishers believe that only the quality of the final product and especially of printed material can affect sales operations of an ELT publishing company and the market in general. Both sides though accept the existence and the role of technology in the classroom activities. In addition, some of the publishers state that the market can be benefited by the use of those technologies by reducing the overall production cost and investing on the production of better quality products.

A general idea about how publishing will continue to operate in the future is that publishers have used technology mainly for marketing reasons that created extra profit to their operations. Therefore, any type of modernization would be welcome by the publishers and the aggregate market if it could be combined by growth, extra profit and costs cut down. The majority of writers' responses disagree with the way that the publishing companies have used technology until today. They believe that it is a corrupted method of promoting books when offers, agreements, and sponsoring gifts have a greater importance than the book itself. In addition they see modern technology as a development of the traditional methods of teaching but not because it can facilitate to teachers' mission.

According to distributors, the affect of possible technological changes into the ELT market can be the possible creation of stronger publishing units but to also the reduction of their number because some of them will not manage to afford the cost of those changes. Distributors commented that their main observable costs are the delivery and storage expenses. Both activities require a high number of employees, large warehouses and high-energy expenses. They state though that a soft form of technological intervention in the ELT market such as with the use of Computer Discs (CDs) and other small portable devices can reduce the cost of distribution and storage. On the other hand, it is commonly accepted that other forms of technological interventions in the ELT sector such as the use of internet and PCs for e-learning operations can be catastrophic for both the distributors and booksellers.

Authors commented on their own future role by stating that there will be less need for their operations since the reputation of each author will have a secondary role when IT in general will be able to differentiate products and hide their weaknesses. Both authors and publishers believe less in the role of bookshops as the future of the ELT book market. They both believe that prices affect the final decision of customers but do not hugely affect the school owners' decision as price is perhaps secondary to content. Some optimistic authors and publishers also believe in the use of e-books in the classrooms during the next decade. They foresee that more activities can be possibly taught if their students' interests are attracted by innovative technological machinery and services.

In contrast to the aforementioned statements, distributors believe that the role of books will continue to be as it is today mainly because the cost of changing the system is not simply financial. Following this, there is very high training cost that cannot be managed by all the existing ELT private institutions because they do not have the resources or they do not believe that they have the abilities to deal with technological changes. According to that perception, teacher's resistance to changes is a very troublesome managerial issue that can lead the changing conditions to a financial breakdown. The most difficult part in a changing business situation is employees' resistance to change. That is a managerial issue with psychological extensions about human behavior.

Regarding technology, the booksellers are the least informed link of the supply chain in the Greek ELT book market. They are least aware of the affects that it can have in the future of the printed books in the market. Their view on the issue is that every link of the existing supply chain is important in order to continue the efficient operation of the market. The difference between all other sectors is that they believe that their role is probably the most important part of the supply chain. Moreover, they agree with the idea that in the future there will be a smaller number of publishing companies and fewer new titles. However, this will not be as a result of new technologies in the market. They strongly believe that the Greek publishing ELT market has a surplus of new titles and publishing companies according to the needs of a maturing market.

The last issue of the interviews was about the possible benefits and detriments that the ELT market and the community can have from the introduction of electronic teaching and learning sources in the education sector. There is a variety of opinions that were contradicting between respondents of the same groups. Therefore, the results are not significant for one to support a hypothesis. There is a pessimistic and an optimistic side according to the personality of each participant and the information that they have about the issue.

There is a belief from a respondents' part that ecologically and practically it is more beneficial to have the existence of printed books. According to them, companies are more secure about their products' safe distribution; there is no need for companies' restructuring and change of employment status, and also they believe that they can secure the culture and the quality of products produced by the publishing companies. The same people believe that there is a better opportunity to recycle and help for a cleaner environment with the use of paper than with the use of machineries. According to that opinion, the use of e-books instead of printed books will bring greater environmental problems due to greater energy needs for the production and the use of each machine. In addition they state that the best way to protect our environment, secure quality and employment positions is to continue using and printing books but with greater emphasis to the paper's recycling part. Finally, they state that pedagogically thinking, books are more appropriate for the education of young ages than any other digital method.

The opposing idea is that the new technologies can definitely help from various perspectives such as financially, ecologically and pedagogically. According to them, the new technologies can deliver information with low cost but at high speed and therefore help on education. More people can have access to education and many more can promote their knowledge to people which are located in distant areas, with a very low operating cost and a similar environmental cost. They also believe that digital technology is the future of education but this can also be the era that bookshops, distributors, and publishers may have a smaller role in the supply chain of an ELT book. Besides, it is believed that authors and individuals in total can have a more essential role in the supply chain of the ELT book sector.

RECOMMENDATIONS

This research has not forecasted when the technological changes may affect the supply chain of the ELT book market because there are no significant results to assume that those changes can take place within a specific time span. The environmental benefits, from the use of electronic sources for replacing the paper use in ELT books and changing businesses operations, do not affect the supply chain participants' decisions. Cost factors as also the lack of strong motives that could create extra profit without creating extra risk, are responsible for rejecting the idea of changing supply chain operations. The paper focused its research to the ELT book market in Greece until the end of 2009. The same research about different book markets in

the region of Greece and globally can be an issue for future research. According to that issue, one can study the motives and the reasons that would lead or force the particular market to change its supply chain operations because of modern technology's use. Finally, it would be important the same research to renew its data according to the financial general conditions of its each market and the global economy.

CONCLUSION

The Greek ELT sector is a mature market that faces a profit decline because of birth rare and student numbers declining number that resulted during the last decades. According to Esplen (2008), private lessons and photocopy activities reduces the operational income of the ELT market while at the same time the publishers' number increased and that increased the competition between publishing companies that enlarged their marketing expenses. The environmental issues of the harmful actions within the ELT book supply chain system is one more reason that made publisher to seek out for possible technological solutions that can reduce the overall product cost, provide faster and better quality of services and products to the market and also reduce the environmental footsteps of their activities. The Greek ELT publishing sector can find solutions to these financial and environmental problems within the functions of green logistics, e-commerce, and e-publishing activities. Government support is considered essential for the successful transition from the traditional to the new supply chain operations. Reverse logistics and recycling are green logistic activities that require employees' training and a lot of effort for changing peoples' behavior. The benefits from the implementation of those activities are multiple and common for businesses and individuals.

The result of the research have shown that the Greek ELT market is moving very fast to changes that many businesses and people from each sector do not seem to be ready to catch up. The new technological teaching and learning resources are the solution for the financial problems that the ELT market has been facing these past years. However, the startup cost for installing such technologies is the main hurdle for publishing companies and school owners. Young ELT school owners and publishers are more informed than older owners about the capabilities and the benefits that they can obtain from the use of electronic forms of teaching. Lower age school owners though usually do not have the resources to install and use such facilities.

According to the statistical analysis younger people are more familiar with the use of technology and therefore motivate their students and their parents to use them also. They recognize that book prices on average are very expensive for their customers but they do not use that criterion for choosing their book list. Furthermore, they may decide to use the entire book list from only one publisher if that publisher would provide them technological facilities for using their books' electronic sources. Current financial crisis increased those activities between publishing companies and school owners in order to have the best possible win-win situation. In addition, school owners who own such facilities stated that they do not always use them during their lessons. The combination of the aforementioned last two statements proves that new technologies have been used from publishers and school owners to attract new customers. Moreover, these technologies expanded faster in the ELT sector because they used them for marketing reasons. This expansion continues because the markets view these technologies as a basic quality characteristic for the services provided from publishers to school owners and from school owners to their students and parents.

In contrast to Dowlatshahi (2005) and Lamming and Hampson (1996), the ecological issue is not the first concern for the adoption of new electronic teaching methods or the traditional because the majority of school owners are not yet well informed about how to use these technologies and full extent of the benefits that they can provide to them.

According to the aforementioned analysis about the market's readiness to accept the changes in the ELT market operations, one can conclude that the market is not easily willing to change. The evidence shows that the basis for installing electronic forms of publishing and education exist but the supply chain members of the ELT market are skeptical of their benefits to the extent that they are unwilling to accept them. The marketing reasons that drove the installation and use of some of the new technologies can become the reason for a fast and furious change. Such changes will likely force reluctant market members to adopt the new ways in order to keep their market share. Distributors and booksellers seem to be the most affected members of these changes because they are not prepared. E-commerce can reduce both sides' facilities and therefore reduce their cost in order to continue providing their services to publishers and individuals more economically. In conclusion, the new learning technologies can possibly affect the ELT supply chain but not by eliminating books' printed versions. The change of the operational system's basis is a matter of training the system's members to accept it and perhaps more importantly to inform the final customers to demand it.

REFERENCES

Armstrong, C. J., Edwards, L., & Lonsdale, R. (2002). Virtually there? E-books in UK academic libraries. *Program: Electronic Library & Information Systems*, *36*(4), 216–227. doi:10.1108/00330330210447181

Banou, C. (2006). Money and taste: New roles for the Greek publishers in a changing era. *The International Journal of the Book*, *3*(2), 39–46.

Banou, G. C., & Kostagiolas, A. P. (2007). Managing expectations for open access in Greece: Perceptions from the publishers and academic libraries. *International Journal of the Book, 3*(2), 39–46.

Banou, G. C., & Phillips, A. (2008). The Greek publishing industry and professional development. *Publishing Research Quarterly, 24*(2), 98–110. doi:10.1007/s12109-008-9070-2

Buzzetto, M., & Sweat, G., & Elobaid. (2007). Reading in a digital age: e-Books are students ready for this learning object? *Interdisciplinary Journal of Knowledge and Learning Objects, 3,* 239–250.

Cigolini, R., Cozzi, M. M., & Perona, A. (2004). New framework for supply chain management conceptual model and empirical test. *International Journal of Operations & Production Management, 24*(1), 7–41. doi:10.1108/01443570410510979

Cox, J. (2004). E-books: Challenges and opportunities. *D-Lib Magazine, 10*(10). Retrieved from www.dlib.org/dlib/october04/cox/10cox.html

Doonan, J., Lanoie, P., & Laplante, B. (2005). Analysis determinants of environmental performance in the Canadian pulp and paper industry: An assessment from inside the industry. *Ecological Economics, 55*(1), 73–84. doi:10.1016/j.ecolecon.2004.10.017

Dowlatshahi, S. (2005). A strategic framework for the design and implementation of remanufacturing operations in reverse logistics. *International Journal of Production Research, 43*(16), 3455–3480. doi:10.1080/00207540500118118

Eagan, P. D., & Kaiser, D. (2002). Can environmental purchasing reduce mercury in US health care? *Environmental Health Perspectives, 110*(9), 847–851. doi:10.1289/ehp.02110847

Esplen, M. (2002). *Greece publishing market profile.* London, UK: The Publishers Association & The British Council.

Esplen, M. (2008). *Greece publishing market profile.* London, UK: The Publishers Association.

Fischer, R., & Lugg, R. (2001). E-book basics. *Collection Building, 20*(3), 119–122. doi:10.1108/01604950110396988

Gallagher, P. (2007). A view from Australia. *Publishing Research Quarterly, 23*(2), 137–140. doi:10.1007/s12109-007-9022-2

Gentry, C. R. (1999). Reducing the cost of returns. *Chain Store Age, 75*(10), 124–125.

Golafshani, N. (2003). Understanding reliability and validity in qualitative research. *The Qualitative Report, 8*(4), 597-607. Retrieved August 18, 2009, from http://www.nova.edu/ssss/QR/QR8-4/golafshani.pdf

Gold, D. J. (1994). An electronic publishing model for academic publishers. *Journal of the American Society for Information Science American Society for Information Science, 45*(10), 760–764. doi:10.1002/(SICI)1097-4571(199412)45:10<760::AID-ASI7>3.0.CO;2-H

Golicic, L. S., Davis, F. D., McCarthy, M. T., & Mentzer, T. J. (2002). The impact of e-commerce on supply chain relationships. *International Journal of Physical Distribution & Logistics Management, 32*(10), 851–871. doi:10.1108/09600030210455447

Green, K., Morton, B., & New, S. (1996). Purchasing and environmental management: Interactions, policies and opportunities. *Business Strategy and the Environment, 5*(5), 188–197. doi:10.1002/(SICI)1099-0836(199609)5:3<188::AID-BSE60>3.0.CO;2-P

Guide, D., Souza, G., Van Wassenhove, L., & Blackburn, J. (2006). Time value of commercial product returns. *Management Science, 52*(8), 1200–1214. doi:10.1287/mnsc.1060.0522

Hoepfl, M. C. (1997). Choosing qualitative research: A primer for technology education researchers. *Journal of Technology Education, 9*(1), 47-63. Retrieved August 18, 2009, from http://scholar.lib.vt.edu/ejournals/JTE/v9n1/pdf/hoepfl.pdf

Khanna, V. K. (2008). An Indian experience of environmental management system. PICMET. *Proceedings of PICMET, 2008,* 1806–1816.

Laband, D., & Hudson, J. (2003). The pricing of economics books. *The Journal of Economic Education,* 360–368. doi:10.1080/00220480309595229

Lamming, R., & Hampson, J. (1996). The environment as a supply chain issue. *British Journal of Management, 7,* 45–62. doi:10.1111/j.1467-8551.1996.tb00147.x

Lin, C. Y. (2007). Adoption of green supply chain practices in Taiwan's logistics industry. *Journal of International Management Studies, 2*(2), 90–98.

Lloyd, S. (2008). A book publisher's manifesto for the twenty-first century: How traditional publishers can position themselves in the changing media flow of a networked era. *Library Trends, 57*(1), 30–42. doi:10.1353/lib.0.0019

Meyer, H. (1999). Many happy returns. *The Journal of Business Strategy, 30*(2), 27–31. doi:10.1108/eb040015

Mikko, P., Yorjola, H., & Halmstrom, J. (2001). Solving the last mile issue: Reception box or delivery box? *International Journal of Physical Distribution & Logistics Management, 31*(6), 427–439. doi:10.1108/09600030110399423

Min, H., & Galle, W. P. (2001). Green purchasing practices of US firms. *International Journal of Operations & Production Management, 21*(9), 1222–1238. doi:10.1108/EUM0000000005923

Mukhopadhyay, S., & Setoputro, R. (2005). Optimal return policy and modular design for build-to-order products. *Journal of Operations Management, 23*(5), 496–506. doi:10.1016/j.jom.2004.10.012

Murphy, P., Poist, R., & Braunschweig, C. (1996). Green logistics: Comparative views of environmental progressives, moderates, and conservatives. *Journal of Business Logistics, 17*(1), 191–211.

Paramasevam, G., Hassan, M., & Mohamed, N. (2001). Cost benefit analysis for implementation of environmental management systems. In *Proceedings of the International Symposium on Environmentally Conscious Design and Inverse Manufacturing,* (pp. 766-768). IEEE.

Peters, A. T. (2001). Gutterda èmmerung (twilight of the gutter margins): e-Books and libraries. *Library Hi Tech, 19*(1), 50–62. doi:10.1108/07378830110384593

Rawlins, G. (1993). Publishing over the next decade. *Journal of the American Society for Information Science American Society for Information Science, 44*(8), 474–479. doi:10.1002/(SICI)1097-4571(199309)44:8<474::AID-ASI6>3.0.CO;2-3

Rogers, D. S., & Tibben-Lembke, R. S. (2002). Differences between forward and reverse logistics in a retail environment. *Supply Chain Management: An International Journal, 7*(5), 271–282. doi:10.1108/13598540210447719

Sarkis, J. (2001). Manufacturing's role in corporate environmental sustainability: Concerns for the new millennium. *International Journal of Operations & Production Management, 21*(5/6), 666–685. doi:10.1108/01443570110390390

Sarkis, J. (2003). A strategic decision framework for green supply chain management. *Journal of Cleaner Production, 11*(4), 397–409. doi:10.1016/S0959-6526(02)00062-8

Sarkis, J., Meade, M. L., & Talluri, S. (2004). E-logistics and the natural environment. *Supply Chain Management: An International Journal, 9*(4), 303–312. doi:10.1108/13598540410550055

Sbihi, A., & Eglese, W. R. (2007). Combinatorial optimization and green logistics. *4OR: A Quarterly Journal of Operations Research, 5*(2), 99-116.

Seeley, M. (2006). Impact of the internet on the services aspect of the STM publishing business. *Information Services & Use, 26*, 173–175.

Srikanta, R. (2009). Antecedents and drivers for green supply chain management implementation in manufacturing environment. *The Icfai University Journal of Supply Chain Management, 6*(1), 20.

Srivastava, S. K., & Srivastava, R. K. (2006). Managing product returns for reverse logistics. *International Journal of Physical Distribution & Logistics Management, 36*(7), 524–546. doi:10.1108/09600030610684962

Stock, J. R. (2001). The 7 deadly sins of reverse logistics. *Material Handling Management, 56*(3), 5–11.

Tan, A., & Kumar, A. (2008). A decision making model to maximise the value of reverse logistics in the computer. *International Journal of Logistics Systems and Management, 4*(3), 297–312. doi:10.1504/IJLSM.2008.017478

Tyan, J., Wang, F. K., & Du, T. (2003). Applying collaborative transportation management models in global third-party logistics. *International Journal of Computer Integrated Manufacturing, 16*(4–5), 283–291. doi:10.1080/0951192031000089183

Vasileiou, M., Hartley, R., & Rowley, J. (2009). An overview of the e-book market place. *Online Information Review, 33*(1), 173–192. doi:10.1108/14684520910944454

Vasileiou, M., & Rowley, J. (2008). Progressing the definition of e-book. *Library Hi Tech, 26*(3), 355–368. doi:10.1108/07378830810903292

Walker, D., Pitt, M., & Thakur, U. J. (2007). Environmental management systems information management and corporate responsibility. *Journal of Facilities Management, 5*(1), 49–61. doi:10.1108/14725960710726346

Watson, K., Klingenberg, B., Polito, T., & Geurts, T. G. (2004). Impact of environmental management system implementation on financial performance: A comparison of two corporate strategies. *Management of Environmental Quality: An International Journal, 15*(6), 622–628. doi:10.1108/14777830410560700

Weissberg, A. (2008). The identification of digital book content. *Publishing Research Quarterly, 24*(4), 255–260. doi:10.1007/s12109-008-9093-8

Zhu, Q., Sarkis, J., & Geng, Y. (2005). Green supply chain management in China: Pressures, practices performance. *International Journal of Operations & Production Management, 25*(5), 449–468. doi:10.1108/01443570510593148

Zhu, Q., Sarkis, J., & Lai, H. (2007). Initiatives and outcomes of green supply chain management implementation by Chinese manufacturers. *Journal of Environmental Management, 85*(1), 179–189. doi:10.1016/j.jenvman.2006.09.003

Chapter 15
ERP Implementation Service Supply Chain:
A Modular Perspective

Yong Lin
University of Greenwich, UK

Zhenkun Zhou
Huazhong University of Science and Technology, China

Li Zhou
University of Greenwich, UK

Shihua Ma
Huazhong University of Science and Technology, China

ABSTRACT

ERP system plays a critical role in gaining competitive advantages; however, the implementation of the ERP system is a critical success factor but a difficult process to both the software providers and the buyers of the ERP system. Designing and delivering the implementation services becomes a key challenge to the ERP suppliers. This chapter applies modular logic into service design in order to reduce complexity and increase the service variety and quality, and develop a conceptual structure of service supply chain for delivering ERP implementation services.

INTRODUCTION

Along with the fast development of technology, information system like ERP (Enterprise Resource Planning) plays an increasingly important strategic role in supply chain and logistics operations of most industries. Moreover, ERP is to some extent regarded as a source of gaining competitive advantage, streamlining operations, and having "lean" manufacturing. However, the implementation of ERP system is still a challenge job to the ERP suppliers, and the failure of the implemen-

DOI: 10.4018/978-1-4666-3914-0.ch015

tation services possibly leads to millions dollar losses. Furthermore, the integration scopes of ERP system have been extended from internal to external covering resources in supply chain level, which enlarges the difficulties of implementation services. Consequently, how to efficiently and effectively *design and deliver ERP implementation services* to customer becomes a critical factor of the sustainable development to the ERP supplier.

In order to improve the quality of ERP implementation services, this chapter aims to develop a framework for designing ERP implementation services by applying modular logic which is commonly used in the field of product design; and to build a conceptual structure of service supply chain for delivering ERP implementation services.

BACKGROUND

ERP Implementation

ERP system is regarded as a key approach to gain competitive advantage, streamline operations, improve business processes, improve communication and interaction, and enhance productivity and working quality (Al-Mashari et al., 2003; Willis and Willis-Brown, 2002). However, managers are often confronting difficulties and challenges in comprehending the full potential advantages and benefits of ERP system (Marnewick and Labuschagne, 2005; Maditinos et al., 2012).

One of the key reasons is because of the complexity of the ERP system itself (Finney and Corbett, 2007; Markus and Tanis, 2000; Somers and Nelson, 2004). Most of the arguments believe that the success of ERP systems largely depend on its implementation (Hong and Kim, 2002; Gargeya and Brady, 2005; Marnewick and Labuschagne, 2005; Finney and Corbett, 2007; Maditinos et al., 2012). Gaining a better understanding of the complexities of ERP implementations is helpful to managers to avoid barriers and increase the likelihood of achieving desired results from the

ERP system (Dezdar and Ainin, 2011). Thus the challenges of ERP solutions lie in the design and management of the implementation services (Muthusamy et al., 2005; Kim et al., 2005; Singla and Goyal, 2006). The ERP implementation service is kind of professional knowledge-intensive complex service and this highly customized service to meet customer's individual requirements. As a complex IT project, ERP system project is not a pure technology work but a program of management reengineering involved information technology, business process, and organizational strategy, which increase the difficulties of the ERP implementation. As a result, better defined implementation services become a key to the success of ERP system project.

In addition to the integration scopes of ERP system have been extended from internal to external covering resources in supply chain level, hence including upstream and downstream partners are required to get involved into the implementation process. Furthermore, EPR implementation actually leads to many positive effects on supply chain performance (Yang and Su, 2009; Forslund and Jonsson, 2010). However, at the same time it enlarges the difficulties of designing and delivering the ERP implementation services (Chen et al., 2008). Obviously, it is important to consider the implementation services delivery from a view of supply chain.

Service Supply Chain

With the increasing focus shift from product production to service offer, service supply chain management emerges as a new focus of the supply chain research (Poole, 2003; Ellram et al., 2004; Sengupta et al., 2006; Baltacioglu et al., 2007). Due to different nature of products and services, there are many differences between manufacturing supply chain and service supply chain (Sengupta et al., 2006; Niranjan and Weaver, 2011). However, not like the comprehensive development of manufacturing supply chain management, the body of knowledge of service supply chain management is still building in progress. Particularly, the research on the structure of the service supply chain is still scare.

There is no common definition on service supply chain and service supply chain management. Service supply chain could be described as "a network of suppliers, service providers, customers and other service partners that transfer resources into services or servitised products delivered to and received by the customers" (Lin et al., 2010, p.1191). Meanwhile, service supply chain management is to manage the "information, processes, capacity, service performance and funds from the earliest supplier to the ultimate customer" (Ellram et al., 2004, p. 25).

Current research has covered services including health care (Cook et al., 2000; Baltacioglu et al., 2007; Lillrank et al., 2011), telecom (Akkermans and Vos, 2003), tourism (Véronneau and Roy, 2009a, 2009b), after-sale (Kim et al., 2007; Saccani et al., 2007; Shih, 2007), consulting (Giannakis, 2011), municipality (Arlbjørn et al., 2011), e-government (Michaelides and Kehoe, 2006), and language school (Zsidisin et al., 2000). However, with the context of ERP implementation services, the research on its service supply chain management is still limited.

Modularity

Due to being regarded as one of the effective methods to manage complexity and deliver product variety to customers (Baldwin and Clark, 1997; Salvador, 2007; Starr, 2010), modular logic is widely applied in product design (Mikkola, 2006), and production (Starr, 1965, 2010) in the manufacturing industry, broadly covering computer (Langlois and Robertson, 1992; Baldwin and Clark, 1997), bicycle (Schilling, 2000), automobile (Cusumano and Nobeoka, 1992; Takeishi and Fujimoto, 2003; Doran, 2004; Ro et al., 2007; Doran et al., 2007; Lin et al., 2009) industries.

After its successful application in the manufacturing industries, modularity is also rapidly being introduced into service industries (Voss and Hsuan, 2009), including finance (Baldwin and Clark, 1997), software design (Kratochvil and Carson, 2005; Griswold et al., 2006), IT outsourcing (Miozzo and Grimshaw, 2005), and logistics services (Pekkarinen and Ulkuniemi, 2008; Lin and Pekkarinen, 2011). In terms of software design, modularity is regarded as a key rule. However, it is only little research on applying modular logic into the design of ERP implementation services.

As complex a system as the supply chain is, modularity is also appropriate to be applied in the supply chain research. It was verified that companies with high levels of product modularity lead to better supply chain integration in terms of product co-development, organizational coordination, and information sharing (Lau et al., 2010). After examining a construction supply chain from module manufacturer through to module client, Doran and Giannakis (2011) highlighted that supply chain integration should be increased to ensure that modular solutions can compete more effectively with traditional, on-site solutions.

FRAMEWORK OF MODULAR ERP IMPLEMENTATION SERVICES

Firstly, this chapter develops a framework of ERP implementation services based on the modular logic and the theory of Product Service System (PSS).

Product Service System and Modularity

A Product Service System (PSS) is an integrated combination of products and services that delivers value in use to the customer (Baines et al., 2007). This conception is motivated by servitization strategy (Vandermerwe and Rada, 1988) that the traditional manufacturing firms combining services with products to provide higher value and profits than sole products to cope with changing market forces. With the conception of PSS, it means that the manufacturing companies are shifting their focus from providing products to offering services in order to achieve competitive advantages and enhance firm operational performance, and finally to satisfy customer's needs.

Based on the modular logic, we could divide the product service system into two subsystems, product subsystem and service subsystem. A modular subsystem tends to be designed and built by modular components and processes. Figure 1 shows the architecture of subsystems for both product and service.

The product subsystem is defined as diverse kinds of multiple product family grounded on firm's production capability, and each product family normally consists of a set of products, and each product could be defined as a product module with a hierarchy view. As a result, the product subsystem is naturally decomposed into individually product modules. Similarly, each module is further decomposed into one or more physical components in the light of functional attribute where physical components implement the functional elements of the product. And the mapping

between functional elements and components may be one-to-one, many-to-one, or one-to-many (Ulrich, 1995). In view of this mixing-and-match diverse component on the one hand makes contribution to product modular global function, on the other hand creates product variety and product architecture choices (Mikkola, 2001). In addition, the manufacturing process of product component is consisted of a succession of production activities step by step. From a functional static view, product component is the smallest building block of the product subsystem. Meanwhile, from a modular dynamic view, physical product component is divided into process activities.

Borrowing this logic applied in product subsystem analysis, service subsystem also can be analyzed with modular logic. Generally, services differ from physical products in terms of their more abstract nature, parallel production and consumption, as well as co-production of the service provider and customer. Services should be regarded as the basis of exchange (Vargo and Lusch, 2008), where value is created for the customer through an interactive, process and experimental relationship between the service provider and the customer. As the same as in the product subsystem, the service subsystem is developed with varieties of

Figure 1. Architecture of product subsystem and service subsystem

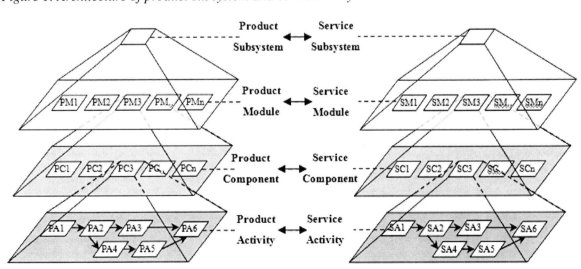

service offering based on firm's service capability. Furthermore, a service provision to the customer is a group of diverse market objects of exchange (Axelsson and Wynstra, 2002), which is visible to a customer and can be combined by one or several service modules (Pekkarinen, 2008). Each service module can be combined according to service functional attribute in many ways from one or several distinct service components (Voss and Hsuan, 2009). Service component is acted as product component did in product subsystem to mix-and-match and make contribution to the service modular global function. In addition, the service process delivering service provision to the final customer includes a set of activities arranged in a specific order (Lin and Pekkarinen, 2011). Therefore, from a rather static point of view, service modules are combination of required service components, and service component is the smallest building block of the service subsystem. While from a further dynamic point of view, service component is completed and performed by a series of processes and activities.

Modular ERP Product Service System

With the modularity applied in the service subsystem, it contributes not only to decrease service complexity, but also to increase service variety offered to the customers, which results in flexible design and enables a company respond to the changing markets and technologies rapidly and cost-effectively. In order to comprehensively analyze both product module and service module, static view is developed to analyze its functional configuration, while dynamic view is applied to analyze the procedure to complete the specific module (See Figure 2).

According to Figure 2, the PPS consists of product subsystem and service subsystem as an essential value-added segment in particular within the context of service sector. Service subsystem is decomposed into various service modules responding to quickly changed customer requirements, that is to say mixing-and-matching service modules could support customized require-

Figure 2. Modular product service system

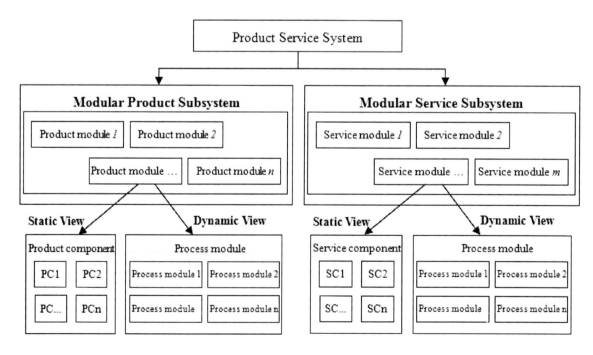

ments at a relatively low cost. From a static view, service module is decomposed into various service components, and each component is a representative of some functional elements of the service module. From a dynamic procedure view, service component includes a set of processes arranged in a specific order which forms the so-called service process.

In terms of ERP, the ERP software system itself is a product subsystem, and the implementation of ERP is the service subsystem. The *product subsystem* is consisted of product modules (specific pre-designed function packages), the product (ERP software) provided to the customer is a combination of these modules. According to the modular logic, each *module* could be decomposed into one or more physical *components* with specific function of the product. From a functional static perspective, product component is regarded as the smallest building block of the product subsystem. Moreover, with a dynamic view, the product component is results of a succession of process modules, and each process module performs specific tasks or activities. Meanwhile, the *service subsystem* includes the services offered to the customers to complete the ERP implementation project, and the service is a combination of different service *module*. Each service module can be combined according to service functional attribute in many ways from one or several distinct service *components*. The same as in the product subsystem, the service components delivering services to the final customers through a set of *processes* arranged in a specific order. Most important thing is that the service subsystem becomes more and more essential to value creation.

An Example of Modular ERP PSS

An example of a modular ERP product service system is described in Figure 3, which includes ERP product subsystem and ERP implementation service subsystem.

Within the modular ERP product service system described in Figure 3, the product subsystem is further decomposed into software (ERP in this case) product families and hardware product families. Each product family includes several product modules (such as database, middleware, technology, server and storage system, and ERP functional applications), and each module consists of several product components matching functional elements. For example, in the module of ERP functional application, procurement and manufacturing correspondently take responsibilities of managing procurement transactions with suppliers and managing the manufacturing processes and activities.

In order to efficiently and effectively install ERP system in a customer company, services provided by the IT provider plays a critical role of its success. Hence, the ERP project in this case is designed with two subsystem modules, not only product subsystem, but also service subsystem. Whilst, the modular service subsystem is decomposed into three service modules, including management consulting service module, implementation service module, and support service module. And each service module without exception is decomposed into several sub modules. For example, support service module includes sub modules like technical support, service updating, critical path fixing (See Figure 3).

In terms of the ERP implementation services, it can be viewed through both static and dynamic angles. From a static view, implementation service modules can be decomposed into a combination of service components covering different functional elements, resources allocations, and service modes. While from a dynamic view, implementation service modules can be regarded as different process modules consisting of different service activities to complete the ERP implementation. The service module is generally including on-site or off-site process modules such as project scope, blueprint design, system building, switch

Figure 3. A framework of a modular ERP product service system

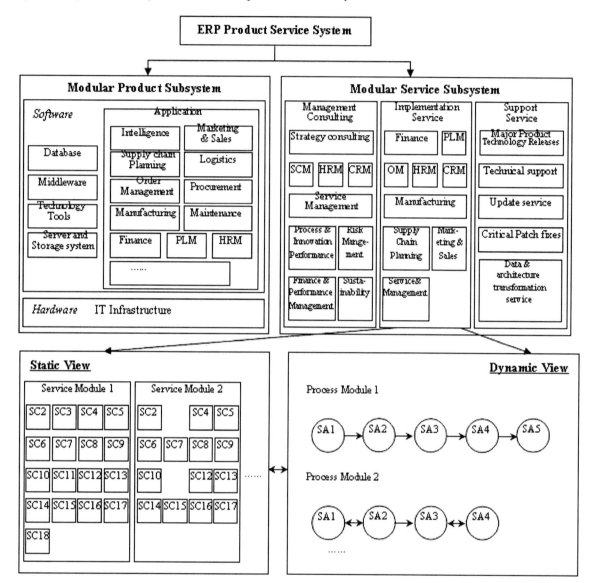

preparation, system switch and continuous support (see Table 1).

Table 1 shows that the ERP implementation service module is decomposed into 18 service components with a static view, and these modules are organized into six stages including project scope, blueprint design, system building, switch preparation, system switch, and continuous support. Each stage consists of a set of different service activities to completely perform a spe-

cific process module in the entire ERP implementation service module.

Breaking down the ERP implementation service process into independent sub-process modules provides the ERP suppliers with a kind of flexibility that effectively customizing service to meet customer's individual requirements and also efficiently controlling the potential implementation service risks.

Table 1. ERP implementation service offering

Implementation Service Module		Project Scope			Blueprint Design				System Building		Switch Preparation			System Switch				Continuous Support			
		SC_1	SC_2	SC_3	SC_4	SC_5	SC_6	SC_7	SC_8	SC_9	SC_{10}	SC_{11}	SC_{12}	SC_{13}	SC_{14}	SC_{15}	SC_{16}	SC_{17}	SC_{18}
1. on-site	1) Consultant				√	√				√			√		√		√	√	
	2) Advanced					√	√		√		√			√		√	√		√
2. off-site	1) Consultant																√		
	2) Advanced			√				√								√			

281

ERP IMPLEMENTATION SERVICE SUPPLY CHAIN

Due to the integration scope of ERP system has been extend from internal to external resources, the ERP implementation services are not limited in a company view but a supply chain view. Furthermore, the ERP software providers cannot complete the ERP project for a big-size company by themselves; that's the reason why they sometimes outsource some of the consulting and implementation services to third party. In order to enhance the delivery of the modular implementation services, an ERP implementation service supply chain is developed (see Figure 4) to support the modular ERP product service system presented in Figure 4. This framework of service supply chain is followed the conceptual service supply chain structure proposed by Lin et al., (2010) and combined with the modular PSS proposed above.

The service supply chain for ERP implementation is a network of ERP suppliers, IT service providers, hardware suppliers, customers and other service partners that transferring resources into services delivered to and received by the customers. The key feature of the service supply chain is customer involvement into the value creation process. In this context, ERP software, its related hardware, and the implementation services are delivered to the customers. Meanwhile, the customer is getting involved into par-

Figure 4. A framework of the ERP implementation service supply chain

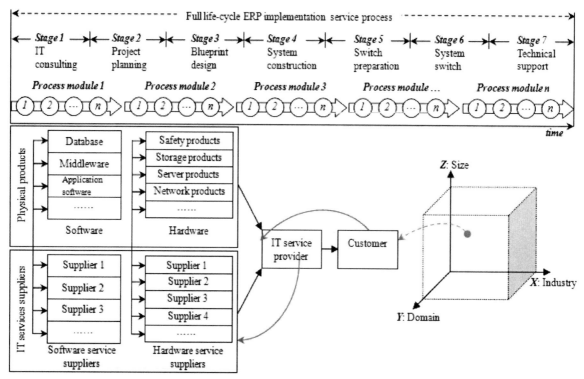

X: Industry — including industries like high technology, professional service, industrial manufacturing, travel and transportation, wholesale distribution.

Y: Domain — covering functions such as manufacturing management, finance management, supply chain management, retail management, human resource management, customer relationship management, business intelligence, PLM, group management

Z: Size — including large enterprise, large-medium enterprise, small-medium enterprise.

ticularly the implementation process. Also the IT service provider is getting involved into the operational process of suppliers who providing IT services and physical products to him.

The customer is severed with customized ERP package (*Y*: Domain) based on its background of industry (*X*: Industry) and enterprise size (*Z*: Size). Such categorization is linked with the modular logic applied in ERP software design and its implementation service design.

In order to provide suitable and effective services to end-customers, the ERP supplier needs to coordinate a series of activities along the service supply chain. These activities could be categorized into four key groups: solutions provision, solutions distribution, service integration, and customer interface. (1) Solution provision covers a set of activities related to the ERP product subsystem. Specifically, these activities include the creation, development, and upgrade of the ERP contents and applications; (2) Solution distribution describes the activities of delivering contents and applications to the end-users; (3) Service integration activities are focused on integrating the services into customer's operations. For example, management consulting service module focuses on developing appropriate processes to integrate the outsourced applications and data into the existing processes; implementation service module ensures leveraging the legacy data, systems, and processes; technical support service module ensures integrating application with the existing IT infrastructure in the end-user companies; (4) Customer interface activities mainly focus on managing the customer relationship during the ERP implementation.

ERP supplier needs to integrate above four groups of service activities to meet customer expectations and satisfy customer requirements, and to efficiently configure the service supply chain considering possible uncertainties. For one thing, ERP supplier will choose qualified service suppliers based on the evaluation of their service capabilities, industry reputation, professional features, implementation characteristic, and price factors. For another, ERP supplier will configure an appropriate service supply chain with suitable service suppliers and partners to perform right service modules.

FUTURE RESEARCH DIRECTIONS

The conceptual frameworks of modular ERP product service system and ERP implementation service supply chain are developed in this chapter. The framework combines the PSS conception and modular logic aims to improve the success and service quality of the ERP implementation. The results provide guidance to managers to ERP implementation services and its supply chain.

With the modular ERP product service system, it is possible to mix different modules to satisfy customers' individual requirement. Hence, it is necessary to further the research on how to define and standardize the service module and process module. Modular organization structure of the company (ERP supplier) needs to be studied to enhance the overall strategic flexibility of the modular ERP product service system. Appropriate tools and approaches should be developed to support the optimization of the process modules. Furthermore, the interface between service module and product module, between different service/process modules should be further studied and defined to increase the efficiency and effectiveness of the ERP implementation. Moreover, customer involvement is one of the key features of service supply chain, the interface between customer and service provider should be further explored to improve the customer experience and service quality.

The results in this chapter are mainly derived from study in the IT industry, it could be extended the research to touch other industries to validate and verify these results, and best practices should be summarized to support its practical application.

CONCLUSION

This chapter proposes a conceptual framework for modular ERP product service system, which explores two views to analyze the modular ERP implementation services. One is from functional static view, the other from dynamic process perspective. A framework of ERP implementation service supply chain is developed based on the conceptual framework of service supply chain (Lin et al., 2010).

The research results will contribute to both academic and practice. It is an extension of the research on PSS and service supply chain, and in particular it is an application of the modular logic in a specific field, ERP implementation service. The results also provide possible directions to managers on how to efficiently and effectively design and deliver ERP implementation services.

REFERENCES

Akkermans, H., & Vos, B. (2003). Amplification in service supply chains: An exploratory case study from the telecom industry. *Production and Operations Management*, *12*(2), 204–223. doi:10.1111/j.1937-5956.2003.tb00501.x

Al-Mashari, M., Al-Mudimigh, A., & Zairi, M. (2003). Enterprise resource planning: A taxonomy of critical factors. *European Journal of Operational Research*, *146*(2), 352–364. doi:10.1016/S0377-2217(02)00554-4

Arlbjørn, J. S., Freytag, P. V., & de Haas, H. (2011). Service supply chain management: A survey of lean application in the municipal sector. *International Journal of Physical Distribution & Logistics Management*, *41*(3), 277–295. doi:10.1108/09600031111123796

Axelsson, B., & Wynstra, F. (2002). *Buying business services*. New York, NY: Wiley.

Baines, T., Lightfoot, H., Evans, S., Neely, A., Greenough, R., & Peppard, J. … Michele, P. (2007). State-of-the-art in product-service systems. *Proceedings of the Institution of Mechanical Engineers - Part B - Engineering Manufacture*, *221*, 1-10.

Baldwin, C. Y., & Clark, K. B. (1997). Managing in an age of modularity. *Harvard Business Review*, *75*(5), 84–93.

Baltacioglu, T., Ada, E., Kaplan, M. D., Yurt, O., & Kaplan, Y. C. (2007). A new framework for service supply chains. *Service Industries Journal*, *27*(2), 105–124. doi:10.1080/02642060601122629

Cook, J. S., DeBree, K., & Feroleto, A. (2001). From raw materials to customers: Supply chain management in the service industry. *SAM Advanced Management Journal*, *66*(4), 14–21.

Cusumano, M. A., & Nobeoka, K. (1992). Strategy, structure and performance in product development: Observations from the auto industry. *Research Policy*, *21*(3), 265–293. doi:10.1016/0048-7333(92)90020-5

Dezdar, S., & Ainin, S. (2011). Examining ERP implementation success from a project environment perspective. *Business Process Management Journal*, *17*(6), 919–939. doi:10.1108/14637151111182693

Doran, D. (2004). Rethinking the supply chain: An automotive perspective. *International Journal of Supply Chain Management*, *9*(1), 102–109. doi:10.1108/13598540410517610

Doran, D., & Giannakis, M. (2011). An examination of a modular supply chain: A construction sector perspective. *Supply Chain Management: An International Journal*, *16*(4), 260–270. doi:10.1108/13598541111139071

Doran, D., Hill, A., Hwang, K. S., & Jacob, G. (2007). Supply chain modularisation: Cases from the French automobile industry. *International Journal of Production Economics, 106*(1), 2–11. doi:10.1016/j.ijpe.2006.04.006

Ellram, L. M., Tate, W. L., & Billington, C. (2004). Understanding and managing the services supply chain. *Journal of Supply Chain Management, 40*(4), 17–32. doi:10.1111/j.1745-493X.2004.tb00176.x

Finney, S., & Corbett, M. (2007). ERP implementation: A compilation and analysis of critical success factors. *Business Process Management Journal, 13*(3), 329–347. doi:10.1108/14637150710752272

Forslund, H., & Jonsson, P. (2010). Selection, implementation and use of ERP systems for supply chain performance management. *Industrial Management & Data Systems, 110*(8), 1159–1175. doi:10.1108/02635571011077816

Gargeya, V. B., & Brady, C. (2005). Success and failure factors of adopting SAP in ERP system implementation. *Business Process Management Journal, 11*(5), 501–516. doi:10.1108/14637150510619858

Giannakis, M. (2011). Management of service supply chains with a service-oriented reference model: The case of management consulting. *Supply Chain Management: An International Journal, 16*(5), 346–361. doi:10.1108/13598541111155857

Griswold, W. G., Shonle, M., Sullivan, K., Song, Y., Tewari, N., Cai, Y., & Rajan, H. (2006). Modular software design with crosscutting interfaces. *IEEE Software, 23*(1), 51–60. doi:10.1109/MS.2006.24

Hong, K., & Kim, Y. (2002). The critical success factors for ERP implementation: An organizational fit perspective. *Information & Management, 40*, 25–40. doi:10.1016/S0378-7206(01)00134-3

Kim, S. H., Cohen, M. A., & Netessine, S. (2007). Performance contracting in after-sales service supply chains. *Management Science, 53*(12), 1843–1858. doi:10.1287/mnsc.1070.0741

Kim, Y., Lee, Z., & Gosain, S. (2005). Impediments to successful ERP implementation process. *Business Process Management Journal, 11*(2), 158–170. doi:10.1108/14637150510591156

Kratochvil, M., & Carson, C. (2005). *Growing modular: Mass customization of complex products, services and software.* Berlin, Germany: Springer.

Langlois, R. N., & Robertson, P. L. (1992). Networks and innovation in a modular system: Lessons from the microcomputer and stereo component industries. *Research Policy, 21*(4), 297–313. doi:10.1016/0048-7333(92)90030-8

Lau, A. K. W., Yam, R. C. M., & Tang, E. P. Y. (2010). Supply chain integration and product modularity: An empirical study of product performance for selected Hong Kong manufacturing industries. *International Journal of Operations & Production Management, 30*(1), 20–56. doi:10.1108/01443571011012361

Lillrank, P., Groop, J., & Venesmaa, J. (2011). Processes, episodes and events in health service supply chains. *Supply Chain Management: An International Journal, 16*(3), 194–201. doi:10.1108/13598541111127182

Lin, Y., & Pekkarinen, S. (2011). QDF-based modular logistics service design. *Journal of Business and Industrial Marketing, 26*(5), 344–356. doi:10.1108/08858621111144406

Lin, Y., Shi, Y. J., & Zhou, L. (2010). Service supply chain: Nature, evolution, and operational implications. *Advances in Intelligent and Soft Computing, Springer-Verlag, 66*, 1189–1204. doi:10.1007/978-3-642-10430-5_91

Maditinos, D., Chatzoudes, D., & Tsairidis, C. (2011). Factors affecting ERP system implementation effectiveness. *Journal of Enterprise Information Management, 25*(1), 60–78. doi:10.1108/17410391211192161

Markus, M. L., & Tanis, C. (2000). The enterprise system experience - From adoption to success. In Zmud, R. W. (Ed.), *Framing the Domains of IT Management: Projecting the Future through the Past* (pp. 173–208). Cincinnati, OH: Pinnaflex Educational Resources.

Marnewick, C., & Labuschagne, L. (2005). A conceptual model for enterprise resource planning (ERP). *Information Management & Computer Security, 13*(2), 144–155. doi:10.1108/09685220510589325

Michaelides, R., & Kehoe, D. (2006). Service supply chain management in e-government operations. *International Journal of Technology Management, 7*(3), 237–252.

Mikkola, J. H. (2001). Portfolio management of R&D projects: Implications for innovation management. *Technovation, 21*(7), 423–435. doi:10.1016/S0166-4972(00)00062-6

Mikkola, J. H. (2006). Capturing the degree of modularity embedded in product architectures. *Journal of Product Innovation Management, 23*(2), 128–146. doi:10.1111/j.1540-5885.2006.00188.x

Miozzo, M., & Grimshaw, D. (2005). Modularity and innovation in knowledge-intensive business services: IT outsourcing in Germany and the UK. *Research Policy, 34*, 1419–1439. doi:10.1016/j.respol.2005.06.005

Muthusamy, S. K., Palanisamy, R., & MacDonald, J. (2005). Developing knowledge management systems for ERP implementation: A case study from service sector. *Journal of Service Research*, 65–92.

Niranjan, T. T., & Weaver, M. (2011). A unifying view of goods and services supply chain management. *Service Industries Journal, 31*(14), 2391–2410. doi:10.1080/02642069.2010.504821

Pekkarinen, S., & Ulkuniemi, P. (2008). Modularity in developing business services by platform approach. *The International Journal of Logistics Management, 19*(1), 84–103. doi:10.1108/09574090810872613

Poole, K. (2003). Seizing the potential of the service supply chain. *Supply Chain Management Review, 7*(4), 54–61.

Ro, Y. K., Liker, J. K., & Fixson, S. K. (2007). Modularity as a strategy for supply chain coordination: The case of U.S. auto. *IEEE Transactions on Engineering Management, 54*(1), 172–189. doi:10.1109/TEM.2006.889075

Ruey-Shun Chen, R. S., Sun, C. M., Helms, M. M., & Jih, W. J. (2008). Role negotiation and interaction: An exploratory case study of the impact of management consultants on ERP system implementation in SMEs in Taiwan. *Information Systems Management, 25*(2), 159–173. doi:10.1080/10580530801941371

Saccani, N., Johansson, P., & Perona, M. (2007). Configuring the after-sales service supply chain: A multiple case study. *International Journal of Production Economics, 110*(1-2), 52–69. doi:10.1016/j.ijpe.2007.02.009

Salvador, F. (2007). Toward a product system modularity construct: literature review and reconceptualization. *IEEE Transactions on Engineering Management, 54*(2), 219–240. doi:10.1109/TEM.2007.893996

Schilling, M. A. (2000). Toward a general modular systems theory and its application to interfirm product modularity. *Academy of Management Review, 25*(2), 312–334.

Sengupta, H., Heiser, R., & Cook, S. (2006). Manufacturing and service supply chain performance: A comparative analysis. *Journal of Supply Chain Management, 42*(4), 4–15. doi:10.1111/j.1745-493X.2006.00018.x

Singla, A. R., & Goyal, D. P. (2006). Managing risk factors in ERP implementation and design: An empirical investigation of the Indian industry. *Journal of Advances in Management Research, 3*(1), 59–67. doi:10.1108/97279810680001239

Somers, T., & Nelson, K. (2004). A taxonomy of players and activities across the ERP project life cycle. *Information & Management, 41*, 257–278. doi:10.1016/S0378-7206(03)00023-5

Starr, M. K. (1965). Modular production-a new concept. *Harvard Business Review, 43*(6), 131–142.

Starr, M. K. (2010). Modular production - A 45-year-old concept. *International Journal of Operations & Production Management, 30*(1), 7–19. doi:10.1108/01443571011012352

Takeishi, A., & Fujimoto, T. (2003). Modularization in the car industry. *The Business of Systems Integration, 1*, 254–279. doi:10.1093/0199263221.003.0013

Ulrich, K. (1995). The role of product architecture in the manufacturing firm. *Research Policy, 24*, 419–440. doi:10.1016/0048-7333(94)00775-3

Vandermerwe, S., & Rada, J. (1988). Servitization of business: Adding value by adding services. *European Management Journal, 6*(4), 314–324. doi:10.1016/0263-2373(88)90033-3

Vargo, S. L., & Lusch, R. F. (2008). Service-dominant logic: Continuing the evolution. *Journal of the Academy of Marketing Science, 36*(1), 1–10. doi:10.1007/s11747-007-0069-6

Véronneau, S., & Roy, J. (2009a). Global service supply chains: An empirical study of current practices and challenges of a cruise line corporation. *Tourism Management, 30*(1), 128–139. doi:10.1016/j.tourman.2008.05.008

Véronneau, S., & Roy, J. (2009b). RFID benefits, costs, and possibilities: The economical analysis of RFID deployment in a cruise corporation global service supply chain. *International Journal of Production Economics, 122*(2), 692–702. doi:10.1016/j.ijpe.2009.06.038

Voss, C., & Hsuan, J. (2009). Service architecture and modularity. *Decision Science Journal, 40*(4), 541–569. doi:10.1111/j.1540-5915.2009.00241.x

Willis, T., & Willis-Brown, A. (2002). Extending the value of ERP. *Industrial Management & Data Systems, 102*(1), 35–38. doi:10.1108/02635570210414640

Yang, C., & Su, Y. F. (2009). The relationship between benefits of ERP systems implementation and its impacts on firm performance of SCM. *Journal of Enterprise Information Management, 22*(6), 722–752. doi:10.1108/17410390910999602

Zsidisin, G. A., Jun, M. J., & Adams, L. L. (2000). The relationship between information technology and service quality in the dual-direction supply chain: A case study approach. *International Journal of Service Industry Management, 11*(4), 312–328. doi:10.1108/09564230010355359

ADDITIONAL READING

Baines, T., Lightfoot, H., Benedettini, O., & Kay, J. M. (2009). The servitization of manufacturing: A review of literature and reflection on future challenges. *Journal of Manufacturing Technology Management*, *20*(5), 547–567. doi:10.1108/17410380910960984

Caridi, M., Pero, M., & Sianesi, A. (2012). Linking product modularity and innovativeness to supply chain management in the Italian furniture industry. *International Journal of Production Economics*, *136*(1), 207–217. doi:10.1016/j.ijpe.2011.11.012

Forslund, H. (2010). ERP systems' capabilities for supply chain performance management. *Industrial Management & Data Systems*, *110*(3), 351–367. doi:10.1108/02635571011030024

Lockett, H., Johnson, M., Evans, S., & Bastl, M. (2011). Product service systems and supply network relationships: An exploratory case study. *Journal of Manufacturing Technology Management*, *22*(3), 293–313. doi:10.1108/17410381111112684

Pil, F. K., & Cohen, S. K. (2004). Modularity: Implications for imitation, innovation, and sustained advantage. *Academy of Management Review*, *31*, 995–1011. doi:10.5465/AMR.2006.22528166

Schilling, M. A. (2000). Toward a general modular systems theory and its application to inter-firm product modularity. *Academy of Management Review*, *25*(2), 312–334.

KEY TERMS AND DEFINITIONS

Enterprise Resource Planning (ERP): The ability to deliver an integrated suite of business applications. ERP tools share a common process and data model, covering broad and deep operational end-to-end processes, such as those found in finance, HR, distribution, manufacturing, service and the supply chain. ERP applications automate and support a range of administrative and operational business processes across multiple industries, including line of business, customer facing, administrative, and the asset management aspects of an enterprise. However, ERP deployments tend to come at a significant price, and the business benefits are difficult to justify and understand (Gartner Group).

Modularity: A general systems concept, typically defined as a continuum describing the degree to which a system's components may be separated and recombined. It refers to both the tightness of coupling between components, and the degree to which the "rules" of the system architecture enable (or prohibit) the mixing and matching of components (Schilling, 2000).

Product Service-System (PSS): An integrated combination of products and services. This western concept embraces a service-led competitive strategy, environmental sustainability, and the basis to differentiate from competitors who simply offer lower priced products (Baines, et al., 2007).

Service Supply Chain: The network of suppliers, service providers, consumers and other supporting units that performs the functions of transaction of resources required to produce services; transformation of these resources into supporting and core services; and the delivery of these services to customers (Baltacioglu, et al., 2007).

Compilation of References

Abdi, F., Shavarini, S. K., & Hoseini, S. M. S. (2006). Glean lean: How to use lean approach in service industries? *Journal of Service Research, 6*, 191–206. Retrieved from http://web.ebscohost.com.ezproxy.liv.ac.uk/ehost/pdfviewer/pdfviewer?hid=18&sid=855e0e21-c986-4197-95a2-32f406d7d4a7%40sessionmgr11&vid=2

Abdullah, D., Radzi, S. M., Jamaluddin, M. R., & Patah, M. O. R. A. (2010). Hotel web site evaluation and business travelers' preferences. In *Proceedings of the ICETC 2010 - 2010 2ⁿᵈ International Conference on Education Technology and Computer*, (pp. 3485-3488). ICETC.

Aberdeen Group. (2008). *The changing role of logistics service providers in today's supply chain*. Retrieved from http://www.aberdden.com

Abood, D., Murdoch, R., N'Diaye, S., Albano, D., Kofmehl, A., & Tung, T. … Whitney, J. (2010). Cloud computing and sustainability: The environmental benefits of moving to the cloud. *Accenture*. Retrieved September 14, 2012, from http://www.accenture.com/us-en/pages/index.aspx

Adams, N. (2009). Perspectives on data mining. *International Journal of Market Research, 52*(1), 11–19. doi:10.2501/S147078530120103X

Ahronovitz, M., et al. (2010). *Cloud computing use cases white paper, version 4.0*. Washington, DC: National Institute of Standards and Technology.

AIM. (2012). *RFID cases*. Retrieved July 02, from http://www.aimglobal.org/casestudies/RFID.asp

Akkermans, H., & Vos, B. (2003). Amplification in service supply chains: An exploratory case study from the telecom industry. *Production and Operations Management, 12*(2), 204–223. doi:10.1111/j.1937-5956.2003.tb00501.x

Al-Mamari, S., & Nunes, M. (2008). Readiness for CRM use in developing countries: Case of Oman. In *Proceedings of the IADIS International Conference - Information Systems*, (pp. 1-12). Algarve, Portugal: IADIS.

Al-Mashari, M., Al-Mudimigh, A., & Zairi, M. (2003). Enterprise resource planning: A taxonomy of critical factors. *European Journal of Operational Research, 146*(2), 352–364. doi:10.1016/S0377-2217(02)00554-4

Al-Mashari, M., & Zairi, M. (2000). Supply-chain re-engineering using enterprise resource planning (ERP) systems: An analysis of a SAP R/3 implementation case. *International Journal of Physical Distribution & Logistics Management, 30*(3-4), 296–313. doi:10.1108/09600030010326064

Amoako-Gyampah, K., & Salam, A. F. (2004). An extension of the technology acceptance model in an ERP implementation environment. *Information & Management, 41*(6), 731–745. doi:10.1016/j.im.2003.08.010

Anderton, A. (2008). *Economics AQA* (5th ed.). Causeway Press.

Angeles, R. (2005). RFID technologies: Supply chain applications and implementation issues. *Information Systems Management, 22*(1), 51–65. doi:10.1201/1078/44912.22.1.20051201/85739.7

Arlbjørn, J. S., Freytag, P. V., & de Haas, H. (2011). Service supply chain management: A survey of lean application in the municipal sector. *International Journal of Physical Distribution & Logistics Management, 4*(3), 277–295. Retrieved from http://www.emeraldinsight.com.ezproxy.liv.ac.uk/journals.htm?issn=0960-0035&volume=41&issue=3&articleid=1917332&show=pdfdoi:10.1108/09600031111123796

Armbrust, M., Fox, A., Griffith, R., Joseph, A., Katz, R., & Konwinski, A. (2010). A view of cloud computing. *Communications of the ACM, 53*(4), 50–58. doi:10.1145/1721654.1721672

Armstrong, C. J., Edwards, L., & Lonsdale, R. (2002). Virtually there? E-books in UK academic libraries. *Program: Electronic Library & Information Systems, 36*(4), 216–227. doi:10.1108/00330330210447181

Arsanjan, A. (2004). Service-oriented modeling and architecture: How to identify, specify, and realize services for your SOA. *IBM Developer Works.* Retrieved from http://www.ibm.com/developerworks/library/ws-soa-design1/

Arvanitoyannis, I. S., Choreftaki, S., & Tserkezou, P. (2005). An update of EU legislation (directives and regulations) on food-related issues (safety, hygiene, packaging, technology, GMOs, additives, radiation, labelling): Presentation and comments. *International Journal of Food Science & Technology, 40*(10), 1021–1112. doi:10.1111/j.1365-2621.2005.01113.x

Ash, C. G., & Burn, J. M. (2001). E-ERP: A comprehensive approach to e-business. In Khosrow-Pour, M. (Ed.), *Managing Information Technology in a Global Economy.* Hershey, PA: IGI Global.

Ash, C., & Burn, J. M. (2001). Managing information technology in a global economy. In Khosrow-Pour, M. (Ed.), *Information Resources Management Association.* Hershey, PA: IGI Global.

Atallah, M. J., Elmongui, H. G., Deshpande, V., & Schwarz, L. B. (2003). Secure supply-chain protocols. In *Proceedings of IEEE International Conference on E-Commerce,* (pp. 293–302). Newport Beach, CA: IEEE Press.

Athanasaki, M. T., & Stefanou, C. J. (2012). Critical success factors for implementing integrated ERP/CRM systems. In *Proceedings of the International Conference on Contemporary Marketing Issues,* (pp. 357-364). Thessaloniki, Greece: IEEE.

Attaran, M. (2012). Critical success factors and challenges of implementing RFID in supply chain management. *Journal of Supply Chain and Operations Management, 10*(1), 144–167.

Avery, S. (2000). E-procurement: A wealth of information for buyers. *Purchasing, 129*(5), 111.

Axelsson, B., & Wynstra, F. (2002). *Buying business services.* New York, NY: Wiley.

Bade, D., Mueller, J., & Youd, B. (1999). *Technology in the next level of supply chain outsourcing: Leveraging the capabilities of fourth party logistics.* Retrieved from http://bade.ascet.com

Bailey, K., & Francis, M. (2008). Managing information flows for improved value chain performance. *International Journal of Production Economics, 111*(1), 2–12. doi:10.1016/j.ijpe.2006.11.017

Baines, T., Lightfoot, H., Evans, S., Neely, A., Greenough, R., & Peppard, J. … Michele, P. (2007). State-of-the-art in product-service systems. *Proceedings of the Institution of Mechanical Engineers - Part B - Engineering Manufacture, 221,* 1-10.

Baldwin, C. Y., & Clark, K. B. (1997). Managing in an age of modularity. *Harvard Business Review, 75*(5), 84–93.

Bales, R. R., Maull, R. S., & Radnor, Z. (2004). The development of supply chain management within the aerospace manufacturing sector. *Supply Chain Management: An International Journal, 9*(3), 250–255. doi:10.1108/13598540410544944

Baltacioglu, T., Ada, E., Kaplan, M. D., Yurt, O., & Kaplan, Y. C. (2007). A new framework for service supply chains. *Service Industries Journal, 27*(2), 105–124. doi:10.1080/02642060601122629

Banou, C. (2006). Money and taste: New roles for the Greek publishers in a changing era. *The International Journal of the Book, 3*(2), 39–46.

Banou, G. C., & Kostagiolas, A. P. (2007). Managing expectations for open access in Greece: Perceptions from the publishers and academic libraries. *International Journal of the Book, 3*(2), 39–46.

Banou, G. C., & Phillips, A. (2008). The Greek publishing industry and professional development. *Publishing Research Quarterly, 24*(2), 98–110. doi:10.1007/s12109-008-9070-2

Basnet, C., & Leung, J. M. Y. (2005). Inventory lot-sizing with supplier selection. *Computers & Operations Research, 32,* 1–14. doi:10.1016/S0305-0548(03)00199-0

Bayles, D. (2002). *E-logistics & e-fulfillment: Beyond the "buy" button*. Paper presented at UNCTAD Workshop 2002. Curaçao, Curaçao.

Beamon, B. M., & Ware, T. M. (1998). A process quality model for the analysis, improvement and control of supply chain systems. *International Journal of Physical Distribution & Logistics Management, 28*(9/10), 704–715. doi:10.1108/09600039810248127

Bechtel, C., & Jayaram, J. (1997). Supply chain management: A strategic perspective. *International Journal of Logistics Management, 8*(1), 15–34. doi:10.1108/09574099710805565

Benton, W. C., & Maloni, M. (2005). The influence of power driven buyer seller relationships on supply chain satisfaction. *Journal of Operations Management, 23*(1), 1–22. doi:10.1016/j.jom.2004.09.002

Berger, P. D., & Zeng, A. Z. (2006). Single versus multiple sourcing in the presence of risks. *The Journal of the Operational Research Society, 57*(3), 250–261. doi:10.1057/palgrave.jors.2601982

Berman, S., Kesterson, L., Marshall, A., & Srivathsa, R. (2012). The power of cloud - Driving business model innovation. *IBM Institute for Business Value*. Retrieved September 14, 2012, from http://www.ibm.com/us/en/

Bertolini, M., Bevilacqua, M., & Massini, R. (2006). FMECA approach to product traceability in the food industry. *Food Control, 17*(2), 137–145. doi:10.1016/j.foodcont.2004.09.013

Bevilacqua, M., Ciarapica, F., & Giacchetta, G. (2008). Business process reengineering of a supply chain and a traceability system: A case study. *Journal of Food Engineering, 93*, 13–22. doi:10.1016/j.jfoodeng.2008.12.020

Bewsell, G., Jamieson, R., Gardiner, A., & Bunker, D. (2005). An investigation of dispute resolution mechanisms on power and trust: A domain study of online trust in e-auctions. *Lecture Notes in Computer Science, 3592*, 288–298. doi:10.1007/11537878_29

Bhasin, S. (2008). Lean and performance measurement. *Journal of Manufacturing Technology Management, 19*(5), 670–684. Retrieved from http://www.emeraldinsight.com.ezproxy.liv.ac.uk/journals.htm?issn=1741-038X&volume=19&issue=5&articleid=1728408&show=pdf doi:10.1108/17410380810877311

Bhasin, S., & Burcher, P. (2006). Lean viewed as a philosophy. *Journal of Manufacturing Technology Management, 17*(1), 56–72. Retrieved from http://www.emeraldinsight.com.ezproxy.liv.ac.uk/journals.htm?issn=1741-038X&volume=17&issue=1&articleid=1532807&show=pdf doi:10.1108/17410380610639506

Bichler, M. (2000). A roadmap to auction-based negotiation protocols for electronic commerce. In *Proceedings of the 33rd Hawaii International Conference on System Sciences*, (pp. 1857-1866). Hawaii, HI: IEEE.

Bichler, M., & Kalagnanam, J. (2005). Configurable offers and winner determination in multi-attribute auctions. *European Journal of Operational Research, 160*(2), 380–394. doi:10.1016/j.ejor.2003.07.014

Bichler, M., Kersten, G., & Strecker, S. (2003). Towards a structured design of electronic negotiations. *Group Decision and Negotiation, 12*(4), 311–335. doi:10.1023/A:1024867820235

Bieberstein, N., Jones, K., Laird, R. G., & Mitra, T. (2008). *Executing SOA: A methodology for service modeling and design*. New York, NY: IBM Press.

Bienstock, C., Mentzer, J., & Bird, M. (1997). Measuring physical distribution service quality. *Journal of the Academy of Marketing Science, 25*, 31–44. doi:10.1007/BF02894507

Blackhurst, J. V., Scheibe, K. P., & Johnson, D. J. (2008). Supplier risk assessment and monitoring for the automotive industry. *International Journal of Physical Distribution & Logistics Management, 38*(2), 143–165. doi:10.1108/09600030810861215

Blanchard, D. (2007). *Supply chain management - Best practices*. Hoboken, NJ: Wiley & Sons Inc.

Bodea, C., & Mogos, R. (2007). An electronic market space architecture based on intelligent agents and data mining technologies. *Informatica Economica Journal, 11*(4), 115–118.

Bodkin, C. D., & Perry, M. (2004). Goods retailers and service providers: Comparative analysis of web site marketing communications. *Journal of Retailing and Consumer Services, 11*(1), 19–29. doi:10.1016/S0969-6989(02)00058-9

Boger, S., Hobbs, J. E., & Kerr, W. A. (2001). Supply chain relationships in the Polish pork sector. *Supply Chain Management: An International Journal, 6*(2), 74–82. doi:10.1108/13598540110387573

Booth, D., & Canyang, L. (2007). *Web services description language (WSDL) version 2.0 part 0: Primer.* Retrieved from http://www.w3.org/TR/2007/REC-wsdl20-primer-20070626

Bose, I., Pal, R., & Ye, A. (2008). ERP and SCM systems integration: The case of a valve manufacturer in China. *Information & Management, 45*(4), 233–241. doi:10.1016/j.im.2008.02.006

Boss, G., Malladi, P., Quan, D., Legregni, L., & Hall, H. (2007). *Cloud computing*. IBM White Paper. New York, NY: IBM.

Bowen, D. E., & Youngdahl, W. E. (1998). Lean service: In defense of a production-line approach. *International Journal of Service Industry Management, 9*(3), 207–225. Retrieved from http://www.emeraldinsight.com.ezproxy.liv.ac.uk/Insight/viewPDF.jsp?contentType=Article&Filename=html/Output/Published/EmeraldFullTextArticle/Pdf/0850090301.pdfdoi:10.1108/09564239810223510

Bowersox, D. J. (1990). The strategic benefits of logistics alliances. *Harvard Business Review, 68*(4), 36–43.

Bradford, M., Mayfield, T., & Toney, C. (2001). Does ERP fit in a lean world? *Strategic Finance, 82*(11), 28-34. Retrieved from http://ehis.ebscohost.com.ezproxy.liv.ac.uk/eds/pdfviewer/pdfviewer?vid=10&hid=6&sid=6cb9fd95-fa0b-417e-9ac6-0034b265e2c9%40sessionmgr11

Brimacombe, A., Cotter, B. C., & Timmermans, K. (2011). *Supplier relationships: Cracking the value code.* Accenture.

Brun, A., Caniato, F., Caridi, M., Castelli, C., Miragliotta, G., & Ronchi, S. (2008). Logistics & supply chain management in luxury fashion retail: Empirical investigation of Italian firms. *International Journal of Production Economics, 114*(2), 554–570. doi:10.1016/j.ijpe.2008.02.003

Bui, Y. N. (2009). *How to write a master thesis.* London, UK: Sage Publications Ltd.

Burgess, K., Singh, P. J., & Koroglu, R. (2006). Supply chain management: A structured literature review and implications for future research. *International Journal of Operations & Production Management, 26*(7), 703–729. doi:10.1108/01443570610672202

Buyya, R., Yeo, C. S., Venugopal, S., Broberg, J., & Brandic, I. (2009). Cloud computing and emerging IT platforms: Vision, hype, and reality for delivering computing as the 5th utility. *Future Generation Computer Systems, 25*(6), 599–616. doi:10.1016/j.future.2008.12.001

Buzzell, R. D., & Ortmeyer, G. (1995). Channel partnerships streamline distribution. *Sloan Management Review, 36*(3), 83–96.

Buzzetto, M., & Sweat, G., & Elobaid. (2007). Reading in a digital age: e-Books are students ready for this learning object? *Interdisciplinary Journal of Knowledge and Learning Objects, 3*, 239–250.

Cagliano, R., Caniato, F., & Spina, G. (2004). Lean, agile and traditional supply: How do they impact manufacturing performance? *Journal of Purchasing and Supply Management, 10*(4-5), 151–164. Retrieved from http://www.sciencedirect.com.ezproxy.liv.ac.uk/science?_ob=MImg&_imagekey=B7579-4FBHW7M-1-1&_cdi=12893&_user=822084&_pii=S147840920500004X&_origin=search&_zone=rslt_list_item&_coverDate=07%2F01%2F2004&_sk=999899995&wchp=dGLzVzb-zSkWB&md5=52954d872906932ed6c3352fbcc7b261&ie=/sdarticle.pdfdoi:10.1016/j.pursup.2004.11.001

Campo, S., Rubio, N., & Jague, M. J. (2010). Information technology use and firm's perceived performance in supply chain management. *Journal of Business-To-Business Marketing, 17*(1), 336–364. doi:10.1080/10517120903574649

Candido, G., Barata, J., Colombo, A. W., & Jammes, F. (2009). SOA in reconfigurable supply chains: A research roadmap. *Engineering Applications of Artificial Intelligence, 22*, 939–949. doi:10.1016/j.engappai.2008.10.020

Carter, C. R., & Ellram, L. M. (2003). Thirty-five years of the journal of supply chain management: Where we have been and where we going? *The Journal of Supply Chain Management, 39*, 27–39. doi:10.1111/j.1745-493X.2003.tb00152.x

Carter, C. R., Kaufmann, L., Beall, S., Carter, P. L., Hendrick, T. E., & Petersen, K. J. (2004). Reverse auctions – Grounded theory from the buyer and supplier perspective. *Transportation Research Part E, Logistics and Transportation Review, 40*(3), 183–270. doi:10.1016/j.tre.2003.08.004

Cauldwell, P., Chawala, R., & Chopra, V. (2001). *Professional XML web services*. Wrox Press.

Cavinato, J. L. (1992). A total cost/value model for supply chain competitiveness. *Journal of Business Logistics, 13*(2), 285–301.

Cearley, D., & Phifer, G. (2009). Case studies in cloud computing. *Gartner*. Retrieved September 14, 2012, from http://www.gartner.com/technology/home.jsp

Chaffey, D. (2012). *E-business and e-commerce management* (3rd ed.). Upper Saddle River, NJ: Pearson Publication.

Chan, C.-K., Chow, H. K. H., Ng, A. K. S., Chan, H. C. B., & Ng, V. T. Y. (2012, March). *An RFID case study for air cargo supply chain management*. Paper presented at the International Multi-Conference of Engineers and Computer Scientists. Hong Kong, China. Retrieved from http://www.iaeng.org/publication/IMECS2012/IMECS2012_pp278-283.pdf

Chang, V. (2003). The role and effectiveness of e-learning: Key issues in an industrial context. In *Proceedings of the First International Conference in the United Nations Information Society*. Geneva, Switzerland: United Nations.

Chang, V. (2006). Web service testing and usability for mobile learning. In *Proceedings of IEEE Computer Society: The First International Conference on Mobile Communications and Learning MCL*. IEEE Press.

Chang, V. (2011). *A proposed cloud computing business framework*. Eighteen-Month Thesis Technical Report. Southampton, UK: University of Southampton.

Chang, V., David, B., Wills, G., & De Roure, D. (2010). A categorisation of cloud business models. In *Proceedings of the 10th International Symposium on Cluster, Cloud and Grid Computing*. Melbourne, Australia: IEEE.

Chang, V., Wills, G., & De Roure, D. (2010). A review of cloud business models and sustainability. In *Proceedings of IEEE Cloud 2010, the 3rd International Conference on Cloud Computing*. Miami, FL: IEEE Press.

Chang, V., Wills, G., & Walters, R. (2011). Towards business integration as a service 2.0 (BIaaS 2.0). In *Proceedings of the IEEE International Conference on e-Business Engineering, The 3rd International Workshop on Cloud Services - Platform Accelerating e-Business*. Beijing, China: IEEE Press.

Chang, V., Wills, G., De Roure, D., & Chee, C. (2010). Investigating the cloud computing business framework - Modelling and benchmarking of financial assets and job submissions in clouds. In *Proceedings of UK e-Science All Hands Meeting 2010, Research Clouds: Hype or Reality Workshop*. Cardiff, UK: IEEE.

Chang, V., De Roure, D., Wills, G., & Walters, R. (2011). Case studies and organisational sustainability modelling presented by cloud computing business framework. *International Journal of Web Services Research, 8*(3), 26–53.

Chang, V., De Roure, D., Wills, G., Walters, R., & Barry, T. (2011). Organisational sustainability modelling for return on investment: Case studies presented by a national health service (NHS) trust UK. *Journal of Computing and Information Technology, 19*(3), 1846–3908. doi:10.2498/cit.1001951

Chang, V., Li, C. S., De Roure, D., Wills, G., Walters, R., & Chee, C. (2011). The financial clouds review. *International Journal of Cloud Applications and Computing, 1*(2), 41–63. doi:10.4018/ijcac.2011040104

Chang, V., Walters, R., & Wills, G. (2012). Business integration as a service. *International Journal of Cloud Applications and Computing, 2*(1). doi:10.4018/ijcac.2012010102

Chang, V., Wills, G., Walters, R., & Currie, W. (2011). Towards a structured cloud ROI: The University of Southampton cost-saving and user satisfaction case studies. In *Sustainable Green Computing: Practices, Methodologies and Technologies*. Hershey, PA: IGI Global.

Chan, S. L. (2000). Information technology in business processes. *Business Process Management Journal, 6*(3), 224–237. Retrieved from http://www.emeraldinsight.com.ezproxy.liv.ac.uk/journals.htm?issn=1463-7154&volume=6&issue=3&articleid=843451&show=pdf&PHPSESSID=3df7d1voc136p4s47cfvd73ig-3doi:10.1108/14637150010325444

Charan, P., Shankar, R., & Baisya, R. K. (2008). Analysis of interactions among the variables of supply chain performance measurement system implementation. *Business Process Management Journal, 14*(4), 512–529. doi:10.1108/14637150810888055

Charikleia, L. (2010). *RFID in the retailing supply chain: A case study on fashion retailing industry.* (Masters Dissertation). Retrieved June 20, from https://gupea.ub.gu.se/bitstream/2077/22606/1/gupea_2077_22606_1.pdf

Chawla, V. (2007). An overview of passive RFID. *IEEE Communications Magazine, 45*(9). Retrieved from http://ieeexplore.ieee.org/xpls/abs_all.jsp?arnumber=4342873doi:10.1109/MCOM.2007.4342873

Chen, J., & Ma Yan, W. (2011). The research of supply chain information collaboration based on cloud computing. *Procedia Environmental Sciences, 10*(A), 875-880.

Chen, X. (2003). *Transportation service procurement using combinatorial auctions.* (Master Thesis). MIT. Cambridge, MA.

Chen, I. J., & Paulraj, A. (2004). Towards a theory of supply chain management: The constructs and measurements. *Journal of Operations Management, 22*(2), 119–150. doi:10.1016/j.jom.2003.12.007

Chiu, B. (2010). *Leveraging visibility technology for business applications.* Oracle White Paper. Redwood Shores, CA: Oracle Corporation.

Chopra, S., & Meindl, P. (2012). *Supply chain management.* London, UK: Pearson Education Limited.

Chow, C., & van der Stede, W. (2006). The use and usefulness of nonfinancial performance measures. *Accounting Management Quarterly, 7*(3), 1–8.

Chow, H. K. H., Choy, K. L., Lee, W. B., & Chan, F. T. S. (2007). Integration of web-based and RFID technology in visualizing logistics operations - A case study. *Supply Chain Management: An International Journal, 12*(3), 221–234. doi:10.1108/13598540710742536

Choy, K. L., Lee, W. B., & Lob, V. (2003). Design of a case based intelligent supplier relationship management system—The integration of supplier rating system and product coding system. *Expert Systems with Applications, 25*, 87–100. doi:10.1016/S0957-4174(03)00009-5

Christopher, M. (2000). The agile supply chain – Competing in volatile markets. *Industrial Marketing Management, 29*(1), 37–44. doi:10.1016/S0019-8501(99)00110-8

Christopher, M. (2005). *Logistics and supply chain management.* London, UK: Prentice Hall.

CIES. (2004). *Implementing traceability in the food supply chain committee on the guidelines for introduction of food traceability systems: Handbook for introduction of food traceability systems* (2nd ed.). Tokyo, Japan: Food Marketing Research and Information Center.

Cigolini, R., Cozzi, M. M., & Perona, A. (2004). New framework for supply chain management conceptual model and empirical test. *International Journal of Operations & Production Management, 24*(1), 7–41. doi:10.1108/01443570410510979

Co, H. C., & Barro, F. (2009). Stakeholder theory and dynamics in supply chain collaboration. *International Journal of Operations & Production Management, 29*(6), 591–611. doi:10.1108/01443570910957573

Cohen, M. A., & Kunreuther, H. (2007). Operations risk management: Overview of Paul Kleindorfer's contributions. *Production and Operations Management, 16*(5), 525–541. doi:10.1111/j.1937-5956.2007.tb00278.x

Coltoman, T., Hadh, R., & Michael, K. (2008). RFID and supply chain management: Introduction to the special issue. *Journal of Theoretical and Applied Electronic Commerce Research, 3*(1).

Consulting, W. C. L. (2006). *Global supply chain overview (consumer goods), ocean carriers.* Retrieved November 16, 2011, from http://www.wclconsulting.com

Conway, G. (2011). Introduction to cloud computing. *Innovation Value Institute.* Retrieved September 14, 2012, from http://ivi.nuim.ie/

Cook, J. S., DeBree, K., & Feroleto, A. (2001). From raw materials to customers: Supply chain management in the service industry. *SAM Advanced Management Journal, 66*(4), 14–21.

Cooper, M. C., & Ellram, L. M. (1993). Characteristics of supply chain management & the implications for purchasing & logistics strategy. *The International Journal of Logistics Management, 4*(2), 13–24. doi:10.1108/09574099310804957

Cooper, M. C., & Gardner, J. T. (1993). Building good relationships – More than just partnering or strategic alliances? *International Journal of Physical Distribution & Logistics Management, 23*(6), 14–26. doi:10.1108/09600039310044876

Cotteleer, M., & Bendoly, E. (2006). Order lead-time improvement following enterprise information technology implementation: An empirical study. *Management Information Systems Quarterly, 30*(3), 643–660.

Cox, J. (2004). E-books: Challenges and opportunities. *D-Lib Magazine, 10*(10). Retrieved from www.dlib.org/dlib/october04/cox/10cox.html

CPTTF CPMA/PMA. (2004). *Traceability best practices: Fresh produce industry (North America).* Traceability Task Force.

Cusumano, M. A., & Nobeoka, K. (1992). Strategy, structure and performance in product development: Observations from the auto industry. *Research Policy, 21*(3), 265–293. doi:10.1016/0048-7333(92)90020-5

Cybulski, J., & Lukaitis, S. (2005). The impact of communications and understanding on the strategic alignment model. In *Proceedings of the 16th Australasian Conference on Information Systems.* Sydney, Australia: IEEE.

Dack, A. (2011). Cloud computing in FedEx. *FedEx.* Retrieved from http://www.apecscmc.org/

Dadzie, K., Chelariu, C., & Winston, E. (2005). Customer service in the internet-enabled logistics supply chain: Website design antecedents and loyalty effects. *Journal of Business Logistics, 26*(1), 53–78. doi:10.1002/j.2158-1592.2005.tb00194.x

Daives, C. (2004). *Preparing for new EU traceability laws.* Supply Chain Europe.

Damgard, I., & Pedersen, M. (2008). RFID security: Trade-offs between security and efficiency. *Computer Science, 4964,* 318-334. Retrieved from http://www.bytopia.dk/blog/wp-content/uploads/2008/08/rfid.pdf

Daniel, E. M., & White, A. (2005). The future of inter-organisational system linkages: Findings of an international delphi study. *European Journal of Information Systems, 14*(2), 188–203. doi:10.1057/palgrave.ejis.3000529

De Toni, A., & Tonchia, S. (1996). Lean organization, management by process and performance measurement. *International Journal of Operations & Production Management, 16*(2), 221–236. Retrieved from http://www.emeraldinsight.com.ezproxy.liv.ac.uk/journals.htm?issn=0144-3577&volume=16&issue=2&articleid=848951&show=pdf&PHPSESSID=p4b9p490euietmkqiqgvdt5l44doi:10.1108/01443579610109947

Demirtas, E. A., & Ustun, O. (2008). An integrated multi objective decision making process for supplier selection and order allocation. *Omega: The International Journal of Management Science, 36,* 76–90. doi:10.1016/j.omega.2005.11.003

Derakhshan, R., Orlowska, M., & Li, X. (2007). RFID data management: Challenges and opportunities. In *Proceedings of the IEEE International Conference on RFID,* (pp. 26-28). IEEE Press. Retrieved from http://130.102.79.1/~xueli/IEEE-RFID-Conf-04143527.pdf

Dery, C., Grant, D., Harley, B., & Wright, C. (2006). work, organisation and enterprise resource planning systems: An alternative research agenda. *New Technology, Work and Employment, 21*(3), 199–214. doi:10.1111/j.1468-005X.2006.00175.x

Dezdar, S., & Ainin, S. (2011). Examining ERP implementation success from a project environment perspective. *Business Process Management Journal, 17*(6), 919–939. doi:10.1108/14637151111182693

Dillon, T., Wu, C., & Chang, E. (2010). Cloud computing: Issues and challenges. In *Proceedings of the 24th IEEE International Conference on Advanced Information Networking and Applications,* (pp. 27-33). IEEE Press.

Dinos, V. (2003). 3PLs and outsourcing in Greece. *Warehouse. Logistics & Transportation, 15,* 34–37.

Dong, T. Y., Zhang, L., Tong, R. F., & Dong, J. X. (2006). Production procedure control in agile supply chain management based on multiple monitoring modes. *Computer Integrated Manufacturing Systems, 12*(1), 117–126.

Doonan, J., Lanoie, P., & Laplante, B. (2005). Analysis determinants of environmental performance in the Canadian pulp and paper industry: An assessment from inside the industry. *Ecological Economics, 55*(1), 73–84. doi:10.1016/j.ecolecon.2004.10.017

Doran, D. (2004). Rethinking the supply chain: An automotive perspective. *International Journal of Supply Chain Management, 9*(1), 102–109. doi:10.1108/13598540410517610

Doran, D., & Giannakis, M. (2011). An examination of a modular supply chain: A construction sector perspective. *Supply Chain Management: An International Journal, 16*(4), 260–270. doi:10.1108/13598541111139071

Doran, D., Hill, A., Hwang, K. S., & Jacob, G. (2007). Supply chain modularisation: Cases from the French automobile industry. *International Journal of Production Economics, 106*(1), 2–11. doi:10.1016/j.ijpe.2006.04.006

Dowlatshahi, S. (2005). A strategic framework for the design and implementation of remanufacturing operations in reverse logistics. *International Journal of Production Research, 43*(16), 3455–3480. doi:10.1080/00207540500118118

Eagan, P. D., & Kaiser, D. (2002). Can environmental purchasing reduce mercury in US health care? *Environmental Health Perspectives, 110*(9), 847–851. doi:10.1289/ehp.02110847

Educause & Nacubo. (2010). *Shaping the higher education cloud.* Educause and Nacubo White Paper. Educause and Nacubo.

Edwards, P., Peters, M., & Sharman, G. (2002). The effectiveness of information systems in supporting the extended supply chain. *Journal of Business Logistics, 22*, 1–28. doi:10.1002/j.2158-1592.2001.tb00157.x

El Amrani, R., Rowe, F., & Geffroy-Maronnat, B. (2006). The effects of enterprise resource planning implementation strategy on cross-functionality. *Information Systems Journal, 16*(1), 79–104. doi:10.1111/j.1365-2575.2006.00206.x

Ellinger, A. E., Lynch, D. F., Andzulis, J. K., & Smith, R. J. (2003). B-to-B e-commerce: A content analytical assessment of motor carrier websites. *Journal of Business Logistics, 24*(1), 119–220. doi:10.1002/j.2158-1592.2003.tb00037.x

Ellram, L. M., & Edis, O. R. V. (1996, September). A case study of successful partnering implementation. *International Journal of Purchasing & Materials Management*, 20-38.

Ellram, L. M., Tate, W. L., & Billington, C. (2004). Understanding and managing the services supply chain. *Journal of Supply Chain Management, 40*(4), 17–32. doi:10.1111/j.1745-493X.2004.tb00176.x

Emiliani, M. L. (2000). Insight from industry: Business-to-business online reverse auctions: Key issues for purchasing process improvement. *Supply Chain Management: An International Journal, 5*(4), 176–186. doi:10.1108/13598540010347299

Emiliani, M. L., & Stec, D. J. (2005). Wood pallet suppliers' reaction to online reverse auctions. *Supply Chain Management: An International Journal, 10*(4), 278–288. doi:10.1108/13598540510612758

Emiliani, M., & Stec, D. (2004). Aerospace parts supplier's reaction to online reverse auctions. *Supply Chain Management, 9*(2), 139–153. doi:10.1108/13598540410527042

Ericsson, D. (2011). *Demand chain management – The evolution.* Retrieved from http://www.orssa.org.za

Esplen, M. (2008). *Greece publishing market profile.* London, UK: The Publishers Association.

European Commission. (2000). *White paper on food safety.* Brussels, Belgium: European Commission.

European Logistics Association. (2001). *The influence of e-commerce on tomorrows logistics.* Retrieved November 20, 2011, from http://www.elalog.org/publications/tno-ebook.pdf

European Union. (2002). Regulation (EC) No 178/2002 of the European parliament and of the council. *Official Journal of the European Communities.* Brussels, Belgium: European Union.

Evangelista, P. (2002). Information and communication technology key factor in logistics and freight transport. In Ferrara, G., & Morvill, A. (Eds.), *Training in Logistics and Freight Transport Industry: The Experience of the European Project ADAPT-FIT* (pp. 15–36). London, UK: Ashgate Ltd.

Evangelista, P., & Kilpala, H. (2007). The perception on ICT use among small logistics service providers: A comparison between Northern and Southern Europe. *European Transport, 35*, 81–98.

Fabbe-Costes, N., & Jahre, M. (2008). Supply chain integration and performance: A review of the evidence. *International Journal of Logistics Management, 19*(2), 130–154. doi:10.1108/09574090810895933

Fabbe-Costes, N., Jahre, M., & Roussat, C. (2009). Supply chain integration: The role of logistics service providers. *International Journal of Productivity and Performance Management, 58*(1), 71–91. doi:10.1108/17410400910921092

Fagui, L., Kun, L., & Yang, Z. (2008). *Semantic web services and its application in third-party logistics*. Paper presented at the 2008 International Workshop on Education Technology and Training & 2008 International Workshop on Geoscience and Remote Sensing. New York, NY.

Fang, L., & Zhang, C.-Q. (2005). *The e-logistics framework in e-commerce*. Retrieved September 1, 2011, from: http://delivery.acm.org/10.1145/1090000/1089626/p408-fang.pdf?ip=83.212.54.165&acc=ACTIVE%20SERVICE&CFID=68228288&CFTOKEN=11031907&__acm__=1330456613_00dd81e149cff1801ff348adad525ff5

Farrell, C. (2008). The role of the internet in the delivery of export promotion services: A web site content analysis. *Journal of Global Marketing, 21*(4), 259–269. doi:10.1080/08911760802206094

Fawcett, S. E., & Magnan, G. M. (2002). The rhetoric and reality of supply chain integration. *Internal Journal of Physical Distribution & Logistics Management, 32*(5), 339–361. doi:10.1108/09600030210436222

Fawcett, S., Stanley, L., & Smith, S. (1997). Developing a logistics capability to improve the performance of international operations. *Journal of Business Logistics, 18*(2), 101–127.

Feder, B. J. (2004, December 28). Wal-Mart edict on radio tags hits snag. *The Denver Post*, p. 6C.

Fingar, P., Kumar, H., & Tarun, S. (2000). *Enterprise e-commerce: The software component breakthrough for business-to-business commerce*. Meghan-Kiffer Press.

Finney, S., & Corbett, M. (2007). ERP implementation: A compilation and analysis of critical success factors. *Business Process Management Journal, 13*(3), 329–347. doi:10.1108/14637150710752272

Fischer, R., & Lugg, R. (2001). E-book basics. *Collection Building, 20*(3), 119–122. doi:10.1108/01604950110396988

Flynn, B. B., Kakibara, S. S., Schroeder, R. G., Bates, K. A., & Flynn, E. J. (1990). Empirical research methods in operations management. *Journal of Operations Management, 9*(2), 250–284. doi:10.1016/0272-6963(90)90098-X

Fogel, R. (2010). *The education cloud: Delivering education as a service*. Intel White Paper. Intel.

Folinas, D., Vlachopoulou, M., Manthou, V., & Manos, B. (2003). A web-based integration of data and processes in agribusiness supply chain. In *Proceedings of the EFITA 2003 Conference*, (vol. 1, pp. 143-150). EFITA.

Folinas, D. K. (2012). *Outsourcing management for supply chain operations and logistics service, handbook*. Hershey, PA: IGI Global. doi:10.4018/978-1-4666-2008-7

Food Standards Agency. (2002). *Traceability in the food chain: A preliminary study*. Food Chain Strategy Division.

Fordice, R. (2004). Under control. *Meat Processing, 11*, 34–40.

Forslund, H., & Jonsson, P. (2010). Selection, implementation and use of ERP systems for supply chain performance management. *Industrial Management & Data Systems, 110*(8), 1159–1175. doi:10.1108/02635571011077816

Foster, I., Zhao, Y., Raicu, I., & Lu, S. Y. (2008). Cloud computing and grid computing 360-degree compared. In *Proceedings of IEEE Grid Computing Environments (GCE08)*. Austin, TX: IEEE.

Frank, S., Ma, S. H., & Michael, B. (2008). *Internationalization of logistics systems: How Chinese and German companies enter foreign markets*. Berlin, Germany: Springer.

Freeman, M. A., & Capper, J. M. (1999). Exploiting the web for education: An anonymous asynchronous role simulation. *Australia Journal of Educational Technology, 15*(1), 95–116.

Fugate, B., Mentzer, J., & Stank, T. (2010). Logistics performance: Efficience, effectiveness and differentiation. *Journal of Business Logistics, 31*(1), 43–62. doi:10.1002/j.2158-1592.2010.tb00127.x

Gallagher, P. (2007). A view from Australia. *Publishing Research Quarterly*, *23*(2), 137–140. doi:10.1007/s12109-007-9022-2

Ganesan, S., George, M., Jap, S., Palmatier, R., & Weitz, B. (2009). Supply chain management and retailer performance: Emerging trends, issues and implications for research and practice. *Journal of Retailing*, *85*(1), 84–94. doi:10.1016/j.jretai.2008.12.001

Garcia, M., Skinner, C., Poole, N., Escribano, J. B., Boente, I., & Bandeiras, P. ... Messaho, D. (2003). *Benchmarking safety and quality management practices in the Mediterranean fresh produce export sector*. Working Paper. London, UK: Imperial College.

Gardner, D. (2009, August 25). How the cloud aids supply chain recalls cloud computing uniquely enables product and food recall processes across supply chains. *Cloud Computing Journal*.

Gargeya, V. B., & Brady, C. (2005). Success and failure factors of adopting SAP in ERP system implementation. *Business Process Management Journal*, *11*(5), 501–516. doi:10.1108/14637150510619858

Garg, S., & Buyya, R. (2012). Green cloud computing and environmental sustainability. In Murugesan, S., & Gangadharan, G. (Eds.), *Harnessing Green IT: Principles and Practices* (pp. 315–340). London, UK: Wiley Press.

Genong, Y., Liping, D., Wenli, Y., Peisheng, Z., & Peng, Y. (2009). Multi-agent systems for distributed geospatial modeling, simulation and computing. In *Handbook of Research on Geoinformatics* (pp. 196–205). Hershey, PA: IGI Global.

Gens, F. (2011). IDC predicts 2012 will be the year of mobile and cloud platform wars as IT vendors vie for leadership while the industry redefines itself. *IDC*. Retrieved September 14, 2012, from http://www.idc.com/

Gentry, C. R. (1999). Reducing the cost of returns. *Chain Store Age*, *75*(10), 124–125.

Gericke, A., Klesse, M., Winter, R., & Wortmann, F. (2010). Success factors of application integration: An exploratory analysis. *Communications of the Association for Information Systems*, *27*(37), 678–694.

Germain, R., & Iyer, K. (2006). The interaction of internal and downstream integration and its association with performance. *Journal of Business Logistics*, *27*(2), 29–52. doi:10.1002/j.2158-1592.2006.tb00216.x

Giampietro, C., & Emiliani, M. L. (2007). Coercion and reverse auctions. *Supply Chain Management: An International Journal*, *12*(2), 75–84. doi:10.1108/13598540710737253

Giannakis, M. (2011). Management of service supply chains with a service-oriented reference model: The case of management consulting. *Supply Chain Management: An International Journal*, *16*(5), 346–361. doi:10.1108/13598541111155857

Giannakis, M., & Croom, S. R. (2004). Towards the development of a supply chain management paradigm: A conceptual framework. *Journal of Supply Chain Management*, *40*(2), 27–36. doi:10.1111/j.1745-493X.2004.tb00167.x

Gill, R. (2007). Lean manufacturing and ERP systems: Different by design. *Ceramic Industry*, *157*(8), 19-20. Retrieved from http://web.ebscohost.com.ezproxy.liv.ac.uk/ehost/pdfviewer/pdfviewer?vid=2&hid=5&sid=95dd27a9-43b5-4713-b92c-d09eacf666f3%40sessionmgr13

Gillis, C. (2011). Visibility through CAT's eyes. *American Shipper Journal*, *53*(12), 8–15.

Ginns, P., & Ellis, R. (2007). Quality in blended learning: Exploring the relationships between on-line and face-to-face teaching and learning. *The Internet and Higher Education*, *10*, 53–64. doi:10.1016/j.iheduc.2006.10.003

Giraud, G., & Halawany, R. (2006). Consumers perception of food traceability in Europe. In *Proceedings of the 98th EAAE Seminar: Marketing Dynamics within the Global Trading System*, (p. 7). Chania, Greece: EAAE.

Giunipero, L. C., Hooker, R. E., Matthews, S. C., Yoon, T. E., & Brudvig, S. (2008). A decade of SCM literature: Past, present and future implications. *Journal of Supply Chain Management*, *44*(1), 66–86. doi:10.1111/j.1745-493X.2008.00073.x

Golafshani, N. (2003). Understanding reliability and validity in qualitative research. *The Qualitative Report*, *8*(4), 597-607. Retrieved August 18, 2009, from http://www.nova.edu/ssss/QR/QR8-4/golafshani.pdf

Golan, E., Krissoff, B., Kuchler, F., Calvin, L., Nelson, K., & Price, G. (2004). *Traceability in the U.S. food supply: Economic theory and industry studies. Agricultural Economic Report, No 830*. Washington, DC: U.S. Department of Agriculture.

Gold, D. J. (1994). An electronic publishing model for academic publishers. *Journal of the American Society for Information Science American Society for Information Science, 45*(10), 760–764. doi:10.1002/(SICI)1097-4571(199412)45:10<760::AID-ASI7>3.0.CO;2-H

Golicic, L. S., Davis, F. D., McCarthy, M. T., & Mentzer, T. J. (2002). The impact of e-commerce on supply chain relationships. *International Journal of Physical Distribution & Logistics Management, 32*(10), 851–871. doi:10.1108/09600030210455447

Goodman, J., & Truss, C. (2004). The medium and the message: Communicating effectively during a major change initiative. *Journal of Change Management, 4*(3), 217–228. doi:10.1080/1469701042000255392

Green, K., Morton, B., & New, S. (1996). Purchasing and environmental management: Interactions, policies and opportunities. *Business Strategy and the Environment, 5*(5), 188–197. doi:10.1002/(SICI)1099-0836(199609)5:3<188::AID-BSE60>3.0.CO;2-P

Green, K., Whitten, D., & Inman, R. (2008). The impact of logistics performance on organizational performance in a supply chain context. *Supply Chain Management: An International Journal, 13*(4), 317–327. doi:10.1108/13598540810882206

Griffis, S., Goldsby, T., Cooper, M., & Closs, D. (2007). Aligning logistics performance measures to the information needs of the firm. *Journal of Business Logistics, 28*(2), 35–56. doi:10.1002/j.2158-1592.2007.tb00057.x

Grimaila, M. (2007). RFID security concerns. *ISSA Journal*. Retrieved from https://dev.issa.org/Library/Journals/2007/February/Grimaila%20-%20RFID%20Security%20Concerns.pdf

Griswold, W. G., Shonle, M., Sullivan, K., Song, Y., Tewari, N., Cai, Y., & Rajan, H. (2006). Modular software design with crosscutting interfaces. *IEEE Software, 23*(1), 51–60. doi:10.1109/MS.2006.24

GS1. (2006). *Official website*. Retrieved from http://www.gs1.org

Gsell, H., & Nagel, R. (2012). *Application integration in the logistics mall*. Washington, DC: Society for Design and Process Science.

Gudmundsson, S. V., & Walczuch, R. (1999). The development of electronic markets in logistics. *The International Journal of Logistics Management, 10*(2), 99–113. doi:10.1108/09574099910806021

Guide, D., Souza, G., Van Wassenhove, L., & Blackburn, J. (2006). Time value of commercial product returns. *Management Science, 52*(8), 1200–1214. doi:10.1287/mnsc.1060.0522

Guide, V., Harrison, T., & Van Wassenhove, L. (2003). The challenge of closed-loop supply chains. *Interfaces: The INFORMS Journal of Operations Research, 33*(6), 3–6.

Gunasekaran, A., & Ngai, E. (2004). Information systems in supply chain integration and management. *European Journal of Operational Research, 159*(1), 269–295. doi:10.1016/j.ejor.2003.08.016

Gunasekaran, A., Patel, C., & McGaughey, R. E. (2004). A framework for supply chain performance measurement. *International Journal of Production Economics, 87*, 333–347. doi:10.1016/j.ijpe.2003.08.003

Gunther, O., & Spiekermann, S. (2005). RFID and the perception of control: The customers view. *Communications of the ACM, 48*(9), 9. doi:10.1145/1081992.1082023

Gurung, A. (2006). A survey of information technologies in logistics management. In *Proceedings of the 2006 Annual Conference*. Oklahoma City, OK: Decision Sciences Institute.

Hahn, C., Kim, K., & Kim, J. (1986). Costs of competition: Implications for purchasing strategy. *International Journal of Purchasing and Materials Management, 22*(3), 2–7.

Haines, M. (2009). Understanding enterprise system customization: An exploration of implementation realities and the key influence factors. *Information Systems Management, 26*(1), 182–198. doi:10.1080/10580530902797581

Halldorsson, A., & Arlbjorn, J. S. (2005). Research methodologies in supply chain management – What do we know? In Kotzab, H., Seuring, S., Muller, M., & Reiner, G. (Eds.), *Research Methodologies in Supply Chain Management* (pp. 107–122). Heidelberg, Germany: Physica-Verlag. doi:10.1007/3-7908-1636-1_8

Hallikas, J., Karvonen, I., Pulkkinen, U., Virolainen, V.-M., & Tuominen, M. (2004). Risk management processes in supplier networks. *International Journal of Production Economics*, *90*, 47–58. doi:10.1016/j.ijpe.2004.02.007

Hanks, P. (1990). *Collins dictionary of the English language* (2nd ed.). London, UK: Collins.

Harland, C. M. (1996). Supply chain management: Relationships, chains and networks. *British Journal of Management*, *7*(1), 63–80. doi:10.1111/j.1467-8551.1996.tb00148.x

Harris, J., & Alter, A. (2010). Cloudrise: Rewards and risks at the dawn of cloud computing. *Accenture*. Retrieved September 14, 2012, from http://www.accenture.com/us-en/pages/index.aspx

Hartley, J. L., Lane, M. D., & Duplaga, E. A. (2006). Exploring the barriers to the adoption of e-auctions for sourcing. *International Journal of Operations & Production Management*, *26*(2), 202–221. doi:10.1108/01443570610641675

Hartley, J. L., Lane, M. D., & Hong, Y. (2004). An exploration of the adoption of e-auctions in supply management. *Proceedings of IEEE Transactions on Engineering Management*, *51*(2), 153–161. doi:10.1109/TEM.2004.826010

Heavey, C., Byrne, P. J., Liston, P., & Byrne, J. (2006). Operational design in VO supply networks creation network- centric collaboration and supporting fireworks. In Camarinha-Matos, L. M., Afsarmanesh, H., & Ollus, M. (Eds.), *Handbook of Network-Centric Collaboration and Supporting Frameworks* (pp. 381–388). Boston, MA: Springer. doi:10.1007/978-0-387-38269-2_40

Helo, P., Xiao, Y., & Jiao, R. (2006). A web-based logistics management system for agile supply demand network design. *Journal of Manufacturing Technology Management*, *17*(8), 1058–1077. doi:10.1108/17410380610707384

Hendricks, K. B., & Singhal, V. R. (2003). The effect of supply chain glitches on shareholder wealth. *Journal of Management*, *21*, 501–522.

Hendricks, K. B., & Singhal, V. R. (2005). Association between supply chain glitches and operating performance. *Management Science*, *51*(5), 695–711. doi:10.1287/mnsc.1040.0353

Hendricks, K. B., & Singhal, V. R. (2005). An empirical analysis of the effect of supply chain disruptions on long-run stock price performance and equity risk of the firm. *Production and Operations Management*, *14*(1), 35–52. doi:10.1111/j.1937-5956.2005.tb00008.x

Hendricks, K. B., Singhal, V. R., & Stratman, J. K. (2007). The impact of enterprise systems on corporate performance: A study of ERP, SCM, and CRM system implementations. *Journal of Operations Management*, *25*, 65–82. doi:10.1016/j.jom.2006.02.002

Herdon, M., Rózsa, T., & Füzesi, I. (2006). *Food traceability solutions in information systems*. Paper presented at the Conference HAICTA 2006: International Conference on: Information Systems in Sustainable Agriculture, Agroenvironment and Food Technology. New York, NY.

Hervani, A., Helms, M., & Sarkis, J. (2005). Performance measurement for green supply chain management. *Benchmarking: An International Journal*, *12*(4), 330–353. doi:10.1108/14635770510609015

Hill Associates, Inc. (2006). *Enterprise applications: A conceptual look at ERP, CRM, and SCM*. Colchester, VT: Copyright Coordinator.

Hines, P., Silvi, R., & Bartolini, M. (2002). *Lean profit potential*. Cardiff, UK: Lean Enterprise Research Centre. Retrieved from http://www.constructingexcellence.biz/pdf/document/Leanprofit.pdf

Hobbs, J. E. (2006). Liability and traceability in agri-food supply chains. In Onderstejn, C. J. M., Wijnands, J. H. M., Huirne, R. B. M., & van Kooten, O. (Eds.), *Quantifying the Agri-Food Supply Chain* (pp. 87–102). Berlin, Germany: Springer. doi:10.1007/1-4020-4693-6_7

Ho, D. C. K., Au, K. F., & Newton, E. (2003). The process and consequences of supply chain virtualization. *Industrial Management & Data Systems*, *103*(6), 423–433. doi:10.1108/02635570310479990

Hoepfl, M. C. (1997). Choosing qualitative research: A primer for technology education researchers. *Journal of Technology Education, 9*(1), 47-63. Retrieved August 18, 2009, from http://scholar.lib.vt.edu/ejournals/JTE/v9n1/pdf/hoepfl.pdf

Hong, K., & Kim, Y. (2002). The critical success factors for ERP implementation: An organizational fit perspective. *Information & Management, 40,* 25–40. doi:10.1016/S0378-7206(01)00134-3

Hope-Ross, D., & Spencer, C. (2001). *SRM is not yet a suite spot.* Washington, DC: Gartner Group.

Horton, W. (2000). *Designing web-based training.* New York, NY: John Wiley & Sons Publisher.

Hosono, S., Hara, T., Shimomura, Y., & Arai, T. (2010). Prioritizing service functions with non-functional requirements. In *Proceedings of the CIRP Industrial Product-Service Systems Conference,* (pp. 133-140). Linkoping, Sweden: CIRP.

Hosono, S., Kuno, A., Hasegawa, M., Hara, T., Shimomura, Y., & Arai, T. (2009). A framework of co-creating business values for IT services. In *Proceedings of the 2009 IEEE International Conference on Cloud Computing.* Bangalore, India: IEEE.

Hoxha, J., Scheuermann, A., & Bloehdorn, S. (2010). An approach to formal and semantic representation of logistics services. In *Proceedings of the ECAI 2010 Workshop on Artificial Intelligence and Logistics,* (pp. 73-78). ECAI.

Huang, S. Y., Huang, S. M., & Wu, T. H. (2009). Process efficiency of the enterprise resource planning adoption. *Industrial Management & Data Systems, 109*(8), 1085–1100. doi:10.1108/02635570910991319

Hull, J. C. (2009). *Options, futures, and other derivatives* (7th ed.). Upper Saddle River, NJ: Prentice Hall.

Hultkrantz, O., & Lumsden, K. (2003). E-commerce and consequences for the logistics Industry. *European Conference of Ministers of Transport Organisation for Economic Co-operation and Development.* Retrieved November 20, 2011, from http://www.oecd.org/dataoecd/3/19/2726935.pdf

Hulzebos, L., & Koenderink, N. (2006). Modeling food supply chain for tracking and tracing. In Smith, I., & Furness, A. (Eds.), *Improving Traceability in Food Processing and Distribution* (pp. 67–87). New York, NY: Woodhead Publishing. doi:10.1533/9781845691233.2.67

Hur, D., Mabert, V. A., & Hartley, J. L. (2007). Getting the most out of reverse e-auction investment. *Omega, 35*(4), 403–416. doi:10.1016/j.omega.2005.08.003

Huynh, M., & Chu, H. (2011). Open-source ERP: Is it ripe for use in teaching supply chain management? *Journal of Information Technology Education: Innovations in Practice, 10*(1), 181–194.

ICAP. (2009). *Sector report: Third party logistics.* ICAP.

IDTechEx. (2005). *An introduction to RFID and tagging technologies.* Retrieved June 30, from http://www.idspackaging.com/Common/Paper/Paper_486/Y9268U8423.pdf

IFS. (2007). *6 steps to ERP implementation success.* MSS Technologies Inc.

Ittner, C., & Larcker, D. (2003). The use and usefulness of nonfinancial performance measures. *Harvard Business Review, 5*(9), 1–10.

Jahre, M., & Fabbe-Costes, N. (2005). Adaptation and adaptability in logistics networks. *International Journal of Logistics: Research and Applications, 8*(2), 143–157. doi:10.1080/13675560500110903

Jansen-Vullers, M. H., van Dorp, C. A., & Beulens, A. J. M. (2003). Managing traceability information in manufacture. *International Journal of Information Management, 23,* 395–413. doi:10.1016/S0268-4012(03)00066-5

Jedermann, R. (2007). Semi-passive RFID and beyond: Steps toward automated quality tracing in the food chain. *International Journal of Radio Frequency Identification Technology and Applications, 1*(3). Retrieved from http://www.sfb637.uni-bremen.de/pubdb/repository/SFB637-B6-07-026-IJ.pdfdoi:10.1504/IJRFITA.2007.015849

Jennings, N., Sycara, K., & Wooldridge, M. (1998). A roadmap of agent research and development. *Journal of Autonomous Agents and Multi-agent Systems, 1*(1), 7–36. doi:10.1023/A:1010090405266

Jericho Forum. (2009). *Cloud cube model: Selecting cloud formations for secure collaboration version 1.0.* Jericho Forum Specification.

Ji, C., Li, M., & Li, L. (2004). Freight transportation system based on web service. In *Proceedings of the IEEE International Conference on Services Computing (SCC 2004)*. IEEE Press.

Jiang, Y., Hu, L., Yang, Z., Yan, G., & Shen, X. (2006). Evaluation of cross-strait public library web site. *Journal of Natural Sciences, 11*(5), 1202–1208.

Jin, M., & Wu, S. D. (2006). Supplier coalitions in on-line reverse auctions: Validity requirements and profit distribution scheme. *International Journal of Production Economics, 100*(2), 183–194. doi:10.1016/j.ijpe.2004.10.017

Johnson, E., & Pyke, D. (1999). *Supply chain management.* (Unpublished M. Ed. Dissertation). Dartmouth College. Hanover, NH.

Johnson, B., Skibo, C., & Young, M. (2003). *Inside Microsoft visual studio. NET 2003.* Redmond, WA: Microsoft Press.

Jolluck, D. & Weich, C. (2010). *An oracle white paper: An introduction to rubee technology.* Oracle White Paper. Redwood Shores, CA: Oracle Corporation.

Jun, C., & Wei, M. Y. (2011). The research of supply chain information collaboration based on cloud computing. *Procedia Environmental Sciences, 10*, 875–880. doi:10.1016/j.proenv.2011.09.140

Kagermann, H., Österle, H., & Jordan, J. M. (2011). *IT-driven business models: Global case studies in transformation.* New York, NY: John Wiley & Sons.

Kaihara, T. (2001). Supply chain management with economics. *International Journal of Production Economics, 73*(1), 5–14. doi:10.1016/S0925-5273(01)00092-5

Kamal, M. M., Themistocleous, M., & Morabito, V. (2009). Justifying the decisions for EAI adoption in LGAs: A validated proposition of factors, adoption lifecycle phases, mapping and prioritisation of factor. In *Proceedings of the 42nd Hawaii International Conference on System Sciences*, (pp. 1-10). Hawaii, HI: IEEE.

Kameshwaran, S., & Narahari, Y. (2001). *Auction algorithms for achieving efficiencies in logistics marketplaces.* Paper presented at the International Conference on Energy, Automation and Information Technology. Kharaghpur, India.

Karakostas, B., & Katsoulakos, T. (2011). A collaborative resource-based cloud architecture for freight logistics. *CLOSER,* 141-144.

Karkkainen, M. (2003). Increasing efficiency in the supply chain for short shelf life goods using RFID tagging. *International Journal of Retail and Distribution Management, 31*, 529–536. doi:10.1108/09590550310497058

Karlsen, K. M., Sørensen, C. F., Forås, F., & Olsen, P. (2011). Critical criteria when implementing electronic chain traceability in a fish supply chain. *Food Control, 22*, 1339–1347. doi:10.1016/j.foodcont.2011.02.010

Kasilingam, R. G., & Lee, C. P. (1996). Selection of vendors-a mixed-integer programming approach. *Computers & Industrial Engineering, 31*, 347–350. doi:10.1016/0360-8352(96)00148-9

Kelepouris, T., Pramatari, K., & Doukidis, G. (2007). RFID-enabled traceability in the food supply chain. *Industrial Management & Data Systems, 107*, 183–200. doi:10.1108/02635570710723804

Kempainen, K., & Vepsalainen, A. P. J. (2003). Trends in industrial supply chains and networks. *Internal Journal of Physical Distribution & Logistics Management, 33*(8), 701–719. doi:10.1108/09600030310502885

Kern, T., & Willcocks, L. (2002). Exploring relationships in information technology outsourcing: The interaction approach. *European Journal of Information Systems, 11,* 3–19. doi:10.1057/palgrave/ejis/3000415

Kersten, G. E., Noronha, S. J., & Teich, J. (2000). *Are all e-commerce negotiations auctions?* Paper presented at the Fourth International Conference on the Design of Cooperative Systems. Sophia-Antipolis, France.

Ketchen, D., & Giunipero, L. (2004). The intersection of strategic management and supply chain management. *Industrial Marketing Management, 33*(1), 51–56. doi:10.1016/j.indmarman.2003.08.010

Khalifa, M., Banerjee, P., & Ma, L. (2003). Strategies for successfully deploying e-markets: Lessons from the China context. In *Proceedings of the 36th Hawaii International Conference on System Sciences (HICSS 2003)*. Hawaii, HI: IEEE.

Khanna, V. K. (2008). An Indian experience of environmental management system. PICMET.*Proceedings of PICMET, 2008*, 1806–1816.

Kim, W., Kim, S., Lee, E., & Lee, S. (2009). Adoption issues for cloud computing. In *Proceedings of MoMM2009*. Kuala Lumpur, Malaysia: MoMM.

Kim, S. H., Cohen, M. A., & Netessine, S. (2007). Performance contracting in after-sales service supply chains. *Management Science, 53*(12), 1843–1858. doi:10.1287/mnsc.1070.0741

Kim, Y., Lee, Z., & Gosain, S. (2005). Impediments to successful ERP implementation process. *Business Process Management Journal, 11*(2), 158–170. doi:10.1108/14637150510591156

Klafft, M. (2006). Including process information in traceability. In Smith, I., & Furness, A. (Eds.), *Improving Traceability in Food Processing and Distribution* (pp. 107–127). New York, NY: Woodhead Publishing. doi:10.1533/9781845691233.2.107

Klassen, K. J., & Willoughby, K. A. (2003). In-class simulation games: Accessing student learning. *Journal of Information Technology Education, 2*.

Kleindorfer, P. R., & Saad, G. H. (2005). Managing disruption risks in supply chains. *Production and Operations Management, 14*(1), 53–68. doi:10.1111/j.1937-5956.2005.tb00009.x

Knemeyer, A. M., Zinn, W., & Eroglu, C. (2009). Proactive planning for catastrophic events in supply chains. *Journal of Operations Management, 27*(2), 141–153. doi:10.1016/j.jom.2008.06.002

Knight, C., Stanley, R., & Jones, L. (2002). Agriculture in the food supply chain: an overview. *Key Topics in Food Science and Technology, 5*, 91–96.

Knoppen, D., & Christiaanse, E. (2007). Supply chain partnering: A temporal multidisciplinary approach. *Supply Chain Management: An International Journal, 12*(2), 164–171. doi:10.1108/13598540710737343

Koenderink, N., & Hulzebos, L. (2006). Dealing with bottlenecks in traceability systems. In Smith, I., & Furness, A. (Eds.), *Improving Traceability in Food Processing and Distribution* (pp. 88–107). New York, NY: Woodhead Publishing. doi:10.1533/9781845691233.2.88

Kourgiantakis, M., Mandalianos, I., Migdalas, A., & Pardalos, P. M. (2006). Optimization in e-commerce. In Resende, M. G. C., & Pardalos, P. M. (Eds.), *Handbook of Optimization in Telecommunications* (pp. 1077–1050). New York, NY: Springer. doi:10.1007/978-0-387-30165-5_35

Krajewska, M. A., & Kopfer, H. (2006). Collaborating freight forwarding enterprises, request allocation and profit sharing. *OR-Spektrum, 28*(3), 301–317. doi:10.1007/s00291-005-0031-2

Kratochvil, M., & Carson, C. (2005). *Growing modular: Mass customization of complex products, services and software*. Berlin, Germany: Springer.

Krcmar, H. (2011). *SAP UCC products / services and their use within university curricula*. Paper presented at the SAP UCC Munich Workshop. Poznan, Germany.

Krutz, R. L., & Dean Vines, R. (2010). *Cloud security: A comprehensive guide to secure cloud computing*. New York, NY: Wiley Publishing.

Kshetri, N. (2010). Cloud computing in developing economics. *IEEE Computer, 43*(10), 47–55. doi:10.1109/MC.2010.212

Kull, T. J., Boyer, K., & Calantone, R. (2007). Last-mile supply chain efficiency: An analysis of learning curves in online ordering. *International Journal of Operations & Production Management, 27*, 409–434. doi:10.1108/01443570710736985

Kumar, P., & Thapliyal, M. P. (2010). Integration of e-business with ERP systems. *International Journal of Computer Science & Communication, 1*(2), 13–17.

Kwon, I. G., & Suh, T. (2004). Factors affecting the level of trust and commitment in supply chain relationships. *The Journal of Supply Chain Management, 40*(2), 4–14. doi:10.1111/j.1745-493X.2004.tb00165.x

Laband, D., & Hudson, J. (2003). The pricing of economics books. *The Journal of Economic Education*, 360–368. doi:10.1080/00220480309595229

Lai, K. H., Ngai, E. W. T., & Cheng, T. C. E. (2004). An empirical study of supply chain performance in transport logistics. *International Journal of Production Economics*, *87*(3), 321–331. doi:10.1016/j.ijpe.2003.08.002

Laios, L. (2004). Logistics outsourcing? *Warehouse & Transportation*, *21*, 59–62.

Lamming, R. (1996). Squaring lean supply with supply chain management. *International Journal of Operations & Production Management*, *16*(2), 183–196. Retrieved from http://www.emeraldinsight.com. ezproxy.liv.ac.uk/journals.htm?issn=0144-3577&volume=16&issue=2&articleid=848948&show=pdfdoi:10.1108/01443579610109910

Lamming, R., & Hampson, J. (1996). The environment as a supply chain issue. *British Journal of Management*, *7*, 45–62. doi:10.1111/j.1467-8551.1996.tb00147.x

Landt, J. (2005). The history of RFID. *IEEE Potentials*, *24*(4), 8–11. doi:10.1109/MP.2005.1549751

Langley, J. C. Jr, & Holcomb, M. C. (1992). Creating logistics customer value. *Journal of Business Logistics*, *13*(2), 1–27.

Langlois, R. N., & Robertson, P. L. (1992). Networks and innovation in a modular system: Lessons from the microcomputer and stereo component industries. *Research Policy*, *21*(4), 297–313. doi:10.1016/0048-7333(92)90030-8

Lau, H. C., & Goh, Y. G. (2002). An intelligent brokering system to support multi-agent web-based 4th-party logistics. In *Proceedings of the 14th IEEE International Conference on Tools with Artificial Intelligence*, (pp. 154-161). IEEE Press.

Lau, A. K. W., Yam, R. C. M., & Tang, E. P. Y. (2010). Supply chain integration and product modularity: An empirical study of product performance for selected Hong Kong manufacturing industries. *International Journal of Operations & Production Management*, *30*(1), 20–56. doi:10.1108/01443571011012361

Laudon, K. C., & Laudon, J. P. (2011). *Managing information systems: Managing the digital firm* (12th ed.). Upper Saddle River, NJ: Pearson.

Laurent, S. (Ed.). (1999). *XML™: A primer* (2nd ed.). New York, NY: MIS Press.

Lazaropoulos, H. (2009). *3PLs in Greece*. Retrieved September 1, 2011, from http://www.plant-management.gr

Ledyard, J. O., Olson, M., Porter, D., Swanson, J. A., & Torma, D. P. (2002). The first use of a combined value auction for transportation services. *Interfaces*, *32*(5), 4–12. doi:10.1287/inte.32.5.4.30

Lee, C. W., Kwon, I., & Severance, D. (2007). Relationship between supply chain performance and degree of linkage among supplier, internal integration, and customer. *Supply Chain Management: An International Journal*, *12*(6), 444–452. doi:10.1108/13598540710826371

Lee, H., Padmanabhan, V., & Whang, S. (1997). Information distortion in a supply chain: The bullwhip effect. *Management Science*, *43*(4), 546–558. doi:10.1287/mnsc.43.4.546

León-Peña, J. (2008). e-Business and the supply chain management. *Business Intelligence Journal*. Retrieved March 1, 2011, from http://www.saycocorporativo.com/saycoUK/BIJ/journal/Vol1No1/article_4.pdf

Leukel, J., Kirn, S., & Schlegel, T. (2011). Supply chain as a service: A cloud perspective on supply chain systems. *IEEE Systems Journal, 5*(1).

Li, J., Shaw, M., Sikora, R., Tan, G., & Yang, R. (2001). *The effects of information sharing strategies on supply chain performance*. (Unpublished M.Ed. Dissertation). University of Illinois. Urban-Champaign, IL.

Li, L. (2010). Empirical study on evaluation of agricultural web sites in China. In *Proceedings of the 2010 International Conference on E-Product E-Service and E-Entertainment, ICEEE2010*. ICEEE.

Liker, J. K. (2004). *The Toyota way: 14 management principles from the world's greatest manufacturer*. New York, NY: McGraw- Hill.

Lillrank, P., Groop, J., & Venesmaa, J. (2011). Processes, episodes and events in health service supply chains. *Supply Chain Management: An International Journal*, *16*(3), 194–201. doi:10.1108/13598541111127182

Lin, F.-H., & Hwang, C.-C. (2009). A content analysis of web-site quality of online auction sellers. In *Proceedings of the IADIS International Conference e-Commerce 2009, Part of the IADIS Multi Conference on Computer Science and Information Systems, MCCSIS 2009*, (pp. 105-112). IADIS.

Lin, C. Y. (2007). Adoption of green supply chain practices in Taiwan's logistics industry. *Journal of International Management Studies, 2*(2), 90–98.

Lindner, M., Galan, F., Chapman, C., Clayman, S., Henriksson, D., & Elmroth, E. (2010). The cloud supply chain: A framework for information, monitoring and billing. In *Proceedings of the 2nd International ICST Conference on Cloud Computing (CloudComp 2010)*. Barcelona, Spain: ICST.

Lindner, M., McDonald, F., Conway, G., & Curry, E. (2011). Understanding cloud requirements – A supply chain lifecycle approach. In *Proceedings of the 2nd International Conference on Cloud Computing, GRIDs and Virtualization*. Rome, Italy: IEEE.

Lin, Y., & Pekkarinen, S. (2011). QDF-based modular logistics service design. *Journal of Business and Industrial Marketing, 26*(5), 344–356. doi:10.1108/08858621111144406

Lin, Y., Shi, Y. J., & Zhou, L. (2010). Service supply chain: Nature, evolution, and operational implications. *Advances in Intelligent and Soft Computing, Springer-Verlag, 66*, 1189–1204. doi:10.1007/978-3-642-10430-5_91

Lin, Y., & Zhou, L. (2011). The impacts of product design changes on supply chain risk: A case study. *International Journal of Physical Distribution & Logistics Management, 41*(2), 162–186. doi:10.1108/09600031111118549

Liu, L., Chen, Z., Yan, D., Lu, Y., & Wang, H. (2010, May). E-business and e-government. In *Proceedings of the ICEE 2010 International Conference*, (pp. 2379-2382). IEEE.

Liu, M., Wang, Z., & Xie, H. (2010). Evaluation of e-government web site. In *Proceedings of the 2010 International Conference on Computer Design and Applications, ICCDA 2010*, (pp. 5432-5434). ICCDA.

Lloyd, S. (2008). A book publisher's manifesto for the twenty-first century: How traditional publishers can position themselves in the changing media flow of a networked era. *Library Trends, 57*(1), 30–42. doi:10.1353/lib.0.0019

Loesch, A., & Lambert, J. S. (2007). Information behaviour in e-reverse auctions: Purchasing in the context of the automobile industry. *Journal of Enterprise Information Management, 20*(4), 447–464. doi:10.1108/17410390710772713

Lunnan, R., & Haugland, S. (2007). Research notes and commentaries: Predicting and measuring alliance performance: A multidimensional analysis. *Strategic Management Journal, 29*(1), 545–556.

Lynag, P., Murphy, P., Poist, R., & Grazer, W. (2001). Web-based informational practices of logistics service providers: An empirical assessment. *Transportation Journal, 40*, 34–45.

Lysons, K., & Gillingham, M. (2003). *Purchasing and supply chain management*. London, UK: Pearson Education Limited.

Macbeth, K. D., & Ferguson, N. (1991). Strategic aspects of supply chain management. *Integrated Manufacturing Systems, 2*(1), 8–12. doi:10.1108/09576069110002699

Maditinos, D., Chatzoudes, D., & Tsairidis, C. (2011). Factors affecting ERP system implementation effectiveness. *Journal of Enterprise Information Management, 25*(1), 60–78. doi:10.1108/17410391211192161

Madlmayr, G. (2008). *NFC devices: Security and privacy*. Retrieved from http://ieeexplore.ieee.org/xpl/login.jsp?tp=&arnumber=4529403&url=http%3A%2F%2Fieeexplore.ieee.org%2Fxpls%2Fabs_all.jsp%3Farnumber%3D4529403

Mahto, R., Davis, S., Pearce, J., Robinson, I. I. Jr, & Richard, B. (2010). satisfaction with firm performance in family businesses. *Entrepreneurship. Theory into Practice, 34*(5), 985–1001.

Manciagli, D. (2001). A supplier's view. *Purchasing, 130*(12), 26–28.

Mangan, J., & Christopher, M. (2005). Management development and the supply chain manager of the future. *International Journal of Logistics Management, 16*(2), 178–191. doi:10.1108/09574090510634494

Markus, M. L., Axline, S., Petrie, D., & Tanis, C. (2000). Learning from adopters experiences with ERP: Problems encountered and success achieved. *Journal of Information Technology, 15*(4), 245–265. doi:10.1080/02683960010008944

Markus, M. L., & Tanis, C. (2000). The enterprise system experience - From adoption to success. In Zmud, R. W. (Ed.), *Framing the Domains of IT Management: Projecting the Future through the Past* (pp. 173–208). Cincinnati, OH: Pinnaflex Educational Resources.

Marnewick, C., & Labuschagne, L. (2005). A conceptual model for enterprise resource planning (ERP). *Information Management & Computer Security, 13*(2), 144–155. doi:10.1108/09685220510589325

Marston, S., Li, Z., Bandyopadhyay, S., Zhang, J., & Ghalsasi, A. (2011). Cloud computing - The business perspective. *Decision Support Systems Journal, 51*(1), 176–189. doi:10.1016/j.dss.2010.12.006

Martin, D., Burstein, M., McIlraith, S., Paolucci, M., & Sycara, K. (2005). OWL-S and agent-based systems. In *Extending Web Services Technologies: The Use of Multi-Agent Approaches* (pp. 53–77). New York, NY: Springer.

Martinelli, E., & Marchi, G. (2007). Enabling and inhibiting factors in adoption of electronic-reverse auctions: A longitudinal case study in grocery retailing. *International Review of Retail, Distribution and Consumer Research, 17*(3), 203–218. doi:10.1080/09593960701368721

Mason, R., Lalwani, C., & Boughton, R. (2007). Combining vertical and horizontal collaboration for transport optimisation. *Supply Chain Management: An International Journal, 12*(3), 187–199. doi:10.1108/13598540710742509

Mathe, H., & Shapiro, R. (1993). *Integrating service strategy in the manufacturing company*. London, UK: Chapman & Hall.

Matthyssens, P., & Van den Bulte, C. (1994). Getting closer and nicer: Partnerships in the supply chain. *Long Range Planning, 27*(1), 72–83. doi:10.1016/0024-6301(94)90008-6

Mcilraith, S., & Son, C. T. (2002). Adapting golog for composition of semantic web services. In *Proceedings of the 8th International Conference on Principles and Knowledge Representation and Reasoning (KR-02)*, (pp. 482-496). San Francisco, CA: Morgan Kaufmann.

McKinnon, A. (1999). The outsourcing of logistical activities. In Walter, D. (Ed.), *Global Logistics and Distribution Planning* (pp. 215–234). London, UK: Kogan Page.

McMullan, A. (1996). Supply chain management practices in Asia Pacific today. *International Journal of Physical Distribution & Logistics Management, 26*(10), 79–95. doi:10.1108/09600039610150479

McPherson, A. (2010). How private equity firms can use software as a service to improve portfolio company management. *IDC Financial Insights*. Retrieved September 14, 2012, from http://www.idc-fi.com/

Media & Entertainment (M&E) Team. (2009). Not just the blue-sky thinking: Cloud computing and the digital supply chain. *Accenture*. Retrieved September 14, 2012, from http://www.accenture.com/us-en/pages/index.aspx

Mell, P., & Grance, T. (2011). The NIST definition of cloud computing. *National Institution of Standards and Technology (NIST)*. Retrieved September 14, 2012, from http://csrc.nist.gov/

Mentzer, J., Gomes, R., & Krapfel, R. (1989). Physical distribution service: A fundamental marketing concept? *Journal of the Academy of Marketing Science, 17*, 53–62. doi:10.1007/BF02726354

Mentzer, J., Stank, T., & Esper, T. (2008). Supply chain management and its relationship to logistics, marketing, production and operations management. *Journal of Business Logistics, 29*(1), 31–46. doi:10.1002/j.2158-1592.2008.tb00067.x

Meyer, H. (1999). Many happy returns. *The Journal of Business Strategy, 30*(2), 27–31. doi:10.1108/eb040015

Michael, K., & McCathie, L. (2005). The pros and cons of RFID in supply chain management. In *Proceedings of the International Conference on Mobile Business*, (pp. 623-629). Retrieved form http://ro.uow.edu.au/cgi/viewcontent.cgi?article=1104&context=infopapers&sei-redir=1&referer=http%3A%2F%2Fscholar.google.co.uk%2Fscholar%3Fq%3DRFID%2Bcost%2Bmanagement%26btnG%3D%26hl%3Den%26as_sdt%3D0%252C5#search=%22RFID%20cost%20management%22

Michaelides, R., & Kehoe, D. (2006). Service supply chain management in e-government operations. *International Journal of Technology Management, 7*(3), 237–252.

Mikkola, J. H. (2001). Portfolio management of R&D projects: Implications for innovation management. *Technovation, 21*(7), 423–435. doi:10.1016/S0166-4972(00)00062-6

Mikkola, J. H. (2006). Capturing the degree of modularity embedded in product architectures. *Journal of Product Innovation Management, 23*(2), 128–146. doi:10.1111/j.1540-5885.2006.00188.x

Mikko, P., Yorjola, H., & Halmstrom, J. (2001). Solving the last mile issue: Reception box or delivery box? *International Journal of Physical Distribution & Logistics Management, 31*(6), 427–439. doi:10.1108/09600030110399423

Min, H., & Galle, W. P. (2001). Green purchasing practices of US firms. *International Journal of Operations & Production Management, 21*(9), 1222–1238. doi:10.1108/EUM0000000005923

Miozzo, M., & Grimshaw, D. (2005). Modularity and innovation in knowledge-intensive business services: IT outsourcing in Germany and the UK. *Research Policy, 34*, 1419–1439. doi:10.1016/j.respol.2005.06.005

Mishra, P., Bolic, M., Mustapha, Y., & Stewart, R. (2012). RFID technology for tracking and tracing explosives and detonators in minding services applications. *Journal of Applied Geophysics, 76*, 33–43. doi:10.1016/j.jappgeo.2011.10.004

Mithas, S., Ramasubbu, N., & Sambamurthy, V. (2011). How information management capability influences firm performance. *Management Information Systems Quarterly, 35*(1), 137–150.

Moe, T. (1998). Perspectives on traceability in food manufacture. *Trends in Food Science & Technology, 5*, 211–214. doi:10.1016/S0924-2244(98)00037-5

Möller, M., & Watanabe, M. (2010). Advance purchase discounts versus clearance sales. *The Economic Journal, 120*(547), 1125–1148. doi:10.1111/j.1468-0297.2009.02324.x

Monczka, R. M., Handfield, R. B., Giunipero, L. C., & Pattercon, J. L. (2009). *Purchasing & supply chain management* (4th ed.). Mason, GA: South-West Cengage Learning.

Morgan, C. (2004). Structure, speed and salience: Performance measurement in the supply chain. *Business Process Management Journal, 10*(5), 522–536. doi:10.1108/14637150410559207

Morgan, R. M., & Hunt, S. D. (1994). The commitment-trust theory of relationship marketing. *Journal of Marketing, 58*, 20–36. doi:10.2307/1252308

Moschuris, S. J., & Apergi, A. (2006). Transportation outsourcing: A survey of Greek practices. *Paradigm, 10*(1), 1–10.

Mukhopadhyay, S., & Setoputro, R. (2005). Optimal return policy and modular design for build-to-order products. *Journal of Operations Management, 23*(5), 496–506. doi:10.1016/j.jom.2004.10.012

Murphy, P., & Daley, J. (2000). An empirical study of internet issues among Internet freight forwarders. *Transportation Journal, 39*, 5–14.

Murphy, P., Poist, R., & Braunschweig, C. (1996). Green logistics: Comparative views of environmental progressives, moderates, and conservatives. *Journal of Business Logistics, 17*(1), 191–211.

Murphy, P., & Wood, D. (2004). *Contemporary logistics*. Upper Saddle River, NJ: Pearson Prentice Hall.

Muthusamy, S. K., Palanisamy, R., & MacDonald, J. (2005). Developing knowledge management systems for ERP implementation: A case study from service sector. *Journal of Service Research*, 65–92.

Nacar, R., & Burnaz, S. (2011). A cultural content analysis of multinational companies' web sites. *Qualitative Market Research, 14*(3), 274–288. doi:10.1108/13522751111137505

Nair, A. (2005). Emerging internet-enabled auction mechanisms in supply chain. *Supply Chain Management: An International Journal, 10*(3), 162–168. doi:10.1108/13598540510606214

Narsing, A. (2005). RFID and supply chain management: An assessment of its economic, technical, and productive viability in global supply chains. *The Journal of Applied Business Research, 21*(2), 75–80.

Nexus, G. T. (2009). Visibility in the import supply chain. *GT Nexus Inc.* Retrieved September 14, 2012, from http://www.gtnexus.com/

Niranjan, T. T., & Weaver, M. (2011). A unifying view of goods and services supply chain management. *Service Industries Journal, 31*(14), 2391–2410. doi:10.1080/02642069.2010.504821

Nix, N. (2004). *Adapting and enhancing links for multiple audiences*. Fort Worth, TX: Texas Christian University.

Norrman, A., & Jansson, U. (2004). Ericsson's proactive risk management approach after a serious sub-supplier accident. *International Journal of Physical Distribution and Logistics Management, 34*(5), 434–456. doi:10.1108/09600030410545463

Oke, A., & Gopalakrishnan, M. (2009). Managing disruptions in supply chains: A case study of a retail supply chain. *International Journal of Production Economics, 118*, 168–174. doi:10.1016/j.ijpe.2008.08.045

Onwubolu, G., & Dube, B. (2006). Implementing an improved inventory control system in a small company: A case study. *Production Planning and Control, 17*(1), 67–76. doi:10.1080/09537280500366001

Panayides, P. (2004). Logistics service providers: An empirical study of marketing strategies and company performance. *International Journal of Logistics: Research and Applications, 7*(1), 1–17. doi:10.1080/1367556031 0001619231

Panella, L. (2001). *Guidelines for redesigning the supply chain: Classification -electronic identification - traceability: Multi-regional operating programme services for trade valorisation of southern Italian agricultural products*. Rome, Italy: Ismea.

Papadopoulou, E. M., Panousopoulou, P., & Manthou, V. (2010). Performance indicators in the freight transportation sector- The case of the Greek market. In *Proceedings of the 12 WCTR*. Lisbon, Portugal: WCTR.

Papoutsakis, E., & Stefanou, C. J. (2012). The evaluation process of CRM systems: A review of the literature. In *Proceedings of the International Conference on Contemporary Marketing Issues*, (pp. 377-383). Thessaloniki, Greece: IEEE.

Paramasevam, G., Hassan, M., & Mohamed, N. (2001). Cost benefit analysis for implementation of environmental management systems. In *Proceedings of the International Symposium on Environmentally Conscious Design and Inverse Manufacturing*, (pp. 766-768). IEEE.

Parry, G., Graves, A., & James-Moore, M. (2006). The threat to core competence posed by developing closer supply chain relationships. *International Journal of Logistics Research and Applications, 9*(3), 295–305. doi:10.1080/13675560600859524

Peck, H., & Juttner, U. (2000). Strategy and relationships: Defining the interface in supply chain contexts. *The International Journal of Logistics Management, 11*(2), 33–44. doi:10.1108/09574090010806146

Pekkarinen, S., & Ulkuniemi, P. (2008). Modularity in developing business services by platform approach. *The International Journal of Logistics Management, 19*(1), 84–103. doi:10.1108/09574090810872613

Perea, E., & Zabala, E. (2005). Measurement campaign and assessment of the quality of supply in Res and Dg facilities in Spain. In *Proceedings of the 18th International Conference on Electricity Distribution*. IEEE.

Persona, A., Regattieri, A., Pham, H., & Battini, D. (2007). Remote control and maintenance outsourcing networks and its applications in supply chain management. *Journal of Operations Management, 25*(6), 1275–1291. doi:10.1016/j.jom.2007.01.018

Peters, A. T. (2001). Gutterda èmmerung (twilight of the gutter margins): e-Books and libraries. *Library Hi Tech, 19*(1), 50–62. doi:10.1108/07378830110384593

Petkovic, D. (2005). *Microsoft SQL server 2005: A beginner's guide*. New York, NY: McGraw-Hill.

Pires, S., & Camargo, J. B. (2010). Using cloud computing to integrate processes in the supply chain. In *Proceedings of the POMS 21ˢᵗ Annual Conference*. Vancouver, Canada: POMS.

Poole, K. (2003). Seizing the potential of the service supply chain. *Supply Chain Management Review, 7*(4), 54–61.

Power, D. (2005). Supply chain management integration and implementation: A literature review. *Supply Chain Management: An International Journal, 10*(4), 252–263. doi:10.1108/13598540510612721

Prajogo, D., & Brown, A. (2006). Approaches to adopting quality in SMEs and the impact on quality management practices and performance. *Total Quality Management, 17*(5), 555–556. doi:10.1080/14783360600588042

Presutti, W. D. (2003). Supply management and e-procurement: Creating value added in the supply chain. *Industrial Marketing Management, 32*, 219–226. Retrieved from http://www.sciencedirect.com.ezproxy.liv.ac.uk/science?_ob=MImg&_imagekey=B6V69-46NX5XJ-5-6&_cdi=5809&_user=822084&_pii=S0019850102002651&_origin=&_coverDate=04%2F30%2F2003&_sk=999679996&view=c&wchp=dGLbVlW-zSkWl&md5=31b671e27f110bb99a241c7a7e1aa9db&ie=/sdarticle.pdfdoi:10.1016/S0019-8501(02)00265-1

Puschmann, T., & Alt, R. (2005). Successful use of e-procurement in supply chains. *Supply Chain Management: An International Journal, 10*(2), 122 – 133. Retrieved from http://www.emeraldinsight.com.ezproxy.liv.ac.uk/journals.htm?issn=1359-8546&volume=10&issue=2&articleid=1464663&show=pdf

Qihai, Z., & Yan, L. (2011). Research on logistics distribution mode for e-commerce businesses. *Advanced Materials Research, 181-182*, 3–8. doi:10.4028/www.scientific.net/AMR.181-182.3

Quesada, G., Rachamadugu, R., Gonzalez, M., & Martinez, F. L. (2008). Linking order winning and external supply chain integration strategies. *Supply Chain Management: An International Journal, 13*(4), 296–303. doi:10.1108/13598540810882189

Rabade, L. A., & Alfaro, J. A. (2006). Buyer-supplier relationship's influence on traceability implementation in the vegetable industry. *Journal of Purchasing and Supply Management, 12*, 39–50. doi:10.1016/j.pursup.2006.02.003

Rabinovich, E., & Knemeyer, A. M. (2006). Logistics service providers in internet supply chains. *California Management Review, 48*(4), 84–108. doi:10.2307/41166362

Rankins, R., Bertucci, P., Gallelli, C., & Silverstein, A. T. (2006). *Microsoft SQL server 2005 unleashed*. New York, NY: Sams Publishing.

Rawlins, G. (1993). Publishing over the next decade. *Journal of the American Society for Information Science American Society for Information Science, 44*(8), 474–479. doi:10.1002/(SICI)1097-4571(199309)44:8<474::AID-ASI6>3.0.CO;2-3

Regan, A., & Song, J. (2000). *An industry in transition: Third party logistics in the information age*. Retrieved November 20, 2011, from http://www.uctc.net/papers/634.pdf

Regattieri, A., Gamberi, M., & Manzini, G. (2006). Traceability of food products: General framework and experimental evidence. *Journal of Food Engineering, 81*, 347–356. doi:10.1016/j.jfoodeng.2006.10.032

Rennolls, K., & Al-Shawabkeh, A. (2008). Formal structures for data mining, knowledge discovery and communication in a knowledge management environment. *Intelligent Data Analysis, 12*(1), 147–163.

Resende-Filho, M. A., & Buhr, B. L. (2008). A principal-agent model for evaluating the economic value of traceability system: A case study with injection: Site lesion control in fed castle. *American Journal of Agricultural Economics, 90*(4), 1091–1102. doi:10.1111/j.1467-8276.2008.01150.x

Richey, R. G., Daugherty, P., & Roath, A. (2007). Firm technological readiness and complementarity: Capabilities impacting logistics serving competency and performance. *Journal of Business Logistics, 28*(1), 195–228. doi:10.1002/j.2158-1592.2007.tb00237.x

Rocha, Á., Victor, A., & Brandão, P. L. (2011). Quality of health web sites: Dimensions for a wide evaluation. *Lecture Notes in Business Information Processing, 90*, 254–266. doi:10.1007/978-3-642-24511-4_20

Rogers, D. S., & Tibben-Lembke, R. S. (2002). Differences between forward and reverse logistics in a retail environment. *Supply Chain Management: An International Journal, 7*(5), 271–282. doi:10.1108/13598540210447719

Ross, D. F. (2003). *Introduction to e-supply chain management: Engaging technology to build market –winning business partnerships*. New York, NY: The St. Lucie Press.

Roussos, G. (2006). Enabling RFID in retail. *IEEE Computer, 39*(3), 25–30. doi:10.1109/MC.2006.88

Roussos, G. A. (2008). *Networked RFID, systems, software and services*. London, UK: Springer-Verlag. doi:10.1007/978-1-84800-153-4

Ro, Y. K., Liker, J. K., & Fixson, S. K. (2007). Modularity as a strategy for supply chain coordination: The case of U.S. auto. *IEEE Transactions on Engineering Management, 54*(1), 172–189. doi:10.1109/TEM.2006.889075

Roy, P., Nei, D., Orikasa, T., Xu, Q., Okadome, H., Nakamura, N., & Shiina, T. (2009). A review of life cycle assessment (LCA) on some food products. *Journal of Food Engineering, 90*(1), 1–10. doi:10.1016/j.jfoodeng.2008.06.016

Ruey-Shun Chen, R. S., Sun, C. M., Helms, M. M., & Jih, W. J. (2008). Role negotiation and interaction: An exploratory case study of the impact of management consultants on ERP system implementation in SMEs in Taiwan. *Information Systems Management, 25*(2), 159–173. doi:10.1080/10580530801941371

Ruiz-Torres, A. J., & Farzad, M. (2007). The optimal number of suppliers considering the costs of individual supplier failures. *Omega: The International Journal of Management Science, 35*(1), 104–115. doi:10.1016/j.omega.2005.04.005

Rutner, S. M., Gibson, B. J., & Williams, S. R. (2003). The impacts of the integrated logistics systems on electronic commerce and enterprise resource planning systems. *Transportation Research Part E, Logistics and Transportation Review, 39*(2), 83–93. doi:10.1016/S1366-5545(02)00042-X

Sabbaghi, A., & Vaidyanathan, G. (2008). Effectiveness and efficiency of RFID technology in supply chain management: Strategic value and challenges. *Journal of Theoretical and Applied Electronic Commerce Research, 3*(2), 71–81. doi:10.4067/S0718-18762008000100007

Saccani, N., Johansson, P., & Perona, M. (2007). Configuring the after-sales service supply chain: A multiple case study. *International Journal of Production Economics, 110*(1-2), 52–69. doi:10.1016/j.ijpe.2007.02.009

Sachan, A., & Datta, S. (2005). Review of supply chain management and logistics research. *International Journal of Physical Distribution & Logistics Management, 35*(9), 664–704. doi:10.1108/09600030510632032

Sage, E. R. P. (2011). *7 steps to building a business case for ERP*. Irvine, CA: Sage ERP.

Salin, V. (1998). Information technology in agri-food supply chains. *International Food and Agribusiness Review, 1*, 329–334. doi:10.1016/S1096-7508(99)80003-2

Salomie, J., Dinsoreanu, M., Bianca Pop, C., & Liviu Suciu, S. (2008). Model and SOA solutions for traceability in logistic chains. In *Proceedings of iiWAS2008*, (pp. 339-344). Linz, Austria: iiWAS.

Salomie, I., Dinsoreanu, M., Pop, C. B., & Suciu, S. L. (2008). Logistic chain generation with traceability features using web services composition. In *Proceedings of the 2008 IEEE International Conference on Automation, Quality and Testing. Robotics*. IEEE Press: *1*, 393–397.

Salvador, F. (2007). Toward a product system modularity construct: literature review and reconceptualization. *IEEE Transactions on Engineering Management, 54*(2), 219–240. doi:10.1109/TEM.2007.893996

Samarawickrema, G., & Stacey, E. (2007). Adopting web-based learning and teaching: A case study in higher education. *Distance Education, 28*(3), 313–333. doi:10.1080/01587910701611344

Sarac, A., Absi, N., & Dauzere-Peres, S. (2009). A literature review on the impact of RFID technologies on supply chain management. *Integrating the Global Supply Chain, 128*(1), 77-95. Retrieved June 30, from http://citeseerx.ist.psu.edu/viewdoc/download?doi=10.1.1.169.7017&rep=rep1&type=pdf

Sarkis, J. (2001). Manufacturing's role in corporate environmental sustainability: Concerns for the new millennium. *International Journal of Operations & Production Management, 21*(5/6), 666–685. doi:10.1108/01443570110390390

Sarkis, J. (2003). A strategic decision framework for green supply chain management. *Journal of Cleaner Production, 11*(4), 397–409. doi:10.1016/S0959-6526(02)00062-8

Sarkis, J., Meade, M. L., & Talluri, S. (2004). E-logistics and the natural environment. *Supply Chain Management: An International Journal, 9*(4), 303–312. doi:10.1108/13598540410550055

Sarmaniotis, C., & Stefanou, C. J. (2005). A framework of CRM development phases and key success factors. In *Proceedings of the 2nd International Conference on Enterprise Systems and Accounting*, (pp. 477-495). Thessaloniki, Greece: IEEE.

Sasazaki, S., Itoh, K., Arimitsu, S., Imada, T., Takasuga, A., & Nagaishi, H. (2004). Development of breed identification markers derived from AFLP in beef cattle. *Meat Science, 67,* 275–280. doi:10.1016/j.meatsci.2003.10.016

Sauvage, T. (2003). The relationship between technology and logistics third-party providers. *International Journal of Physical Distribution and Logistics Management, 33*(3), 236–253. doi:10.1108/09600030310471989

Sawik, T. (2011). Selection of supply portfolio under disruption risks. *Omega: The International Journal of Management Science, 39,* 194–208. doi:10.1016/j.omega.2010.06.007

Sawik, T. (2011). Selection of a dynamic supply portfolio in make-to-order environment with risks. *Computers & Operations Research, 38,* 782–796. doi:10.1016/j.cor.2010.09.011

Sbihi, A., & Eglese, W. R. (2007). Combinatorial optimization and green logistics. *4OR: A Quarterly Journal of Operations Research, 5*(2), 99-116.

Scheer, F. P. (2006). Optimizing supply chains using traceability systems. In Smith, I., & Furness, A. (Eds.), *Improving Traceability in Food Processing and Distribution* (pp. 52–64). New York, NY: Woodhead Publishing. doi:10.1533/9781845691233.1.52

Schilling, M. A. (2000). Toward a general modular systems theory and its application to interfirm product modularity. *Academy of Management Review, 25*(2), 312–334.

Schoenherr, T. (2008). Diffusion of online reverse auctions for B2B procurement: An exploratory study. *International Journal of Operations & Production Management, 28*(3), 259–278. doi:10.1108/01443570810856189

Schoenherr, T., & Mabert, V. A. (2007). Online reverse auctions: Common myths versus evolving reality. *Business Horizons, 50*(5), 373–384. doi:10.1016/j.bushor.2007.03.003

Schramm, T., Nogueira, S., & Jones, D. (2011). Cloud computing and supply chain: A natural fit for the future. *Logistics Management.* Retrieved September 14, 2012, from http://www.logisticsmgmt.com/

Schramm, T., Wright, J., Seng, D., & Jones, D. (2010). Six questions every supply chain executive should ask about cloud computing. *Accenture.* Retrieved September 14, 2012, from http://www.accenture.com/us-en/pages/index.aspx

Schrödl, H., & Turowski, K. (2011). SCOR in the cloud – Potential of cloud computing for the optimization of supply chain management systems. In *Proceedings of the European, Mediterranean & Middle Eastern Conference on Information Systems.* Athens, Greece: IEEE.

Schubert, P., & Williams, S. P. (2009). An extended framework for comparing expectations and realized benefits of enterprise systems implementations. In *Proceedings of the 15th Americas Conference on Information Systems.* San Francisco, CA: IEEE.

Schubert, H., Jeffery, K., & Neidecker-Lutz, B. (2010). *The future for cloud computing: Opportunities for European cloud computing beyond 2010.* Expert Group.

Schuldt, A., Hribernik, K. A., Gehrke, J. D., Thoben, K.-D., & Herzog, O. (2011). Towards fourth-party logistics providers: A business model for cloud-based autonomous logistics. In *Proceedings of CLOSER 2011.* CLOSER.

Schwagele, F. (2005). Traceability from a European perspective. *Meat Science, 71,* 164–173. doi:10.1016/j.meatsci.2005.03.002

Scott, W., & Watson, R. (2012). The value of green IT: A theoretical framework and exploratory assessment of cloud computing. In *Proceedings of the 25th Bled eConference - eDependability: Reliable and Trustworthy eStructures, eProcesses, eOperations and eServices for the Future.* Bled, Slovenia: IEEE.

Scott, C., & Westbrook, R. (1991). New strategic tools for supply chain management. *International Journal of Physical Distribution & Logistics Management, 21*(1), 22–23. doi:10.1108/09600039110002225

Seddon, J., & O'Donavan, B. (2010). Rethinking lean service. *Management Services, 54*(1), 34-37. Retrieved from http://web.ebscohost.com.ezproxy.liv.ac.uk/ehost/pdfviewer/pdfviewer?hid=18&sid=4d80a25b-7da8-47cf-89f7-bcf273aba0d5%40sessionmgr12&vid=3

Seeley, M. (2006). Impact of the internet on the services aspect of the STM publishing business. *Information Services & Use, 26,* 173–175.

Seferlis, P., & Giannelos, N. F. (2004). A two-layered optimization-based control strategy for multi-echelon supply chain networks. *Computers & Chemical Engineering, 28*, 799–809. doi:10.1016/j.compchemeng.2004.02.022

Sengupta, H., Heiser, R., & Cook, S. (2006). Manufacturing and service supply chain performance: A comparative analysis. *Journal of Supply Chain Management, 42*(4), 4–15. doi:10.1111/j.1745-493X.2006.00018.x

Setijono, D., & Dahlgaard, J. J. (2007). Customer value as a key performance indicator (KPI) and a key improvement indicator (KII). *Measuring Business Excellence, 11*(2), 44-61. Retrieved from http://www.emeraldinsight.com.ezproxy.liv.ac.uk/journals.htm?issn=1368-3047&volume=11&issue=2&articleid=1610500&show=pdf

Sharif, A. M., & Irani, Z. (2005). Emergence of ERPII characteristics within an ERP integration context. In *Proceedings of the Eleventh Americas Conference on Information Systems*, (pp. 1-9). Omaha, NE: IEEE.

Sharma, S. K., & Kitchens, F. (2003). Assessing technology integration. In *Proceedings of the 7th Pacific Asia Conference on Information Systems*. Adelaide, Australia: IEEE.

Sharma, H., Lavania, D., & Gupta, N. (2011). ERP + e-business = an emerging relationship. *International Journal of Managing Value and Supply Chains, 2*(2).

Sheffi, Y. (1990). Third party logistics: Present and future prospects. *Journal of Business Logistics, 11*(2), 27–39.

Sheffi, Y. (2004). Combinatorial auctions in the procurement of transportation services. *Interfaces, 34*(4), 245–252. doi:10.1287/inte.1040.0075

Simatupang, T. M., & Sridharan, R. (2008). Design for supply chain collaboration. *Business Process Management Journal, 14*(3), 401–418. doi:10.1108/14637150810876698

Singh, B., Garg, S. K., & Sharma, S. K. (2010). Development of index for measuring leanness: Study of an Indian auto component industry. *Measuring Business Excellence, 14*(2), 46-53. Retrieved from http://www.emeraldinsight.com.ezproxy.liv.ac.uk/journals.htm?issn=1368-3047&volume=14&issue=2&articleid=1863916&show=pdf

Singla, A. (2008). Impact of ERP systems on small and mid-sized public sector enterprises. *Journal of Theoretical and Applied Information Technology, 14*(1), 119–131.

Singla, A. R., & Goyal, D. P. (2006). Managing risk factors in ERP implementation and design: An empirical investigation of the Indian industry. *Journal of Advances in Management Research, 3*(1), 59–67. doi:10.1108/97279810680001239

Smart, A. (2010). Exploring the business case for e-procurement. *International Journal of Physical Distribution & Logistics Management, 40*(3), 181–201. Retrieved from http://www.emeraldinsight.com.ezproxy.liv.ac.uk/journals.htm?issn=0960-0035&volume=40&issue=3&articleid=1852848&show=pdfdoi:10.1108/09600031011035083

Smeltzer, L. R., & Carr, A. (2002). Reverse auctions in industrial marketing and buying. *Business Horizons, 45*(2), 47–52. doi:10.1016/S0007-6813(02)00187-8

Smeltzer, L. R., & Carr, A. S. (2003). Electronic reverse auctions promises, risks and conditions for success. *Industrial Marketing Management, 32*(6), 481–488. doi:10.1016/S0019-8501(02)00257-2

Somers, T., & Nelson, K. (2004). A taxonomy of players and activities across the ERP project life cycle. *Information & Management, 41*, 257–278. doi:10.1016/S0378-7206(03)00023-5

Soni, G., & Kodali, R. (2011). A critical analysis of supply chain management content in empirical research. *Business Process Management, 17*(2), 238–266. doi:10.1108/14637151111122338

Soroor, J., Tarokh, M., & Keshtgary, M. (2009). Preventing failure in IT-enabled systems for supply chain management. *International Journal of Production Research, 47*(23), 6543–6557. doi:10.1080/00207540802314837

Srikanta, R. (2009). Antecedents and drivers for green supply chain management implementation in manufacturing environment. *The Icfai University Journal of Supply Chain Management, 6*(1), 20.

Srivastava, S. K., & Srivastava, R. K. (2006). Managing product returns for reverse logistics. *International Journal of Physical Distribution & Logistics Management, 36*(7), 524–546. doi:10.1108/09600030610684962

Starr, M. K. (1965). Modular production-a new concept. *Harvard Business Review, 43*(6), 131–142.

Starr, M. K. (2010). Modular production - A 45-year-old concept. *International Journal of Operations & Production Management*, *30*(1), 7–19. doi:10.1108/01443571011012352

Stefanou, C. J., & Athanasaki, M. T. (2012). The adoption and selection process of CRM software: A review of the literature. In *Proceedings of the International Conference on Contemporary Marketing Issues*, (pp. 390-399). Thessaloniki, Greece: IEEE.

Stefanou, C. J. (2001). Organizational key success factors for implementing SCM/ERP systems to support decision making. *Journal of Decision Systems*, *10*(1), 49–64. doi:10.3166/jds.10.49-64

Stefanou, C. J. (2001). A framework for the ex-ante evaluation of ERP software. *European Journal of Information Systems*, *10*, 204–212. doi:10.1057/palgrave.ejis.3000407

Stefanou, C. J., Sarmaniotis, C., & Stafyla, A. (2003). CRM and customer-centric knowledge management: An empirical research. *Business Process Management Journal*, *9*(5), 617–634. doi:10.1108/14637150310496721

Stevens, J., Weich, C., & GilChrist, R. (2010). RuBee (IEEE 1902.1) – The physics behind, real-time, high security wireless asset visibility networks in harsh environments. *Viable Assets, Inc.* Retrieved from http://www.rubee.com/White-SEC/RuBee-Security-080610.pdf

Stevens, J. (2002). *Applied multivariate statistics for social sciences* (4th ed.). Hoboken, NJ: Lawrence Erlbaum Associates Publisher.

Stock, J. R. (2001). The 7 deadly sins of reverse logistics. *Material Handling Management*, *56*(3), 5–11.

Stough, R. R. (2001). New technologies in logistics management. In Brewer, (Eds.), *Handbook of Logistics and Supply Chain Management* (p. 517). London, UK: Elsevier Science Limited.

Sugak, D. B. (2011). Rankings of a university's web sites on the internet. *Scientific and Technical Information Processing*, *38*(1), 17–19. doi:10.3103/S014768821101014X

Sujay, R. (2011). Hybrid cloud: A new era. *International Journal of Computer Science and Technology*, *2*(2), 323–326.

Sullivan, D. (2010). *Has Facebook's active user growth dropped 25% to 50*. Search Engine Land.

Survey System. (2010). *Sample size calculator.* Retrieved from http://www.surveysystem.com/sscalc.htm

Swaminathan, J., & Tayur, S. (2003). Models for supply chains in e-business. *Management Science*, *49*(10). doi:10.1287/mnsc.49.10.1387.17309

Sykes, A. O. (2012). *An introduction to regression analysis.* Retrieved from http://www.law.uchicago.edu/files/files/20.Sykes_.Regression.pdf

Takeishi, A., & Fujimoto, T. (2003). Modularization in the car industry. *The Business of Systems Integration*, *1*, 254–279. doi:10.1093/0199263221.003.0013

Tan, A., & Kumar, A. (2008). A decision making model to maximise the value of reverse logistics in the computer. *International Journal of Logistics Systems and Management*, *4*(3), 297–312. doi:10.1504/IJLSM.2008.017478

Tang, C. S. (2006). Perspectives in supply chain risk management. *International Journal of Production Economics*, *103*, 451–488. doi:10.1016/j.ijpe.2005.12.006

Tassabehji, R., Taylor, W. A., Beach, R., & Wood, A. (2006). Reverse e-auctions and supplier-buyer relationships: An exploratory study. *International Journal of Operations & Production Management*, *26*(2), 166–184. doi:10.1108/01443570610641657

Teich, J. E., Wallenius, H., Wallenius, J., & Koppius, O. R. (2004). Emerging multiple issue e-auctions. *European Journal of Operational Research*, *159*(1), 1–16. doi:10.1016/j.ejor.2003.05.001

Terzi, S., Cassina, J., & Panetto, H. (2004). Development of a metamodel to foster interoperability along the product lifecycle traceability. In *Proceedings of INTEROP 2004.* INTEROP.

Themistocleous, M., & Irani, Z. (2003). Integrating cross-enterprise systems: An innovative framework for the introduction of enterprise application integration. In *Proceedings of the Eleventh European Conference on Information Systems.* Naples, Italy: IEEE.

Themistocleous, M., Mantzana, V., & Morabito, V. (2009). Achieving knowledge management integration through EAI: A case study from healthcare sector. *International Journal of Technology Management, 47*(1/2/3), 114–126.

Theurer, J. (1998). Seven pitfalls to avoid when establishing performance measures. *Public Management, 80*(7), 21–24.

Tilanus, B. (1997). *Information systems in logistics and transportation.* London, UK: Pergamon.

Tinham, B. (2010). Driving up efficiency: Lean processes and IT. *Works Management, 63*(4), 34-37. Retrieved from http://ehis.ebscohost.com.ezproxy.liv.ac.uk/eds/pdfviewer/pdfviewer?vid=9&hid=6&sid=6cb9fd95-fa0b-417e-9ac6-0034b265e2c9%40sessionmgr11

Tomlin, B. (2009). Impact of supply learning when suppliers are unreliable. *Manufacturing & Service Operations Management, 11*(2), 192–209. doi:10.1287/msom.1070.0206

Tomlin, B., & Wang, Y. (2005). On the value of mix flexibility and dual sourcing in unreliable newsvendor networks. *Manufacturing & Service Operations Management, 7*(1), 37–57. doi:10.1287/msom.1040.0063

Torre, L., Boella, G., & Verhagen (Eds.). (2008). Normative multi-agent systems. *Journal of Autonomous Agents and Multi-Agent Systems, 17*(1).

Trienekens, J. H., Wognum, P. M., Beulens, A. J. M., & van der Vorst, J. G. A. J. (2012). Transparency in complex dynamic food supply chains. *Advanced Engineering Informatics, 26*, 55–65. doi:10.1016/j.aei.2011.07.007

Tyan, J., Wang, F. K., & Du, T. (2003). Applying collaborative transportation management models in global third-party logistics. *International Journal of Computer Integrated Manufacturing, 16*(4–5), 283–291. doi:10.1080/0951192031000089183

Ulrich, K. (1995). The role of product architecture in the manufacturing firm. *Research Policy, 24*, 419–440. doi:10.1016/0048-7333(94)00775-3

Ustundag, A. (2010). Evaluating RFID investment on a supply chain using tagging cost sharing factor. *International Journal of Production Research, 48*(9), 2549–2562. doi:10.1080/00207540903564926

Ustun, O., & Demirtas, E. A. (2008). An integrated multi-objective decision making process for multi-period lot sizing with supplier selection. *Omega: The International Journal of Management Science, 36*, 509–521. doi:10.1016/j.omega.2006.12.004

Uwizeyemungu, S., & Raymond, L. (2010). Linking the effects of ERP to organizational performance: Development and initial validation of an evaluation method. *Information Systems Management, 27*(1), 25–41. doi:10.1080/10580530903455122

Van der Putten, S., Robu, V., Poutré, H. L., Jorritsma, A., & Gal, M. (2006). Automating supply chain negotiations using autonomous agents: A case study in transportation logistics. In *Proceedings of the 5th International Conference on Autonomous Agents and Multi Agent Systems,* (pp. 1506-1513). ACM Press.

Van der Vaart, T., & van Donk, D. P. (2008). A critical review of survey-based research in supply chain integration. *International Journal of Production Economics, 111*(1), 42–55. doi:10.1016/j.ijpe.2006.10.011

Van der Vorst, J. G. A. J. (2004). *Performance levels in food traceability and the impact on chain design: Results of an international benchmark study.* Paper presented at the 6th International Conference on Chain and Network Management in Agribusiness and the Food Industry. Ede, The Netherlands.

Van der Vorst, J., & Beulens, A. (2002). Identifying sources of uncertainty to generate supply chain redesign strategies. *International Journal of physical Distribution and Logistics Management, 32*(6), 409-430.

Van Dorp, C. A. (2004). *Reference-data modelling for tracking and tracing.* (Ph.D. Thesis). Wageningen University. Wageningen, The Netherlands.

Van Hoek, R. (2001). E-supply chains-virtually non-existing. *Supply Chain Management International Journal, 6*, 21–28. doi:10.1108/13598540110694653

Vandermerwe, S., & Rada, J. (1988). Servitization of business: Adding value by adding services. *European Management Journal, 6*(4), 314–324. doi:10.1016/0263-2373(88)90033-3

Vargo, S. L., & Lusch, R. F. (2008). Service-dominant logic: Continuing the evolution. *Journal of the Academy of Marketing Science, 36*(1), 1–10. doi:10.1007/s11747-007-0069-6

Vasileiou, M., Hartley, R., & Rowley, J. (2009). An overview of the e-book market place. *Online Information Review, 33*(1), 173–192. doi:10.1108/14684520910944454

Vasileiou, M., & Rowley, J. (2008). Progressing the definition of e-book. *Library Hi Tech, 26*(3), 355–368. doi:10.1108/07378830810903292

Verdenius, F. (2006). Using traceability systems to optimise business performance. In Smith, I., & Furness, A. (Eds.), *Improving Traceability in Food Processing and Distribution* (pp. 26–51). New York, NY: Woodhead Publishing. doi:10.1533/9781845691233.1.26

Véronneau, S., & Roy, J. (2009). Global service supply chains: An empirical study of current practices and challenges of a cruise line corporation. *Tourism Management, 30*(1), 128–139. doi:10.1016/j.tourman.2008.05.008

Véronneau, S., & Roy, J. (2009). RFID benefits, costs, and possibilities: The economical analysis of RFID deployment in a cruise corporation global service supply chain. *International Journal of Production Economics, 122*(2), 692–702. doi:10.1016/j.ijpe.2009.06.038

Veryfields.com. (2012). *How do RFID tags work?* Retrieved June 30 from http://www.veryfields.net/how-do-rfid-tags-work

Voss, C., & Hsuan, J. (2009). Service architecture and modularity. *Decision Science Journal, 40*(4), 541–569. doi:10.1111/j.1540-5915.2009.00241.x

Vouk, M. (2008). Cloud computing – Issues, research and implementations. *Journal of Computing and Information Technology, 16*(4), 235–246.

Vouxaras, N., & Folinas, D. (2010). Logistics outsourcing: Methodology for the selection of the suitable 3PL partner. *Supply Chain & Logistics, 34*, 54–55.

Walker, D., Pitt, M., & Thakur, U. J. (2007). Environmental management systems information management and corporate responsibility. *Journal of Facilities Management, 5*(1), 49–61. doi:10.1108/14725960710726346

Wamaba, S., & Boeck, H. (2007). Enhancing information flow in a retail supply chain using RFID and the EPC network: A proof-of-concept approach. *Journal of Theoretical and Applied Electronic Commerce Research, 3*(1), 92–105.

Wamaba, S., & Chatfield, A. (2009). A contingency model for creating value from RFID in supply chain network projects in logistics and manufacturing environments. *European Journal of Information Systems, 18*(6), 615–636. doi:10.1057/ejis.2009.44

Wang, M., Liu, J., Shen, J., Tang, Y., & Zhou, N. (2012). Security issues of RFID technology in supply chain management. *Advanced Materials Research, 2*. Retrieved from http://www.scientific.net/AMR.490-495.2470

Wang, N., Zhang, N., & Wang, M. (2006). Wireless sensors in agriculture and food industry-Recent development and future perspective. *Computers and Electronics in Agriculture, 50*, 1–14. doi:10.1016/j.compag.2005.09.003

Ward, M., & Kranenburg, R. (2006). RFID: Frequency, standards, adoption and innovation. *JISC Technology and Standards Watch*. Retrieved from http://www.jisc.ac.uk/uploaded_documents/TSW0602.doc

Waters, D. (2008). *Quantitative methods for business* (4th ed.). Upper Saddle River, NJ: Prentice Hall.

Watkins, B. (2010). Cloud computing: Theirs, mine, ours. *FedEx*. Retrieved September 14, 2012, from http://itri.uark.edu/

Watson, G. S. (1964). Smooth regression analysis. *Sankhyā: The Indian Journal of Statistics, Series A, 26*(4), 359–372. Retrieved from http://www.jstor.org.ezproxy.liv.ac.uk/stable/pdfplus/25049340.pdf?acceptTC=true

Watson, K., Klingenberg, B., Polito, T., & Geurts, T. G. (2004). Impact of environmental management system implementation on financial performance: A comparison of two corporate strategies. *Management of Environmental Quality: An International Journal, 15*(6), 622–628. doi:10.1108/14777830410560700

Weiming, S., Qi, H., Shuying, W., Yinsheng, L., & Hamada, G. (2007). An agent-based service-oriented integration architecture for collaborative intelligent manufacturing. *Robotics and Computer-integrated Manufacturing, 23*, 315–325. doi:10.1016/j.rcim.2006.02.009

Weinstein, R. (2005). IRFID: A technical overview and its application to enterprise. *IT Professional, 7*(3), 27–33. Retrieved from http://ieeexplore.ieee.org/xpls/abs_all.jsp?arnumber=1490473&tag=1doi:10.1109/MITP.2005.69

Weissberg, A. (2008). The identification of digital book content. *Publishing Research Quarterly, 24*(4), 255–260. doi:10.1007/s12109-008-9093-8

Whang, S. (2010). Timing of RFID adoption in a supply chain. *Management Science, 56*(2), 343–355. doi:10.1287/mnsc.1090.1121

White, B. (2000). *Dissertation skills for business and management students*. Andover, MI: Cengage Learning.

White, R., & James, B. (1998). *The outsourcing manual*. London, UK: Grower House.

Wieder, B., Booth, P., Matolcsy, Z. P., & Ossimitz, M. (2006). The impact of ERP systems on firm and business process performance. *Journal of Enterprise Information Management, 19*(1), 13–29. doi:10.1108/17410390610636850

Wilding, R., & Humphries, A. S. (2006). Understanding collaborative supply chain relationships through the application of the Williamson organisational failure framework. *International Journal of Physical Distribution & Logistics Management, 36*(4), 309–329. doi:10.1108/09600030610672064

Willis, T., & Willis-Brown, A. (2002). Extending the value of ERP. *Industrial Management & Data Systems, 102*(1), 35–38. doi:10.1108/02635570210414640

Wilson, M. M. J., & Roy, R. M. (2009). Enabling lean procurement: A consolidation model for small- and medium-sized enterprises. *Journal of Manufacturing Technology Management, 20*(6), 817–833. Retrieved from http://www.emeraldinsight.com.ezproxy.liv.ac.uk/journals.htm?issn=1741-038X&volume=20&issue=6&articleid=1801230&show=pdfdoi:10.1108/17410380910975096

Wilson, T. P., & Clarke, W. R. (1998). Food safety and traceability in the agricultural supply chain: Using the internet to deliver traceability. *Supply Chain Management, 3*, 127–133. doi:10.1108/13598549810230831

Wincel, J. P. (2004). *Lean supply chain management: A handbook for strategic procurement*. New York, NY: Productivity Press.

Wognum, P. M., Bremmers, H., Trienekens, J. H., van der Vorst, J. G. A. J., & Bloemhof, J. M. (2011). Systems for sustainability and transparency of food supply chains – Current status and challenges. *Advanced Engineering Informatics, 25*, 65–76. doi:10.1016/j.aei.2010.06.001

Womack, J. P. (2007). Moving beyond the tool age (lean management). *IET Manufacturing Engineer, 86*(4), 4-5. Retrieved from http://web.ebscohost.com.ezproxy.liv.ac.uk/ehost/pdfviewer/pdfviewer?hid=18&sid=ab420297-1492-4a61-953f-1df158c7a222%40sessionmgr11&vid=2

Womack, J. P., & Jones, D. T. (2003). *Lean thinking*. New York, NY: Free Press.

Wongvasu, N. (2001). Methodologies for providing rapid and effective response to request for quotation (RFQ) of mass customization products. (Dissertation). Northeastern University. Boston, MA.

World Resources Institute. (2007). *GDP: Percent GDP from services 2006 for Europe*. Retrieved from http://earthtrends.wri.org/searchable_db/index.php?step=countries&ccID%5B%5D=2&theme=5&variable_ID=216&action=select_years

Wu, D., & Olson, D. L. (2008). Supply chain risk, simulation, and vendor selection. *International Journal of Production Economics, 114*, 646–655. doi:10.1016/j.ijpe.2008.02.013

Wu, G., & Feng, Y. (2005). Study on workflow-based open competitive bidding e-procurement mechanism. *Services Systems and Services Management, 1*(1), 791–796.

Xiao, Y. M., & Wang, X. Y. (2008). Early-warning analysis on stability of supply chain based on entropy theory. *Journal of Industrial Engineering and Engineering Management, 3*, 57–63.

Xia, W., & Wu, Z. (2007). Supplier selection with multiple criteria in volume discount environments. *Omega: The International Journal of Management Science, 35*, 494–504. doi:10.1016/j.omega.2005.09.002

Xing, Y., Grant, D. B., McKinnon, A. C., & Fernie, J. (2011). The interface between retailers and logistics service providers in the online market. *European Journal of Marketing, 45*(3), 334–357. doi:10.1108/03090561111107221

Xu, X. (2012). From cloud computing to cloud manufacturing. *Robotics and Computer-integrated Manufacturing*, 28, 75–86. doi:10.1016/j.rcim.2011.07.002

Xu, Y. T., & Zhang, S. L. (2001). The supervision and control system research of SCM based on process enterprise. *Basic Automation*, 8(4), 12–14.

Yang, C., & Su, Y. F. (2009). The relationship between benefits of ERP systems implementation and its impacts on firm performance of SCM. *Journal of Enterprise Information Management*, 22(6), 722–752. doi:10.1108/17410390910999602

Yongbin, H., & Qifeng, W. (2010). Study on the forth party logistics information service platform based on web services. In *Proceedings of the International Conference on Innovative Computing and Communication and 2010 Asia-Pacific Conference on Information Technology and Ocean Integration Architecture for Collaborative Intelligent Manufacturing. Robotics and Computer-integrated Manufacturing*, IEEE, 23, 315–325.

Zhang, K., Xu, R., Zhang, Y., Sai, Y., & Wang, X. (2008). An ontology supported semantic web service composition method in enterprise. In *Proceedings of the IEEE International Multi-Symposiums on Computer and Computational*, (pp. 222-227). IEEE Press.

Zhang, C., & Li, S. (2006). Secure information sharing in internet-based supply management systems. *Journal of Computer Information Systems*, 46(4), 18–24.

Zhang, K., Chai, Y., Yang, S. X., & Weng, D. L. (2011). Pre-warning analysis and application in traceability systems for food production supply chains. *Expert Systems with Applications*, 38(3), 2500–2507. doi:10.1016/j.eswa.2010.08.039

Zhang, Q., Cheng, L., & Boutaba, R. (2010). Cloud computing: State-of-the-art and research challenges. *Journal of Internet Services and Applications*, 1(1), 7–18. doi:10.1007/s13174-010-0007-6

Zhang, Y. (2002). The characteristic analysis of finance supervision in supply chain management. *Shanghai Accounting*, 11, 31–32.

Zheng, J., Harland, C., Lamming, R., Johnsen, T., & Wynstra, F. (2000). Networking activities in supply networks. *Journal of Strategic Marketing*, 8, 161–181.

Zhou, L., Xie, Y., Wild, N., & Hunt, C. (2008). Learning and practising supply chain management strategies from a business simulation game: A comprehensive supply chain simulation. In *Proceedings of the Winter Simulation Conference 2008*. IEEE.

Zhou, L., Zhu, Y., Lin, Y., & Bentley, Y. (2012). Cloud supply chain: A conceptual model. In *Proceedings of International Working Seminar on Production Economics*. Innsbruck, Austria: IEEE.

Zhu, Q., Sarkis, J., & Geng, Y. (2005). Green supply chain management in China: Pressures, practices performance. *International Journal of Operations & Production Management*, 25(5), 449–468. doi:10.1108/01443570510593148

Zhu, Q., Sarkis, J., & Lai, H. (2007). Initiatives and outcomes of green supply chain management implementation by Chinese manufacturers. *Journal of Environmental Management*, 85(1), 179–189. doi:10.1016/j.jenvman.2006.09.003

Zsidisin, G. A., Jun, M. J., & Adams, L. L. (2000). The relationship between information technology and service quality in the dual-direction supply chain: A case study approach. *International Journal of Service Industry Management*, 11(4), 312–328. doi:10.1108/09564230010355359

About the Contributors

Deryn Graham is currently a Senior Lecturer in Information Systems at the Business School, and a former Visiting Fellow at the School of Computing and Mathematical Sciences, University of Greenwich. Dr. Graham's background and qualifications are in Computer Science and Artificial Intelligence. Deryn Graham's teaching and research interests are in the areas of E-Logistics, E-Learning and Teaching, Human-Computer Interaction and Interaction Design, Visualisation, and Artificial Intelligence, areas in which she has both published and held national and international grants such EU FP5. Dr. Graham is a European Engineer, and a Fellow of both the British Computer Society (FBCS) and the Higher Education Academy (HEA). She holds a PhD (Artificial Intelligence) and masters degrees in Computer Science (MSc) and in Education (MA). Deryn Graham is also a Chartered Engineer (C. Eng.) and Chartered IT Professional (CITP).

Ioannis Manikas is a Senior Lecturer on Logistics and Supply Chain Management in the Department of System Management and Strategy of the University of Greenwich Business School. Dr. Manikas holds a Master of Science in Food Science and Technology from Aristotle University, and a Master of Science in the field of Logistics, from Cranfield University. He holds a PhD from the Department of Agricultural Economics at Aristotle University of Thessaloniki and his primary interests include supply chain management, logistics, and agribusiness management. He has conducted research for projects regarding supply chain modelling, development of IT solutions for agrifood supply chain management and traceability both in Greece and the UK. He has a wide experience in the elaboration of research proposals under FP6, FP7, and Eurostars-Eureka funding mechanisms, Life Long Learning oriented programs such as Leonardo, and Interregional Development programs such as Interreg III and Interreg IVC. His work as a self employed project manager and consultant in the Agrifood sector includes the design and development of regional operational programs, analysis of regional needs, and respective development policies focused on rural and food production, definition of funding areas and financing resources, definition of strategic goals for regional development and formulation of respective performance monitoring systems, and assessment (ex-ante, on-going, ex-post) of the implementation of EC and national funding mechanisms in national and regional level. Dr Manikas has published his work in over 30 peer reviewed journals and international conferences.

Dimitrios Folinas holds a Ph.D. in e-Logistics from the Department of Applied Informatics, University of Macedonia, Greece, and is an expert in e-logistics, e-supply chain, logistics information systems, and virtual organisations. He is an Assistant Professor at the Department of Logistics of ATEI-TH. and has held various teaching posts with the ATEI-TH., and University of Macedonia. He is the author and co-author of over 120 research publications, and as a researcher he has prepared, submitted, and managed a number of projects funded by National and European Union research entities.

* * *

Eirini Aivazidou is an undergraduate student at the Industrial Management Division of the Department of Mechanical Engineering of the Aristotle University of Thessaloniki. Her studies cover the fields of mechanical design and manufacturing, energy efficiency, as well as industrial engineering. She is specifically interested in operations research, logistics engineering, and supply chain management, with a major focus on green logistics and new technologies in supply chain management. Mrs. Aivazidou has been awarded by the State Scholarship Foundation of Greece for her performance as a student of Mechanical Engineering for the academic year 2009-2010. She is also a member of the Greek Association of Supply Chain Management (GASCM) since 2011.

Antonios Antoniou is an undergraduate student at the Industrial Management Division of the Department of Mechanical Engineering of the Aristotle University of Thessaloniki. His research interests specialize in the field of Logistics and Supply Chain Management. He is a member of the Greek Association of Supply Chain Management (GASCM). Mr. Antoniou has also attended numerous local as well as international events and conferences on logistics and supply chain management.

Konstantinos Arvanitopoulos-Darginis is an undergraduate student at the Design and Structures Division of the Department of Mechanical Engineering of the Aristotle University of Thessaloniki. His interests lie in the fields of vehicle dynamics and machine design, with a focus on new technologies and software. He is also a member of SAE International and Institution of Mechanical Engineers (IMechE). Mr. Arvanitopoulos-Darginis is currently a member of Aristotle Racing Team (ART), a student team that designs and builds a single-seater race car and participates in Formula SAE series (3rd place overall in Formula ATA 2012, Italy).

Sophia Asprodini has studied at the University of Sheffield International Faculty, City College, Greece. She has a Bachelor's Degree in Management and a Master's Degree in Supply Chain Management and Logistics. She has a considerable working experience in the logistics field, specifically in purchasing, forwarding, and warehouse management.

Victor Chang was an IT Manager/IT Lead in one of NHS Trusts, UK. He is working as a Senior Lecturer at Leeds Metropolitan University since September 2012. He previously worked as a Lecturer and IT Architect at Business School, University of Greenwich, while doing and completing his part-time research with the University of Southampton and also part-time PGCert with the University of Greenwich. CCBF is part of his research and consultancy to help organisations in achieving good Cloud design, deployment, and services. He has 22 publications in his PhD, and offers 100% effort for his full-time work. With 14 years of IT experience, he is one of the most active practitioners and researchers in Cloud in England.

Richard Forster is a PhD student at the University of Liverpool Management School. His thesis focuses on the use of commercially relevant technologies and their application within Small to Medium Enterprises (SMEs). He studied for a BSc in e-Business at the University of Liverpool Management School and went onto to do his MSc in e-Business Systems and Strategy at the same institution. His areas of interest include e-business and e-commerce, logistics and supply chain integration, m-commerce, enterprise resource planning, and emergent Web 2.0 ontologies. Within each of these areas he has a particular focus on their adoption and integration within SMEs.

Sudhanshu Joshi is an expert in the area of Supply Chain and Information Systems. He obtained his Masters degrees in Computer Applications and Finance. He did his Doctoral in the area of Supply Chain Information Systems and subsequently obtained his Post Doctoral in Supply Chain Optimization in Service Industry with special reference to Banking Sector among BRIC nations. Dr. Sudhanshu Joshi has 35 international research papers, 5 books, and 7 book chapters to his name. His area of research is supply chain optimization, supply chain integration, and modelling.

Bill Karakostas is a Senior Lecturer in School of Informatics at City University London. Bill received the MSc and PhD in Software Engineering from University of Manchester, United Kingdom. Bill has published over 150 research papers and three books on systems requirement engineering, model-driven service engineering, and service customization. His research interests include Cloud and service computing. He is a member of the ACM and IEEE Computer Society.

Athanasios Kelemis is an Associate Professor in ATEI-TH in Department of Logistics in Katerini. His main research areas include Distributed Systems and Internet Applications in trade and economy. He is also an Honorary Professor in the University of Applied Sciences in Thessaloniki, Department of Logistics. Until 2008, he was the Chief Consultant of German-Hellenic Chamber of Commerce (DGIHK), responsible for Knowhow Transfer in the Area of Environmental Technologies and Renewable Energy Sources. He was responsible in several EU-projects since 1996; more than 15 years of experience in commercial and strategic management, BPM, organisation, and production flow structuring, generation of ITC strategies. He has 15 years working experience of professional activities in Germany and Greece before joining the ATEI in the present position. Finally, he is the author of numerous reports and presentations as well as 17 professional publications in journals and handbooks on the subject of knowledge and strategic information management in commercial or industrial work environments.

Carina Nicole Leistner earned her diploma in Business Administration (Diplom Betriebswirtin [BA]) focussing on logistics and finance from the German University of Co-operative Education Ravensburg in 2007. While pursuing her degree, Carina N. Leistner has worked at various sites in Germany and the UK and within several departments relating to supply chain management, legal, and finance of a large European aeronautical company. Initially commencing in a position as Financial Controller, Carina N. Leistner has changed to procurement in 2008. In the following years she gained substantial experience in the field of operational and strategic procurement, mainly relating to the commodities of IT Hardware, Software, and Services. During that time she also pursued a post-graduate Master's degree in Supply Chain Management and Operations awarded by the University of Liverpool in 2011. Carina N. Leistner is currently employed as Strategic Buyer for IT Application Services with transnational area of responsibility and a yearly spend of 25M€. In her spare time she enjoys running, reading, and travelling.

Guo Li is currently working as an Associate Professor in School of Management and Economics at Beijing Institute of Technology, Beijing, China. He graduated from Central South University in 2003 and obtained his Master's degree in Hunan University in 2005. In 2009, he received his Doctor's degree in Management Science and Engineering from Huazhong University of Science and Technology, Wuhan, China. His areas of interest are supply logistics and algorithm for NP-hard problems, data-mining technology, risks management in supply chain. He has published more than 30 journal papers as first author. Among them more than 15 journal papers are indexed by SCI-EXPANDED or EI. In recent years, he has taken charge of many projects mainly supported by National Natural Science Foundation of China, and Beijing Natural Science Foundation. He is also the reviewer of refereed international magazines and journals.

Yong Lin is a Senior Lecturer in Operations Management in the Business School, University of Greenwich. His research interests lie in the field of modularity, service operations management, and logistics management. In addition to the PhD on Management, he has earned an MSc in Industrial Engineering and a BSc in Enterprise Management. Before joining the University of Greenwich, he worked as an Associate Professor in the Huazhong University of Science and Technology in China. He spent many years in teaching and research, including in charge of several consulting projects and research funds from NSFC (Natural Science Foundation of China) and National 863 Plan. He also had been a Visiting Researcher in the University of Cambridge and a Research Assistant in the Hong Kong University of Science and Technology.

Shihua Ma is a Professor in the Management School of the Huazhong University of Science and Technology, and also the Vice Dean of the school. His research expertise lies on the field of supply chain management, logistics management, and operations management. He has worked as Principal Investigator in several projects funded by the NSFC (National Science Foundation of China) and the 863 Program (National High Technology Research and Development Program of China).

Zenon Michaelides is Lecturer and Director of Studies for the MSc E-Business Systems and Strategy Programme at the University of Liverpool Management School. He studied Aeronautical Engineering at Chelsea College, UK, and completed his PhD from the Department of Engineering at Liverpool University, UK. His areas of research include e-business, logistics and supply chain integration, planning and control, and Enterprise Resources Planning (ERP). His special area of interest is air transport management and production systems, and he has extensive experience in working with international aerospace companies. He is a visiting Lecturer at the Ecoles des Mines Nantes, one of Frances Grand Ecoles, and City College Thessaloniki, an International Faculty of the University of Sheffield.

Fotios Misopoulos is a Senior Lecturer at the Business Administration and Economics Department at The University of Sheffield International Faculty, City College, Greece. He has an extensive teaching and consulting experience. He is teaching Logistics and Supply Chain Management courses at undergraduate, postgraduate, and MBA level in a number of countries of South-Eastern Europe. His has a strong background in Information Technology, teaching relevant courses at various higher education institutions. Additional work includes consultancy for various enterprises in Indianapolis, USA, and Thessaloniki, Greece, and has participated in a variety of projects (Sepve, Icap, etc.). He is a member of the South-East European Research Center (SEERC), EPY, and EEL.

Kamalendu Pal works for School of Informatics at City University London. Kamalendu received the MSc degree in Software Systems Technology from Sheffield University, MPhil degree in Computer Science from University College London, and MBA degree from University of Hull, United Kingdom. He has published more than dozen research papers. His research interests includes knowledge-based systems, decision support systems, computer integrated design, software engineering, and service computing. He is member of the British Computer Society and the Institution of Engineering and Technology.

Eleni-Maria Papadopoulou, PhD, is a Visiting Lecturer at ATEI of Thessaloniki (Katerini Branch) – Department of Logistics, with teaching experience in Logistics and Total Quality Management. She has a degree in Shipping, as well as an MBA with specialization in TQM from the University of Piraeus. She has obtained her Doctoral degree from the University of Macedonia. She has been occupied in the field of transportation and logistics since 2005, and more specifically she has worked in a freight forwarding company, in hotel warehousing, as well as a freelancer of logistics consulting services. Her research interests include transportation, logistics, and total quality management.

Constantinos J. Stefanou is Professor of Business Information Systems and the Director of the Laboratory of Enterprise Resources (LabER), which he established in 2004, of the Department of Accounting, Alexander Technological Educational Institute (ATEI) of Thessaloniki, Greece. Prof. Stefanou holds an MSc degree in Economics, University of London, and a PhD in Information Systems, Brunel University, London. Currently, he is also associate tutor at the Hellenic Open University and teaches Enterprise Resource Planning at a postgraduate level. Prof. Stefanou has supervised a large number of students' theses at both undergraduate and postgraduate levels as well as several PhD dissertations. He publishes, speaks at conferences and seminars, and has authored four books on Business Software Applications, ERP (SAP R/3) Systems, Enterprise Systems, and Financial Analysis using Excel. He has been on the editorial boards of international journals and currently joins the editorial board of the *International Journal of Accounting Information Systems*. He is the founder and the chair of the Organizing Committee of the International Conference on Enterprise Systems, Accounting, and Logistics (ICESAL).

Dimitrios Terzidis has broad experience of ELT Consultations in Greece and also internationally. He has a general business academic background: MSc in Banking and Finance and the MBA in Logistics degrees of the University of Sheffield, also a BA in Business Economics with Human Resource Management degree from Middlesex University.

Agorasti Toka is a Doctoral Student and member of the Laboratory of Quantitative Analysis, Logistics, and Supply Chain Management of the Industrial Management Division, Department of Mechanical Engineering, Aristotle University of Thessaloniki, Greece. She is a researcher in the field of Biomass Logistics and Supply Chain Management and her Ph.D. Thesis has been co-funded by the European Union and Greek National Funds through the Operational Program "Education and Lifelong Learning" of the National Strategic Reference Framework (NSRF) – Research Funding Program: Heracleitus II. She has published her work in a number of scientific journals and conference proceedings. Mrs. Toka is the General Director of the Greek Association of Supply Chain Management (GASCM) since March 2012.

Zhaohua Wang is working as a Professor in School of Management and Economics, Beijing Institute of Technology. He has been engaged in post-doctoral research work in Tsinghua University. Owing to his outstanding efforts in research work, he gained the chance in the program of "Beijing-Funded Plan for Talents," "Funding Scheme for Outstanding Young Teachers in Beijing Institute of Technology," and "Program for New Century Excellent Talents in University" by MOE. Dr. Wang has published 2 academic books and 70 papers in his research field. Most of his papers were published on the famous journal in China and some high level conference proceedings, such as *Journal of Management World*, *Journal of Industrial Economics in China*, *Journal of Reform*, and so on. Dr. Wang conducts several research projects. These projects are sponsored by National Nature Science Foundation, National Social Science Foundation, National Soft Science Research Planning Foundation of the MOST, Humanities and Social Sciences Foundation of MOE, and so on.

Gary Wills is an Associate Professor in Computer Science at the University of Southampton. He is a Visiting Professor at the Cape Peninsular University of Technology. Gary's research projects revolve around System Engineering and applications for industry, medicine, and education. These systems are underpinned by SOA, adaptive systems, advanced knowledge technologies, and Cloud Computing.

Xiang Zhang received his Ph.D. degree in 2007 from Huazhong University of Science and Technology. He is Associate Professor of Operations Management in the School of Management and Economics, Beijing Institute of Technology. Dr. Zhang is Principal Investigator on many research programs, including those awarded by National Nature Science Foundation, the Humanities and Social Sciences Research Funds for Young Scholars of the Ministry of Education, Beijing Excellent Talent Development Foundation, the State-Sponsored Scholarship Program of China Scholarship Council, etc. He has published more than 30 academic articles, including those appeared on international journals listed in ISI and Ei Compendex, and has coauthored three books.

Li Zhou is a Senior Lecturer and a Programme Leader with a MA in E-Logistics and Supply Chain Management, MSc Project Management for Logistics. In addition to the PhD, Li has earned an MSc and a BSc in Engineering. She had been a Post-Doctoral Researcher, a Visiting Scholar, and an Associate Professor and Assistant Director. Li has over 20 years teaching and research experience in various universities in China, Sweden, and UK. At present, Li's principal research interests lie in the field of operation management, specifically in supply chain management and reverse logistics.

Zhenkun Zhou is a Ph.D student in the Management School of the Huazhong University of Science and Technology. Her research interests lie in logistics service and IT service, service supply chain management. She worked in a top ERP company in China for several years.

Index